June 12, 2014
Edinburgh, UK

I0050995

**Association for
Computing Machinery**

Advancing Computing as a Science & Profession

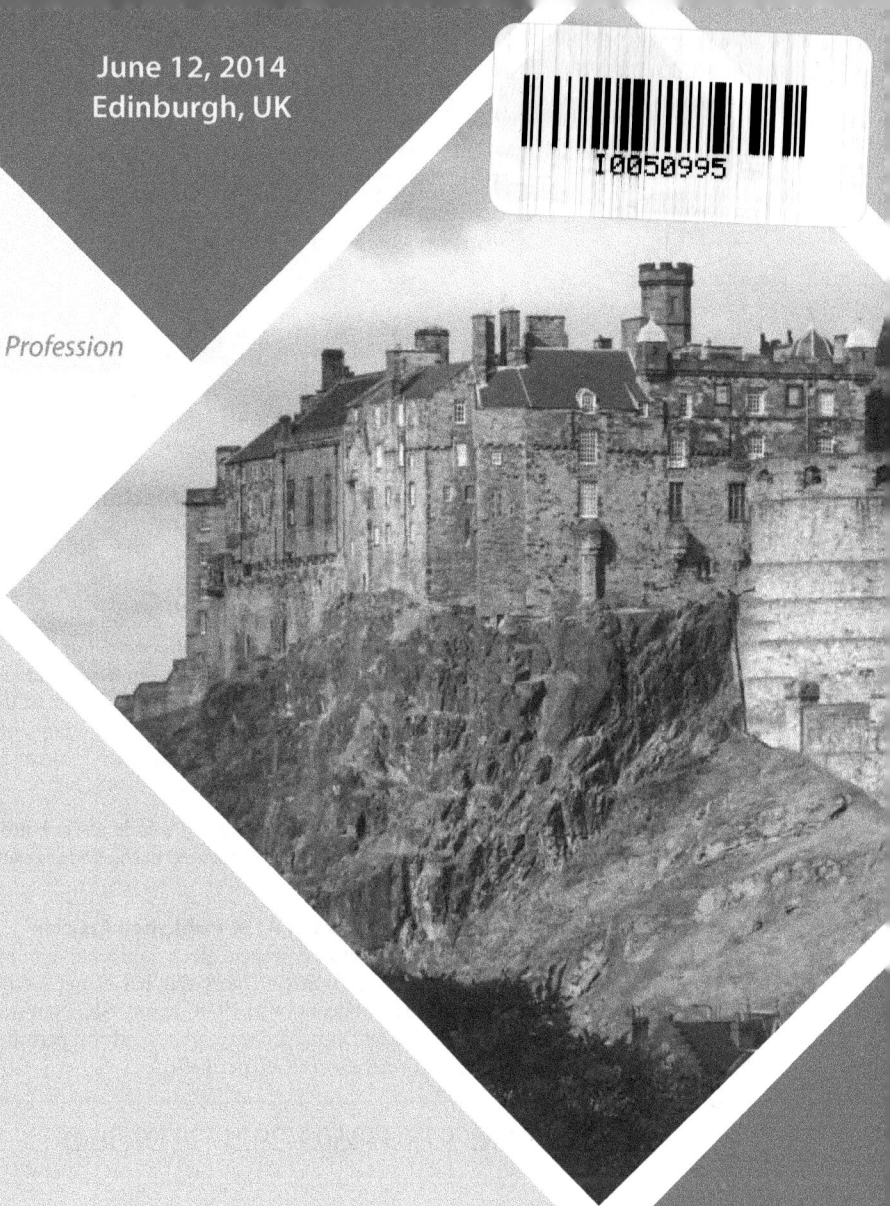

ISMM'14
Proceedings of the 2014 ACM SIGPLAN
International Symposium
on Memory Management

Sponsored by:
ACM SIGPLAN

Supported by:
Microsoft Research & IBM Research

Association for Computing Machinery

Advancing Computing as a Science & Profession

The Association for Computing Machinery
2 Penn Plaza, Suite 701
New York, New York 10121-0701

Notice to Past Authors of ACM-Published Articles
ACM intends to create a complete electronic archive of all articles and/or other material previously published by ACM. If you have written a work that has been previously published by ACM in any journal or conference proceedings prior to 1978, or any SIG Newsletter at any time, and you do NOT want this work to appear in the ACM Digital Library, please inform permissions@acm.org, stating the title of the work, the author(s), and where and when published.

ISBN: 978-1-4503-2921-7 (Digital)

ISBN: 978-1-4503-3085-5 (Print)

Additional copies may be ordered prepaid from:

ACM Order Department
PO Box 30777
New York, NY 10087-0777, USA

Phone: 1-800-342-6626 (USA and Canada)
+1-212-626-0500 (Global)
Fax: +1-212-944-1318
E-mail: acmhelp@acm.org
Hours of Operation: 8:30 am – 4:30 pm ET

Printed in the USA

ISMM 2014 Chairs' Welcome

It is our great pleasure to welcome you to the *2014 ACM International Symposium on Memory Management*. This year the call for papers attracted 22 submissions from around the world, representing research from academia and industry. The program committee selected 11 of these papers for presentation and publication in the conference. The acceptance rate is similar to prior years and reflects the generally high quality of submissions to ISMM.

We encourage participants to attend the opening keynote by Tony Printezis:

- *Use of the JVM at Twitter: A Bird's Eye View,* Tony Printezis, Twitter, Inc.

Tony spent 10 years at Sun Microsystems (now Oracle) working on garbage collection and virtual machine technology, on both the research side and product side. Now at Twitter, Tony will talk about the special demands placed on VMs and memory managers by the Twitter infrastructure and how his team is addressing them.

Many people contributed to ISMM 2014. We first thank the authors for submitting their research for publication in this symposium, which keeps it a top-quality venue for memory-related research of all kinds. We are grateful to the program committee and the external program committee, who worked very hard in reviewing papers and providing feedback for authors. Finally, we thank our sponsors, ACM SIGPLAN and our generous corporate supporters, IBM Research, and Microsoft Research.

We hope that you will find the program engaging and thought-provoking and that the symposium will provide you with a valuable opportunity to share ideas with other researchers and practitioners from institutions around the world.

David P. Grove
ISMM 2014 General Chair
IBM Research

Samuel Z. Guyer
ISMM 2014 Program Chair
Tufts University

Table of Contents

Keynote Address I
Session Chair: Samuel Z. Guyer *(Tufts University)*

Session: Software

Session: Concurrency

Session: Hardware

ISMM 2014 Symposium Organization

General Chair: David Grove *(IBM Research, USA)*

Program Chair: Samuel Z Guyer *(Tufts University, USA)*

Publicity Chair: Jeremy Singer *(University of Glasgow, Scotland)*

Steering Committee Chair: Martin Vechev *(ETH Zurich, Switzerland)*

Steering Committee: David Bacon *(IBM Research, USA)*
Hans J Boehm *(Google, USA)*
Perry Cheng *(IBM Research, USA)*
Doug Lea *(SUNY Oswego, USA)*
Kathryn S. McKinley *(Microsoft Research, USA)*
Erez Petrank *(Technion, Israel)*
Jan Vitek *(Purdue University, USA)*

Program Committee: David Bacon *(IBM Research, USA)*
Emery Berger *(UMass Amherst, USA)*
Laurent Daynes *(Oracle Labs, France)*
Diego Garbervetsky *(University of Buenos Aires, Argentina)*
Doug Lea *(SUNY Oswego, USA)*
Shan Lu *(University of Wisconsin, USA)*
Rob O'Callahan *(Mozilla, New Zealand)*
Melissa O'Neill *(Harvey Mudd College, USA)*
Polyvios Pratikakis *(FORTH ICS, Greece)*
Tony Printezis *(Twitter, USA)*
Tomoharu Ugawa *(UEC Tokyo, Japan)*
Harry Xu *(UC Irvine, USA)*

External Review Committee: Eddie Aftandilian Simon Marlowe
Michael Bond Milo Martin
Tim Harris Nick Mitchell
Tony Hosking Eliot Moss
Richard Jones Jennifer Sartor
Ondrej Lhotak

Sponsor:  acm SIGPLAN

Supporters: Microsoft Research   IBM Research

Use of the JVM at Twitter: A Bird's Eye View

Tony Printezis
Twitter
Boston, MA, USA
tony@printezis.net

Abstract

Specialties:15+ years of virtual machine implementation experience with special focus on memory management / garbage collection. Close to 20 years of C/C++ experience. 15+ years of Java experience. Expert in concurrent/parallel programming.

ACM Classification:
D.3.4 Software, PROGRAMMING LANGUAGES, Processors: Run-time environments; Memory management (garbage collection)

Author Keywords: JVM

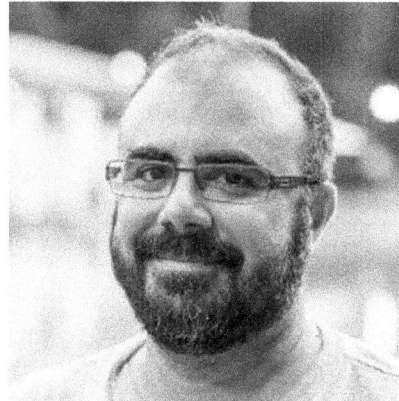

ISMM'14, June 12, 2014, Edinburgh, UK.
ACM 978-1-4503-2921-7/14/06.
http://dx.doi.org/10.1145/2602988.2619208

M³: High-Performance Memory Management from Off-the-Shelf Components

David Terei
Stanford University
dterei@cs.stanford.edu

Alex Aiken
Stanford University
aiken@cs.stanford.edu

Jan Vitek
Purdue University
jv@cs.purdue.edu

Abstract

Real-world garbage collectors in managed languages are complex. We investigate whether this complexity is really necessary and show that by having a different (but wider) interface between the collector and the developer, we can achieve high performance with off-the-shelf components for real applications. We propose to assemble a memory manager out of multiple, simple collection strategies and to expose the choice of where to use those strategies in the program to the developer. We describe and evaluate an instantiation of our design for C. Our prototype allows developers to choose on a per-type basis whether data should be reference counted or reclaimed by a tracing collector. While neither strategy is optimised, our empirical data shows that we can achieve performance that is competitive with hand-tuned C code for real-world applications.

Categories and Subject Descriptors D.3.4 Programming Languages [*Processors*]: Memory management (garbage collection); D.3.3 Programming Languages [*Language Constructs and Features*]: Dynamic storage management

General Terms Algorithms, Design, Experimentation, Languages, Performance

Keywords Memory Management; Garbage Collection; Tracing; Mark-Sweep; Reference Counting

1. Introduction

Automatic memory management, as supported by modern managed languages such as Java, Ruby and Go, offers a great deal of safety and productivity to developers. Through a simple interface, an entire class of difficult bugs is removed, improving security and reliability. Moreover, the best collectors are competitive, both in throughput and latency, with explicit memory management. However, the complexity of highly-tuned collectors and the engineering effort involved in creating them is staggering. For Java, hundreds of man years were invested into the various collectors that are part of the Hotspot virtual machine. One reason for this complexity is that most memory management strategies have pathologies, particular workloads that will make them perform sub-optimally. To avoid these, best-of-breed collectors incorporate sophisticated optimisations designed to reduce the likelihood of triggering worst case behaviour.

The price for all this is a substantial engineering cost, a cost that puts high-performance memory management out of the reach of many systems. Languages that are developed by small communities, such as Ruby, Python or R, young industrial languages such as Go, or languages such as C for which automated memory management is not the preferred route, cannot afford such sophisticated solutions. Implementations of these languages are forced to get by with basic reference counting or mark-sweep collectors. This complexity also makes tuning a modern collector to work well across a wide range of benchmarks, or to a specific application, a difficult task.

In this paper, we investigate whether this complexity is really necessary. We show that through a different (but wider) interface between the developer and garbage collector we can achieve high performance from off-the-shelf components. We modify the developer's memory management interface in two ways. Firstly, we allow multiple memory management strategies to co-exist in the same program, and secondly we give developers control of the policy decision of which program values are managed by which strategy. We refer to this interface as a multi-memory-management (M^3) system.

While this extension adds some burden at the language level, it allows for a drastic reduction in the complexity of the underlying runtime system. Instead of highly tuned collectors that require substantial compiler support, off-the-shelf collector designs can be used. Furthermore, the design we are proposing is completely opt-in. If developers specify no annotations, then a default collector manages all memory, essentially reducing to the current state of affairs.

We have implemented a prototype M^3 system for C that provides developers the choice between a naive reference counting collector, or a basic mark-sweep collector. Despite the simplicity of the components, we are able to achieve close to, or in one case better than, the performance of explicit memory management. We chose C for two reasons. First, it allows us to compare directly with carefully written manual memory management for performance-oriented applications. Second, our implementation is an existence proof that it is straightforward to build an M^3 prototype from scratch from off-the-shelf components.

Our work also suggests that through this wider interface, higher performance with less effort is achievable for language implementations willing to ask developers for more information. By allowing developers to guide the memory management policy at the language level, the collector strategy can be customized to the specific application, improving performance and avoiding any worst case behaviour that a fixed policy collector will have.

ISMM'14, June 12, 2014, Edinburgh, United Kingdom.
Copyright is held by the owner/author(s). Publication rights licensed to ACM.
ACM 978-1-4503-2921-7/14/06... $15.00.
http://dx.doi.org/10.1145/2602988.2602995

We do not expect M^3 to be universally applicable, but believe that in the hands of more experienced developers building systems where performance is a concern, it can be simpler and achieve stronger results than current approaches. These are situations where a great deal of times is already spent tweaking the exposed garbage collector and run-time settings on deployment.

In addition to describing the design of our system, we conduct case studies of three programs and evaluate the performance of our system on each. Our contributions are as follows:

- We identify the benefits in extending the memory management interface and the requirements a new interface should satisfy.

- We detail one specific design that satisfies this interface.

- We conduct an evaluation of this design on three programs: Memcached, MOSS and a synthetic web middleware.

The paper is organized as follows. In Section 2, we motivate the problem with one particular program we believe is ill-served by current garbage collectors. In Section 3 we detail the requirements of an M^3 system and describe one design point in the space. In Section 4 we present three case studies, describing how to use an M^3 system with them and evaluate the performance impact. We describe related work in Section 5 and conclude in Section 6.

2. Background

In this section we provide some background on the performance characteristics of modern memory management systems and some further indications that a simpler implementation that provides more control to developers would have advantages.

Firstly, designers of automatic memory management implementations are interested in providing collectors that work well across a broad range of client systems and metrics of success are usually expressed in terms of average behaviour across a set of standard benchmarks [13]. And, on average modern collectors work very well. However, previous work has shown that the efficacy of a memory management system is highly dependent on the behaviour of the application and available resources [4, 19, 32]. For example, Soman et al. [32] showed in their work on the dynamic selection of the best garbage collector for a specific application that no single collector was optimal for all benchmarks. In fact, the optimal collector often varies over the life-time of the application. All of this leads to considerable variance in collector performance over the set of applications that developers care about.

Anecdotally we have heard stories of software projects that discovered after writing a large amount of code in a particular language with a managed implementation that the collector performed poorly in at least some (and sometimes, many) of the project's important use cases. Unfortunately, these projects had few options for addressing the problem, as memory managers generally expose control over only a few decisions (e.g., the size of the generations in a generational collector). Short of the hugely expensive task of rewriting the code to target a different platform with a different garbage collector, these projects are effectively stuck with serious performance issues they cannot address.

We argue that a collector built from off-the-shelf components but with a wider interface between the developer and the memory manager would help address some of these issues. By giving developers a simpler system with easier-to-understand performance, as well as more control, developers can better reason in advance about how a proposed system would perform and better address problems as they arise by changing the collector's policy.

2.1 An Example: Memcached

In this section we use Memcached as an example of the challenges facing modern memory management systems. It is also one of our

```
typedef struct {
    uint size;        // sizes of items
    void *free;       // free list
    uint free_size;   // total free items in list
    void **slabs;     // array of slab pointers
    uint slab_size;   // # of allocated slabs
    uint slab_limit;  // size of slabs array
} slabclass_t;

// global holding our slab classes
static slabclass_t slabclass[MAX_SLAB_CLASSES];
```

Figure 1. Type and management of slab classes in Memcached.

case studies. Memcached is a high-performance, distributed, in-memory key-value store, widely used for the task of caching temporary data in modern web architectures [2]. For example, Facebook and Twitter make extensive use of the technology to reduce load on relational database servers and rely on a 99% hit rate to scale to the massive user bases that they serve [3]. Memcached uses an event-based architecture, scaling to a large number of cores. The server is accessed over the network using a client library. Efficient memory management is critical as Memcached deals with very large heap sizes and is used in performance sensitive situations where 99th percentile latency matters. Being able to provide consistent performance at all times and with high heap utilization is a necessity.

Memcached is a challenging program for a garbage collector due to its absolute emphasis on performance and the unpredictable lifetimes of items in the system. Key-value pairs in the system are only deallocated for one of three reasons:

1. The client issues a `delete` command

2. The client issues a `set` command to update an existing item. Internally Memcached treats this as a `delete` and `new` command, never updating items in place.

3. The maximum memory usage is hit and Memcached frees the least-recently-used key-value pair to make room for the next one.

These properties generally make applying the generational hypothesis efficiently very difficult, as the lifetimes are either unpredictable or the oldest items in the system are being deallocated. Heap sizes in the 10's of GB and a requirement for low latency make the problem even more difficult. We believe these characteristics have prevented systems like Memcached from moving to safer, more productive languages.

In fact, one of our coauthors tried writing a Memcached-like system in the garbage-collected Go programming language [22] and ran into exactly these problems. By the time the problems were apparent, it was too late to consider rewriting the entire code base, so the system was modified to use a custom allocator and reference counting scheme written using unsafe primitives. This doubled the size of the code base and introduced more bugs than had been encountered in the entire development process up to that point. In this situation a simpler collector with the usual safety guarantees but more performance transparency and developer control would have been much better than the ultimate solution.

Memcached is written in C and uses explicit memory management and a few custom allocators to improve performance and handle fragmentation. For the bulk of memory, the key-value store itself, it uses a slab allocator with a number of fixed sized allocation classes for meeting requests, trading external for internal fragmentation, giving $O(1)$ allocation and deallocation routines. The code for a slab class is shown in Figure 1.

While challenging, we believe that software such as Memcached would be suitable for automatic memory management if the developer was able to express the program's properties to the memory manager. In our proposed design, the developer can specify that the memory associated with the key-value store is managed by a reference counting system while the rest of the system is managed by a tracing collector. This design is already partially captured in the Memcached code base, with manual reference counting being performed on key-value items.

3. Design

In this section we explore the design space for M^3 systems and offer one concrete design. An M^3 system must make choices on the following axes:

- Memory management strategies: multiple approaches for allocation and deallocation of memory.

- Composability: rules and restrictions for composing strategies in the same program.

- Granularity: the data items to which a strategy can be attached.

- Staging: the times at which a strategy can be selected.

These four dimensions map out the main design choices that must be addressed by a multi-memory-management proposal. We contend that with the right design, an M^3 system can be built from off-the-shelf components while still allowing developers to achieve the performance characteristics that they desire.

It is worth pointing out the relation between M^3 systems and the policies implemented by various generational garbage collectors. Generational collectors offer more than one strategy for allocating and recovering memory, e.g., a young generation using a semi-space copying collector with a bump-point allocator and an old generation managed using a mark-sweep collector with free-lists for allocation. However, the decision of when to move memory from one generation to the other is not exposed to the developer and each object can only change policy once. Instead, after-the-fact administrators will attempt to tweak a few knobs such as generation sizing to improve throughput or latency. This work generalizes these ideas and gives developers control over the choice of strategy.

3.1 Our Design

We present a concrete design of an M^3 system inspired by our case studies. Our design targets C and strives for simplicity, both in its implementation and cognitive complexity for the developer:

- Two memory management strategies are supported: naive reference counting and tracing garbage collection.

- The strategies can be freely composed in the same computation.

- The granularity of the strategies is at the type level. We expect the common case to be that all values of the same type are managed by the same policy, but developers can choose per allocation site.

- Strategies are selected at allocation and stay in place for the lifetime of the data.

3.1.1 Granularity: Using Types

Types are a natural place to attach memory management choices and they provide a hint to the compiler to generate efficient code for memory accesses. In our design, each type defaults to tracing collection, but all types have two implicit variants that give the developer control. For example, a type `stats` can be used as follows:

	Tracing	Ref. Counting
Strategy	Batch	Incremental
Mutation cost	None	High
Throughput	Low	High
Pauses	Long	Short
Cycles?	Yes	No

Table 1. Tracing Vs. Reference Counting. Taken from Bacon et al. [7].

	Tracing	Ref. Counting
Num. of In-Bound Refs.	Large	Small
Num. of Out-Bound Refs.	Small	Large
Expected Lifetime	Short	Long
Mutation Rate of Refs.	High	Low
Utilisation of Memory	Low	High

Table 2. Ideal properties for a node to perform well with Tracing Vs. Reference Counting

```
stats      st;  // default to tracing collector
rc::stats st;  // use of reference counting
gc::stats st;  // use of tracing collector
```

Types already capture commonality in the code and this commonality usually extends to the best way to manage the underlying memory. While for some very common types, such as primitive types like `int` and `char*`, a single ideal memory management strategy doesn't exist for all values, simple type aliasing functionality is sufficient to deal with this, to allow further specialisation by use-case. We will discuss the use of types further in Section 3.1.3.

3.1.2 Memory Management Strategies

While there are countless variations on how memory can be reclaimed in a system we eventually settled on offering the choice between the two primary viewpoints in today's systems: reference counting and tracing.

The reduction of our initial scope to these two strategies is not surprising in hind-sight, especially when viewing these two strategies as duals of one-another as suggested by Bacon et al. [7]. The strength and weaknesses of each one complements the other, as shown in Table 1 where we summarise the trade-offs of each strategy and in Table 2 where we specify the kinds of nodes in a heap that work best with one strategy.

3.1.3 Implementation Considerations

For an implementation of our design a number of questions arise, primarily on what memory management code to generate for a function and how to deal with pointers crossing from one heap to the other. A schematic diagram of our design is in Figure 2. Here we outline the scope of a complete compiler, however, our current prototype does not automate everything. We also do not evaluate the performance of pointers crossing heap boundaries thoroughly at this time. Please refer to Section 4.1 for an overview of the current prototype.

Code Generation Naive reference counting requires insertion of code around pointer operations to atomically update reference counts. A tracing garbage collector does not require any barriers around pointer accesses. The simplest strategy for combining the two is to emit checks around all pointer operations. These checks perform a switch on both where the pointer resides and where it points to select the appropriate code to execute. The four choices and the corresponding actions are outlined in Table 3. While these checks are expensive, we do not expect it to be the common case:

Stored To	Points To	Action
Traced Heap	Traced Heap	Nothing
Traced Heap	RC Heap	Add to remembered set
RC Heap	RC Heap	Perform reference counting
RC Heap	Traced Heap	Perform reference counting

Table 3. Decision of code to execute for creation of new pointers

instead we have found that a division of the types into the reference counted or traced heap can be easily found that minimises or eliminates the need for the general case. However, the general case does provide a simple and safe programming model for the developer.

To improve the performance of the common case, we attack it as a simple optimisation problem: how to specialise code to one memory management strategy? Currently in our prototype this is done with a very simple optimiser: we look at all uses of a type in the code base and if it is only ever used as a traced type then we can specialise all the code for that type to tracing. If it is used as both a traced and reference counted type then we optionally issue a warning and leave the code unspecialised. This design requires whole program compilation. A straightforward extension would be to add per-module declarations that certain types are only used with a specific memory management strategy, enabling separate compilation.

Heap Boundaries The second issue that we must deal with is how to handle pointers that reside in one heap but point to values in the other heap. This boundary crossing problem is exactly the same issue dealt with in generational collectors where we must be aware of all pointers from the old generation pointing into the young generation. We have two cases to handle:

1. Pointers in the traced heap (*TH*) pointing to the reference counted heap (*RC*); and

2. Pointers in the reference counted heap pointing to the traced heap.

TH to RC Pointers For the first case, we simply update the tracing collector to be aware of reference counting and perform the appropriate decrements as a finalization step on collected objects that point into the reference counted heap. While this approach has a cost (the tracing collector now exhibits some of the behaviour of a reference counting implementation, where tracing dead objects and freeing is a potentially unbounded operation) we do not expect this to be an issue in practice. Our assumption is that pointers crossing heap boundaries will be rare and that a large number of them is a sign of an inappropriate decision by the developer on how to specialise the types.

RC to TH Pointers For the second case, we adopt a similar solution to generational collectors and make use of a remembered set for augmenting the root set of the tracing collector. We can do this efficiently as we are expecting most code to be specialised to a specific memory management strategy and as such will not pay the cost of a software or hardware write barrier for all heap operations. Instead we can simply insert the appropriate code where needed. There is a significant complication compared to the typical use of remembered sets in generational garbage collectors, which is that our remembered set can never be cleared. In a generational collector, the remembered set grows between old generation collections but is reset on each full collection. As we never wish to scan the reference counted heap, we must instead both add entries to and remove entries from our remembered sets and in the worst case they can grow unbounded. As before, we argue that such a large number of pointer crossings is a sign of an inappropriate decision by the developer on how to specialise the types.

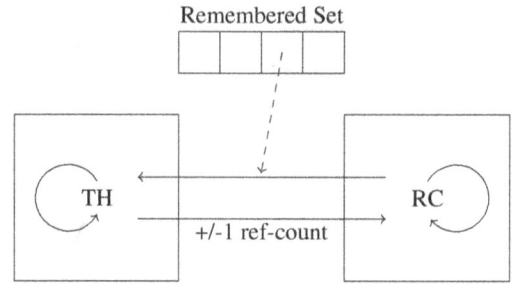

Figure 2. Schematic of our Multi-Memory-Management Design

4. Case Studies

In order to both shape our design and evaluate it, we undertook case studies of a number of programs, the results of which we explore in this section. The studies include Memcached, a high-performance in-memory key-value store, MOSS, a plagiarism detection tool and finally a synthetic example that models the behaviour of a typical middleware service in a modern web stack. For each of these studies, we specify the heap organization, how we divided it up in our system and the results of a performance evaluation.

As our implementation is for C, we evaluate each of our case studies against an explicit memory management version. This sets an accurate and very competitive baseline. The small delta between the explicit memory management version and our M^3 version shows the performance achievable with our approach. It also suggests that M^3 could be used by developers of currently explicit memory management systems to improve safety while retaining performance.

4.1 Implementation

As we have set out to explore the viability of a memory management system using off-the-shelf components, we have pursued a simple implementation. Despite this, even in its current state it is able to show competitive performance.

For our mark-sweep tracing collector we use the Boehm-Weiser garbage collector [14, 15]. For our reference counting implementation we utilize C++11's `shared_ptr` feature [25]. To handle pointers from the traced to RC heap we manually add a finalizer onto the traced object at allocation, where the finalizer knows how to decrement the RC pointer. In a complete implementation, the tracing collector would instead perform the decrement directly to the RC object during the sweep phase.

The Boehm-Weiser collector provides a mature implementation that supports parallel and incremental collection [16]. It is a conservative collector designed to operate against C/C++ programs. We use the collector in parallel mode with incremental collection disabled to keep it as simple as possible.

Our reference counting implementation using `shared_ptr`'s provides a naive reference counting collector. Shared pointers implement reference counting by adding a second level of indirection, with the reference count being stored at this second level and the managed object left unmodified. This is costly in terms of the second indirection we pay on these pointers but provides a very simple and easy way to integrate it with the rest of the system since the underlying representation of values isn't changed. This also allows easy handling of interior pointers, as a `shared_ptr` acts as a fat pointer, retaining both a pointer to the start of the object and one to the current offset.

Unless otherwise noted, memory for the mark-sweep heap is allocated using the allocator provided by the Boehm-Weiser collector while memory for the reference counted heap is allocated using the `malloc` and `free` routines provided by GNU C library (glibc) 2.18.1 [1].

4.2 Memcached

Memcached is a high-performance, distributed, in-memory key-value store that is widely used for the task of caching temporary data in modern web architectures. We introduced Memcached in Section 2.1.

The heap of Memcached can be largely divided into two distinct components: the management of the key-value pairs themselves and the rest. The key-value pairs are managed by a typical slab-allocator design, giving $O(1)$ allocation and deallocation behaviour by trading external fragmentation for internal fragmentation. The rest consists of thread data structures, configuration details, server statistics, and connection and buffer handling. These are all managed by a variety of free-list allocators for each type. Some client commands, such as statistics collection, also generate variable and short lived data. A schematic of the heap organization can be seen in Figure 3.

4.2.1 Applying a Multi-Memory-Management System

We split the heap of Memcached in a simple way: memory retrieved from the slab allocator for use in storing key-value pairs is reference counted, while the rest of the system is traced. We achieve this by having the slab allocator return reference counted pointers and using a destructor method for them that returns memory to the appropriate slab.

This design removes the bulk of the memory from consideration by the tracing collector, which allows us to scale to very large heap sizes with high utilization while maintaining low latency and high throughput. We remove the use of free-lists for managing the rest of the memory such as connections and buffers, instead simply relying on the tracing collector. The modifications needed to the types and allocation routines to achieve this are shown in Figure 4.

The traced and reference counted heaps are largely separated in this design, with only one pointer potentially existing per connection from the traced heap to the reference counted heap. Each connection object holds a pointer to an item in the key-value store that corresponds to the item the connection is currently processing for either a `get` or `set` request. As such, the number of these pointers is in practice bound to a fairly low number as it isn't reasonable to expect a Memcached server to deal with much in excess of a few thousand connections.

4.2.2 Evaluation

We evaluate the results of our system with Memcached using two different metrics, the total throughput of the server and the worst-case latency. For Memcached we evaluate three different variants; firstly, the original, explicit memory management version; secondly, a fully traced version; and thirdly, the M^3 version. We use two servers for the evaluation, one running Memcached and one running the client. Both are 12 core 2.27GHz Intel Xeon L5640 machines connected via 10 gigabit Ethernet.

The throughput results are presented in Table 4. In this setup we initially load 100,000 key-value pairs into the server and then perform as many `get` requests as possible for a 5 minute period. For the tracing garbage collector, we invoke a collection every 10 seconds. The small heap size however makes this very cheap and indeed we can increase the frequency further with no impact. The main point is to measure the cost of using reference counting in our M^3 system.

The results demonstrate that all three versions are able to achieve the same level of throughput with approximately 1.73M requests per second.

```
// new aliases for RC.
typedef char* slab_t;
typedef slab_t* slablist_t;

typedef struct {
    uint size;         // sizes of items
    slab_t free;       // free list
    uint free_size;    // total free items in list
    slablist_t slabs;  // array of slab pointers
    uint slab_size;    // # of allocated slabs
    uint slab_limit;   // size of slabs array
} slabclass_t;

// global holding our slab classes
static slabclass_t slabclass[MAX_SLAB_CLASSES];

// slab allocation
static int slabs_alloc(const unsigned int id) {
    // declare reference counted allocation
    rc::slab_t ptr;

    slabclass_t *p = slabclass[id];
    if ((mem_malloced + len > mem_limit && p->slab_size > 0) ||
        (grow_slab_list(id) == 0) ||
        ((ptr = malloc((size_t)len)) == 0)) {
        MEMCACHED_SLABS_SLABCLASS_ALLOCATE_FAILED(id);
        return 0;
    }
    p->slabs[p->slab_size++] = ptr;
    mem_malloced += len;
    MEMCACHED_SLABS_SLABCLASS_ALLOCATE(id);
    return 1;
}
```

Figure 4. Modifications to the slab Type's and allocation routines. Compare with Figure 1.

Memcached Version	Request Per Second
Explicit	1,728,240
Full Tracing	1,722,577
M^3	1,730,996

Table 4. Throughput performance of the various versions of Memcached. We performed `get` requests with a 50MB heap and manually invoked the tracing collector every 10 seconds.

For measuring latency we model the behaviour of Memcached in a production environment under increasing heap sizes. To do this, we utilise a third machine to generate load, performing 400,000 requests per second with a mixture of 90% `get` and 10% `set` requests. Performing this over a 7 minute window grows the heap in a linear fashion from nothing to 4GB. Our original client now functions as a latency sampler, sending 5,000 `get` requests per second during the experiment and recording the 20 worst latency samples. A graph of the additions into this set over the course of the experiment is shown in Figure 5. Here we let the tracing collector decide on its own when to collect. The 5 worst samples are shown in Table 5. Here we see where our M^3 system can bring real benefits, with latency largely matching the performance of explicit memory management and greatly improving on the full tracing design. It is also worth pointing out that our evaluation only went to a heap of 4GB, a small size when modern servers come with 40GB - 1TB of memory.

7

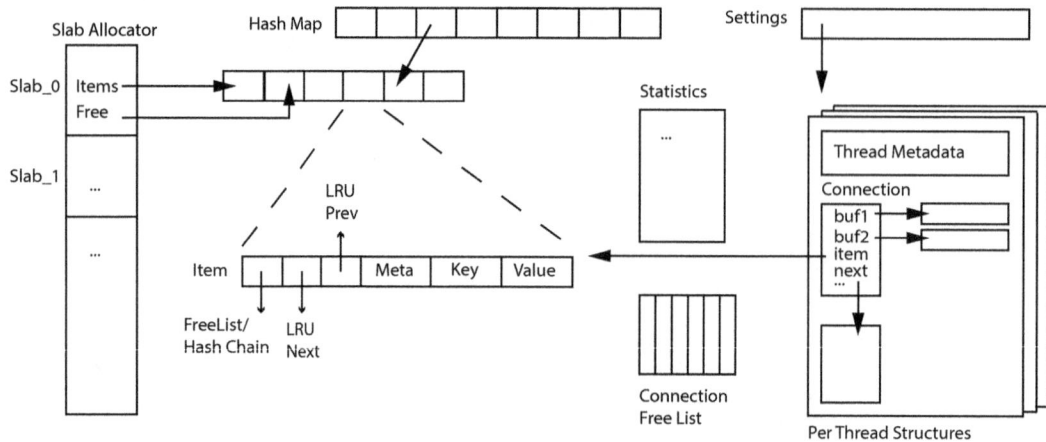

Figure 3. Memcached Heap Organization

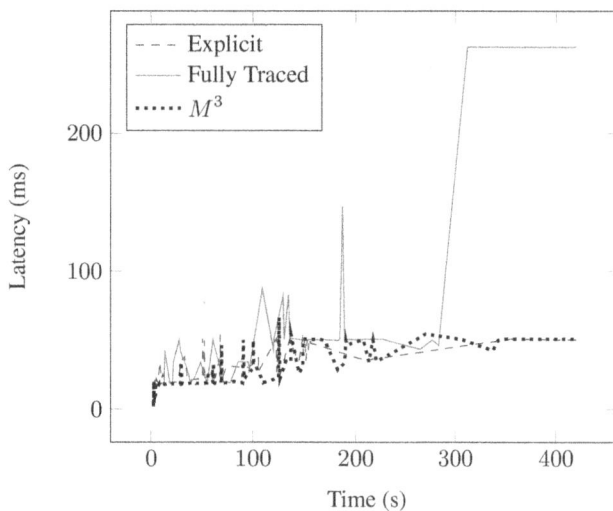

Figure 5. Latency of worst response-time as we slowly increase the heap of Memcached by performing a mix of 90% `get` requests and 10% `set` requests at an approximate rate of 400,000 requests per second.

Memcached Version	5	4	3	2	1
Explicit	51	51	54	54	66
Full Tracing	83	88	147	263	263
M^3	51	51	51	51	53

Table 5. The 5 worst latency measurements (ms) for different versions of Memcached. These were taken over the course of 7 minutes as we increased the heap from nothing to 4GB.

4.3 MOSS

MOSS is a widely-used plagiarism detection tool in use since 1994 for evaluating the similarity of programs [30]. It is written in C and uses Gay and Aiken's region memory manager [20, 21].

What we are proposing is less work for the developer than using regions, which have been used by systems developers for decades in C/C++ (often under different names, usually "arenas" or "zones"). So there is plenty of evidence that developers can deal with this. The main savings is that the developer does not need to specify where data should be freed, which is typically the developer's responsibility in region-based systems. A cost is that you do not get the locality benefits of regions—we're not doing anything about fragmentation. As future work, regions could be incorporated as another choice of memory management policy into our approach.

MOSS's heap organization consists of the following principle regions:

1. **database**: A potentially very large array storing information about the various passages of program text that MOSS is processing. An internally linked list is threaded through the array as well for various ordering operations.

2. **index**: A secondary array that stores a searchable index for efficiently looking up the passages in the text database. It is sized at 1/8th of the text database.

3. **files**: Stores information about the various files being processed.

4. **matches**: Stores information on matches among files; largely a collection of arrays and linked lists.

5. **temporary regions**: A variety of short lived regions are created for operations such as sorting subsets of much larger arrays and linked lists.

The database, index and files regions all have a lifetime equal to the program itself and as such only ever grow in size and require allocation but not deallocation. The matches and various temporary regions are much shorter lived, being created and destroyed throughout the execution. A diagram of MOSS's heap organization can be seen in Figure 6.

4.3.1 Applying a Multi-Memory-Management System

We simply put the text database into the reference counted heap and the rest is put under the control of the tracing collector. Similar to Memcached, the bulk of the data is stored in the text database and little mutation occurs here except for some re-ordering of passages using the internal linked list. It is not useful moving the index to the reference counted heap as the indexes are stored as relative array offsets, not actual pointers, so the tracing collector can deal efficiently with the index regardless of its size. This requires creating a new alias for the type involved, `passage`, but is an easy change to make given the isolated and limited way the database is used.

With this division we only end up with a few instances of pointers crossing heap boundaries. For the traced to reference counted direction, which can be handled very efficiently, a pointer for each

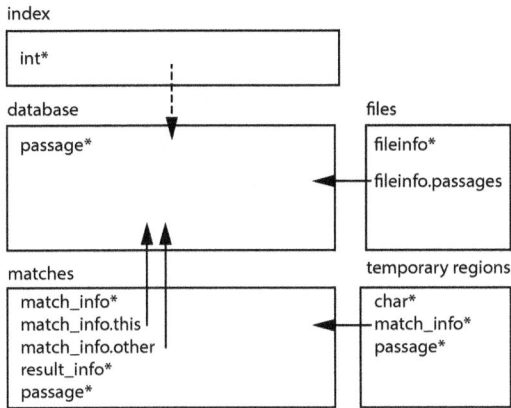

Figure 6. MOSS Heap Organization. Solid lines represent pointers, dotted lines implicit pointers through array offsets. The types stored in each region are also listed.

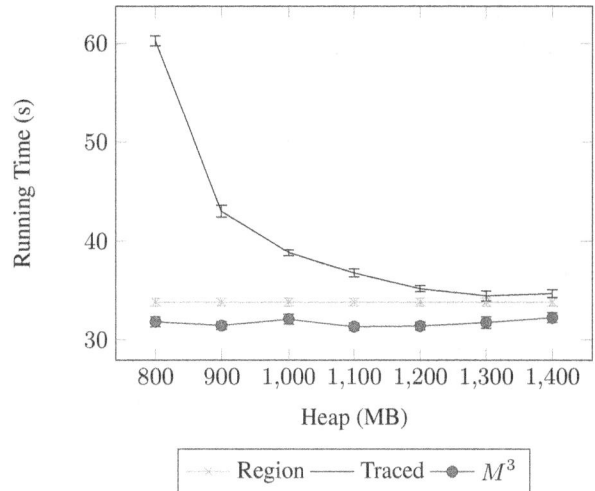

Figure 7. Performance of the various versions of MOSS

file read points to its corresponding passages array in the database. Secondly, for each match we find between two files, a pointer is created to each passage. No pointers from the reference counted heap to the traced heap are ever created, as while `passage` values exist in both, the existing code already copies such values from the reference counted database so that it can perform isolated mutation.

4.3.2 Evaluation

The results from an evaluation of MOSS under various configurations are presented in Figure 7. The evaluation is performed by running MOSS over two different versions of a large source code repository consisting of 1,255 files and 845,122 lines of code. Processing all of this causes MOSS to allocate 2,441MB of memory. For the versions of MOSS using a collector, we run the experiment over a range of heap sizes, from 800MB, the minimum that all versions can use, up to 1,400MB. For the M^3 version, we size the reference counted heap at a fixed 670MB, the maximum size it needs at any point, and the remaining is assigned to the tracing collector.

We see that at all heap sizes the M^3 version of MOSS achieves the strongest results with a running time of 31.82 seconds on average across all heap sizes. The region version of MOSS has a running time of 33.4 seconds and the traced version of MOSS has a running time between 34.6 - 60.24 seconds. The M^3 variant surprisingly achieves a faster time than the explicit, region version. This appears to be due to the cost of creating many small temporary regions compared to the performance of parallel mark-sweep.

The M^3 variant is unaffected by the heap size in the range shown as with the passage database removed from the tracing collectors heap, its collection policy triggers a collection less frequently and each collection is faster. With the collector set to trigger at 85% heap utilization, the traced version of MOSS with an 800MB heap is constantly at that limit since the passage database is 670MB in size, occupying 83.75% of the heap. With the M^3 version, the tracing collector runs without regard for the passage database since it resides in the reference counted heap, allowing it to make better policy decisions. This leads the traced version to run the garbage collector 86 times compared to the M^3 version where it runs only 17 times. While tweaking the policy of the tracing collector could help, this is exactly what we have achieved in the M^3 version! Also, even at a 900MB heap when the traced version runs with a comparable number of collections (15), the higher cost of

collection for tracing the passage database means the traced version has a running time of 44.4 seconds.

4.4 Synthetic Middleware

Our third case study is a synthetic program that models the behaviour of a typical middleware service in a distributed web stack. This example is distilled from what is known about a persistent memory management performance issue in a commercial Internet service.

The basic design is a request-response architecture that further generates RPC calls to backend services. Our program has a number of parameters that can be tuned, all demonstrating various challenges for memory management systems:

1. **Allocation Per Request**: We perform a certain amount of allocation for every request received. Currently we use a tunable normal distribution for deciding the amount.

2. **RPC Delay**: We model the RPC calls by inserting delays in processing. In the production system, the RPC backend is a separate system.

3. **Long Lived Global State**: For each request that comes in we choose a random user id to assign the request to. For each user in the system we keep statistics at the service on the number and type of requests performed. The number of users in the system is tunable.

We believe these parameters accurately model the challenges of automated memory management in modern systems code and highlight the complex policy decisions that collectors need to deal with. The program causes problems for most generational collectors in the following way:

1. Firstly, the data allocated per request should ideally never be promoted to the old generation. It is by its nature short lived and bounded by the number of connections and requests that a server will handle at any time. However, due to the 99th percentile latencies present in a distributed system, it is extremely hard to size generations correctly to capture these properties.

2. Secondly, as the amount allocated per request can vary, this presents a problem when it is promoted to the old generation due to fragmentation and the use of free-lists in nearly all old generations.

9

3. Finally, these two properties over time cause the old generation to fill up with fragmented and ill-aged data, eventually triggering a worst-case stop the world compaction collection in many collector designs (e.g., HotSpot JVM's CMS collector).

The difficulty of getting the aging policy right through the knobs provided is key to this issue. The commercial Internet company, for example, runs a number of their services with 12GB young generations compared to 4GB old generations in an attempt to never have memory incorrectly promoted. While this helps, in the presence of huge variance in 99th percentile latencies and high throughput it only delays the inevitable.

Unfortunately due to limitations with our implementation we are unable to demonstrate the effects of varying the 99th percentile latency of RPC calls and the amount of data allocated per request. This is because the effect of these parameters, incorrect promotion of memory and fragmentation of the old generation, are only applicable in a generational system with two styles of collection and allocation. While the Boehm-Weiser collector has some generational behaviour in its incremental collection implementation, this provides neither a separate allocation mechanism nor tracing behaviour. Despite these limitations, we are able to show an improvement for our approach over pure tracing or reference counting.

4.4.1 Applying a Multi-Memory-Management System

While we cannot illustrate the specific problem outlined above because we do not have a generational tracing collector, the synthetic middleware is still an instructive benchmark. We apply our M^3 design in a straightforward manner: short-lived data associated with requests are managed by the tracing collector, as are connections themselves, while the longer lived global state is managed by the reference counted heap.

While one could object that a generational collector with a tracing, bump-pointer allocator for the young generation and a reference counting collector for the old generation would also suffice, we disagree. This would only hold if the aging policy could be tuned exactly right, a hard problem we believe when considering the variability of 99th percentile latency in these systems. Even if the aging and generations can be adjusted to prevent premature aging, it is likely that this configuration is non-optimal for the bulk of data that should be handled by the tracing collector that has a narrow distribution of life-times.

The key point here is the difficulty of tuning a program with a fixed collection policy. Rather than struggle to do that after the program has been developed with limited tools (e.g., setting the generation sizes), we are advocating allowing developers to use their knowledge of the application-specific characteristics to set the overall collection policy. That is, instead of a more complex collector to handle this workload, we show that our M^3 system can achieve high performance from our simple implementation with only a small amount of developer input.

4.4.2 Evaluation

As with Memcached, we evaluate our M^3 system for this case study on two metrics: throughput and latency. We use the same setup as before, two machines, one running the synthetic middleware service and the other the client for load generation and sampling. Both machines are 2.27GHz Intel Xeon L5640 connected via 10 gigabit Ethernet.

For throughput we evaluate two different configurations, one with no bytes allocated per request and another with a fixed 10 bytes allocated per request. These results can be seen in Figure 8. In both configurations the explicit memory management, full tracing and M^3 versions achieve the same level of performance at 1.86M req/s. The full reference counting version however only achieves 93% of the performance in the first configuration and 90% in the

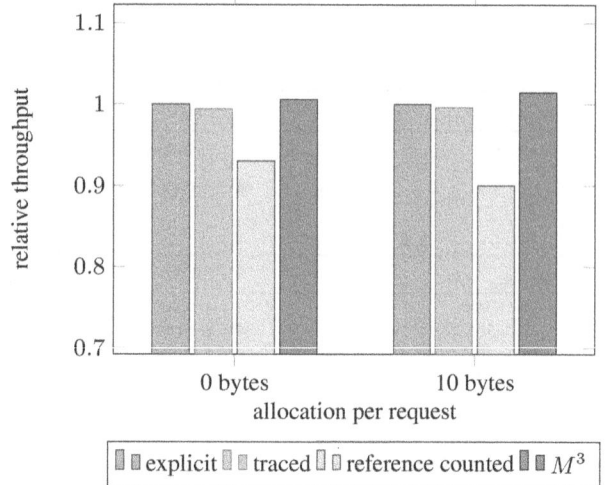

Figure 8. Throughput performance of various versions of our synthetic middleware service. Performance is relative to the explicit memory management version and consists of two different configuration. Firstly, with no allocation per requests and secondly, with a fixed 10 bytes allocated per request.

second configuration. It is worth highlighting the minimal impact on performance when we are allocating per-request for the tracing collector configurations. The work of the mark phase is proportional to the amount of live data and in this system that is bounded by the number of live requests we are dealing with. While the sweep phase is proportional to the allocation rate, the cost is far cheaper than marking due to the memory access patterns.

For evaluating the impact on latency we collected the 10 worst latency samples across a range of sizes for the number of users (or long lived data) in the system. We utilize three machines, one to run the service, one to generate load of 300,000 req/s across 2,000 connections and the final machine for sampling latency by generating 2,000 req/s. We run the experiment for 10 minutes, invoking the tracing garbage collector every 1 minute to evaluate pause times.

The result of the worst recorded latency measure is shown in Figure 9. As expected the latency of the traced version gets progressively worse as we increase the number of users in the system. The other three versions all have acceptable latency profiles, staying flat across the range of heap sizes. The explicit memory management version achieves a worst case of 2.5ms, the reference counted version a worst case of 3.1ms and the M^3 version a worst case of 4.5ms. While the M^3 version achieves the worst of the three, it is within acceptable bounds and its throughput performance is 10% greater than the reference counted version. Critically though, we have as developers chosen just one point in the possible space of policies for the M^3 version. A developer valuing latency more than throughput could easily reference count the entire heap.

Our results demonstrate that the M^3 version is able to achieve better latency than the traced version and better throughput than the reference counted version. Indeed, it is within a small constant latency overhead of the throughput and latency performance of the explicit memory management version.

4.5 Summary

In all three of our case studies, the M^3 system performs well, with a flat latency profile and throughput equal to the explicit memory management or traced version. We believe the key conclusions from these results are:

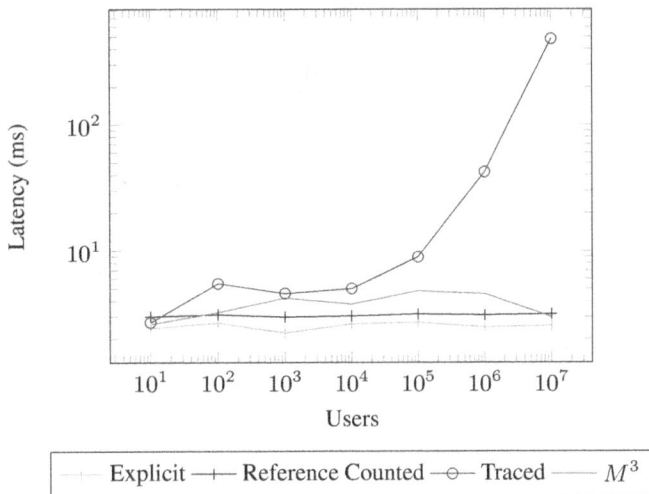

Figure 9. Latency of worst response-time as we increase the amount of users in the system. This corresponds to more permanent, long-lived data.

1. An M^3 system can achieve great performance. In each of our case studies, our M^3 version achieves as good throughput as the traced version and a flat latency profile very close to the behaviour of the reference counted version.

2. A little developer control goes a long way. We are able to achieve the competitive performance that we do with a very simple implementation that uses off-the-shelf components.

3. An M^3 system allows the policy to be expressed by the developer so that the collector can be customized to the program and done so after initial program development. While some may object that the right traditional collector design would achieve similar results to our M^3 design, designing a policy that is exactly right for all programs is at least very difficult; certainly such a policy has yet to be demonstrated.

5. Related Work

Customisable Memory Management   Our closest related work is by Attardi, Flagella and Idlio on their Customisable Memory Management framework for C++ [5, 6]. Their work is motivated by performance and the observation that there is no single ideal collector. Like us, their design gives developers the ability to customize the memory management policy by exposing multiple heaps and allowing developers to choose, on a type-by-type bases, which heap is responsible for values of that type. They make use of C++ features such as inheritance and operator overloading to provide a framework that can be customised and extended for mixing various garbage collection strategies. Unlike our work however, they only consider tracing collectors, looking at abstracting a mark-sweep and semi-space collector for example. They also take the approach of tracing across heap boundaries. Tracing heap A will trace the reachable set of all pointers starting from the roots of A, regardless of if traced objects reside in a different heap. Their system also doesn't consider language level support, instead designing a conservative collector that can work with the existing C++ language.

Memory Management Toolkits   There is a rich history of work in providing customizable memory allocators through either a richer interface than `malloc` or composable layers of simple allocation routines [8, 33]. They are similar to M^3 in their widening of the interface between the developer and memory manager. However, they only deal with allocation and unsafe interfaces while our focus

is on safe memory management and choosing between reclamation strategies.

Similar work has been done for managed languages, providing toolkits of composable code that can be used to easily build garbage collectors [11, 24]. We believe this work is complementary to ours as it would allow rapid experimentation of different collector strategies. It also somewhat addresses the complexity of modern garbage collectors. Our work differs though in it focus and advocating of a wider interface between the developer and memory manager, something not explicitly considered by these toolkits.

Garbage Collection for C/C++   The Boehm-Weiser collector [14, 15] for C/C++ has been designed with the assumption that it does not control the entire heap of a program. The collector provides considerable flexibility, safely allowing calls to the libc `malloc` and `free` API's, as well as the ability to add individual pointers to the root set. The Boehm-Weiser collector essentially provides developers two choices of memory management policy: a value can be placed in the explicitly managed heap or in the GC-managed heap. There is no language-level support and so the developer must be very careful not to store the only pointer to a live object in the traced heap into the explicitly managed heap.

The work of Ellis and Detlefs [18] provides a design of a language extension to C++ for allowing garbage collection to be safely integrated with the language. They propose dealing with GC pointers stored in the explicitly managed heap in the same manner as us, by using write barriers and remembered sets. Broader in scope, it also includes the design of a safe subset of C++ that can support garbage collection efficiently. This proposal has apparently never been implemented or evaluated.

Hinted Collection   Reames and Necula have recently published work [29] on *hinted collection*, where the developer can provide deallocation hints. In their system, a deallocation hint acts as a performance optimization and has no impact on the correctness of a program. The collector simply uses the hints to optimize the ordering and scope for tracing the heap, achieving a reduction in pause times. They have a single tracing collector managing the whole heap, rather than exposing different strategies with different trade-offs as we propose. The work is complementary to ours and could be used to further optimize the behaviour of the tracing collector in our system.

Pretenuring   Pretenuring [10, 12, 17, 27] allocates objects directly into the old generation or permanent space in a generation collector. The performance benefits can be significant if the right objects are pretenured, as it avoids costs associated with promoting them from the young generation. The overall memory management policy is still fixed. Pretenuring is also done through profiler information, either online or pre-recorded, and doesn't attempt to widen the garbage collection interface for developers.

Garbage Collection Selection   Work has been done on the automatic selection of a garbage collection algorithm for a particular program [19, 32]. Based on characteristics of the program (e.g., obtained by profiling) a specific GC algorithm is selected. In some cases, the choice can be changed dynamically at certain safe execution points. These works are motivated by the problem that no single GC provides the best results for all programs. While we believe M^3 provides a plausible solution to this issue, our motivation is in exploring the benefits of using several simple strategies to avoid the complexity associated with modern garbage collectors. In approach, this line of work exposes no control to the developer and does not allow different GC designs to be mixed within the same program.

Reference Counting and Tracing Collectors   Previous work has explored the relationship between reference counting and tracing collectors. The work of Bacon, Cheng and Rajan [7] showed that tracing and reference counting can be seen as duals of each other. Tracing finds live data and is batch driven in nature, while reference counting finds dead data and is incremental in nature. Various collector designs can be seen as combining elements of both to achieve low latency and high throughput.

The work of Blackburn and McKinley on a garbage collection design called 'Ulterior Reference Counting' [9] explores a generational collector that traces the young generation and reference counts the old generation. It is likely that some of our case studies would perform well with their collector. However, we have no doubt that there are other realistic systems where their approach would not perform especially well. Our main point is that the problem of efficient memory management can be simplified and more easily achieved if developers are given a modicum of control over setting the collection policy.

The state-of-the-art for pure reference counting collectors, such as the work of Shahriyar et al. [31] shows very promising results with a single collector being competitive across a range of benchmarks. This work though focuses on pushing the performance of reference counting collectors and as such greatly increases their complexity over naive reference counting, counter to our own aim. The work also doesn't look at latency, a principle concern in two of our case studies.

Safe Explicit Memory Management The prior work of Jim et al. with their safe dialect of C, the Cyclone programming language [23, 26], addresses the problem of safe memory management with strong developer control. Their work adopts a region-based type system to provide static safety for memory management. This type system provides a unifying framework for several forms of memory management, including stack allocation, arena regions, reference counting and tracing collection.

Recently, Mozilla has started working on a new programming language, Rust [28], that is similar in some ways to the memory management design of Cyclone. It uses a linear type system to provide a number of different management policies. These include unique pointers, reference counted pointers and traced pointers, allowing for stack allocation, reference counting and tracing.

These systems all differ from our work in their emphasis on a strong static typing discipline with the memory management strategy encoded into pointer types. An advantage of this approach is that it can express more sophisticated strategies with finer granularity of control. Our approach is very different as we are motivated by exploring the power of using off-the-shelf components as a response to increased complexity in runtimes and compilers. Part of our motivation is also to explore solutions for existing languages without such complex type systems as deployed by Cyclone and Rust.

6. Conclusion

Real-world garbage collectors in managed languages are becoming increasingly complex. We investigated whether this complexity is really necessary and show that by having a different (but wider) interface between the collector and the developer, we can get high performance with off-the-shelf components for real applications. Our interface, M^3, provides developers with the choice of multiple memory management strategies that can coexist, allowing them to select the best combination of policies for their program and change that choice at any time. We do not expect M^3 to be universally applicable, but believe that in the hands of experienced developers dealing with performance sensitive code it can be simpler and achieve stronger results than current approaches. To investigate the feasibility of M^3 we conducted case studies of three different programs: Memcached, MOSS and a synthetic mid-

dleware. For all three we achieved performance results equal to or better than any of the single memory management strategies we had available and were competitive with explicit memory management. Finally, we remark that while our design used a mark-sweep and reference counting collector, we do not believe this is necessary for an M^3 system. Instead, systems should be designed with trade-offs between memory managers carefully chosen and their integration well managed.

Acknowledgments

This work is funded by the DARPA Clean-Slate Design of Resilient, Adaptive, Secure Hosts (CRASH) program and by a gift from Google.

References

[1] GNU C Library, 2.18.1. https://www.gnu.org/software/libc/, 2013.

[2] Memcached. http://memcached.org/, 2014.

[3] B. Atikoglu, Y. Xu, E. Frachtenberg, S. Jiang, and M. Paleczny. Workload Analysis of a Large-scale Key-value Store. In *International Conference on Measurement and Modeling of Computer Systems*, SIGMETRICS '12. ACM, 2012.

[4] C. R. Attanasio, D. F. Bacon, A. Cocchi, and S. Smith. A Comparative Evaluation of Parallel Garbage Collector Implementations. In *Workshop on Languages and Compilers for Parallel Computing*, LCPC'01, 2001.

[5] G. Attardi and T. Flagella. A Customizable Memory Management Framework. In *USENIX C++ Conference*, 1994.

[6] G. Attardi, T. Flagella, and P. Iglio. A Customisable Memory Management Framework for C++. In *Software Practice and Experience*, SPE'98, 1998.

[7] D. F. Bacon, P. Cheng, and V. Rajan. A Unified Theory of Garbage Collection. In *Object-Oriented Programming, Systems, Languages & Applications*, OOPSLA'04. ACM SIGPLAN, 2004.

[8] E. D. Berger, B. G. Zorn, and K. S. McKinley. Composing High-Performance Memory Allocators. In *Conference on Programming Language Design and Implementation*, PLDI'01. ACM SIGPLAN, 2001.

[9] S. M. Blackburn and K. S. McKinley. Ulterior Reference Counting: Fast Garbage Collection without a Long Wait. In *Object-Oriented Programming, Systems, Languages & Applications*, OOPSLA'03. ACM SIGPLAN, 2003.

[10] S. M. Blackburn, S. Singhai, M. Hertz, K. S. McKinely, and J. E. B. Moss. Pretenuring for Java. In *Object-Oriented Programming, Systems, Languages & Applications*, OOPSLA'01. ACM SIGPLAN, 2001.

[11] S. M. Blackburn, P. Cheng, and K. S. McKinley. Oil and Water? High Performance Garbage Collection in Java with JMTk. In *International Conference on Software Engineering*, ICSE'04. IEEE, 2004.

[12] S. M. Blackburn, M. Hertz, K. McKinley, J. E. B. Moss, and T. Yang. Profile-Based Pretenuring. In *Transactions on Programming Languages and Systems*, TPLS'07. ACM SIGPLAN, 2007.

[13] S. M. Blackburn, K. S. McKinley, R. Garner, C. Hoffmann, A. M. Khan, R. Bentzur, A. Diwan, D. Feinberg, D. Frampton, S. Z. Guyer, M. Hirzel, A. Hosking, M. Jump, H. Lee, J. E. B. Moss, A. Phansalkar, D. Stefanovik, T. VanDrunen, D. von Dincklage, and B. Wiedermann. Wake Up and Smell the Coffee: Evaluation Methodology for the 21st Century. *Commun. ACM*, 2008.

[14] H. Boehm. Space Efficient Conservative Garbage Collection. In *Conference on Programming Language Design and Implementation*, PLDI'93. ACM SIGPLAN, 1993.

[15] H. Boehm and M. Weiser. Garbage Collection in an Uncooperative Environment. In *Software Practice and Experience*, SPE'88, 1988.

[16] H. Boehm, A. Demers, and S. Shenker. Mostly Parallel Garbage Collection. In *Conference on Programming Language Design and Implementation*, PLDI'91. ACM SIGPLAN, 1991.

[17] P. Cheng, R. Harper, and P. Lee. Generational Stack Collection and Profile-Driven Pretenuring. In *Conference on Programming Language Design and Implementation*, PLDI'98. ACM SIGPLAN, 1998.

[18] J. R. Ellis and D. L. Detlefs. Safe, Efficient Garbage Collection for C++. In *C++ Technical Conference*, CTEC'94. USENIX, 1994.

[19] R. Fitzgerald and D. Tarditi. The Case for Profile-Directed Selection of Garbage Collectors. In *International Symposium on Memory Management*, ISMM'00. ACM SIGPLAN, 2000.

[20] D. Gay and A. Aiken. Memory Management with Explicit Regions. In *Conference on Programming Language Design and Implementation*, PLDI'98. ACM SIGPLAN, 1998.

[21] D. Gay and A. Aiken. Language Support for Regions. In *Conference on Programming Language Design and Implementation*, PLDI'01. ACM SIGPLAN, 2001.

[22] Google. The Go Programming Language. http://golang.org/, 2014.

[23] D. Grossman, G. Morrisett, T. Jim, M. Hicks, Y. Wang, and J. Cheney. Region-based Memory Management in Cyclone. In *Conference on Programming Language Design and Implementation*, PLDI'02. ACM SIGPLAN, 2002.

[24] R. L. Hudson, J. E. Moss, A. Diwan, and C. F. Weight. A Language-Independent Garbage Collector Toolkit. Technical report, Amherst, MA, USA, 1991.

[25] International Organization for Standards. Programming Language C++. ISO/IEC 14882:2011(E), 2011.

[26] T. Jim, G. Morrisett, D. Grossman, M. Hicks, J. Cheney, and Y. Wang. Cyclone: A Safe Dialect of C. In *USENIX Annual Technical Conference*, ATC'02. USENIX, 2002.

[27] M. Jump, S. M. Blackburn, and K. S. McKinley. Dynamic Object Sampling for Pretenuring. In *International Symposium on Memory Management*, ISMM'04. ACM SIGPLAN, 2004.

[28] Mozilla. The Rust Programming Language. http://www.rust-lang.org/, 2014.

[29] P. Reames and G. Necula. Towards Hinted Collection. In *International Symposium on Memory Management*, ISMM'13. ACM SIGPLAN, 2013.

[30] S. Schleimer, D. S. Wilkerson, and A. Aiken. Winnowing: Local Algorithms for Document Fingerprinting. In *International Conference on Management of Data*, COMAD'03. ACM SIGMOD, 2003.

[31] R. Shahriyar, S. M. Blackburn, X. Yang, and K. S. McKinley. Taking Off the Gloves with Reference Counting Immix. In *Object-Oriented Programming, Systems, Languages & Applications*, OOPSLA'13. ACM SIGPLAN, 2013.

[32] S. Soman, C. Krintz, and D. F. Bacon. Dynamic Selection of Application-Specific Garbage Collectors. In *International Symposium on Memory Management*, ISMM'04. ACM SIGPLAN, 2004.

[33] K.-P. Vo. Vmalloc: A General and Efficient Memory Allocator. *Software Practice and Experience*, v26:1–18, 1996.

Allocation Folding Based on Dominance

Daniel Clifford   Hannes Payer   Michael Starzinger   Ben L. Titzer

Google

{danno,hpayer,mstarzinger,titzer}@google.com

Abstract

Memory management system performance is of increasing importance in today's managed languages. Two lingering sources of overhead are the direct costs of memory allocations and write barriers. This paper introduces *allocation folding*, an optimization technique where the virtual machine automatically folds multiple memory allocation operations in optimized code together into a single, larger *allocation group*. An allocation group comprises multiple objects and requires just a single bounds check in a bump-pointer style allocation, rather than a check for each individual object. More importantly, all objects allocated in a single allocation group are guaranteed to be contiguous after allocation and thus exist in the same generation, which makes it possible to statically remove write barriers for reference stores involving objects in the same allocation group. Unlike object inlining, object fusing, and object colocation, allocation folding requires no special connectivity or ownership relation between the objects in an allocation group. We present our analysis algorithm to determine when it is safe to fold allocations together and discuss our implementation in V8, an open-source, production JavaScript virtual machine. We present performance results for the Octane and Kraken benchmark suites and show that allocation folding is a strong performance improvement, even in the presence of some heap fragmentation. Additionally, we use four hand-selected benchmarks JPEGEncoder, NBody, Soft3D, and Textwriter where allocation folding has a large impact.

Categories and Subject Descriptors   D3.4 [*Programming Languages*]: Processors   compilers, memory management (garbage collection), optimization

General Terms   Algorithms, Languages, Experimentation, Performance, Measurement

Keywords   Dynamic Optimization, Garbage Collection, Memory Managment, Write barriers, JavaScript

1. Introduction

Applications that rely on automatic memory management are now everywhere, from traditional consumer desktop applications to large scale data analysis, high-performance web servers, financial trading platforms, to ever-more demanding websites, and even billions of mobile phones and embedded devices. Reducing the costs

of automatic memory management is of principal importance in best utilizing computing resources across the entire spectrum.

Automatic memory management systems that rely on garbage collection introduce some overhead in the application's main execution path. While some garbage collection work can be made incremental, parallel, or even concurrent, the actual cost of executing allocation operations and write barriers still remains. This is even more apparent in collectors that target low pause time and require heavier write barriers.

This paper targets two of the most direct costs of garbage collection overhead on the application: the cost of allocation bounds checks and write barriers executed inline in application code. Our optimization technique, *allocation folding*, automatically groups multiple object allocations from multiple allocation sites in an optimized function into a single, larger *allocation group*. The allocation of an allocation group requires just a single bounds check in a bump-pointer style allocator, rather than one check per object. Even more importantly, our flow-sensitive compiler analysis that eliminates write barriers is vastly improved by allocation folding since a larger region of the optimized code can be proven not to require write barriers.

Allocation folding relies on just one dynamic invariant:

Invariant 1. *Between two allocations A_1 and A_2, if no other operation that can move the object allocated at A_1 occurs, then space for the object allocated at A_2 could have been allocated at A_1 and then initialized at A_2, without ever having been observable to the garbage collector.*

Our optimization exploits this invariant to group multiple allocations in an optimized function into a single, larger allocation. Individual objects can then be carved out of this larger region, without the garbage collector ever observing an intermediate state.

Allocation folding can be considered an optimization local to an optimized function. Unlike object inlining [5], object fusing [21], or object colocation [11], the objects that are put into an allocation group need not have any specific ownership or connectivity relationship. In fact, once the objects in a group are allocated and initialized, the garbage collector may reclaim, move, or promote them independently of each other. No static analysis is required, and the flow-sensitive analysis is local to an optimized function. Our technique ensures that allocation folding requires no special support from the garbage collector or the deoptimizer and does not interfere with other compiler optimizations. We implemented allocation folding in V8 [8], a high-performance open source virtual machine for JavaScript. Our implementation of allocation folding is part of the production V8 code base and is enabled by default since Chrome M30.

The rest of this paper is structured as follows. Section 2 describes the parts of the V8 JavaScript engine relevant to allocation folding, which includes the flow-sensitive analysis required for allocation folding and relevant details about the garbage collector and write barriers. Section 3 describes the allocation folding algorithm and shows how allocation folding vastly widens the scope of write barrier elimination. Section 4 presents experimental results for allocation folding across a range of benchmarks which include the Octane [7] and Kraken [13] suites. Section 5 discusses related work followed by a conclusion in Section 6.

2. The V8 Engine

V8 [8] is an industrial-strength compile-only JavaScript virtual machine consisting of a quick, one-pass compiler that generates machine code that simulates an expression stack and a more aggressive optimizing compiler based on a static single assignment (SSA) intermediate representation (IR) called Crankshaft, which is triggered when a function becomes hot. V8 uses runtime type profiling and hidden classes [9] to create efficient representations for JavaScript objects. Crankshaft relies on type feedback gathered at runtime to perform aggressive speculative optimizations that target efficient property access, inlining of hot methods, and reducing arithmetic to primitives. Dynamic checks inserted into optimized code detect when speculation no longer holds, invalidating the optimization code. Deoptimization then transfers execution back to unoptimized code[1]. Such speculation is necessary to optimize for common cases that appear in JavaScript programs but that can nevertheless be violated by JavaScript's extremely liberal allowance for mutation. For example, unlike most statically-typed object-oriented languages, JavaScript allows adding and removing properties from objects by name, installing getters and setters (even for previously existing properties), and mutation of an object's prototype chain at essentially any point during execution. After adapting to JavaScript's vagaries, Crankshaft performs a suite of common classical compiler optimizations, including constant folding, strength reduction, dead code elimination, loop invariant code motion, type check elimination, load/store elimination, range analysis, bounds check removal and hoisting, and global value numbering. It uses a linear-scan SSA-based register allocator similar to that described by Wimmer [20].

V8 implements a generational garbage collector and employs write barriers to record references from the old generation to the young generation. Write barriers are partially generated inline in compiled code by both compilers. They consist of efficient inline flag checks and more expensive shared code that may record the field which is being written. For V8's garbage collector the write barriers also maintain the incremental marking invariant and record references to objects that will be relocated. Crankshaft can statically elide write barriers in some cases, e.g. if the object value being written is guaranteed to be immortal and will not be relocated, or if the object field being written resides in an object known to be in the young generation. The analysis for such elimination is given in Section 2.3.1.

2.1 Crankshaft IR

Crankshaft uses an SSA sparse-dataflow intermediate representation which is built directly from the JavaScript abstract syntax tree (AST). All important optimizations are performed on this IR. Instructions define values rather than virtual registers, which allows an instruction use to refer directly to the instruction definition, making move instructions unnecessary and improving pattern matching. Instructions are organized into basic blocks which are themselves organized into a control flow graph with branches and gotos, and PHI instructions merge values at control flow join points. SSA form guarantees that every instruction I_n is defined exactly once.

Instruction	Dep	Chg
I_n = PARAMETER[K]		
I_n = CONSTANT[K]		
I_n = ARITH(I, I)		
I_n = LOAD[field](object)	Ψ	
I_n = STORE[field](object, value)		Ψ
I_n = ALLOC[space](size)	Λ	Λ
I_n = INNER[offset, size](alloc)		
I_n = CALL(I...)	*	*
I_n = PHI(I...)		

Table 1: Simplified Crankshaft IR Instructions.

Every definition must dominate its uses, except for the inputs to PHI instructions.

Table 1 shows a simplified set of Crankshaft instructions that will be used throughout this paper. Statically known parts of an instruction, such as the field involved in a LOAD or STORE, or the value of a constant, are enclosed in square brackets []. The inputs to an instruction are given in parentheses () and must be references to dominating instructions. The table also lists the effects changed and depended on for each instruction. Effects will be discussed in Section 2.2.2. We elide the discussion of the more than 100 real Crankshaft instructions which are not relevant to this paper.

2.2 Global Value Numbering

The analysis required to detect opportunities for allocation folding is implemented as part of the existing flow-sensitive global value numbering (GVN) algorithm in Crankshaft. Global value numbering eliminates redundant computations when it is possible to do so without affecting the semantics of the overall program. Extending GVN to handle impure operations gives the necessary flow-sensitivity for identifying candidates for allocation folding.

2.2.1 GVN for Pure Operations

GVN traditionally targets *pure* computations in the program such as arithmetic on primitives, math functions, and accesses to immutable data. Because such operations always compute the same result and neither produce nor are affected by side-effects, it is safe to hoist such computations out of loops or reuse the result from a previous occurrence of the same operation on the same inputs.

For each basic block in the method, the value numbering algorithm visits the instructions in control flow order, putting pure instructions into a value numbering table. In our simplified Crankshaft instruction set depicted in Table 1, we consider all arithmetic instructions $\text{ARITH}(I_i, I_j)$ to be pure instructions[2]. Two instructions are *value-equivalent* if they are the same operation (e.g. both ADD or both SUB) and the inputs are identical SSA values. If a value-equivalent instruction already exists in the table, then the second instruction is redundant. The second instruction is removed, and all of its uses are updated to reference the first instruction.

Crankshaft uses the dominator tree of the control flow graph to extend local value numbering to the entire control flow graph. The dominator tree captures the standard dominance relation for basic blocks: a basic block D *dominates* basic block B if and only if D appears on every path from the function entry to B. It is

---

[1] V8 might be considered the most direct descendant of the Smalltalk $\rightarrow$ Self $\rightarrow$ HotSpot lineage of virtual machines that pioneered these techniques.

[2] In JavaScript, all operations are untyped. Arithmetic on objects could result in calls to application-defined methods that have arbitrary side-effects. In V8, a complex system of type profiling with inline caches, some static type inference during compilation, and some speculative checks in optimized code guard operations that have been assumed to apply only to primitives.

straightforward to extend the dominator relation on basic blocks to instructions, since instructions are ordered inside of basic blocks.

GVN applies local value numbering to each basic block in dominator tree order, starting at the function entry. Instead of starting with an empty value numbering table at the beginning of each block, the value numbering table from a dominating block D is copied and used as the starting table when processing each of its immediately dominated children B. By the definition of dominance, a block D dominating block B appears on every control flow path from the start to B. Therefore any instruction I_2 in B which is equivalent to I_1 in D is redundant and can be safely replaced by I_1. Since Crankshaft's SSA form guarantees that every definition must dominate its usages, the algorithm is guaranteed to find all fully redundant computations[3].

2.2.2 GVN for Impure Operations

Crankshaft extends the GVN algorithm to handle some instructions that *can* be affected by side-effects, but are nevertheless redundant if no such side-effects can happen between redundant occurrences of the same instruction. Extending GVN to impure instructions by explicitly tracking side-effects is the key analysis needed for allocation folding.

We illustrate the tracking of side-effects during GVN with a simple form of redundant load elimination. A load $L_2 = \texttt{LOAD}[\texttt{field}](O_i)$ can be replaced with a previous load of the same field $L_1 = \texttt{LOAD}[\texttt{field}](O_i)$ if L_1 dominates L_2 and no intervening operation could have modified the field of the object on any path between L_1 and L_2.

For load elimination, we consider $\texttt{LOAD}$ and $\texttt{STORE}$ instructions and an abstraction of the state in the heap. For the sake of illustration, in this section we will model all the state in the heap with a single effect Ψ, but for finer granularity, one could model multiple non-overlapping heap abstractions with individual side-effects Ψ_f, e.g. one for each field $\texttt{f}$[4]. Stores *change* Ψ and loads *depend* on Ψ. $\texttt{CALL}$ instructions are conservatively considered to change all possible side-effects, so we consider them to also change Ψ.

While previously only pure instructions were allowed to be added to the value numbering table, now we also allow instructions that depend on side-effects to be added to the table, and each entry in the value numbering table also records the effects on which the instruction depends. When processing a load $L_1 = \texttt{LOAD}[\texttt{field}](O_i)$, it is inserted into the table and marked as depending on effect Ψ. A later load $L_2 = \texttt{LOAD}[\texttt{field}](O_i)$ might be encountered. Such a load is redundant if the value numbering table contains L_1. When an instruction that *changes* a side-effect is encountered, any entry in the value numbering table that *depends* on that effect is invalidated. Thus any store $S_1 = \texttt{STORE}[\texttt{field}](O_i, V_j)$ causes all instructions in the table that depend on Ψ to be removed, so that subsequent loads cannot reuse values from before the store.

We would like to use the idea above to perform global value numbering for instructions that can be affected by side-effects across the entire control flow graph. Unfortunately, it is not enough just to rely on the effects we encounter as we walk down the dominator tree, as we did in the previous algorithm. The dominator tree only guarantees that a dominator block *appears* on every path from the start to its dominated block, but other blocks can appear between the dominator and the dominated block. To correctly account for side-effects, we must process the effects on *all* paths from a dominator block to its children blocks.

---

[3] By induction on the structure of instructions.

[4] The actual load elimination algorithm in Crankshaft models several non-overlapping heap memory abstractions and also performs a limited alias analysis.

To perform this analysis efficiently, we first perform a linear pass over the control flow graph, computing an unordered set of effects that are produced by each block. Loops require extra care. Assuming a reducible flow graph, each loop has a unique header block which is the only block from which the loop can be entered. A loop header block is marked specially and contains the union of effects for all blocks in the loop. When traversing the dominator tree, if the child node is a loop header, then all instructions in the value numbering table that depend on the loop effects are first invalidated.

Armed with the pre-computed effect summaries for each block, the GVN algorithm can process the effects on all paths between a dominator and its children by first starting at the child block and walking the control flow edges backward, invalidating entries in the value numbering table that depend on the summary effects from each block, until the dominator block is reached. Such a walk is worst-case $O(E)$, since the dominator block may be the start block and the child block may be the end block, leading to an overall worst-case of $O(E * N)$, where E is the number of edges and N is the number of blocks. In practice, most dominator-child relationships have zero non-dominating paths, so this step is usually a no-op. Our implementation also employs several tricks to avoid the worst-case complexity, such as memoizing some path traversals and terminating early when the value numbering table no longer contains impure instructions, but the details are not relevant to the scope of this paper.

2.2.3 Side-Effect Dominators

Each effect ϵ induces a global flow-sensitive relation on instructions that depend on ϵ and instructions that change ϵ. We call this relation ϵ-dominance.

Definition 1. *For a given effect ϵ, instruction D ϵ-dominates instruction I if and only if D occurs on every path from the function entry to I, and no path from D to I contains another instruction $D' \neq D$ that changes ϵ.*

Given this new definition, it is easy to restate load elimination.

Predicate 1. *A load $L_2 = \texttt{LOAD}[\texttt{field}_j](O_i)$ can be replaced with $L_1 = \texttt{LOAD}[\texttt{field}_j](O_i)$ if L_1 Ψ-dominates L_2.*

We can also define an ϵ-*dominator*.

Definition 2. *For a given effect ϵ, instruction D is the ϵ-dominator of instruction I if and only if D ϵ-dominates I and D changes ϵ.*

It follows immediately from the definition of ϵ-dominance that an instruction can have at most one ϵ-dominator.

GVN for impure values computes both ϵ-dominance and the unique ϵ-dominator during its traversal of the instructions. It provides the ϵ-dominator as an API to the rest of the compiler. Crankshaft uses it for both allocation folding and for write barrier elimination, both of which are detailed in the following sections.

2.3 Write Barriers

V8 employs a generational garbage collector, using a semi-space strategy for frequent minor collections of the young generation, and a mark-and-sweep collector with incremental marking for major collections of the old generation. Write barriers emitted inline in compiled code track inter-generational pointers and maintain the marking invariant between incremental phases. Every store into an object on the garbage collected heap may require a write barrier, unless the compiler can prove the barrier to be redundant. This section details the tasks a write barrier must perform and some of the implementation details to understand the runtime overhead introduced by write barriers, and then explores conditions under which it is permissible to statically eliminate write barriers (Section 2.3.1).

Write barriers in V8 perform three main tasks to ensure correct behavior of the garbage collector while mutators are accessing objects on the garbage collected heap.

- **Track Inter-generational Pointers**: References stored into the old generation pointing to an object in the young generation are recorded in a store buffer. The store buffer becomes part of the root-set for minor collections, allowing the garbage collector to perform a minor collection without considering the entire heap. Every mutation of an object in the old generation potentially introduces an old-to-young reference.

- **Maintain Marking Invariant**: During the marking phase of a major collection, a standard marking scheme gives each object one of three colors: white for objects not yet seen by the garbage collector, gray for objects seen but not yet scanned by the garbage collector, and black for objects fully scanned by the garbage collector. The marking invariant is that black objects cannot reference white objects. To reduce the pause time of major collections, V8 interleaves the marking phase with mutator execution and performs stepwise incremental marking until the transitive closure of all reachable objects has been found. The write barrier must maintain the marking invariant for objects in the old generation, since every mutation of an object in the old generation could potentially introduce a black-to-white reference. Newly allocated objects are guaranteed to be white and hence cannot break the marking invariant.

- **Pointers into Evacuation Candidates**: To reduce fragmentation of certain regions of the heap, the garbage collector might mark fragmented pages as evacuation candidates before the marking phase starts. Objects on these pages will be relocated onto other, less fragmented pages, freeing the evacuated pages. The marking phase records all references pointing into these evacuation candidates in a buffer so that references can be updated once the target object has been relocated. As before, objects in the young generation are fully scanned during a major collection and their references don't need to be recorded explicitly. Every mutation of an object in the old generation potentially introduces a reference pointing to an evacuation candidate.

```
 1 store:
 2   mov      [$obj+field], $val
 3 barrier:
 4   and      $val, 0xfff00000
 5   test_b   [$val+PAGE_FLAGS], VALUES_INTERESTING
 6   jz       skip
 7   mov      $val, 0xfff00000
 8   and      $val, $obj
 9   test_b   [$val+PAGE_FLAGS], FIELDS_INTERESTING
10   jz       skip
11   call     RecordWriteStub($obj, field)
12 skip:
13   ...
```

Listing 1: Inlined write barrier assembly on IA32

The above three tasks require an efficient yet compact implementation of the write barrier code. This is achieved by splitting the write barrier into two parts: one that is emitted inline with the compiled code, and out-of-line code stubs. The assembly code in Listing 1 shows the instructions being emitted inline for an IA32 processor. After performing the store to the field (Line 2), the write barrier first checks whether the referenced object $val is situated on a page where values are considered interesting (Lines 4 to 6). It then checks whether the receiver object $obj is situated on a page whose fields are considered interesting (Lines 7 to 10). These checks perform bit mask tests of the page flags for the pages[5] on which the respective objects are situated. The code stubs recording the store are only called in case both checks succeed (Line 11). The write barrier can be removed if the compiler can statically determine that at least one of the checks will always fail.

During execution the garbage collector may change the page flags VALUES_INTERESTING and FIELDS_INTERESTING which are continuously checked by write barriers.

2.3.1 Write Barrier Elimination

Under some conditions it is possible to statically remove write barriers. Stores whose receiver object is guaranteed to be newly allocated in the young generation never need to be recorded. Such stores cannot introduce old-to-young references, they cannot break the marking invariant as newly allocated objects are white, and finally their fields will be updated automatically in case they point into evacuation candidates.

Using the GVN algorithm which handles side-effecting instructions, we introduce a new effect Λ, which tracks the last instruction that could trigger a garbage collection. We say that allocations, meaning instructions of the form $I_1 = \texttt{ALLOC}[\texttt{s}](K_1)$, both *change* and *depend on* Λ. We consider all `CALL` instructions to have uncontrollable effects, so they implicitly also change Λ, as with Ψ.

With Λ, it is easy for Crankshaft to analyze store instructions and remove write barriers to objects guaranteed to be newly allocated in the young generation:

Predicate 2. $S_1 = \texttt{STORE}[\texttt{field}](O_1, V_1)$ *does not require a write barrier if* O_1 *has the form* $O_1 = \texttt{ALLOC}[\texttt{young}](I_1)$ *and* O_1 Λ-*dominates* S_1.

This approach to write barrier elimination is limited in that it can only remove write barriers for the most recently allocated young space object. As we will see in the next section, allocation folding enlarges the scope for write barrier elimination.

3. Allocation Folding

Allocation folding groups multiple allocations together into a single chunk of memory when it is safe to do so without being observable to the garbage collector. In terms of Crankshaft IR instructions, this means replacing some `ALLOC` instructions with `INNER` instructions. `ALLOC` allocates a contiguous chunk of memory of a given size, performing a garbage collection if necessary. `INNER` computes the effective address of a sub-region within a previously allocated chunk of memory and has no side-effects. According to Invariant 1, we can fold two allocations together if there is no intervening operation that can move the first allocated object. We can use that dynamic invariant to formulate the allocation folding opportunities on Crankshaft IR:

Predicate 3. *Allocations* $A_1 = \texttt{ALLOC}[\texttt{s}](K_1)$ *and* $A_2 = \texttt{ALLOC}[\texttt{s}](K_2)$ *are candidates for allocation folding if* A_1 *is the* Λ-*dominator of* A_2.

When candidates are identified, allocation folding is a simple local transformation of the code. If allocation $A_1 = \texttt{ALLOC}[\texttt{s}](K_1)$ is the Λ-dominator of allocation $A_2 = \texttt{ALLOC}[\texttt{s}](K_2)$, then a single instruction $A_{\texttt{new}} = \texttt{ALLOC}[\texttt{s}](K_1 + K_2)$ can be inserted immediately before A_1, and A_1 can be replaced with $A_1' = \texttt{INNER}[\#0, K_1](A_{\texttt{new}})$ and A_2 can be replaced with $A_2' = \texttt{INNER}[K_1, K_2](A_{\texttt{new}})$.

Figure 1 presents an example control flow graph before allocation folding has been performed. The dominator tree is shown in light gray and is marked with the effects for each block. Blocks

---

[5] All pages in the collected heap are aligned at megabyte boundaries, hence computing the page header from an arbitrary object reference is a single bitmask.

```
B0
I1 = PARAMETER[0]
I2 = PARAMETER[1]
I3 = CONSTANT[#16]
I4 = ALLOC[young](I3)
I4  I5 = STORE[a](I4, ...)
I4      IF I2 -> B1, B2
```

```
       B0
        Λ
   B1   B2   B3
    Λ    Λ    Λ
```

```
B1
I4  I6 = CONSTANT[#8]
I4  I7 = ALLOC[young](I6)
I7  I8 = STORE[w](I7, ...)
I7  I9 = STORE[b](I4, I7)
I7      GOTO -> B3
```

```
B2
I4  I10 = CONSTANT["name"]
I4  I11 = STORE[b](I4, I10)
I4      GOTO -> B3
```

```
B3
    I12 = CONSTANT[#12]
    I13 = ALLOC[young](I12)
I13 I14 = STORE[z](I13, ...)
I13 I15 = STORE[c](I4, I13)
I13     RET I4
```

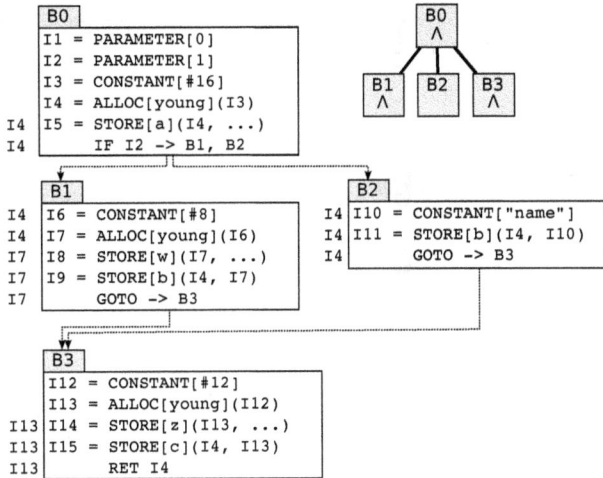

Figure 1: Example CFG before allocation folding.

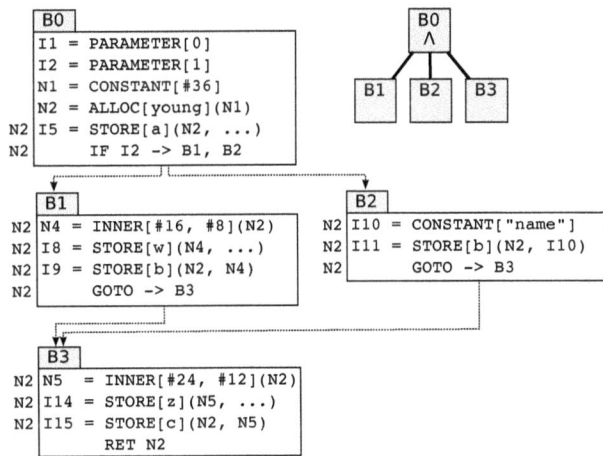

```
B0
I1 = PARAMETER[0]
I2 = PARAMETER[1]
N1 = CONSTANT[#36]
N2 = ALLOC[young](N1)
N2  I5 = STORE[a](N2, ...)
N2      IF I2 -> B1, B2
```

```
       B0
        Λ
   B1   B2   B3
```

```
B1
N2  N4 = INNER[#16, #8](N2)
N2  I8 = STORE[w](N4, ...)
N2  I9 = STORE[b](N2, N4)
N2      GOTO -> B3
```

```
B2
N2  I10 = CONSTANT["name"]
N2  I11 = STORE[b](N2, I10)
N2      GOTO -> B3
```

```
B3
N2  N5  = INNER[#24, #12](N2)
N2  I14 = STORE[z](N5, ...)
N2  I15 = STORE[c](N2, N5)
        RET N2
```

Figure 2: Example CFG after allocation folding.

B0, B1, and B3 each contain an allocation instruction, therefore each is marked as changing Λ. The Λ-dominator is shown to the left of each instruction, outside the basic block. Note that some instructions, such as I12 and I13 do not have a Λ-dominator. In Figure 1, we can see that some, but not all, write barriers can be eliminated through local analysis. Write barriers associated with stores I8, I11, and I14 can be eliminated, since we can see that their Λ-dominator is the receiver of the store, and that receiver is an allocation in the young generation. However, write barriers associated with stores I9 and I15 cannot be eliminated because their Λ-dominator does not match the receiver object of the store.

Figure 2 shows the control flow graph from Figure 1 after allocation folding has been performed. Some instructions have been removed, and new instructions N_n have been inserted. The allocations in blocks B0, B1, and B3 have been folded into one larger allocation[6] in B0 and are replaced by INNER instructions that carve out individual objects from the allocation group. We can see that removing these allocations removes the Λ from these

---

[6] Note that allocation I13 has no Λ-dominator until allocation I7 has been folded into I4. In general, allocation folding can be applied again whenever it introduces a new Λ-dominator for an allocation that previously did not have one due to merges in the control flow.

blocks because INNER instructions do not change Λ. By replacing ALLOC instructions with INNER instructions the number of program points at which garbage collection can happen is reduced. This then increases the opportunities for local write barrier elimination. The opportunities are evident in the changes to the Λ-dominators for each instruction. After allocation folding, the single, larger allocation Λ-dominates all the stores. All stores in the example are now into objects allocated from the same allocation group, which is allocated in the young generation. Since we know that stores into objects in the young generation cannot introduce old-to-young references, all write barriers in this example can be removed.

In this example we can see how allocation folding can give rise to memory fragmentation. If at runtime the code follows the path B0 → B2 → B3, then the space reserved for the inner allocation at N4 will have been allocated but not be used because we do not overlap the space reserved for the folded allocations. A straightforward approach to avoiding this source of memory fragmentation is to only fold allocations in the same basic block. We compare allocation folding with and without the basic block restriction and study the overhead of fragmentation by measuring the amount of each allocation group that is actually used, or the *allocation group utilization*, in Section 4.

Memory fragmentation gives rise to uninitialized memory regions between objects in the heap. This requires the garbage collector to be capable of handling a non-iterable heap. As a consequence a mark-and-sweep garbage collector must store the mark bits outside objects.

3.1 Allocation Folding in Crankshaft

We present the pseudo-code of the allocation folding algorithm in Crankshaft in Listing 2. We perform allocation folding as part of GVN, after performing aggressive inlining, so that the maximum number of folding opportunities are available.

```
1  HAllocate::HandleSideEffectDominator(dominator):
2    if !dominator->IsAllocate():
3      return;
4    if AllocationFoldingBasicBlockMode() &&
5       this->BlockID() != dominator->BlockID():
6      return;
7    dominator_size = dominator->Size();
8    size = this->Size();
9    if !dominator_size->IsConstant() ||
10      !size->IsConstant():
11     return;
12   new_size = dominator_size + size;
13   if this->DoubleAligned():
14     if !dominator->DoubleAligned():
15       dominator->SetDoubleAligned(true);
16     if IsDoubleAligned(dominator_size):
17       dominator_size += DoubleSize()/2;
18       new_size += DoubleSize()/2;
19   if new_size > MaxAllocationFoldingSize():
20     return;
21   new_size_instruction =
22     HConstant::CreateAndInsertBefore(
23       new_size, dominator);
24   dominator->UpdateSize(new_size_instruction);
25   inner_allocated_object_instruction =
26     HInnerAllocatedObject::New(
27       dominator, dominator_size);
28   this->DeleteAndReplaceWith(
29     inner_allocated_object_instruction);
```

Listing 2: Allocation folding algorithm

A given allocation instruction can only be folded into its Λ-dominator if that Λ-dominator is itself an allocation instruction (Line 2). If the basic block restriction is enabled (Line 3), then only allocations in the same basic block will be folded (Line 4).

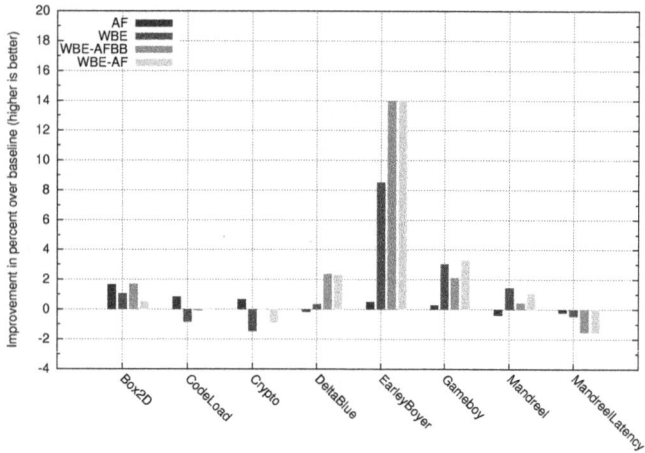

(a) Part 1

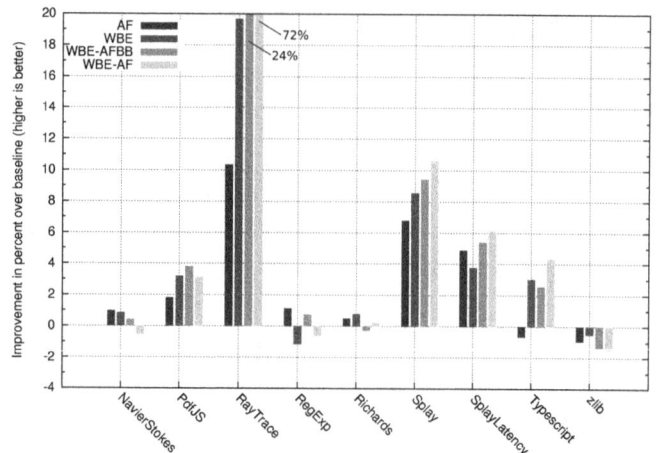

(b) Part 2

Figure 3: Improvement in percent of all configurations over the baseline on the Octane suite running on X64.

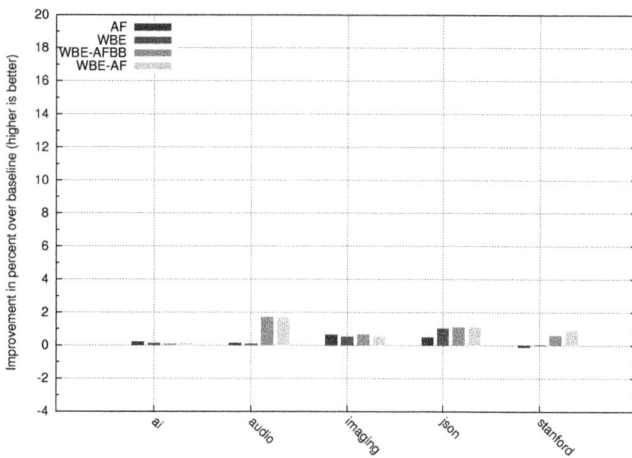

Figure 4: Improvement in percent of all configurations over the baseline on the Kraken suite running on X64.

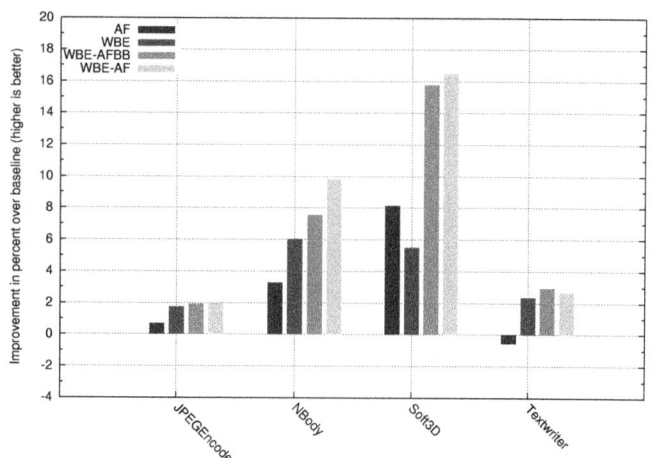

Figure 5: Improvement in percent of all configurations over the baseline on hand-selected benchmarks running on X64.

The allocation size must be a constant[7] (Line 9 and Line 10). The size of the the new dominator allocation instruction is the sum of the sizes of the given allocation instruction and its Λ-dominator (Line 12). If the given allocation instruction requires double alignment (Line 10) the Λ-dominator must be aligned as well and the extra space accounted for if necessary (Line 17 and Line 18). If the new allocation would be larger than a maximum size (a constant determined based on the size of the young generation) then the algorithm will not do the folding (Line 19). If all criteria are satisfied, the algorithm increases the size of the Λ-dominator allocation instruction (Line 24) and creates a new inner-allocate (INNER) instruction which refers to the end of the previous allocation group (Line 25). All uses of the previous instruction are replaced with uses of the new inner-allocate instruction (Line 28).

---

[7] Folding non-constant size allocations is possible in principle, but the gritty details means a lot of graph rewriting, since the computed sizes also need to be hoisted.

4. Experiments

We ran V8 revision r18926 on an X64 server machine with an Intel Core i5-2400 quad-core 3.10GHz CPU and 80GB of main memory running Linux. We performed the same experiments on IA32 and ARM, but found that the performance results were in such close agreement with X64 that we gained no new insights. We therefore chose to omit redundant data for space reasons.

For our experiments we used the complete Octane 2.0 [7] and Kraken 1.1 [13] suites, two standard JavaScript benchmarks which are designed to test specific virtual machine subsystems. In both cases we run each benchmark 20 times, each run in a separate virtual machine in order to isolate their effects from each other and report the average of these runs. We ran many other benchmarks where we measured no observable impact from allocation folding, but found no benchmarks where allocation folding was a measurable detriment to performance. However, we did find that for four other benchmarks, allocation folding had significant improvement: (1) a JPEGEncoder [16] written in JavaScript encoding an image, (2) NBody [10] solving the classical N-body problem, (3) a

JavaScript software 3D renderer Soft3D [12], and (4) the JavaScript benchmark Textwriter [1] originally designed to test string operation speed.

We use five configurations of V8 for our experiments: (1) *baseline* generates optimized code without write barrier elimination or allocation folding, (2) *allocation folding (AF)* is the baseline configuration with allocation folding only, (3) *write barrier elimination (WBE)* is the baseline configuration with write barrier elimination only, (4) *write barrier elimination and allocation folding on basic blocks (WBE-AFBB)*, performs write barrier elimination and allocation folding only on basic blocks, and (5) *write barrier elimination and allocation folding (WBE-AF)* is the previous configuration without the basic block restriction.

The WBE-AF configuration is the one used in production code and on average yields the biggest performance improvement. The other configurations are used to investigate the independent impact of the optimizations on the baseline performance without taking the positive interplay of allocation folding and dominator-based write barrier elimination into account.

4.1 Throughput

Figures 3-5 show relative throughout improvement for each of the benchmarks on X64. Allocation folding has the most impact on `RayTrace`, and here we measured a trend that is common to several benchmarks. In `RayTrace`, we measured an improvement with AF of more than 10% from saving bump-pointer allocation costs, with WBE of more than 20% from doing only dominator-based write barrier elimination, with WBE-AFBB of 23% from allocation folding at the basic block level, and with WBE-AF of more than 70% from allocation folding without the basic block restriction. WBE-AF improves `EarleyBoyer` by about 14%, `Splay` by over 10%, and `TypeScript` by about 4%. `DeltaBlue`, `PdfJS`, and `Gameboy` also improve by about 2-3%. The throughput improvement is less than 1% for most of the Kraken benchmarks. Other benchmarks had significant improvements with WBE-AF, such as `NBody` (10%) and `Soft3D` (16%).

With many benchmarks we see the same trend where the improvement from allocation folding alone is measurable, even significant, but the largest gains are from eliminating the cost of write barriers, as seen in `EarlyBoyer`, `RayTrace`, `Gameboy`, `NBody`, and `Soft3D`. Also notable is `DeltaBlue`, which only benefits from the combined effects of allocation folding and write barrier elimination, and sees almost no benefit from either independently. We also see that in several cases allocation folding on basic blocks gives results as good as the complete dominator-based algorithm.

Tables 2-4 show the proportion of folded and non-folded allocation sites in optimized code in our benchmarks.

4.2 Write Barrier Frequency

Tables 5, 6 and 7 show the static number of write barrier sites compiled into the optimized code as well as the dynamic number of write barriers executed.

There is a strong correlation between throughput improvement and fewer executed write barriers due to folded allocations. For example, in `RayTrace`, WBE eliminates about 38% of write barriers for a 20% speedup, and WBE-AF eliminates about 96% of write barriers resulting in a throughput improvement of 72%. `EarleyBoyer` executes even fewer write barriers in comparison to the baseline, with 98% eliminated and throughput improvement by 14% using WBE-AF. In `Soft3D` allocation folding reduced the number of executed write barriers by 86% for a speedup of 16% using WBE-AF. In `NBody` allocation folding removed the most write barriers, about 99% in WBE-AF. The results are consistent across the remaining benchmarks, with those that have the most write barriers eliminated experiencing the largest gains in throughput.

	AFBB	AF
Benchmark	Folded in %	Folded in %
Box2D	21	35
CodeLoad	28	28
Crypto	33	42
DeltaBlue	37	47
EarleyBoyer	26	42
Gameboy	3	3
Mandreel	38	38
MandreelLatency	38	38
NavierStokes	18	18
PdfJS	29	31
RayTrace	11	65
RegExp	27	27
Richards	26	65
Splay	22	40
SplayLatency	22	40
Typescript	6	12
zlib	82	82

Table 2: Static proportion of folded allocation instructions in Octane.

	AFBB	AF
Benchmark	Folded in %	Folded in %
ai	25	25
audio	37	38
imaging	0	0
json	0	0
stanford	23	24

Table 3: Static proportion of folded allocation instructions in Kraken.

	AFBB	AF
Benchmark	Folded in %	Non-folded in %
JPEGEncoder	18	55
NBody	76	88
Soft3D	56	58
Textwriter	8	17

Table 4: Static proportion of folded allocation instructions in hand-selected benchmarks.

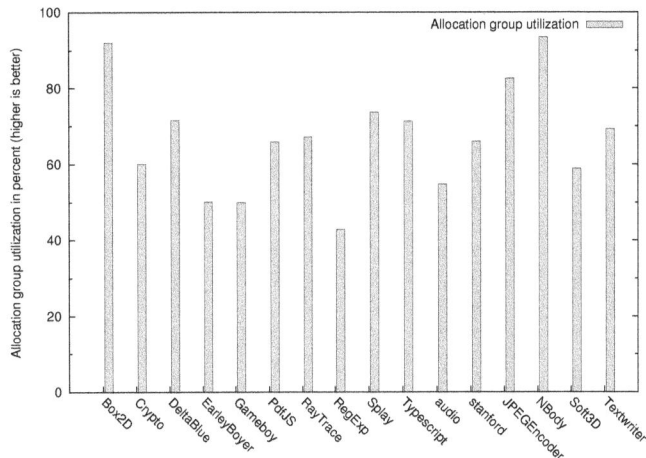

Figure 6: Allocation group utilization on X64.

	Static					Dynamic				
Benchmark	Baseline	AF	WBE	WBE-AFBB	WBE-AF	Baseline	AF	WBE	WBE-AFBB	WBE-AF
Box2D	3,166	3,103	2,446	2,449	2,188	41,083,162	41,083,425	25,453,150	25,432,225	20,811,285
Codeload	46,956	46,929	46,780	46,814	46,793	300,295	300,447	186,482	186,487	186,491
Crypto	720	717	353	257	237	1,690,104	1,692,164	494,311	329,287	312,298
DeltaBlue	518	516	307	209	187	472,408,298	472,408,568	329,751,772	251,689,699	197,782,399
EarleyBoyer	774	777	215	196	196	1,374,515,484	1,374,515,775	28,122,342	28,029,928	28,039,744
Gameboy	4,019	3,984	3,634	3,692	3,685	8,714,289	8,773,082	8,321,467	8,176,195	8,145,726
Mandreel	107	107	39	36	36	18,668	18,668	1,744	1,744	1,744
MandreelLatency	127	127	41	36	36	18,668	18,668	1,744	1,744	1,744
NavierStokes	218	216	111	109	109	27,887	27,887	26,039	26,039	26,039
PdfJS	4,983	5,186	4,165	4,173	4,091	215,806,576	216,156,555	38,048,742	39,857,551	38,115,351
RayTrace	998	998	621	614	238	1,188,216,950	1,188,216,565	741,557,641	741,554,567	54,467,024
RegExp	423	423	330	323	323	73,182,468	73,182,384	62,449,266	62,446,183	62,446,138
Richards	429	429	206	189	185	593,493,156	593,462,983	589,364,534	588,980,038	588,831,690
Splay	1,658	1,649	1,533	1,497	1,574	477,647,218	477,647,182	464,248,939	438,256,053	438,258,244
SplayLatency	1,641	1,678	1,519	1,503	1,515	477,646,746	477,646,841	464,241,636	438,255,521	438,256,651
Typescript	19,326	19,770	16,542	15,467	17,395	36,257,098	36,241,445	30,485,767	30,412,861	30,454,115
zlib	309	309	185	176	176	17,078	17,078	14,812	14,767	14,767

Table 5: Static and dynamic number of write barriers in optimized code in the Octane suite.

	Static					Dynamic				
Benchmark	Baseline	AF	WBE	WBE-AFBB	WBE-AF	Baseline	AF	WBE	WBE-AFBB	WBE-AF
ai	80	80	26	26	26	145,579	145,579	126,795	126,341	126,296
audio	261	261	78	70	63	125,518	126,034	55,694	33,364	30,990
imaging	40	40	2	2	2	1,967	1,967	51	51	51
json	40	40	2	2	2	1,910	1,910	51	51	51
stanford	773	766	489	455	441	1,780,963	1,766,298	847,108	730,193	717,309

Table 6: Static and dynamic number of write barriers in optimized code in the Kraken suite.

	Static					Dynamic				
Benchmark	Baseline	AF	WBE	WBE-AFBB	WBE-AF	Baseline	AF	WBE	WBE-AFBB	WBE-AF
JPEGEncoder	178	178	96	94	92	5,979,914	6,001,312	5,775,179	5,786,586	5,766,983
NBody	528	527	314	33	33	41,969,426	43,652,671	27,032,795	10,399	10,300
Soft3D	490	490	276	206	206	298,331,060	344,663,928	155,663,705	43,997,228	42,900,118
Textwriter	665	670	351	333	332	111,465,619	114,906,407	93,684,228	90,337,194	90,710,264

Table 7: Static and dynamic number of write barriers in optimized code in the hand-selected benchmarks.

4.3 Allocation Group Utilization

Allocation instructions folded into a given dominator from different branch successors may result in unused memory, which can be considered fragmentation. Figure 6 shows the percentage of memory allocated for the allocation group that is actually used as live objects by the program for the AF and WBE-AF configurations. Benchmarks with 100% allocation group utilization are elided for conciseness. Here we only consider memory dynamically allocated in allocation groups by optimized code, and do not count the memory allocated in normal allocations *outside* of allocation groups or in unoptimized code. Therefore this should not be considered a measurement of total heap fragmentation. Our measurements show that most of the benchmarks utilize between 50% and 80% of the memory allocated in allocation groups, with the exception of RegExp using only 42%, and Box2D and NBody using more than 90%. Lower memory utilization in the young generation results in more frequent young generation collections. We investigate this effect in the next section.

4.4 Garbage Collection Overhead

Intuitively, more frequent collections that result from higher memory fragmentation should lead to higher garbage collection overhead, but is this effect real, and is it more significant than the benefits from allocation folding? We studied this question by recording a number of garbage collection statistics, including the number of minor garbage collections, number of major garbage collections, and garbage collection time in milliseconds of the baseline, WBE, WBE-AFBB, AF, and WBE-AF configurations. We report the raw numbers in Table 8, Table 9, and Table 10. These numbers show that in most cases, there is almost no increase in garbage collection overhead, even though many benchmarks see a small increase in the number of minor collections. This is because the cost of scavenging is proportional to the size of live objects, so a small amount of fragmentation, which is by definition not live, has little cost other than cache effects and appears not to be measurable. However, in some cases we see the total garbage collection time increase, for example by 48 ms in Soft3D and by about 41 ms in PdfJS, with the former due to more minor collections and the latter due to more major collections. Even with the added garbage collection overhead of 56 additional minor collections, allocation folding is still an overall throughput improvement in Soft3D. The throughput of PdfJS slightly degrades in the AF and WBE-AF configurations, due to three additional major collections.

5. Related Work

Are write barriers really that expensive? This question was studied extensively by Blackburn and Hosking in 2004 [3], and a followup study in 2012 [22]. Their reported experimental results indicate average write barrier overheads in the range of 1-6% for the Java programs they study, for most of the write barrier types. At first glance,

	Baseline, WBE, WBE-AFBB (no fragmentation)			AF, WBE-AF (fragmentation)		
Benchmark	#Minor GCs	#Major GCs	GC time in ms	#Minor GCs	#Major GCs	GC time in ms
Box2D	111	5	99.37	111	5	100.97
CodeLoad	14	5	137.45	14	5	136.22
Cyrpto	62	0	2.25	69	0	1.5
DeltaBlue	585	0	44.57	587	0	45.11
EarleyBoyer	856	0	770.58	856	0	763.82
Gameboy	37	18	112.99	37	19	116.51
Mandreel	106	6	12.84	106	6	12.91
MandreelLatency	106	6	12.84	106	6	12.91
NavierStokes	16	0	2.18	16	0	2.26
PdfJS	555	26	772.54	555	29	813.28
RayTrace	2599	0	18.5	2610	0	22.11
RegExp	959	0	20.49	956	0	18.91
Richards	63	0	0.56	63	0	0.56
Splay	311	194	416.69	313	194	419.1
SplayLatency	311	194	416.69	313	194	419.1
Typescript	51	6	444.77	51	6	449.11
zlib	1	1	2.41	1	1	2.35

Table 8: Number of minor collections, major collections, and total garbage collection time in ms with and without allocation folding in the Octane suite on X64.

	Baseline, WBE, WBE-AFBB (no fragmentation)			AF, WBE-AF (fragmentation)		
Benchmark	Minor GCs	Major GCs	GC time in ms	Minor GCs	Major GCs	GC time in ms
ai	4	1	6.55	4	1	6.49
audio	42	6	18.37	43	6	18.31
imaging	2	4	6.45	2	4	6.33
json	21	2	4.16	21	2	4.26
stanford	45	4	16.96	45	4	16.97

Table 9: Number of minor collections, major collections, and total garbage collection time in ms with and without allocation folding in the Kraken suite on X64.

	Baseline, WBE, WBE-AFBB (no fragmentation)			AF, WBE-AF (fragmentation)		
Benchmark	Minor GCs	Major GCs	GC time in ms	Minor GCs	Major GCs	GC time in ms
JPEGencoder	18	1	17.89	18	1	17.51
NBody	597	0	0.31	620	0	0.31
Soft3D	437	0	57.44	493	0	105.67
TextWriter	2213	0	6.28	2230	0	10.13

Table 10: Number of minor collections, major collections, and total garbage collection time in ms with and without allocation folding in the hand-selected benchmarks on X64.

the large speedups for some benchmarks yielded by our optimization technique would seem to contradict their estimate of write barrier overheads. However, a close reading of their data tables show several important outliers, and we believe these outliers are exactly the cases where our optimization technique works best. First, V8's garbage collector is incremental, requiring a heavier write barrier than any of those studied in these two papers. V8's write barrier is closest to the "zone" barrier reported in their study, which, though no attention was called to it in their discussion, shows between 10-50% performance overhead for several DaCapo benchmarks. This larger write barrier overhead is in closer agreement to the optimization potential exploited in this paper using allocation folding. Second, we believe that some of the applications in Octane are much more allocation intensive than those in DaCapo, if only by virtue of JavaScript's numerical model leading to excessive amounts of boxing double numbers in V8, which is extreme in the case in RayTrace. Third, garbage collection designs with heavier write barrier costs are becoming more important as language implementations pursue reducing latency versus maximum throughput. We showed allocation folding to be of particular benefit to V8, which has an expensive write barrier to support incremental marking.

Previous optimizations related to allocation folding fall into two categories: static analysis during compilation to reduce barriers and techniques to combine object allocations.

Barth [2] discusses minimizing the expense of reference-counted garbage collection through static analysis during compilation and is suggestive of later write barrier elimination based on static analysis [23]. Although eliding unnecessary reference-count decrement on freshly allocated objects is specifically mentioned, implementation details and empirical results are not presented as the author considered the technique impractical for the time.

Nandivada and Detlefs [14] present a static analysis pass to minimize write barriers at compile time for a snapshot-at-the-beginning style of garbage collector and document the empirical improvement of generated code using their techniques. Their approach bears similarities to ours as it exploits the property of freshly allocated objects always being colored white to remove write barriers. However, it is unable to leverage this property for multiple objects allocated in close proximity and the algorithm's ability to remove write barriers can actually diminish with objects allocated in clusters. Rogers [17] studies the problem of read barriers in a concurrent collector and uses techniques similar to partial redundancy elimination to hoist or sink potentially redundant parts of barriers. Pizlo et al.

[15] generate multiple copies of the code, with different versions of read/write barriers specialized to different phases of collection, but they do not describe the complete removal of barriers. Vechev and Bacon [18] study conditions under which write barriers may be redundant for concurrent collectors and study program traces. Their work may prove to be complimentary in that allocation folding could present even more covering conditions than previously known.

Automatic object inlining is well studied [4] [6] [5], however it relies on parent-child relationships between objects to make decisions to combine allocations. Object colocation [11] allocates related objects together in the same space, but requires explicit support from the garbage collector and is intended to reduce the cost of collection rather than to improve the efficiency of compiled code. Object and array fusing [21] uses colocation to improve the efficiency of accessing one object through the field of another in compiled code, but also requires explicit support from the garbage collector. Object combining [19] is closest to allocation folding in that it has fewer restrictions, but works best with patterns where an indirection can be eliminated, and the opportunity for eliminating write barriers was not recognized at the time.

6. Conclusion

In this paper we introduced allocation folding, a compiler optimization where multiple memory allocation operations in optimized code are folded together into a single, larger allocation group. Folding allocations together reduces the per-object allocation overhead and widens the scope for write barrier removal. Unlike previous work on object inlining, fusion, and colocation, allocation folding requires no particular connectivity or ownership relationship among objects, only a control-flow relation within a single optimized function. We presented a flow-sensitive analysis based on GVN with side-effects that computes the necessary dominance information to determine allocation folding candidates.

We implemented allocation folding in V8, a high-performance open-source JavaScript virtual machine and evaluated its effectiveness across a variety of standard benchmarks. Our results demonstrated that allocation folding can make a large improvement in throughput for allocation and write-barrier intensive programs. We measured the benefits of reducing bump-pointer operations and write barriers both independently and together. We found that memory fragmentation arising from allocation folding has negligible cost in most cases.

7. References

[1] C. Authors. Textwriter. http://www.chrome.org.

[2] J. M. Barth. Shifting garbage collection overhead to compile time. *Communications of the ACM*, 20(7):513–518, July 1977.

[3] S. M. Blackburn and A. L. Hosking. Barriers: friend or foe? In *Proceedings of the International Symposium on Memory Management*, ISMM '04, pages 143–151, New York, NY, USA, 2004. ACM.

[4] J. Dolby. Automatic inline allocation of objects. In *Proceedings of the Conference on Programming Language Design and Implementation*, PLDI '97, pages 7–17, New York, NY, USA, 1997. ACM.

[5] J. Dolby and A. Chien. An automatic object inlining optimization and its evaluation. *SIGPLAN Notices*, 35(5):345–357, May 2000.

[6] J. Dolby and A. A. Chien. An evaluation of automatic object inline allocation techniques. In *Proceeding of the Conference on Object-Oriented Programming Systems, Languages, and Applications*, OOPSLA '98, pages 1–20. ACM Press, 1998.

[7] Google Inc. Octane. https://developers.google.com/octane, 2013.

[8] Google Inc. V8. https://code.google.com/p/v8, 2013.

[9] Google Inc. V8 design. https://code.google.com/p/v8/design, 2013.

[10] I. Gouy. Nbody. http://shootout.alioth.debian.org.

[11] S. Z. Guyer and K. S. McKinley. Finding your cronies: static analysis for dynamic object colocation. In *Proceedings of the Conference on Object-oriented Programming, Systems, Languages, and Applications*, OOPSLA '04, pages 237–250, New York, NY, USA, 2004. ACM.

[12] D. McNamee. Soft3d, 2008.

[13] Mozilla. Kraken. https://krakenbenchmark.mozilla.org, 2013.

[14] V. K. Nandivada and D. Detlefs. Compile-time concurrent marking write barrier removal. In *Proceedings of the International Symposium on Code Generation and Optimization*, CGO '05, pages 37–48, Washington, DC, USA, 2005. IEEE Computer Society.

[15] F. Pizlo, E. Petrank, and B. Steensgaard. Path specialization: reducing phased execution overheads. In *Proceedings of the International Symposium on Memory Management*, ISMM '08, pages 81–90, New York, NY, USA, 2008. ACM.

[16] A. Ritter. JPEGEncoder. https://github.com/owencm/javascript-jpeg-encoder, 2009.

[17] I. Rogers. Reducing and eliding read barriers for concurrent garbage collectors. In *Proceedings of the Workshop on Implementation, Compilation, Optimization of Object-Oriented Languages, Programs and Systems*, ICOOOLPS '11, pages 5:1–5:5, New York, NY, USA, 2011. ACM.

[18] M. T. Vechev and D. F. Bacon. Write barrier elision for concurrent garbage collectors. In *Proceedings of the International Symposium on Memory Management*, ISMM '04, pages 13–24, New York, NY, USA, 2004. ACM.

[19] R. Veldema, J. H. Ceriel, F. H. Rutger, and E. Henri. Object combining: A new aggressive optimization for object intensive programs. In *Proceedings of the Conference on Java Grande*, JGI '02, pages 165–174, New York, NY, USA, 2002. ACM.

[20] C. Wimmer and M. Franz. Linear scan register allocation on SSA form. In *Proceedings of the International Symposium on Code Generation and Optimization*, CGO '10, pages 170–179, New York, NY, USA, 2010. ACM.

[21] C. Wimmer and H. Mössenbösck. Automatic feedback-directed object fusing. *ACM Transactions on Architecture and Code Optimization*, 7(2):7:1–7:35, Oct. 2010.

[22] X. Yang, S. M. Blackburn, D. Frampton, and A. L. Hosking. Barriers reconsidered, friendlier still! In *Proceedings of the International Symposium on Memory Management*, ISMM '12, pages 37–48, New York, NY, USA, 2012. ACM.

[23] K. Zee and M. Rinard. Write barrier removal by static analysis. In *Proceedings of the Conference on Object-oriented Programming, Systems, Languages, and Applications*, OOPSLA '02, pages 191–210, New York, NY, USA, 2002. ACM.

Push-Pull Constraint Graph for Efficient Points-to Analysis

Bollu Ratnakar and Rupesh Nasre

IIT Madras, Chennai, India

{ratna, rupesh}@cse.iitm.ac.in

We present techniques for efficient computation of points-to information for C programs. Pointer analysis is an important phase in the compilation process. The computed points-to information and the alias information is useful for client analyses from varied domains such as bug finding, data-flow analysis, identifying security vulnerabilities, and parallelization, to name a few. Former research on pointer analysis has indicated that the main bottleneck towards scalability is manifested by the presence of complex constraints (load $p = *q$ and store $*p = q$ constraints) in the program. Complex constraints add edges to the *constraint graph* in an unpredictable manner and are responsible for initiating propagation of large amounts of points-to information across edges. We identify that the root cause to this issue is in the homogeneous structure in the constraint graph, due to which existing analyses treat loads and stores in a uniform manner. To address these issues, we present two techniques. First, we represent a constraint graph in a non-homogeneous manner, treat loads and stores in different ways, and employ a *push-pull* model for non-uniform propagation. Second, we propose *lazy propagation* which propagates information in the constraint graph only when necessary. We illustrate the effectiveness of our techniques using six large open-source programs and show that they improve the analysis time over a state-of-the-art BDD-based analysis by 33% and over Deep Propagation by 21%.

Categories and Subject Descriptors D.3.4 [*Programming Languages*]: Processors-Optimization

General Terms Algorithms, Languages

Keywords constraint graph, points-to analysis, push-pull, lazy propagation, propagation patterns

1. Introduction

Points-to analysis is a method to statically find out if two pointers in a program may point to the same memory location at runtime. If they do, then the two pointers are said to be aliases of each other.

Points-to analysis is an enabler for several compiler optimizations and continues to be a key static analysis. Because of its importance, a large number of points-to analysis algorithms have been proposed in literature [1–3, 11, 28, 30]. Enormous growth of the code bases in proprietary and open source software systems demands scalability of heap analyses over millions of lines of code.

ISMM'14, June 12, 2014, Edinburgh, UK.
Copyright © 2014 ACM 978-1-4503-2921-7/14/06. . . $15.00.
http://dx.doi.org/10.1145/2602988.2602989

Algorithm 1 Points-to Analysis using Constraint Graph

Require: set C of points-to constraints
1: Process address-of constraints
2: Add edges to constraint graph G using copy constraints
3: **repeat**
4:     Propagate points-to information in G
5:     Add edges to G using load and store constraints
6: **until** fixed-point

The efficiency of pointer analysis is paramount, as its computed information directly affects the effectiveness of client analyses such as traditional optimizations, slicing, array-bounds checking, etc.

For analyzing a general purpose C program in a flow-insensitive manner, it is sufficient to consider all pointer statements of the following forms: address-of assignment (p = &q), copy assignment (p = q), load assignment (p = *q) and store assignment (*p = q) [25]. Load and store assignments are also referred to as complex assignments. A heap allocation is represented using an address-of assignment. We deal with context-insensitive (which ignores the calling context of a function), flow-insensitive (which ignores control-flow), field-insensitive (which assumes that access to a field of an aggregate is to the whole aggregate) inclusion-based (Andersen-style) points-to analysis in this work.

A flow-insensitive analysis iterates over a set of points-to constraints until a fixed-point is obtained. Typically, the flow of points-to information is represented using a constraint graph G, in which a node denotes a pointer variable and a directed edge from node n_1 to node n_2 represents propagation of points-to information from n_1 to n_2. Each node is initialized with the points-to information computed by evaluating the *address-of* constraints. Edges are added to G initially by *copy* constraints and then by *complex* (*load* and *store*) constraints as the analysis progresses. This is because the edges introduced by *complex* constraints depend upon the availability of points-to information at nodes which, in turn, depends upon the propagation. In effect, evaluation of complex constraints and propagation of points-to information are cyclically dependent. Thus, as the analysis performs an iterative progression of the points-to information propagation, new edges get introduced in G due to the evaluation of the complex constraints, resulting in the computation of more and more points-to information at its nodes. When no more edges can be added and no more points-to information can be computed, the constraint graph G gets stabilized and a fixed-point (points-to information at the nodes) is reached. The information can then be used by various clients (e.g., for program understanding, identifying security vulnerabilities, parallelization, etc.). An outline of this analysis is given in Algorithm 1.

Techniques have been developed for efficient propagation of the points-to information across the edges of a constraint graph. Online cycle elimination [4] detects cycles in G on-the-fly and collapses all the nodes in a cycle into a representative node. Cycle collapsing is possible because all the nodes in a cycle eventually contain the same points-to information. This significantly reduces the number of pointers tracked and speeds up the overall analysis. Wave and Deep Propagation [25] techniques perform a topological ordering of the edges and propagate only the difference in the points-to information in breadth-first or depth-first manner respectively. These propagation orders significantly improve the points-to analysis time. In yet another method, various heuristics like Greatest Input Rise, Greatest Output Rise, and Least Recently Fired [12] work on the amount and recency of information computed at various nodes in the constraint graph to achieve a quicker fixed-point.

Unfortunately, existing optimizations need to restrict themselves to intra-iteration techniques of Algorithm 1. This is because the complex constraints are capable of adding edges arbitrarily in the constraint graph. Therefore, it is difficult to predict where in the constraint graph an edge would be added. This, for instance, restricts propagation orders to deal with the *current state of the graph* and not carry forward propagation order across iterations when more edges are added. Had there been an oracle that informs where the future edges would be added, the propagation could have taken it into account to choose a better order. As an example, if an edge $b \rightarrow c$ exists in the graph right now (in iteration i), then an existing algorithm is going to propagate points-to information of b to c in this iteration. However, if the algorithm had known that in the next iteration $(i+1)$, edge $a \rightarrow b$ would be added, then propagation from b to c could have been delayed to a later iteration. In absence of this oracle, the algorithm ends up propagating information via edge $b \rightarrow c$ twice, once in iteration i and once in iteration $i + 1$.

We propose a non-homogeneous technique that allows an algorithm to partially infer where future edges would be added to the constraint graph. This is based on a simple but critical observation that for a load statement $p = *q$, although the source of the new edges is unknown, the target node is known; that is p. Thus, any new edge added by the load constraint would be of the form $X \rightarrow p$ where X is another hitherto unknown node in the graph. Similarly, for a store statement $*p = q$, although the target node is unknown, the source is always node q. With this observation, we have partial information about the placement of the next set of edges, which can help us focus on edges following this pattern and ignore other patterns. This phenomenon is discussed in Section 2.2.

Using the edge addition pattern, the propagation in the constraint graph becomes non-homogeneous; that is, we can now transform the propagation in Step 4 of Algorithm 1 to perform *information push* at known sources (for stores) and perform *information pull* at known targets (for loads). Since the number of loads and stores is known and fixed prior to running the analysis, the number of known sources and targets is also fixed. With such a processing, the analysis can now make more intelligent decisions while propagating information in this push-pull constraint graph.

An interesting aspect of partially predictable propagation is that the information can now be lazily propagated if not absolutely necessary. Thus, if an edge $b \rightarrow c$ is added but there is no constraint containing $*c$, then the propagation of information across edge $b \rightarrow c$ may be delayed if c does not have any outgoing edges. This helps in reduced propagation, for instance, when edge $a \rightarrow b$ is added later. This delayed propagation helps improve the overall analysis time. Using the mechanism of push-pull constraint graph and lazy propagation, we develop an efficient context-insensitive flow-insensitive points-to analysis for C programs.

Our contributions are summarized below.

- The study of the nature of the dynamic constraint graph to predict edge addition. We find that by tracking sources and targets of the constraint graph, we can partially predict the placement of future edges. This predicted information can be used to augment existing techniques for improved propagation.

- An efficient context-insensitive flow-insensitive points-to analysis exploiting two key techniques: *push-pull constraint graph* and *lazy propagation*. The non-homogeneous processing of the push-pull constraint graph improves the work-efficiency of the algorithm, while lazy propagation reduces the overall propagation of points-to information in the constraint graph.

- Detailed experimental evaluation of the points-to analysis algorithm using six large open-source programs (namely, *tshark*, *linux*, *hphp*, *gimp*, *gdb* and *gs*). Our context-insensitive points-to analysis is 33% faster than BDD-based Lazy Cycle Detection [7], 46% faster than Andersen's analysis [1], and 21% faster than Deep Propagation [25].

The paper is organized as below. We briefly explain constraint graph and our modifications to it using an example in Section 2. Using this modified push-pull constraint graph, we present our context-insensitive points-to analysis algorithm in Section 3. We evaluate the effectiveness of our approach in Section 5 by running it on six large benchmarks and comparing against the-state-of-the-art methods. We contrast our work with the relevant related work in Section 6 before concluding in Section 7.

2. Our Approach

We first illustrate the functioning of a constraint graph in base Andersen's analysis and how points-to information is propagated using a running example. Then, we formulate the notion of push-pull constraint graph and illustrate how it improves efficiency. Finally, we present lazy propagation and illustrate how it can reduce points-to information propagation in a push-pull constraint graph.

2.1 Running Example

Consider the following set of statements obtained from a C program after removing the control-flow (since we are dealing with flow-insensitive points-to analysis). We also ignore types.

$a = \&x; b = \&y; p = \&a; *p = e; b = *q;$
$q = \&c; p = \&p; *q = a; e = b;$

The points-to information for this set of statements is computed by Algorithm 1 as shown in Figure 1. The figure shows the state of the constraint graph and the points-to information for each node (which represents a pointer in the program) for each iteration.

Initially, due to address-of constraints, a points to x, b points to y, p points to a and p itself, and q points to c. We add copy edges to the constraint graph: for constraint $e = b$, we add edge $b \rightarrow e$.

In Iteration 1, we first propagate information across the only edge, making e point to y. We then add edges using the complex constraints: $*p = e$ adds edges $e \rightarrow a, e \rightarrow p$, $b = *q$ adds edge $c \rightarrow b$, while $*q = a$ adds edge $a \rightarrow c$. This creates a cycle between nodes a, c, b, e. If online cycle detection is triggered at this point, the cycle would be collapsed into a single node.

In Iteration 2, we propagate information along all the existing edges making all nodes in the cycle point to x, y. In addition, p's points-to set becomes $\{a, p, x, y\}$. We then add edges using the complex constraint: $*p = e$ adds edges $e \rightarrow x, e \rightarrow y$. Other constraints do not add any new edge in the constraint graph.

In Iteration 3, we propagate information along all the edges making x, y point to $\{x, y\}$. We try adding more edges using the complex constraints, but cannot add any new edges.

When no more edges can be added and no more points-to information can be propagated, the algorithm reaches a fixed-point. The points-to sets computed for each pointer constitutes the points-to information for the example program. Thus, the final set of points-to facts computed using this inclusion-based analysis is: $a, b, c, e, x, y \rightarrow \{x, y\}; p \rightarrow \{a, p, x, y\}; q \rightarrow \{c\}$.

We observe the following properties.

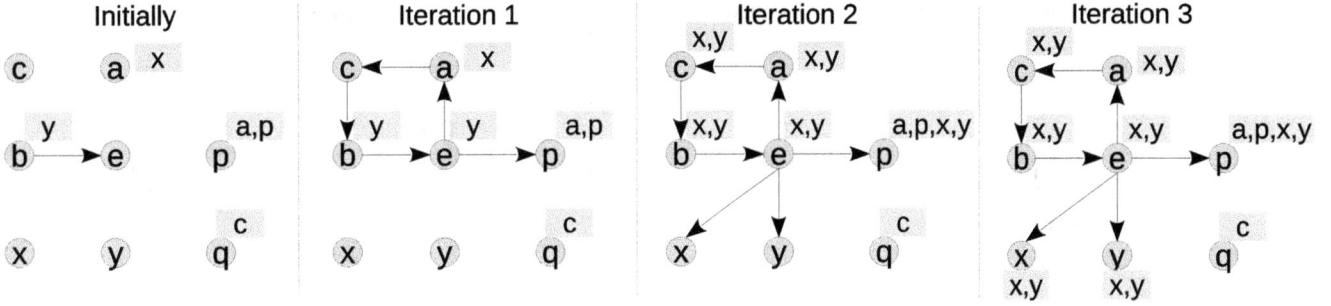

Figure 1. Constraint graph in each iteration for the running example

Property 1. *Every constraint graph edge added by a load statement $p = *q$ is incident on node p, that is, it has p as its target. Similarly, every constraint graph edge added by a store statement $*p = q$ originates at node q, that is, it has q as its source.*

In other words, every load has a *known target* whereas every store has a *known source*. We further say that loads have *unknown sources* and stores have *unknown targets*. Unknown sources and targets are generated by *starred* variables (e.g., $*p$).

Property 2. *If $\mathcal{S}$ is the set of unknown sources across all loads and $\mathcal{T}$ is the set of unknown targets across all stores, then $\forall s \in \mathcal{S}, s \in \mathcal{A}$ and $\forall t \in \mathcal{T}, t \in \mathcal{A}$, where $\mathcal{A}$ is the set of all address-taken variables in the program.*

Property 2 suggests that the set of unknown sources and targets is a subset of the address-taken variables in the program. For instance, variable p is address-taken in $q = \&p$ and whenever we dereference q in a load or a store, it refers to p.

In general, the number of address-taken variables is often only a small fraction of the total number of program variables. For instance, for our set of programs (details in Section 5), there are only 16% address-taken variables on an average. This means, although future edges added by a complex statement could be arbitrary in the worst case, in real-world programs, such edges are confined to a small subset of source-target pairs, and can be partially predicted.

2.2 Push-Pull Constraint Graph

Based on our observations on how complex statements may add future edges, we alter the constraint graph to encode this information. Each known source *pushes* information via its outgoing edges, while each known target *pulls* information via its incoming edges. This makes information propagation non-homogeneous in the new constraint graph. Due to the non-homogeneity of the push-pull constraint graph, it is not evident that points-to facts would be correctly propagated across nodes, and whether the fixed-point computed would match that of the original constraint graph. In particular, all the edges in the original constraint graph were homogeneous, so propagating information across a path of edges (say, $a \rightarrow b \rightarrow c$) was straightforward. However, in our new graph, it is unclear if the information being pushed from node a to b would reach c unless either b is also a push node or c is a pull node.

Effective handling of this issue necessitates dividing nodes into various categories (we formally prove correctness in Section 4).

1. *Push nodes:* These are the known sources in the push-pull constraint graph. We denote their set as $\mathcal{S}$.

2. *Pull nodes:* These are the known targets in the push-pull constraint graph. We denote their set as $\mathcal{T}$.

3. *PushPull nodes:* These nodes appear as both sources and targets, and can be computed as $\mathcal{S} \cap \mathcal{T}$.

4. *AddressTaken nodes:* These variables appear on the right hand side of address-of statements. We denote their set as $\mathcal{A}$.

5. *Starred nodes:* These variables are dereferenced in a complex statement. We denote their set as $\mathcal{R}$.

6. *Simple nodes:* All **other** variables. For a statement $p = q$, we refer to p and q as *Simple Target* and *Simple Source* respectively.

Note that a variable may be both Push / Pull as well as AddressTaken (in our implementation, we mark such nodes as Push / Pull). Similarly, a variable may be both Starred and Push / Pull or Starred and AddressTaken (we mark such nodes as Starred). However, a Simple variable cannot be Push or Pull or AddressTaken or Starred, and *vice versa*. The reason for dividing the variables in such a manner is discussed later in this subsection, but briefly, it helps us categorize structural patterns in the constraint graph leading to effective prioritization for propagating information.

In our running example, a and e are the Push nodes, b is a Pull node, x, y, a, c, p are AddressTaken and p, q are Starred nodes.

It should be noted that all the above categories are static and do not change as points-to analysis progresses. This means, program variables can be classified *once* into these categories prior to running the analysis, and this classification remains fixed.

Above categorization leads to the following properties.

Property 3. *No new edges get incident from and to a Simple node due to evaluation of a complex constraint.*

New edges added by a complex constraint are always from a Push node to an AddressTaken node, or from an AddressTaken node to a Pull node. Since Simple nodes do not belong to any of these categories, no new edges can be added to them.

Categorizing Simple nodes is important, as we observe that ~64% nodes are Simple in our set of benchmarks. This means complex constraints target only one third of the constraint graph.

Efficiency of a points-to analysis is significantly influenced by online cycle detection [23]. Cycle elimination collapses cycles and reduces the number of pointers tracked. However, repeated cycle detection in a large constraint graph is expensive. So, it is essential to control how often and when cycle detection is triggered [7]. Our formulation of different kinds of nodes can help online cycle detection and elimination, as evident by the following property.

Property 4. *For a Simple node to be a part of a future online cycle, it must be reachable from an AddressTaken node and an AddressTaken node must be reachable from the Simple node.*

Since the only edges to be added to the constraint graph in future are added by evaluating the complex constraints (loads and stores), all future edges would be added from a Push node to an AddressTaken node or from an AddressTaken node to a Pull node. This means, if a Simple node s was to become a part of a cycle, there must be a path from an AddressTaken node a to node s prior

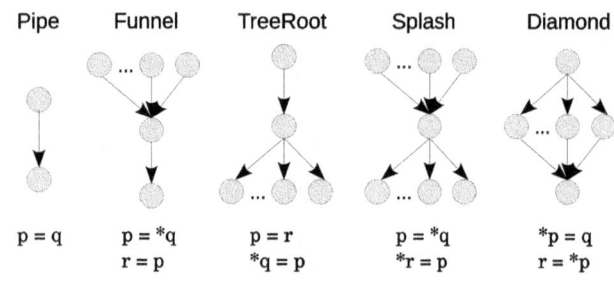

Figure 2. Patterns in Push-Pull Constraint Graph

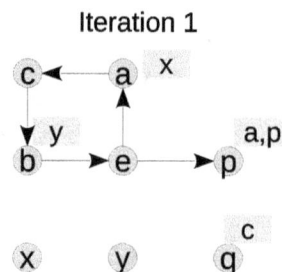

Figure 3. Lazy Propagation on our running example

to evaluating any complex constraint. Additionally, to complete the cycle, the node s must also have a path to some AddressTaken node b (node a may become reachable from b by future edges).

As a corollary, if all the nodes in a directed acyclic forest of the constraint graph are Simple, then none of the forest nodes ever becomes part of any cycle. This is because, since the nodes are neither AddressTaken nor Push/Pull, no new edges would be incident on them. In other words, if Simple nodes form an isolated coalition, then an online cycle detection algorithm can avoid traversing them.

Property 4 and the above corollary can be used to focus graph traversal to a subset of the constraint graph edges in order to improve the efficiency and the false positive rate of online cycle detection (a false positive occurs when cycle detection gets triggered even when no cycle currently exists in the constraint graph).

The above categorization of nodes and the associated properties enable us extract patterns in the push-pull constraint graph that help us propagate information more intelligently. We explain these patterns below. They are visually illustrated in Figure 2.

1. *Pipe:* A directed edge exists between two Simple nodes.

2. *Funnel:* A directed edge connects a Pull node to a Simple node.

3. *TreeRoot:* A directed edge connects a Simple node to a Push node.

4. *Splash:* A directed edge connects a Pull node to a Push node. A PushPull node is also a Splash.

5. *Diamond:* The same Starred node is connected to a Push as well as a Pull node (e.g., $*p = \ldots$ and $\ldots = *p$).

Pipes are conservative and contribute to a small amount of information propagation. Pipes occur in abundance in real-world programs, as we observe in Section 5. Funnels and TreeRoots often result in a considerable amount of data flow across the constraint graph. However, at the end of a Funnel, the amount of flow gets streamlined and often reduced (due to duplicates across incoming points-to sets). At the end of a TreeRoot, information starts spreading rapidly. However, the real culprits are Splashes; they collect large amount of information from multiple sources and spread it across multiple (possibly different) targets. Therefore, the information propagation via Splashes (as well as TreeRoots) contributes significantly to the overall efficiency of the points-to analysis. Diamonds create controlled spreads of information; points-to facts are propagated from its source node to a set of nodes and the collective information then leaves the Diamond via its sink node.

These patterns provide us insights into what type of nodes lead to more propagation. TreeRoots and Splashes are the most expensive patterns to occur in the constraint graph. Both are manifested by Push nodes, which are an artifact of store statements. Therefore, store statements are often responsible for propagating huge amounts of points-to information during the analysis. For instance, in the example from Section 2.1, store statement $*p = e$ adds four outgoing edges to e shown in Figure 1, creating a TreeRoot.

2.3 Lazy Propagation

In a traditional constraint graph, points-to information is propagated eagerly, that is, during propagation, the analysis computes a fixed-point of the information, with the current set of edges. However, the fixed-point is required only in the end – not during all the intermediate iterations. We exploit this observation to delay propagation of certain points-to facts in our push-pull constraint graph.

For instance, consider our running example from Figure 1 again. In Iterations 1 and 2, the analysis propagates partial information (first set $\{y\}$ and then set $\{x, y\}$) across the cycle edges. If we delay the propagation in Iteration 1, then the constraint graph appears as shown in Figure 3. Complex constraints $*p = e, b = *q, *q = a$ add edges $e \rightarrow p, e \rightarrow a, c \rightarrow b, a \rightarrow c$. Contrasting it with Iteration 1 of Figure 1, we observe that the propagations have not occurred but still the cycle $a \rightarrow c \rightarrow b \rightarrow e$ has been formed. In effect, the analysis has successfully avoided propagating partial information across edges. If now the propagation happens, then all the cycle nodes have the same points-to information in one go – improving the efficiency. Another possibility at this stage is that an analysis may decide to trigger cycle detection and collapse the cycle nodes. In any case, lazy propagation has reduced the amount of points-to information propagation in the constraint graph.

Arbitrarily delaying the propagation may result in delaying the fixed-point itself – since future propagation and placement of edges depend upon the current points-to information. Therefore, lazy propagation must be done carefully. We crucially exploit the following fact for effective lazy propagation.

Property 5. *For a directed constraint graph edge $u \rightarrow v$, propagation can be delayed if more edges may get added onto u or if more edges may emanate from v in future.*

Thus, if delaying the propagation is going to be beneficial in combining multiple propagations, then only lazy propagation should be triggered; otherwise not. On the other hand, if no edges are going to be incident on u in future (e.g., if it is a Simple node) and no edges are going to emanate from v in future (e.g., if it is a Pull node and not an AddressTaken node), then delaying the propagation is unlikely to result in combining multiple propagations.

In general, predicting the future edges is difficult, but due to our push-pull constraint graph and the identified patterns, our analysis can identify edges for lazy propagation. Thus, for a Funnel or TreeRoot or Splash or Diamond (Figure 2), it is helpful to delay propagation so that the points-to information can be accumulated at the Push or Pull nodes before propagating further. In contrast, it is okay to perform eager propagation for Pipes. One way to implement lazy propagation is to identify such patterns (note that these patterns can be identified offline from the points-to constraints), and then delaying propagation at the appropriate nodes. However, a common characteristic in the last four patterns of Figure 2 is the presence of Push or Pull variables. Therefore, we can use Push/Pull nodes to decide lazy propagation. We use the following heuristics to delay the propagation of points-to information.

- If a node is Pull or PushPull, the information is lazily propagated across all its incident edges.
- Else if a node is Push or AddressTaken, the information is lazily propagated across all its incident edges.
- Else if a node is Starred or Simple, then the information is eagerly propagated across all its incident edges.

The rationale behind lazy propagation via Push/Pull nodes is to reduce the propagation across Load/Store edges ($p = *q$ and $*p = q$). Starred nodes accumulate points-to information and new edges are added because of them. To avoid delaying the fixed-point, we allow edges to be added eagerly – hence information is eagerly propagated across Starred nodes. Further, the cost of edge addition is very small compared to that of propagation.

Implementation and Parameter Tuning. Lazy propagation can be modeled by avoiding propagation for a controlled period of time across an edge. One way to implement it is by avoiding propagation for a fixed number of iterations. However, we found that avoiding propagation for more than one iteration often delays the fixed-point and increases analysis time. Therefore, such a method is difficult to fine-tune, and we employ an improved strategy.

We implement lazy propagation based on the amount of points-to information computed. Thus, we delay propagation across an edge $u \rightarrow v$ until u accumulates an additional threshold amount of points-to information. This makes sense because the very purpose of lazy propagation is to wait for more points-to information, combine the old and the new points-to facts, and propagate them together. Unfortunately, a fixed threshold (say, 50 points-to facts) is unsuitable for different programs. Therefore, we attempted setting the threshold based on the number of variables (pointers) and the number of constraints in the program.

$$\text{Lazy Threshold} = (m + n)/s$$

where s is a normalization constant based on the program size. In our experiments, we set it to 1000 since we deal with programs with several kilo lines of code. For programs larger than we study, the normalization constant should also be increased. While the above formula took care of varied program sizes, for a single program, this threshold posed challenges. On closer inspection, we found that the points-to information does not change linearly for a pointer during the analysis. Therefore, a fixed value throughout the analysis does not work well in practice.

Fortunately, there is a clear pattern in which most constraints add new points-to information in real-world programs. During early part of the analysis (say, upto iteration it_1), a typical constraint adds more and more new points-to facts. This continues for a while after which the newly added points-to information gradually reduces (say, after iteration it_2). This phenomenon has been observed before and used for prioritizing constraint evaluation [20]. We exploit it for deciding the lazy threshold.

$$
\begin{aligned}
\text{Lazy Threshold} &= it * (m + n)/2 * s \text{ if } it \leq it_1 \\
&= (it_2 - it) * (m + n)/4 * s \text{ if } it_1 + 1 \leq it \leq it_2 \\
&= 0 \text{ otherwise}
\end{aligned}
$$

where it is the iteration number of the analysis, it_1 is the iteration upto which the points-to information only increases, and it_2 is the iteration after which the cost of lazy propagation outweighs its benefits. Thus, for the first few iterations (in $1..it_1$), the threshold is linearly increased. For the next several iterations (in $it_1 + 1..it_2$), the threshold is linearly reduced (with a different slope). This approximates the changes in the points-to sets across iterations.

Algorithm 2 Inclusion-based Points-to Analysis using Push-Pull Constraint Graph

Require: set C of points-to constraints, set V of variables
Ensure: each variable in V has a set of values indicating its points-to set
1: Process address-of constraints
2: Add edges to constraint graph G using copy constraints
3: Identify Push, Pull, PushPull, AddressOf, Starred and Simple nodes from load / store constraints {Algorithm 3}
4: **repeat**
5:     Lazily propagate points-to information in G {Algorithm 4}
6:     Add edges to G using load / store constraints
7:     **if** no information was propagated in Step 5 and no new edges added in Step 6 **then**
8:         Eagerly propagate points-to information in G
9:     **end if**
10: **until** fixed-point

Towards the later iterations ($it > it_2$) the amount of information being computed reduces and lazy propagation is not advisable. Hence, we set the threshold to zero resulting in eager propagation.

Empirically, we found that the performance is best on an average for $it_1 = 3$ and $it_2 = 8$ for our set of programs. Unlike the normalization constant s, the values of it_1 and it_2 are not readily dependent on the program size. They depend upon the program structure which guides the number of analysis iterations and the nature of the points-to propagation. For instance, a program such as *176.gcc* from SPEC 2000 benchmark suite which requires 18 iterations to reach the fixed-point should have a larger value of it_2.

3. Points-to Analysis Algorithm

Equipped with the push-pull mechanism and lazy propagation, we develop a flow-insensitive context-insensitive inclusion-based points-to analysis, presented in Algorithm 2. The algorithm works on a set of points-to constraints C and a set of variables V to compute a fixed-point solution. It starts with processing the address-of constraints in Line 1, which initializes the initial points-to sets. We then start building the push-pull constraint graph G by adding directed copy edges corresponding to the copy statements. Thus, for each constraint of the form $p = q$, we add a copy edge $q \rightarrow p$ in G. Till this step, the processing is similar to the traditional inclusion-based points-to analysis (as outlined in Algorithm 1).

Next, we process the load / store constraints to classify the nodes in G as Push, Pull, PushPull, AddressOf, Starred and Simple. This is presented as a subroutine in Algorithm 3. After these initializations, the `repeat-until` loop at Lines 4–10 of Algorithm 2 computes a fixed-point points-to information. The loop performs two steps: it lazily propagates points-to information in G and adds more copy edges using load / store constraints. Lazy propagation is presented in Algorithm 4. It performs a topological traversal of G and at each node checks if it is a Push, Pull, PushPull or AddressTaken node (Line 2 of Algorithm 4). If yes, then the node is eligible for lazy propagation. However, if the points-to information for the node has not been propagated since a while (based on the LazyThreshold), or if the node is Starred or Simple, then the information is propagated in an eager manner (Lines 5–13). Note that for Pull and PushPull nodes, we need to pull information from the incoming sources (Lines 5–8), while for all kinds of nodes, we need to push information via the outgoing edges (Lines 11–13). We also update the size of the old points-to information for future use (Line 9).

It is possible that due to laziness, no new information is propagated in the constraint graph in some iteration and no new edges may get added to it either. Our `repeat-until` loop may infer this

---

Algorithm 3 Identify Node Types

1: **for all** variables v
2:     $v.type$ = Simple
3: **for all** constraints c **do**
4:     **if** c is of the form $p = *q$ {load} **then**
5:         **if** $p.type$ == Push **then**
6:             $p.type$ = PushPull
7:         **else**
8:             $p.type$ = Pull
9:         **if** $q.type$ == Simple **then**
10:            $q.type$ = Starred
11:     **else if** c is of the form $*q = p$ {store} **then**
12:         **if** $p.type$ == Pull **then**
13:             $p.type$ = PushPull
14:         **else**
15:             $p.type$ = Push
16:         **if** $q.type$ == Simple **then**
17:            $q.type$ = Starred
18:     **else if** c is of the form $q = \&p$ {address-of} **then**
19:         **if** $p.type$ == Simple **then**
20:            $p.type$ = AddressTaken
21:     **end if**
22: **end for**

Algorithm 4 Lazy Propagation

1: **for all** $v \in G$ in topological order **do**
2:     **if** $v.type \in$ {Push, Pull, PushPull, AddressTaken} **and** sizeof($v.ptsto$) - $v.oldsizeptsto \leq$ *LazyThreshold* **then**
3:         ; {lazy propagation}
4:     **else**
5:         **if** $v.type$ == Pull **or** $v.type$ == PushPull **then**
6:             **for all** incoming edges $u \rightarrow v$ **do**
7:                 $v.ptsto = v.ptsto \cup u.ptsto$
8:             **end for**
9:             $v.oldsizeptsto$ = sizeof($v.ptsto$)
10:         **end if**
11:         **for all** outgoing edges $v \rightarrow w$ **do**
12:             $w.ptsto = w.ptsto \cup v.ptsto$ {eager propagation}
13:         **end for**
14:     **end if**
15: **end for**

---

situation to be a fixed-point, which is incorrect. Hence, when such a situation arises (that is, there are no changes to the data-structures), the algorithm performs an eager propagation in G and then checks for the fixed-point. This is shown in Lines 7–9 in Algorithm 2.

4. Correctness, Precision and Complexity

In this section we prove that our push-pull graph-based formulation is sound and analyze its precision and complexity.

4.1 Correctness

We prove that using push-pull constraint graph CG_{pp} and lazy propagation, the points-to information computed is a superset of that obtained using a standard constraint graph (CG_{std}) based method. In the absence of lazy propagation, CG_{pp} is simply a different implementation of CG_{std}. Due to flow-insensitivity, the order of propagation in CG_{std} does not matter from a correctness perspective; any propagation order produces the same fixed-point as long the propagations continue following the subset constraints. That is, whenever source of an edge contain an additional points-to fact than the destination node, the points-to fact is propagated. This

means, given subsets $E_1, E_2, ..., E_k$ such that $E_i \in E$ where E is the set of all edges in CG_{std}, the processing order of E_i does not change the fixed-point. CG_{pp} is a specific way of chunking the edge-subsets: for a known source, all its outgoing edges are chunked into a subset for propagation, and for a known target, all its incoming edges are chunked into another subset for propagation. Since arbitrarily dividing E into subsets does not compromise soundness, a specific division such as in CG_{pp} also does not lead to loss of information. Therefore, CG_{pp} (alone) preserves correctness.

Lazy propagation in CG_{pp} could lead to an unsound analysis. This is because, if a points-to fact is lazily propagated, it would be held with the source without getting propagated (Line 3 in Algorithm 4), which could lead to a false fixed-point. However, note that in such a case, our analysis would invoke eager propagation (Line 8 in Algorithm 2), forcing the source node to release the newly added information through its outgoing edges. In theory, such a sequence may recur; that is, every lazy propagation may falsely indicate a fixed-point which would be followed by an eager propagation in every iteration. However, in any scenario, eager propagation (combined with lazy propagation) would make sure that the subset constraints are met for every CG_{pp} edge *eventually*. The only way in which a loss of information may occur is when an address-of fact is originally not recorded with a node in CG_{pp}. This cannot happen because address-of constraints are processed before any lazy propagation is performed (Line 1 of Algorithm 2). Therefore, lazy propagation in CG_{pp} does not lead to a loss of information. Hence, our analysis from Algorithm 2 leads to a sound analysis.

4.2 Precision

Algorithm 2 produces the same points-to information as that computed by Andersen's analysis [1]. Since we proved that our algorithm computes a superset of the information computed by Andersen's analysis (Subsection 4.1), it suffices to prove that every points-to fact computed by our algorithm is also computed by Andersen's analysis. Let us assume for the sake of contradiction that a points-to fact f is spuriously computed by Algorithm 2, and not computed by Andersen's analysis. This means lazy propagation in our CG_{pp} propagated f in Algorithm 2. Lazy propagation only delays propagation and does not add any extra information, as evident from Algorithm 4. In addition, propagation order of the points-to information does not affect the precision of a flow-insensitive analysis, which CG_{pp} and lazy propagation alter. Therefore, every points-to fact computed by our algorithm must be present in the eager propagation-based Andersen's analysis. In other words, Algorithm 2 is at least as precise as Andersen's analysis.

Combining the correctness and precision arguments above, we can conclude that our analysis computes exactly the same points-to information as Andersen's inclusion-based analysis.

4.3 Complexity

Let m and n be the number of edges and nodes in CG_{pp}. Let us first analyze Algorithm 4. Topological sort requires $O(m+n)$ time. The outermost *for* loop at Line 1 executes n times, while inner *for* loops at Lines 6 and 11 execute over the outgoing edges of nodes. Combined with the outermost loop, the loop bodies of the inner loops need $O(m + n)$ time. The union of points-to information at Lines 7 and 12 require worst-case $O(n)$ time since that is the maximum points-to information a pointer may have. Therefore, the overall complexity of Algorithm 4 is $O(m * n)$. This makes the complexity of Algorithm 2 to be $O(m * n^2)$, which in the worst case is $O(n^4)$. However, due to difference propagation [22] (not shown in the Algorithm), only new facts get propagated avoiding duplicate propagation. This reduces the complexity to $O(n^3)$, same as that of other algorithms compared with in the next section.

5. Experimental Evaluation

We implemented our points-to analysis in Low Level Virtual Machine (LLVM) framework [13] as a pass. We evaluate the effectiveness of our approach using six large open source programs, namely, *tshark, linux, hphp, gimp, gdb* and *gs*. Most of these benchmarks are formerly used in literature [8, 16, 18]. The benchmark characteristics (lines of unprocessed source code, number of points-to constraints in the intermediate representation (IR) and number of pointers in the IR) are given in Figure 4. The programs were run using the *opt* tool of LLVM on an Intel Xeon machine with 2 GHz clock and 16 GB RAM running Debian GNU/Linux 5.0.

We compare our push-pull constraint graph based context-insensitive points-to analysis, called as *pp*, with the following highly optimized implementations. All these implementations are flow-insensitive and context-insensitive.

- *anders*: This is our set constraint-based implementation of the base Andersen's algorithm [1] which is field-insensitive, flow-insensitive and context-insensitive. It uses sparse bitmaps to store points-to information.

- *bddlcd*: This is the context-insensitive *Lazy Cycle Detection* (LCD) algorithm implemented using Binary Decision Diagrams (BDD) from Hardekopf and Lin [7] (downloaded from Hardekopf's website [5]).

- *bmaplcd*: This is the context-insensitive LCD algorithm from Hardekopf and Lin [7] which uses bitmaps to store the points-to information. The authors have shown that the bitmap version works faster than the BDD based version.

- *deep*: This is the context-insensitive Deep Propagation method from Pereira and Berlin [25] (downloaded from Pereira's website [24]). This method propagates points-to information in the constraint graph to all the reachable nodes in a depth-first manner along a path, before the other paths are considered. It uses a sparse bitmap representation to store points-to sets and has been shown to scale well.

Since *bddlcd* and *bmaplcd* were written for LLVM 2.2, we ran their variants with that version; all other implementations use LLVM 3.4 (*bddlcd* and *bmaplcd* do not compile with LLVM 3.4). We could run *deep* without making any modifications. However, *deep* expects input in a special *.gen* format. Therefore, we converted points-to constraints from LLVM IR into *.gen* format using a simple LLVM pass. As is the standard practice, we time only the initialization and the solving phases for each method.

It is difficult to fairly compare various implementations, since they use different algorithms and often different storage representation. The implementation of *pp* originated with that of *deep*. Therefore, although we compare overall performance with several implementations, the effect of push-pull constraint graph and lazy propagation can be isolated best by comparing *pp* against *deep*.

5.1 Performance Comparison

We compare the performance of our context-insensitive points-to analysis *pp* against other analyses in Figure 4. From the results, it is clear that *pp* is almost 46%, 33%, 25% and 21% faster than *anders*, *bddlcd*, *bmaplcd* and *deep* respectively. This happens mainly due to the reduction in the number of propagations of points-to sets in the constraint graph due to lazy propagation. *pp* delays information via Push/Pull nodes and allows the points-to facts to get accumulated, propagating all of them together at once after the lazy threshold is crossed. Note that *pp* continues propagating information eagerly via Simple and Starred nodes, and also does not delay adding edges (which is relatively inexpensive). These strategic decisions make sure that the fixed-point is not unnecessarily delayed.

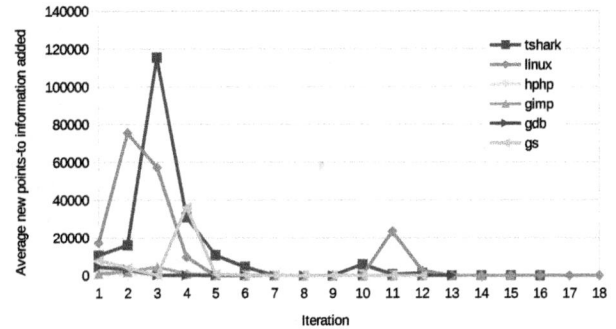

Figure 5. Choosing Parameters for Lazy Threshold

It is interesting to note performance differences across various methods. *anders* uses a set-constraint based analysis and does not exploit structural properties of a constraint graph. Hence it is the slowest of all the evaluated methods. Lower performance of *bddlcd* is due to the complex logic in enumerating points-to facts via BDDs. Since there are a substantial number of loads and stores in our programs, time for points-to enumeration logic adds up to reduce overall efficiency. In contrast, sparse bitmap-based lazy cycle detection *bmaplcd* avoids this complex logic and improves the analysis time. Especially for C programs, bitmaps have been shown to provide better efficiency over BDDs [7].

The memory requirement of *pp* is almost the same as that of *anders* and *bmaplcd*, with minor improvement due to reduced propagations. For the same reason, the memory requirement of *pp* is also relatively smaller than that of *deep*. Note that all these versions use bitmaps for storing points-to information. However, in terms of memory requirement, *bddlcd* performs the best. All the other four context-insensitive versions require at least twice the memory consumed by *bddlcd*. Unfortunately, the reduced storage of *bddlcd* comes at the price of reduced time efficiency.

5.2 Selection of Parameters

An important factor in choosing the Lazy Threshold is deciding the transitioning iterations it_1 and it_2 as discussed in Section 2.3. In this subsection, we discuss the behavior of our benchmarks which leads to the selection of specific values for these parameters. Recall that we divide our analysis into three phases. The first phase is the increasing phase wherein the average points-to information newly added by a constraint goes on increasing. The second phase is the decreasing phase wherein the average points-to information newly added by a constraint goes on reducing. The last phase is the low-activity phase wherein the cost of lazy propagation is high compared to the gain in performance. We would prefer to have an increasing threshold in the first phase, a reducing threshold in the second phase and avoid lazy propagation in the third phase.

Figure 5 shows the average number of new points-to facts added by our analysis in each iteration for our benchmarks. We can clearly see a high activity in the first few iterations. Further, even during the high activity, the points-to information goes on increasing first, reaches a maximum point around iterations 2–4 and then gradually drops. Our lazy threshold follows such a distribution, which has been shown to occur in real-world programs [20]. Therefore, we set our iteration thresholds accordingly as $it_1 = 3$ and $it_2 = 8$. Also note that the change in points-to information can be well approximated with a linear function. Therefore, we choose lazy threshold as a linear function of the iteration number.

31

B/M	KLOC	Cons(K)	Vars(K)	Time (seconds)					Memory (MB)				
				anders	bddlcd	bmaplcd	deep	pp	anders	bddlcd	bmaplcd	deep	pp
tshark	1946	1789	1952	12.6	11.6	10.2	9.7	8.2	868	501	964	1049	844
linux	1503	420	2071	118.3	95.4	84.4	83.8	64.6	1430	537	1322	1893	1355
hphp	877	682	853	49.4	33.8	25.1	27.6	22.5	648	375	626	865	639
gimp	877	649	752	21.9	20.3	18.4	16.7	14.3	795	482	789	764	784
gdb	475	362	529	36.7	33.7	34.5	27.8	21.5	463	256	459	447	463
gs	438	489	639	29.5	22.9	21.0	18.3	14.4	374	185	350	349	365
average	1019.3	731.8	1132.7	44.7	36.3	32.3	30.7	24.3	763	389	752	895	742

Figure 4. Comparison with various algorithms (B/M = benchmark)

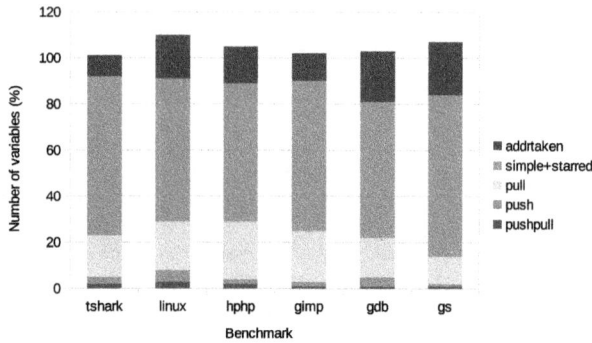

Figure 6. PushPull Constraint Graph Statistics

5.3 Constraint Graph Statistics

Figure 6 shows push-pull constraint graph statistics for each benchmark. Various types of graph nodes (*addresstaken, simple+starred, pull, push, pushpull*) are stacked and the length of each sub-bar represents the percentage of nodes of a particular type. Note that the number of nodes do not sum to 100, since some variables belong to two types (e.g., a Push node could also be AddressTaken). We observe that more than half the nodes are Simple. This means a majority of the constraint graph has a simple Pipe structure – easing points-to information propagation. The number of address-taken variables differs across benchmarks (between 9–23% for our set of programs). Usually, larger the number of address-taken variables, higher is the probability of large points-to sets and more propagation. However, this is not a strict rule, since propagation also depends upon the percentage of push/pull nodes and where they add edges. The number of Push-only nodes is only a small percentage across benchmarks. This means the number of unique source pointers in store statements is small. Considering that the number of stores in these programs is 3–13%, each pointer appears in multiple store statements. Similarly, the number of PushPull nodes is also very small. This suggests that the same variable being used as a source of store and target of load is not very common. In contrast, the number of Pull nodes is relatively high (12 – 25%). This matches well with the number of loads in these programs.

6. Related Work

Survey on pointer analysis techniques is presented by Hind and Pioli [10].

Inclusion based algorithms incur cubic computational complexity. A naive implementation of Andersen's analysis turns out to be inefficient in practice. Therefore, several novel techniques have been developed to improve upon the original Andersen's analysis [2, 9, 15, 29]. Binary Decision Diagrams (BDD) [2, 29] are used to store points-to information in a succinct manner. Although the space reduction using BDD is significant, it also incurs a perfor-

mance penalty over sparse bitmaps, since accessing and merging points-to information involve a complex logic. The idea of *bootstrapping* [11] uses a divide-and-conquer strategy to first divide the large problem of pointer analysis by partitioning the set of pointers into disjoint alias sets using a fast and less precise algorithm (e.g., [28]) and later, a more precise algorithm analyzes each partition. Due to the small partition sizes, the overall analysis scales well with the program size. The analysis over the alias partitions can be done in parallel. Nasre et al. [19] convert points-to constraints into a set of linear equations and solve it using a standard linear solver. Storing complete calling context information achieves a good precision, but at the cost of storage and analysis time. For a complete context-sensitive analysis, potentially, the storage requirement and the analysis time can be exponential in the number of functions in the program making it non-scalable. Therefore, approximate representations have been introduced to trade off precision for scalability. Das [3] proposed *one level flow*, Lattner et al. [14] unified contexts while Nasre et al. [21] hashed contexts to alleviate the need to store the complete context information.

Inclusion based analysis can be improved using several novel enhancements proposed in literature. Online cycle elimination [4] breaks dependence cycles amongst pointer variables on the fly. Offline variable substitution [26] and set-based pre-processing [27] operate over constraints prior to the constraint evaluation to find pointer equivalent variables and rewrites constraints with the reduced set of variables to improve the analysis time. Hardekopf and Lin [6] provide a suite of offline analyses based on Hash-based Value Numbering to further improve the effectiveness of offline methods. Our work is complementary to these approaches.

Wave and Deep Propagation techniques [25] perform a breadth-wise and depth-wise propagation of points-to information in a constraint graph. Various techniques proposed for worklist management [12] also identify heuristics to reach the fixed-point faster. Prioritized constraint evaluation [20] dynamically orders constraints to produce useful edges early in the constraint graph. Dominator-based analysis [17] exploits structural properties of dominator trees to find pointer-equivalent variables. Although all of these techniques work on the constraint graph, they rely on homogeneous and eager propagation of points-to information. Further, they restrict themselves to an intra-iteration processing. This is due to the fact that these techniques make a pessimistic assumption that directed edges could be added arbitrarily in the constraint graph. In contrast, our push-pull constraint graph is based on the partial prediction of edge placement across nodes and hence can span iterations of the analysis for a more efficient and lazy propagation.

7. Conclusion

We presented two techniques for speeding up flow-insensitive context-insensitive inclusion-based points-to analysis. Our techniques are based on non-homogeneity in representing the dynamic constraint graph and delaying information propagation as much as possible. These result in partial prediction of where in the constraint graph future edges would be added, using which the analysis makes informed decisions towards points-to information propagation. Based on various propagation patterns that edges create in the constraint graph, we developed intelligent heuristics to lazily propagate information. As an overall effect, the analysis can considerably reduce unnecessary flow of information in the constraint graph. Based on these techniques, we developed a context-insensitive points-to analysis which offers considerable benefits over the state-of-the-art methods. We believe our techniques can prove helpful to other analysis forms such as incremental and on-demand analyses as well.

Acknowledgments

We thank the reviewers and our shepherd whose comments improved the paper substantially. This work is supported by IIT Madras Initiation Grant CSE/13-14/812/NFIG/RUPS.

References

[1] L. O. Andersen. Program Analysis and Specialization for the C Programming Language. PhD thesis, DIKU, University of Copenhagen, May 1994. (DIKU report 94/19).

[2] M. Berndl, O. Lhoták, F. Qian, L. Hendren, and N. Umanee. Points-to analysis using BDDs. In Proc. Conf. on Programming Language Design and Implementation (PLDI), pages 103–114, New York, NY, USA, 2003. ACM. ISBN 1-58113-662-5. .

[3] M. Das. Unification-based pointer analysis with directional assignments. In PLDI, pages 35–46, 2000.

[4] M. Fähndrich, J. S. Foster, Z. Su, and A. Aiken. Partial online cycle elimination in inclusion constraint graphs. In Proc. Conf. on Programming Language Design and Implementation (PLDI), pages 85–96, New York, NY, USA, 1998. ACM. ISBN 0-89791-987-4. .

[5] B. Hardekopf. Bdd based lazy cycle detection, http://www.cs.ucsb.edu/ benh/research/downloads.html.

[6] B. Hardekopf and C. Lin. Exploiting pointer and location equivalence to optimize pointer analysis. In SAS, pages 265–280, 2007.

[7] B. Hardekopf and C. Lin. The ant and the grasshopper: fast and accurate pointer analysis for millions of lines of code. In PLDI, pages 290–299, 2007.

[8] B. Hardekopf and C. Lin. Flow-sensitive pointer analysis for millions of lines of code. In Proceedings of the 9th Annual IEEE/ACM International Symposium on Code Generation and Optimization, CGO '11, pages 289–298, Washington, DC, USA, 2011. IEEE Computer Society. ISBN 978-1-61284-356-8. URL http://dl.acm.org/citation.cfm?id=2190025.2190075.

[9] N. Heintze and O. Tardieu. Ultra-fast aliasing analysis using cla: a million lines of c code in a second. SIGPLAN Not., 36(5):254–263, 2001. ISSN 0362-1340. .

[10] M. Hind and A. Pioli. Which pointer analysis should i use? In ISSTA, pages 113–123, 2000.

[11] V. Kahlon. Bootstrapping: a technique for scalable flow and context-sensitive pointer alias analysis. In Proc. Conf. on Programming Language Design and Implementation (PLDI), pages 249–259, New York, NY, USA, 2008. ACM. ISBN 978-1-59593-860-2. .

[12] A. Kanamori and D. Weise. Worklist management strategies for dataflow analysis, MSR Technical Report, MSR-TR-94-12, 1994.

[13] C. Lattner and V. Adve. LLVM: A Compilation Framework for Lifelong Program Analysis & Transformation. In Proceedings of the 2004 International Symposium on Code Generation and Optimization (CGO'04), Palo Alto, California, Mar 2004.

[14] C. Lattner, A. Lenharth, and V. Adve. Making context-sensitive points-to analysis with heap cloning practical for the real world. In PLDI, pages 278–289, 2007.

[15] O. Lhoták and L. Hendren. Scaling Java points-to analysis using Spark. In G. Hedin, editor, Compiler Construction, 12th International Conference, volume 2622 of LNCS, pages 153–169, Warsaw, Poland, April 2003. Springer.

[16] M. Mendez-Lojo, M. Burtscher, and K. Pingali. A gpu implementation of inclusion-based points-to analysis. In Proceedings of the 17th ACM SIGPLAN symposium on Principles and Practice of Parallel Programming, PPoPP '12, pages 107–116, New York, NY, USA, 2012. ACM. ISBN 978-1-4503-1160-1. . URL http://doi.acm.org/10.1145/2145816.2145831.

[17] R. Nasre. Exploiting the Structure of the Constraint Graph for Efficient Points-to Analysis. In Proceedings of the 2012 International Symposium on Memory Management, ISMM '12, pages 121–132, New York, NY, USA, 2012. ACM. ISBN 978-1-4503-1350-6. . URL http://doi.acm.org/10.1145/2258996.2259013.

[18] R. Nasre. Time- and space-efficient flow-sensitive points-to analysis. ACM Trans. Archit. Code Optim., 10(4): 39:1–39:27, Dec. 2013. ISSN 1544-3566. . URL http://doi.acm.org/10.1145/2541228.2555296.

[19] R. Nasre and R. Govindarajan. Points-to Analysis As a System of Linear Equations. In Proceedings of the 17th International Conference on Static Analysis, SAS'10, pages 422–438, Berlin, Heidelberg, 2010. Springer-Verlag. ISBN 3-642-15768-8, 978-3-642-15768-4. URL http://dl.acm.org/citation.cfm?id=1882094.1882120.

[20] R. Nasre and R. Govindarajan. Prioritizing constraint evaluation for efficient points-to analysis. In Proceedings of the 9th Annual IEEE/ACM International Symposium on Code Generation and Optimization, CGO '11, pages 267–276, Washington, DC, USA, 2011. IEEE Computer Society. ISBN 978-1-61284-356-8. URL http://dl.acm.org/citation.cfm?id=2190025.2190073.

[21] R. Nasre, K. Rajan, R. Govindarajan, and U. P. Khedker. Scalable Context-Sensitive Points-to Analysis Using Multi-dimensional Bloom Filters. In Proceedings of the 7th Asian Symposium on Programming Languages and Systems, APLAS '09, pages 47–62, Berlin, Heidelberg, 2009. Springer-Verlag. ISBN 978-3-642-10671-2.

[22] D. J. Pearce, P. H. J. Kelly, and C. Hankin. Online cycle detection and difference propagation: Applications to pointer analysis. Software Quality Control, 12(4):311–337, Dec. 2004. ISSN 0963-9314. . URL http://dx.doi.org/10.1023/B:SQJO.0000039791.93071.a2.

[23] D. J. Pearce, P. H. J. Kelly, and C. Hankin. Online cycle detection and difference propagation: Applications to pointer analysis. Software Quality Control, 12:311–337, December 2004.

[24] F. Pereira. Wave propagation / deep propagation website, http://compilers.cs.ucla.edu/fernando/projects/pta/home/.

[25] F. M. Q. Pereira and D. Berlin. Wave propagation and deep propagation for pointer analysis. In CGO '09: Proceedings of the 2009 International Symposium on Code Generation and Optimization, pages 126–135, Washington, DC, USA, 2009. IEEE Computer Society. ISBN 978-0-7695-3576-0. .

[26] A. Rountev and S. Chandra. Off-line variable substitution for scaling points-to analysis. In Proc. Conf. on Programming Language Design and Implementation (PLDI), pages 47–56, New York, NY, USA, 2000. ACM. ISBN 1-58113-199-2. .

[27] Y. Smaragdakis, G. Balatsouras, and G. Kastrinis. Set-based Preprocessing for Points-to Analysis. In Proceedings of the 2013 ACM SIGPLAN International Conference on Object Oriented Programming Systems Languages & Applications, OOPSLA '13, pages 253–270, New York, NY, USA, 2013. ACM. ISBN 978-1-4503-2374-1. . URL http://doi.acm.org/10.1145/2509136.2509524.

[28] B. Steensgaard. Points-to analysis in almost linear time. In POPL '96: Proceedings of the 23rd ACM SIGPLAN-SIGACT symposium on Principles of programming languages, pages 32–41, New York, NY, USA, 1996. ACM. ISBN 0-89791-769-3. .

[29] J. Whaley and M. S. Lam. An efficient inclusion-based points-to analysis for strictly-typed languages. In SAS, 2002.

[30] J. Whaley and M. S. Lam. Cloning-based context-sensitive pointer alias analysis using binary decision diagrams. In Proc. Conf. on Programming Language Design and Implementation (PLDI), pages 131–144, New York, NY, USA, 2004. ACM. ISBN 1-58113-807-5. .

Sticky Tries: Fast Insertions, Fast Lookups,
No Deletions for Large Key Universes

Pramod G. Joisha

Hewlett-Packard, USA
pramod.joisha@hp.com

Abstract

We present the sticky trie, a new variant of the standard trie data structure that achieves high-performing atomic insertions and lookups for large key universes by precluding deletions. It has applications in several areas, including address tracking, logging, and garbage collection. By leveraging features of a modern operating system, we show how a runtime can exploit the absence of deletions to realize an efficient sticky-trie implementation.

We report on an evaluation of two representative uses—compelling Bloom-filter alternative and fast substitute for a garbage collector's sequential store buffer (SSB). We demonstrate that a sticky trie, when compared with what is perhaps among the simplest Bloom filters, can be over 43% faster, scale substantially better with increasing threads, and yet be free of false positives. By introducing the concept of an ideal SSB, we also demonstrate that a sticky trie could be competitive in performance with a class of SSBs.

Categories and Subject Descriptors   E.1 [*Data Structures*]

Keywords   Trie; Set; Address-Space API; Memory Management

1.   Introduction

A data structure that abstracts a set from which elements cannot be removed has many applications in computing. This paper describes the *sticky trie*, a data structure for large key universes that attains high-performing atomic insertions and lookups by precluding deletions. We define a sticky trie as a standard trie [26] that disallows deletion. Like a standard trie, its key universe is the set of all u-bit strings. Unlike a standard trie, it retains keys until it is destroyed.

The above definition admits a variety of sticky tries, each distinguished by the operation ensemble that it provides. This paper discusses a class of sticky tries that supports two principal operations: INSERT(k,s) inserts a key k into a sticky trie s, and LOOKUP(k,s) returns 1 if and only if s contains a key whose initial $u - c$ bits match that of k. (Efficient ordered traversals are easily supported.) c is a configurable nonnegative integer. It is chosen per s, before s is created, and remains fixed until s is destroyed. We say that a sticky trie is "exact" when its c is 0, and inexact otherwise.

ISMM'14, June 12, 2014, Edinburgh, UK.
Copyright © 2014 ACM 978-1-4503-2921-7/14/06. . . $15.00.
http://dx.doi.org/10.1145/2602988.2602998

A sticky trie is an apposite choice for situations in which data is continually accumulated and analyzed, but not discarded. Such situations may occur as phases in a program so that any discarding happens at the end of a phase. As an example, a sticky trie could be used to record all of the virtual addresses written by a running program. The granularity could be in parameterized subpage chunks of 2^c bytes, where $c \geq 0$. Only the changed program state could then be checkpointed [12] or flushed to non-volatile RAM [43].

The absence of deletion helps in four ways. First, and perhaps foremost, it enables simple, efficient and atomic implementations of INSERT and LOOKUP. We know of no way of simultaneously achieving these three attributes if concurrent deletions were allowed. A case in point is the recent Ctrie data structure [33]. While it supports atomic insertion, lookup and deletion, its insertion and lookup are more complex, at least in part because they have to contend with the possibility of level removal as a result of deletion. Levels once created in a sticky trie, however, remain until the sticky trie is destroyed. Second, atomicity is achieved for an *arbitrary* key width u, not just up to some machine-word size. Third, the sticky trie can be grown incrementally and on demand without incurring the overhead of checking on each insertion. Fourth, node parts that are identical or cannot logically change can be transparently detected and merged in the background, i.e., in parallel and without interfering with the actions of the client employing the sticky trie.

If conventional data structures were used in situations free of deletion, much could be left on the table. For instance, concurrent insertions into the GNU C++ Library's `unordered_set` container must be synchronized, even in the absence of deletions [19].

If no deletions, why not allocate just an array? Unfortunately, this may fail for large key universes. Our evaluation was for a 48-bit key universe. Current x86-64 platforms cannot allocate a 2^{48}-byte array (Section 7.1.1). And a 2^{48}-*bit* array would be insufficient for realizing an atomic insertion by using simple byte stores alone.

There is prior work on the *static set* and *static dictionary* abstractions [2, 34, 38, 40]. Essentially, these are sets that impose restrictions beyond disallowing deletion. For example, Purdin's static dictionaries disallow insertion after their construction [34].[1] Tarjan and Yao's double-displacement compression scheme [40] requires insertion to precede lookup. Our sticky trie, however, allows insertion to succeed lookup. Moreover, both operations can occur concurrently without synchronization, which, as far as we know, no past work on static sets or static dictionaries has considered.

1.1   Contributions, and Overview

We present four techniques, abbreviated as TTG, FLM, SLM and SLMLite, for implementing an efficient sticky trie. TTG uses trapping to grow the sticky trie incrementally and on demand without incurring the overhead of checking on each insertion. FLM, SLM

---
[1] A well-known textbook on algorithms similarly defines a static set [14].

and SLMLite detect node parts that either cannot logically change or are identical, and then merge their physical storage in the background. SLMLite is a simple yet powerful approximation of SLM that is achieved by invoking a single system call on certain nodes. It is shown that TTG, when compared to a check-based approach to incremental and on-demand growth, can be up to 21% faster.

Various sticky-trie and Bloom-filter implementations, and the GNU C++ Library's `unordered_set`, were compared. We show that the sticky trie implemented by using TTG and SLMLite performs the best among them. An exact sticky trie, despite being ordered and free of false positives, can on average be over 43% faster than what is possibly one of the simplest Bloom filters. This is mainly because of SLMLite's compression. Additionally, we show that this trie can scale substantially better with increasing threads.

Also, we introduce the ideal trap-based sequential store buffer (SSB) whose performance upper bounds the class of trap-based SSBs. We show that in two out of three benchmarks, an exact sticky trie implemented by using TTG and SLMLite can reach parity with, or always outperform, an ideal trap-based SSB. This suggests that it could be an advantageous replacement for any trap-based SSB.

The chief contribution of this work is demonstrating that the purposeful preclusion of deletion can lead to a high-performing concurrent set-like data structure for large key universes.

The rest of this paper is organized as follows. Section 2 provides background on the sticky trie. Sections 3 and 5 explain the TTG, FLM, SLM and SLMLite techniques. Section 4 gives a node-sizing heuristic. Section 6 describes two representative uses. Section 7 reports experimental results. Section 8 discusses limitations. Last, Section 9 covers other related work and Section 10 concludes.

2. Preliminaries

The key universe can be viewed as a hierarchy of "spans". This hierarchy has a standard trie structure, in which spans correspond to trie nodes and span levels correspond to trie levels.

2.1 The Span Hierarchy

Levels are numbered upward from 0. There is one span at Level 0; we call it the L_0 span and it covers the entire key universe. When the hierarchy has at least two levels, an L_0 span is made up of smaller L_1 spans at Level 1. In general, an L_i span resides at Level i, where $0 \leq i \leq \theta$. The nonnegative integer θ is the hierarchy's *leaf level*.

When $0 \leq i < \theta$, an L_i span is a contiguous sequence of two or more L_{i+1} spans. When $i = \theta$, it is a contiguous sequence of two or more *cards*. (The card was proposed by Sobalvarro [37], in the context of garbage collection, as a division of memory that can be finer than a page. In modern garbage-collection parlance, it is a 2^c-byte contiguous region aligned on a 2^c-byte boundary.) In this work, a card is a contiguous sequence of 2^c keys that begins at a multiple of 2^c, where c is as defined in Section 1. There are 2^λ cards in an L_θ span and $2^{l_{i+1}}$ L_{i+1} spans in an L_i span, where the integers λ and l_{i+1} ($0 \leq i < \theta$) can be arbitrarily chosen so long as

$$\lambda \geq 1, \qquad l_{i+1} \geq 1, \qquad \lambda + \sum_{i=0}^{\theta-1} l_{i+1} = u - c. \quad (1)$$

Every span except the L_0 span has a parent. A span that has a parent also has an index that indicates its position within its parent. Given an integer j such that $1 \leq j \leq \theta$, the L_j *index* of the key $k = k_{u-1} \cdots k_0$ is the position within the parent L_{j-1} span of the L_j span that contains k. For instance, the uppermost substring $k_{u-1} \cdots k_{u-l_1}$ is the L_1 index of k—it indicates the position within the L_0 span of the L_1 span that contains k. The substring $k_{u-l_1-l_2-\cdots-l_\theta-1} \cdots k_{u-l_1-l_2-\cdots-l_\theta-\lambda}$ is the *card index* of k—it indicates the position within an L_θ span of the card that contains k.

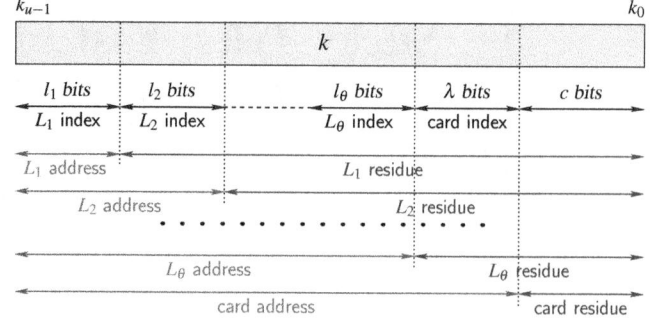

Figure 1. Parts of a u-bit key k. Its least and most significant bits are k_0 and k_{u-1}. There are 2^{l_j} L_j spans in an L_{j-1} span ($1 \leq j \leq \theta$), 2^λ cards in an L_θ span, and 2^c keys in a card.

Also, for all $1 \leq j \leq \theta$, k has an L_j *residue* that is its position within its L_j span. This is the substring $k_{u-l_1-l_2-\cdots-l_j-1} \cdots k_0$. Figure 1 shows how these substrings constitute a key.

Since the substring $k_{u-1} \cdots k_{u-l_1-l_2-\cdots-l_j}$ locates the *particular* L_j span containing k, it is called the L_j *address* of k. The substring formed by the remaining bits of k, namely $k_{u-l_1-l_2-\cdots-l_j-1} \cdots k_0$, is called the L_j *residue* of k. It determines the position of k within the L_j span that contains k. Similarly, $k_{u-1} \cdots k_c$ is called the *card address* of k because it locates the particular card containing k. And $k_{c-1} \cdots k_0$ is called the *card residue* of k because it determines the position of k within the card that contains k.

2.2 A Standard Trie Structure on the Span Hierarchy

An L_i *node* in a standard trie [26], which is the starting point for our sticky trie, is a *leaf* if $i = \theta$ and an *internal node* otherwise (i.e., if $0 \leq i < \theta$). An L_i node corresponds to an L_i span. A leaf is an array of 2^λ bytes in which distinct bytes represent distinct keys in the corresponding L_θ span. Bytes are initially 0 and become 1 as keys get inserted. An internal node is an array of $2^{l_{i+1}}$ *branch pointers* that either are null or target other nodes (leaf or internal).

3. Incremental Growth by Using Traps

Our departure from a standard trie begins with the initial value used for a branch pointer. Rather than the typical null, it is an encoding whose form is a virtual address in protected memory. It therefore generates a trap when dereferenced. However, its construction is such that when used with any valid offset in a base-plus-displacement style of addressing, a trap handler can incrementally grow the trie through its location in memory, by using information from the faulting instruction alone. We call this the TTG (Trap-based Trie Growth) technique. We refer to implementations of INSERT and LOOKUP that use TTG as INSERTT and LOOKUPT.

Consider a branch-pointer slot *st* in an L_i node x ($0 \leq i < \theta$). Its initial content is a pointer e into kernel space that encodes three things: the virtual address a of *st*, an "asynchrony" bit for concurrency control, and $i + 1$, where i is the level of x. We call e a "salt" (Slot-plus-Asynchrony-plus-Level-encoded Trapping) pointer. On a v-bit machine in which the operating system takes up the upper half of the virtual-address space, e can be constructed by first setting it to a, then setting its high bit to 1, and finally stuffing $i + 1$ and the asynchrony bit into its low $\log_2(v) - 3$ bits. (This implies that $\theta < v/16$.) Hence, a salt pointer is a kind of tagged pointer.

A trap handler, on fielding the trap that is generated on dereferencing a validly displaced e, inspects a base register *reg* in the faulting instruction to obtain e. By applying masks on e, it determines a and $i + 1$. It then creates an L_{i+1} node, "swizzles" the contents of *st*

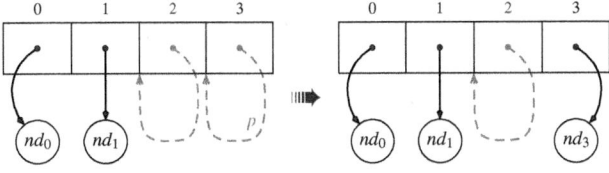

Figure 2. A sticky trie with salt pointers, just before and just after a growth increment. The increment is triggered by dereferencing p.

```
1 l1_ix := k >> (l2+λ+c)      7 card_ix := l2_re >> c
2 s1  := s[l1_ix]            *8 byte := leaf[card_ix]
3 l1_re := k & L1_R_KMSK      9 if (byte = 0)
4 l2_ix := l1_re >> (λ+c)    10    leaf[card_ix] := 1
*5 leaf := s1[l2_ix]         11 endif
6 l2_re := k & L2_R_KMSK
```

Figure 3. Pseudocode for INSERTT(k,s) when $\theta = 2$. Lines prefixed by a star fault only when the base register holds a salt pointer.

```
41 l1_ix := k >> (l2+λ+c)    48 leaf := s1[l2_ix]
42 s1  := s[l1_ix]           49 if (leaf & HI_VMSK)
43 if (s1 & HI_VMSK)         50    return 0
44    return 0               51 endif
45 endif                     52 l2_re := k & L2_R_KMSK
46 l1_re := k & L1_R_KMSK    53 card_ix := l2_re >> c
47 l2_ix := l1_re >> (λ+c)   54 return leaf[card_ix]
```

Figure 4. Pseudocode for LOOKUPT(k,s) when $\theta = 2$.

and reg to point to that node, and returns.[2] A trap, in essence, occurs when a validly displaced salt pointer is dereferenced, causes a branch-pointer slot and a base register to be patched, and results in an irreversible growth increment of one node. Subsequent accesses through that slot are unimpeded since they get the patched value.

In figures, we portray the salt pointer e by $-\rightarrow$, with the arrowhead aimed at the containing slot st, i.e., the virtual address a encoded in e. As an example, Figure 2 displays a sticky trie s for which $\theta \geq 1$ and $l_1 = 2$. It shows the layout of s just before and just after a growth increment. Consider the four slots of the L_0 node on the left. While Slots 0 and 1 contain swizzled pointers that target L_1 nodes, Slots 2 and 3 contain salt pointers, such as p. On fielding the trap that is generated on dereferencing p, the trap handler can determine from p the *next* level at which a child node nd_3 must be created. It can also determine from p the virtual address of Slot 3. Thus, it can patch that slot with a normal pointer to nd_3.

The salt pointer e has two noteworthy features. First, if d is any valid displacement for a, i.e., if $a+d$ is in user space, then $e+d$ will be in kernel space. Second, by targeting kernel space, the protection of user-space memory, via the `mprotect` system call, is avoided.

3.1 The INSERTT and LOOKUPT Subroutines

Figures 3 and 4 show the INSERTT and LOOKUPT subroutines in pseudocode, when $\theta = 2$.[3] Lines that can fault are prefixed by a star. Displaced salt pointers are dereferenced only within INSERTT. They are only read in other contexts, such as LOOKUPT and TRAPHANDLER. Hence, all faulting lines are confined to INSERTT.

Masks in the pseudocode are one of two types—those that are used to extract parts of a key and those that are used to extract parts of a virtual address. Names of the former end in *KMSK* and names of the latter end in *VMSK*. For instance, while *L1_R_KMSK* and *L2_R_KMSK* are used to extract the L_1 and L_2 residues, *HI_VMSK*, *ASYNC_VMSK* and *LEVEL_VMSK* are used to extract the high and asynchrony bits, and the level number of a child node. Their respective values are $2^{u-l_1} - 1$, $2^{u-l_1-l_2} - 1$, $2^v - 1$, $v/16$ and $(v-16)/16$.

Consider INSERTT(k,s). By using the L_1 and L_2 indices, Lines 1 through 5 traverse a chain of branch pointers from the root to the leaf that contains k. Lines 6 through 11 then extract k's card index to conditionally set the leaf byte corresponding to it to 1. Because the branch-pointer slots $s + \text{l1\_ix}$ and $s_1 + \text{l2\_ix}$ can be updated asynchronously (by the trap handler), they are marked as volatile. This prevents the improper register-caching of their contents.

Compared with a conditional version of itself, INSERTT offers three advantages. First, it is largely free of conditional code. For all θ, INSERTT has exactly one check. The conditional version (say, INSERTC) has θ *additional* checks. They guard lines corresponding to the starred lines in Figure 3. The INSERTT code path for obtaining the desired leaf byte is free of checks. (Line 9 is optional; as explained in Sections 3.2.1 and 5.2, it exists for entirely different reasons.) Second, calls to the concurrency-control code and allocation code for INSERTC come in *each* of the slow paths of the θ additional checks. For INSERTT, all concurrency control is in the trap handler. Third, INSERTT can be mapped to efficient machine code. When $u = 48$ and $c = 0$, the length of the `gcc 4.7.0` x86-64 code for it is 8, 12 and 16 machine instructions at $\theta = 1, 2$ and 3. The corresponding lengths for INSERTC are 17, 28 and 37. Code length matters under inlining as it can influence the instruction cache.

Consider LOOKUPT(k,s). It returns the leaf byte corresponding to k if one exists, and has a code structure resembling that of INSERTT(k,s). It, however, does not fault. It returns 0 as soon as a salt pointer is encountered on traversing the aforementioned chain. LOOKUPT is similar to a standard trie's lookup subroutine, except that the latter tests for null pointers instead of salt pointers. When $u = 48$ and $c = 0$, the length of the `gcc 4.7.0` x86-64 code for LOOKUPT is 10, 17 and 22 machine instructions at $\theta = 1, 2$ and 3.

It is clear from the pseudocode why an initial value of null for a branch pointer would not have worked. Lines 5 and 8 could still fault but they do not have enough information to enable a trap handler to establish the containing branch-pointer slot. And examining other instructions to establish this is not an option because a compiler can always reorder code. With salt pointers, there is no need to maintain auxiliary information against a faulting instruction.

Note that neither does Line 2 fault nor is there a check guarding Line 42. This is because we preallocate root nodes. Without preallocation, Line 2 would incur the cost of a one-time fault, and Line 42 would incur the cost of a check on *every* call of LOOKUPT. These costs are wasteful if most sticky tries are nonempty.

3.2 Concurrency

Since deletions are absent and since reads and writes of bytes and pointers are atomic, multiple threads can simultaneously execute INSERTT and LOOKUPT without holding locks. The trap handler in Figure 5 manages the concurrency, by using the asynchrony bit.

The *ucntxt* argument represents an interrupted "thread context". It includes a snapshot of the machine's registers at the time of the trap. From *ucntxt*, Line 81 gets the salt pointer e in the faulting instruction's base register reg. Line 82 extracts the virtual address a of the branch-pointer slot st containing e. The loop in Lines 83 through 90 then attempts to gain ownership of st by atomically setting the asynchrony bit at a to 1. This bit is first 0 when a salt pointer

---

[2] Traditionally, pointer swizzling has referred to pointer translation from a secondary-memory to a primary-memory format (e.g., from object identifiers on disk to virtual addresses in RAM) [44]. It has also referred to pointer translation between differently protected regions of primary memory [11].

[3] We adhere to the C programming model and largely follow C notation.

```
81  e := GETBASEREGCONTENT(ucntxt)
82  a := e & ~(HI_VMSK | ASYNC_VMSK | LEVEL_VMSK)
83  while ((e & ASYNC_VMSK)
84      || !ATOMICCMPSWAP(a,e,e | ASYNC_VMSK))
85      e := *a
86      if (~(e & HI_VMSK))
87          y := e
88          goto 92 // already grown; just patch base register
89      endif
90  endwhile
91  *a := y := CREATENODE(e & LEVEL_VMSK)
92  PATCHBASEREG(ucntxt,y) // for normal instruction resumption
```

Figure 5. Pseudocode for TRAPHANDLER(*ucntxt*).

---

is installed in *st*. It changes to 1 when some thread gains ownership of *st*. It changes back to 0 when that thread installs a normal pointer in *st*. Ownership is changed only within TRAPHANDLER.

If a thread *td* gains ownership of *st*, it will create the node *y* at the next level, in Line 91. If another thread *td′* already owns *st*, then *td* will spin in the loop, eventually picking up the normal pointer that *td′* installs. Either way, TRAPHANDLER patches *reg* before returning. The net effect is that INSERTT is atomic with respect to other calls of INSERTT. It is also atomic with respect to LOOKUPT since LOOKUPT dereferences only normal pointers.

3.2.1 Eliminating the Ping-Ponging of Leaf-Byte Cache Lines

INSERTT would continue to work correctly if Line 9 were omitted. But that could result in the unnecessary ping-ponging of cache lines. Suppose INSERTT(k,s) and INSERTT($k′,s$) were indefinitely invoked in parallel on two CPUs, where $k \neq k′$. If the leaf bytes that they correspond to map to the same cache line, the cache-coherence protocol could cause that line to indefinitely go back and forth between the CPUs. The check in Line 9 eliminates this effect.

4. A Heuristic for Sizing a Sticky Trie's Nodes

There is a rich body of mathematical analyses of various "parameters" of a standard trie, such as "size", path length, stack-size, and profile (e.g., [13, 31, 32, 35] and the references therein). A trie's size is the number of its internal nodes [13, 35]. Its path length is the sum of the levels of its leaves [13]. Its stack-size is the recursion depth of an optimized preorder traversal of it [31]. Its profile is the number of nodes that are at a given distance from its root [32].

In a sticky trie that uses the TTG technique in Section 3, all of the branch-pointer slots in the internal nodes from the root to a particular leaf would have been initialized with salt pointers when INSERTT makes the first mark in that leaf. We define a parameter called the *path volume* to model the cost of this initialization. It is the storage in bytes for a root-to-leaf path. Because all leaves in a sticky trie are at the same distance θ from the root, *PV* can be computed as a nonstatistical measure. The smaller the *PV*, the better the chance of accommodating a root-to-leaf path in the levels of the memory hierarchy closest to the CPU.

4.1 Minimizing the Path Volume

On a v-bit machine, a branch-pointer slot is $v/8$ bytes long. Thus,

$$PV = (2^{l_1} + 2^{l_2} + \cdots + 2^{l_\theta})\frac{v}{8} + 2^\lambda. \quad (2)$$

By using the arithmetic mean–geometric mean inequality, it can be shown that *PV* is minimized when $l_i = {}^{\min}l$ and $\lambda = {}^{\min}\lambda$, where

$$^{\min}l = \frac{u - c - \log_2(v/8)}{\theta + 1}, \qquad ^{\min}\lambda = \frac{u - c + \theta\log_2(v/8)}{\theta + 1}. \quad (3)$$

To illustrate, if $u = 64$, $\theta = 2$, $c = 4$ and $v = 64$, then $^{\min}l = 19$ and $^{\min}\lambda = 22$. The optimal size for all nodes then would be 4MB.

5. Transparently Compressing Leaf Pages

A leaf is $2^{\lambda - g}$ pages long, where 2^g is the page size in bytes. When $g = 12$, this can be in the thousands for large key universes (Section 4). We present two techniques to optimize a leaf's physical storage. Both are grounded in the notion of a *change*, which occurs when a byte in a leaf page is written. The change is qualified as *logical* if the byte's values before and after the write are different.

The first technique monitors leaves for pages that cannot logically change. The second technique monitors leaves for pages that are identical. Both merge the identified pages by using special threads called *compressors* that run concurrently with the clients of the sticky trie. The techniques operate in ways that do not impede later accesses into a compressed leaf by the clients. In particular, later accesses do not entail either a decompression or the execution of a code path different from prior accesses. Because the techniques do not affect virtual addresses, the problem of flushing stale pointers in registers and caches does not exist.

If the entire key universe were inserted, then all leaves could theoretically be reduced to one physical page after compression.

5.1 The FLM (Fully-filled Leaf-page Merging) Technique

Because a leaf byte once marked 1 (when a key is inserted) remains 1, a fully-filled leaf page cannot logically change. A compressor remaps such pages atomically to the same physical page, by using a kernel-provided feature called a *nonlinear memory mapping* [10].

5.1.1 Nonlinear Memory Mappings

A memory mapping is an association of pages between two regions of memory. It is linear if the association is a sequentially ordered, one-to-one correspondence; it is nonlinear otherwise [10]. Either type of mapping can be created by using the mmap system call alone. While a single invocation suffices for the former, multiple invocations are needed for the latter. This is because in the standard mmap approach to creating a nonlinear mapping, each invocation alters part of an initially created linear mapping. This, however, is inefficient because every such invocation allocates a kernel object referred to as the VMA (Virtual Memory Area) [10]. Hence, a nonlinear mapping created through mmap alone can cause performance to deteriorate due to the allocation and use of numerous VMAs.

To address the above performance inefficiency, Linux has provided the remap_file_pages system call since kernel version 2.5.46 for the sole purpose of creating a nonlinear mapping. remap_file_pages does not allocate VMAs; instead, it accomplishes its task by directly manipulating page-table entries [10].

5.1.2 The FLM Compression Algorithm

Client threads create leaves when they handle traps due to salt pointers in $L_{\theta-1}$ nodes. Before returning from a trap-handler invocation that creates a leaf z, the client hands off z to another thread called the "preparer". The preparer sets up the compression metadata md for z and then hands off z to the compressor. This handing off is by using any one-sided blocking container, i.e., the producer never blocks and the consumer blocks only on an empty container.

There are M preparers and N compressors per sticky trie. In our implementation, M and N are 1. This was sufficient for capturing profitable compression opportunities in the workloads we studied.

Preparer actions. The preparer begins by allocating and initializing the components of md for the handed leaf z: md.pgoff, md.remapv, md.basepg and md.rc. These are the offset of a fully-filled page within z, a vector denoting the pages in z that have been merged, the virtual address of the first page in z, and a reference count to garbage collect md. The preparer views z as a contiguous sequence of "sections". Each section is a contiguous sequence of pages. For each section, the preparer creates a "work unit" that contains a pointer to md and the virtual address of the last page in the section. After creating work units for all of the sections in z, the preparer hands them off to a compressor, which puts them into a thread-local queue cqueue of unfinished work units.

Compressor actions. Each compressor executes a loop. On each iteration, it checks if its cqueue is empty. If so, it blocks waiting for work from the preparer. If not, it removes a work unit w from cqueue, processes w, and continues onto the next iteration.

The processing of w begins by checking if md.pgoff is set to the offset of a fully-filled page *ffpg* within z. If not, the section *sn* corresponding to w is scanned for an *ffpg*. If an *ffpg* is still not found, w is added back to cqueue and the compressor continues onto the next iteration of the loop. Otherwise, md.pgoff is atomically set to the offset from md.basepg of the found *ffpg*.

If md.pgoff is set to the offset of an *ffpg*, the compressor reads each page pg in *sn* to determine if pg is fully filled. If so, and if md.remapv[pg] = 0 and the offset of pg is not md.pgoff, then md.remapv[pg] is atomically set to 1 and pg is remapped to the page at md.pgoff by using remap_file_pages.

After scanning *sn*, w is added back to cqueue only if the number of remapped pages in *sn* is below a configurable threshold. If w is not added back, md.rc is atomically decremented. The compressor then continues onto the next iteration.

5.2 The SLM (Same Leaf-page Merging) Technique

If two leaf pages contain the same sequence of bytes, not necessarily all 1, their physical storage could be merged. However, merged pages can subsequently change due to updates by clients. But since deletions are absent, and since leaf bytes can transition only from 0 to 1, these changes will all be logical. (There are no transitions from 1 to 1 because of the check in Line 9. And there are no transitions from 0 to 0 because once a leaf is mmap-ed, 0 is never written to it.) Therefore, the number of changes that a leaf page can undergo is bounded—it cannot be more than the number of bytes in a page.

Compressors can use a COW (Copy-On-Write) mechanism to unmerge pages that are updated by a client. Since the number of changes is bounded, COW will not be used indefinitely. Once physical storage is restored to it, an unmerged page can again be brought into consideration for future merging. To further avoid wasteful merging, this reconsideration can be after increasingly extended periods of time—e.g., after multiplicatively-growing durations.

5.2.1 Approximating SLM with Linux's KSM

Since kernel version 2.6.32, Linux provides a page-merging feature called KSM (Kernel Samepage Merging) [5, 41]. With KSM, a simple yet powerful approximation of SLM, called SLMLite, is possible. KSM uses kernel threads to periodically scan registered memory regions for identical pages. Their physical storage is replaced by a single COW page so that physical storage can be automatically restored should one of the merged pages later change.

KSM uses two red-black trees, referred to as unstable and stable, to merge pages [5]. The first tracks pages that could be merged but are not merged yet. The second tracks pages that are merged; these pages are also write-protected. A page pg that is under consideration for merging is first compared with pages in the stable tree. If a match is found, pg is merged and freed. If not found, a checksum is computed for pg. If it is different from the previous checksum for pg, then pg is discarded from further consideration in the current scan. If the checksums are equal, pg is compared with pages in the unstable tree. If a match is not found, pg is inserted

into the unstable tree. But if found, pg is merged with the found page, which is then moved from the unstable to the stable tree.

The motivation for KSM was to accommodate more virtual machines by sharing identical pages of data between them [41].

To use KSM, it must first be enabled through a kernel configuration setting. Next, the KSM daemon, which does the merging, must be running. Finally, an application must register the virtual-address ranges of the memory regions of interest by invoking the madvise system call with the *MADV_MERGEABLE* advice argument [41].

5.2.2 The SLMLite Approximation

SLMLite is a simple extension to a sticky trie's design. The extension is to just invoke madvise with *MADV_MERGEABLE* on the created leaves. It is complementary to the TTG technique (Section 3). There is no userland compressor creation and management because KSM's kernel threads are the compressors. There is no userland COW or merging logic. Thus, KSM is cleanly leveraged to realize an approximation of SLM that, algorithmically, is considerably simpler than FLM. Despite this simplicity, the approximation can be more powerful because it goes after more compression opportunities (merging of identical pages versus merging of only fully-filled pages). Experimental evidence from a prototype shows that an exact SLMLite sticky trie, when compared with an exact FLM sticky trie, can have an insertion performance that is 252% better, and a lookup performance that is 237% better (Section 7.4).

6. Some Uses

We describe two representative uses of a sticky trie in this section.

6.1 Bloom-Filter Alternative

The classic Bloom filter [9] resembles a sticky trie in its interface—insertion, lookup, and no deletion. But it is unordered. It is also a randomized data structure [25]—i.e., its behavior is dependent on randomly selected hash functions. A sticky trie is neither unordered nor randomized nor reliant on hashing. And unlike an exact sticky trie, a practical Bloom filter can never be free of false positives.

6.2 SSB Substitute

An SSB is used by garbage collectors to quickly record the addresses of interesting references, either as a front-end to a remembered set or as a remembered set itself [4, 8, 15, 23, 24]. The SSB and its attendant remembered set—if it has one—could be viewed as a compound data structure that supports insertion (e.g., mutator records the addresses of old-to-young generational references by using barriers) and lookup (e.g., collector retrieves the recorded addresses). The remembered-set component can be discarded once it is consumed by the collector, perhaps after copying a subset of it to another remembered set. Since there is no need for deletion, the compound data structure can be substituted by a sticky trie.

At its core, an SSB is a block of pointer-sized slots along with a free-slot pointer. "Recording the address of a reference" means inserting the address of the location holding the reference. This is usually accomplished by storing the address through the free-slot pointer. If the block overflows, it is first either drained into a remembered set [23, 24] or linked to an empty block [8, 15].

SSB variants typically detect overflow by using traps [4, 15, 23, 24]. An exception is the Jikes RVM variant [8], which checks for overflow on each insertion. Comparing the sticky trie with all possible SSB variants is not a point of this paper. However, we do show that the sticky trie could be competitive with an artificial SSB whose performance upper bounds the class of trap-based SSBs.

Consider a trap-based SSB with the "reset" overflow action: its trap handler only initializes anew the free-slot pointer, thereby always ignoring the block's contents. This trap-based reset SSB's *measured* time $\tau^*(i)$ for recording i addresses can be modeled as

$$\tau^*(i) \approx \tau(i) = \frac{i\alpha}{b} + i\beta + b\gamma, \qquad (4)$$

where b is the block size in slots, α is the time for a trap, β is the time to store into a slot and update the free-slot pointer, and γ is the per-slot time for moving data through a memory hierarchy. For a given $i > b$, if b is too small, there will be too many traps; if b is too large, there will be too much of traffic in the memory hierarchy. Clearly from Equation (4), there is a b that minimizes $\tau(i)$ for an i.

We say that a trap-based reset SSB for recording i addresses in a program P is *ideal* for P if its b minimizes $\tau^*(i)$ for P. This artificial SSB, by construction, upper bounds the performance of *any* trap-based SSB for recording i addresses in P. By experimentally comparing it to the sticky trie (Section 7.4.1), we show that the sticky trie could be competitive with any trap-based SSB.

Equation (4) is inadequate for modeling check-based SSBs because it considers the cost of a trap as the dominant cost of an overflow. In the absence of a similar equation for a check-based SSB, we would have to consider specific implementations to draw comparisons between sticky tries and check-based SSBs.

6.2.1 Automatic Elimination of Duplicates

Several SSB variants do not eliminate a duplicate when storing into a slot—e.g., [4, 15, 23, 24]. For instance, Hosking et al. [23] subsequently use a circular hash table to eliminate duplicates. A sticky trie has the advantage that a duplicate is automatically eliminated.

The Jikes RVM variant eliminates duplicates differently: A bit in the object's header indicates SSB inclusion [8]. Such an SSB, however, would imprecisely record the addresses of field and array-element references as the address of the containing object. A sticky trie whose $c \leq \log_2(v/8)$ would not have this imprecision.

6.2.2 Enumeration

For retrieving the recorded addresses en masse, an enumeration operation can be supported. Essentially, enumeration is a trie traversal. A run of skippable bytes in a node can be traversed by using multiword machine instructions. A possible enhancement is to have a "leap vector" of marks for each node. A mark signifies a longer run of skippable bytes, such as a page. For example, it could indicate a fully-filled leaf page. Initially, none of the leaf pages has a mark because none is fully filled. The task of marking a leaf's leap vector could be relegated to a dedicated thread or piggybacked on the compressors.[4] Thus, as the vector gets populated, the client's leaf-byte enumeration speed could improve.

An internal node's leap vector could be marked by the client itself, incrementally, when growing the trie.

The leap-vector approach has its costs. One is the memory for maintaining the vectors. Another is the time for accessing them. If there are no sufficiently long runs of skippable bytes, the enumeration time could be more than that without the leap vector.

Another possibility for improving enumeration speed is to traverse subtries in parallel. This could be particularly useful when the enumeration order is unimportant.

7. Experimental Results

The sticky trie has been implemented as a C library called Forceps. Its performance was evaluated on three benchmarks. The evaluation comprised four classes of experiments: 1) code-size comparisons of the compiled insertion and lookup subroutines; 2) run-time comparisons of single-thread insertions and lookups; 3) run-time comparisons of multithread insertions and lookups; and 4) resident

set size (RSS) and page-sharing comparisons. These were made by using nine data structures with each benchmark: 1) TTG—sticky trie that uses the TTG technique; 2) cn—sticky trie that uses conditional code instead of traps; 3) F+T—sticky trie that uses FLM and TTG; 4) S+T—sticky trie that uses SLMLite and TTG; 5) BSi—bit-array Bloom filter that uses two simple hash functions; 6) BSy—byte-array version of BSi; 7) BLy—byte-array Bloom filter that uses more advanced hash functions; 8) ut—the GNU C++ Library's unordered_set container (version 3.4.16); and 9) ITSSB—an ideal trap-based SSB (Section 6.2).

7.1 Setup

Our test bed was a 64-bit single-socket desktop with an AMD A10-5800B quad-core, 16GB of RAM, and running Ubuntu 12.04.3 LTS (kernel release 3.5.0). The processor's cache line, L1 instruction and data caches, and L2 cache, are 64B, 128KB, 64KB, and 4MB.

The A10-5800B can dynamically scale its frequency from 1.4GHz to 3.8GHz. We used the CPUFreq kernel subsystem and its "performance governor" configuration to keep the clock at a constant 3.8GHz (see cpufreq-set man page).

Every timing measurement in this paper (in CPU cycles or seconds) is the mean of the last five of an eight-run experiment.

The KSM daemon, which is used for realizing SLMLite (Section 5.2.2), was run only when S+T was used. KSM was toggled by writing to /sys/kernel/mm/ksm/run [41]. None of the other files that controls KSM behavior was changed.

Revision 173836 of gcc was used, which is a version series 4.7 pre-release. The ld version was 2.22. Both support LTO (Link-Time Optimization), which was always kept on along with -O3.

7.1.1 Benchmarks

Our synth, atrack and ctrack benchmarks perform i insertions followed by j lookups on each run. They generate sequences of 48-bit keys for their insertion and lookup workloads. Our interest in 48-bit keys is because one application area for sticky tries, which is explored by atrack and ctrack, is the tracking of 64-bit virtual addresses in software. Current x86-64 platforms use only the low 48 bits by complying with the "canonical address form" property [1, Pages 120, 131–136]. Therefore, the sticky tries in all of our experiments were configured with $u = 48$.

Indeed, because current x86-64 platforms use only the low 48 bits of a virtual address, any attempt to mmap a 2^{48}-byte array in them will fail, irrespective of the /proc/sys/vm/overcommit_memory setting. Thus, in such platforms, a simple byte-array representation of a 48-bit key universe will not work.

synth's insertion and lookup workloads are synthesized by randomly picking from clusters of over four million distinct keys. A cluster's origin is itself randomly picked from a 48-bit key universe.

atrack's insertion workload is the sequence of low 48-bit virtual addresses of elements accessed by a quicksort of a million-element randomly populated array. Each array element is 32 bytes long, so any two distinct keys are at least 32 units apart. atrack's lookup workload is the sequence of low 48-bit virtual addresses of randomly picked elements in the array.

ctrack's insertion workload is the sequence of low 48-bit virtual addresses of a payload field f_0 accessed by a linear traversal of a 2^{17}-node circular linked list *cll*. Hence, a key is revisited after every 2^{17} insertions. After all insertions, 2^{12} nodes are randomly spliced into *cll*. The lookup workload is the sequence of low 48-bit virtual addresses of f_0 accessed by a linear traversal of *cll* after the splicing. A node has four payload fields and is 16 bytes long, so the insertion workload is from a range of at least 2^{21} distinct keys and the lookup workload is from a range of at least 2^{33} distinct keys.

While synth is synthetic, atrack and ctrack are realistic in the sense that they represent a software-based access-tracking

---

[4] For instance, md.remapv in Section 5.1.2 could be taken out of md so that it doubles as a leap vector and is not garbage collected.

application. We chose the three because we are unaware of benchmark suites that focus on insertion and lookup performance alone.

7.1.2 Compared Data Structures

The sticky tries in all of our experiments were configured with $\theta = 1$. Their leaves and internal nodes were sized to 64MB and 4MB by using Equation (3). INSERTT and LOOKUPT are the insertion and lookup subroutines for TTG, F+T and S+T (Figures 3 and 4). The insertion and lookup subroutines for cn are those for a standard trie—they are based on conditional code. The former was outlined as INSERTC in Section 3.1. The latter is similar to LOOKUPT except that it tests for null pointers instead of salt pointers.

BSi, BSy and BLy are nonpartitioned Bloom filters that use either bits (BSi) or bytes (BSy, BLy) as marks. Byte marks permit the realization of lockless atomic insertion and lookup by using atomic byte-store machine instructions. The only difference between BSi and BSy is the bit or byte representation of marks.

The number of hash functions in a Bloom filter affects its false-positive probability in two opposing ways: as more are used, the chance that a lookup is a true hit increases; but as more are used, the number of bits set to 1 for the same number of insertions also increases, which decreases the chance that a lookup is a true hit. The hash-function count additionally affects performance, in a more direct way: as more are used, insertion and lookup times both increase. Therefore, as a compromise between performance and false-positive probability, all of our filters use two hash functions. This choice was also motivated by a theoretical result that shows that only two hash functions are needed to implement a Bloom filter without losing on the asymptotic false-positive probability [25]. It should be emphasized that whatever is the hash-function count, the false-positive probability is always nonzero—this is intrinsic to a Bloom filter and is a fundamental departure from a sticky trie.

BSi and BSy use the modulo and quotient-modulo hash functions: if m is a filter's mark count, then a key k is hashed to $k \bmod m$ and $\lfloor k/m \rfloor \bmod m$. In our experiments, m was set to a power of 2 (i.e., 2^{26}). This enabled modulo and quotient-modulo to be implemented with shift and bit-masking machine instructions alone. For the chosen m, the filter size was 8MB for BSi and 64MB for BSy.

BLy uses modulo forms of the well-known SDBM and DJB hash functions. They are more complex when compared with the hash functions in BSi and BSy, and were chosen to explore the costs incurred by greater sophistication in the hash function.

A hash table underlies the unordered_set of the GNU C++ Library [19]. Our unordered_set instance used gcc's trivial hash function, which simply returns its argument. It also used preallocation, i.e., it was constructed with at least 2^{23} buckets.

7.1.3 A Note on Memory Allocation for Sticky-Trie Nodes

The sticky-trie nodes were allocated by directly invoking mmap. They were nearly always mapped as *anonymous* private [10], partly because KSM merges only anonymous-private pages [41]. The only exception was the leaves under FLM—they were mapped as anonymous shared. This was because remap_file_pages currently only works with shared mappings [10].

Hence, because leaves are always mmap-ed as anonymous, they will be automatically initialized with 0 at creation time. Furthermore, Linux initially uses a single "zero page" for anonymous memory [10]. On the first write to an anonymous page, COW replaces the underlying zero page by a new physical page. Thus, a 64MB leaf never up front consumes 64MB of physical memory.

7.2 Cycle Cost of a Trap

Table 1 shows the mean cycle counts for traps generated on accessing different parts of the virtual-address space. These were measured by using the x86 rdtsc instruction. Thus, the mean cycle

| model | | kernel | CPU cycles per trap | | | | | |
| | | | salt pointer | | null pointer | | mprotect | |
name	GHz		mean	CV	mean	CV	mean	CV
A10-5800B	3.80	3.5.0	5554	0.56%	5773	0.92%	5860	1.00%
E7330	2.40	2.6.18	3870	0.73%	3938	4.23%	4154	1.72%
8354	2.20	2.6.18	1976	0.87%	2214	0.87%	2194	0.57%
X5355	2.66	2.6.18	3680	1.16%	3958	1.15%	3911	1.07%

Table 1. Average CPU cycles per trap in some platforms.

| | TTG, F+T, S+T | | cn | | BSi | BSy | BLy | ut | ITSSB |
	$c=0$	$c=2$	$c=0$	$c=2$					
I	8	9	17	19	18	7	56	266	5
L	10	11	10	11	19	10	66	21	N/A

Table 2. x86-64 instruction counts for insertion (I) and lookup (L).

count for a trap that is generated on dereferencing a salt pointer was 5554 in our test bed. This was 5.51% less than the mean cycle count for a trap that is generated on dereferencing a pointer into mprotect-ed space, and 3.94% less than the mean cycle count for a trap that is generated on dereferencing the null pointer. To quantify the variability in the measurements, we calculated the well-known Coefficient of Variation, which is the ratio of the standard deviation to the mean. This is shown in the 'CV' columns.

Cycle-count measurements in three other platforms are also shown in Table 1. They had older 64-bit processors and kernel. The E7330 and X5355 are Intel Xeon processors; the 8354 is an AMD Third Generation Opteron processor. Hence, a salt-pointer-induced trap had the lowest average cycle cost in all four platforms.

7.3 Insertion and Lookup Compiled Code Sizes

Table 2 shows the x86-64 code sizes for the gcc-compiled insertion and lookup subroutines in the compared data structures. All instructions except xchg %rax, %rax and nop were counted.

TTG, F+T and S+T have the same code sizes because their insertion and lookup subroutines are identical. Their performance differences (Section 7.4) are due to compression and compressor overhead. And for a given c, their lookup code size matches the cn lookup code size because the only difference between them is that the former tests for salt pointers, by using bt and jb, whereas the latter tests for null pointers, by using cmp and jbe. We see that ITSSB has the smallest insertion subroutine, and that TTG, F+T, S+T (all at $c=0$) and BSy have the smallest lookup subroutines.

In all except cn's and ut's insertion subroutine, the compiler inlined all internal calls. The single call in the slow path of cn's insertion subroutine was not inlined. Several calls were not inlined in ut's insertion subroutine, such as those of the new and delete operators and those of the catch, rethrow and ceilf functions.

BSy's insertion subroutine has a total of seven instructions even though its modulo and quotient-modulo hash functions have three and four instructions. This is because of register-reuse opportunities from inlining. The major contributors to the code sizes of BLy's insertion and lookup subroutines are the SDBM and DJB hash functions, which have 22 and 28 instructions. Thus, in some sense, BSi and BSy are among the simplest possible Bloom filters.

7.4 Relative Single-Thread Performance

Figure 6 plots the relative performance $T_{BSi}(i)/T_D(i)$ of a data structure D's insertion (lookup) subroutine against the left axis,

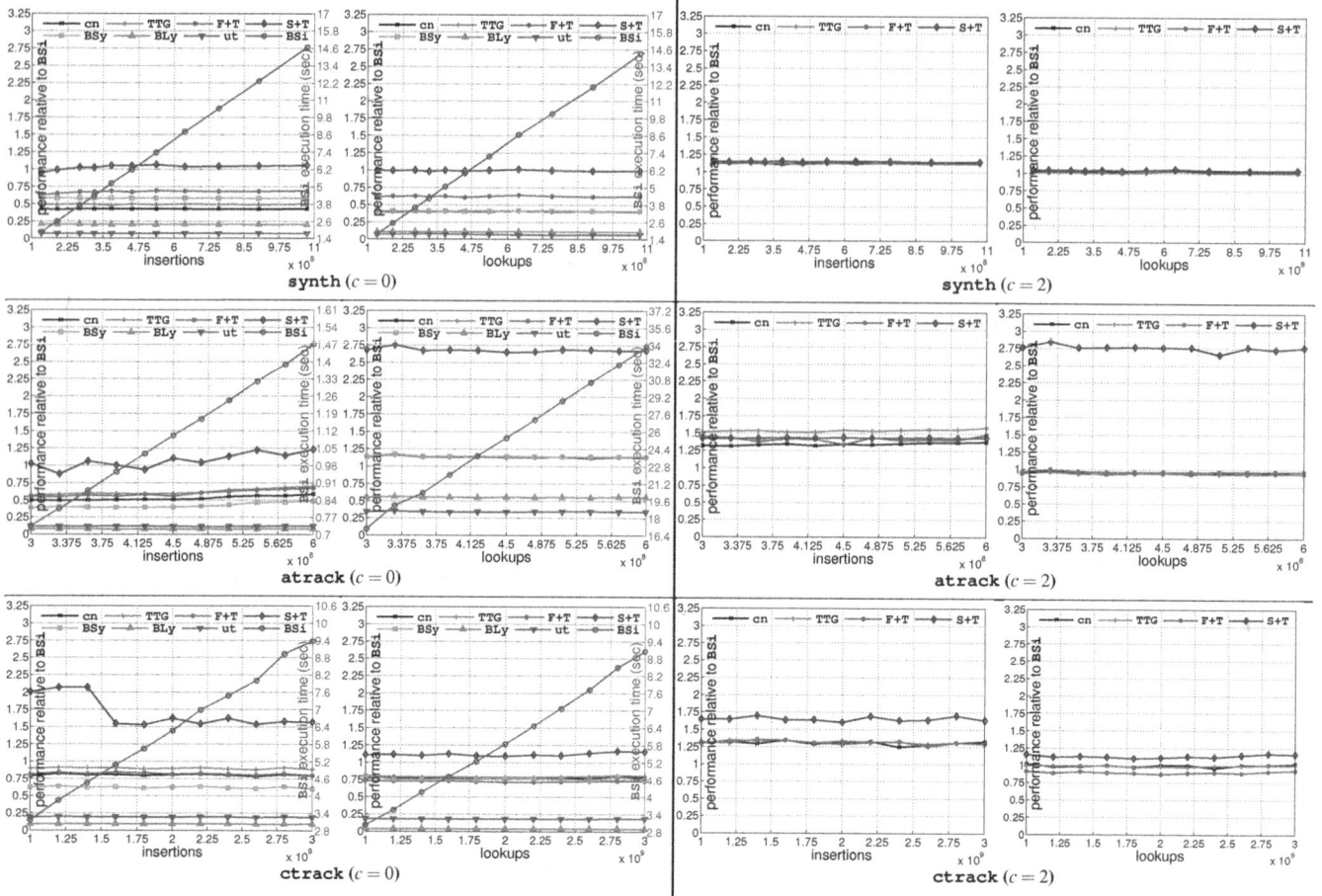

Figure 6. Single-thread performance of a data structure's insertion and lookup relative to BSi's insertion and lookup.

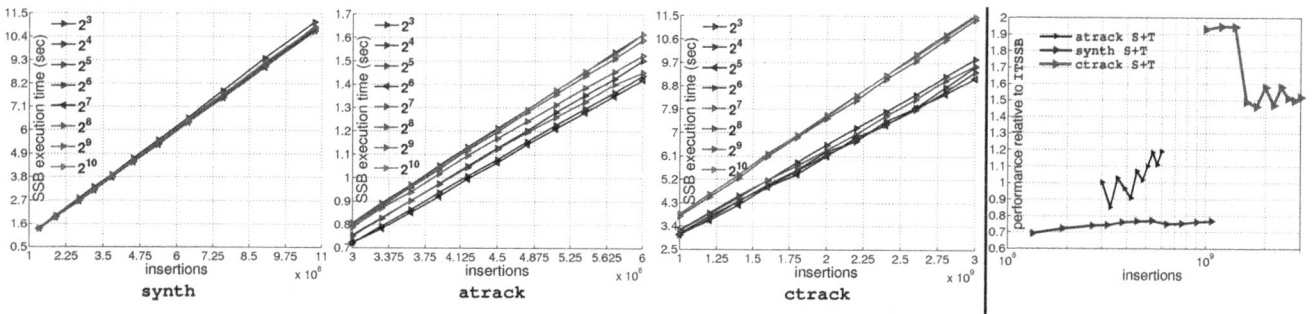

Figure 7. Single-thread insertion times of a trap-based reset SSB, and single-thread insertion performance of S+T relative to ITSSB.

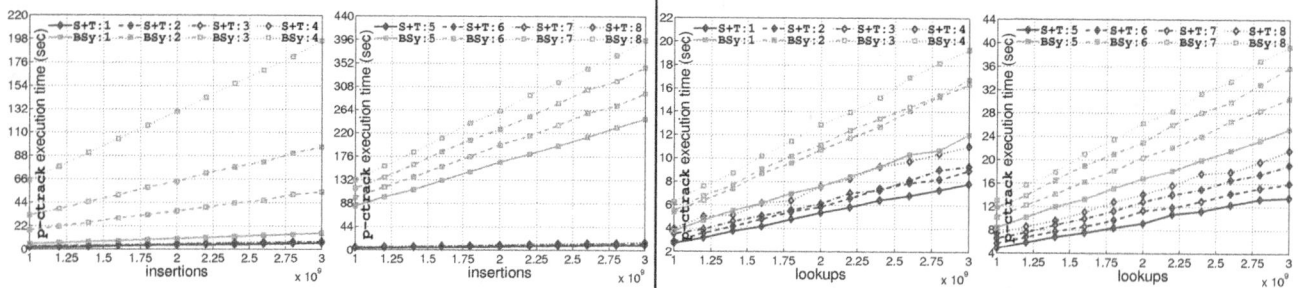

Figure 8. Scaling of the insertion and lookup times of S+T and BSy on p-ctrack as the thread count n is increased from 1 to 8.

where $T_D(i)$ and $T_{BSi}(i)$ are the single-thread run times for i insertions (lookups) into D and BSi. D is cn, TTG, F+T, S+T, BSy, BLy or ut. $T_{BSi}(i)$ is plotted against the right axis. While a row's left half shows relative performance on a benchmark when $c = 0$, its right half shows the same when $c = 2$ for only cn, TTG, F+T and S+T because BSy, BLy, ut and BSi are unaffected by c.

We observe the following at $c = 0$. Lookup performance of S+T was always the best on atrack and ctrack—it was up to 275% of the second best (BSi). On synth, S+T's lookup performance relative to BSi ranged between 98% and 101%. Insertion performance of S+T was always the best on ctrack, being up to 207% of the second best (BSi). On atrack and synth, it was up to 123% and 107% of the second best (BSi). The mean relative performance on synth, atrack and ctrack was 99%, 268% and 112% for lookups, and 103%, 107% and 170% for insertions. The mean over all benchmarks for lookups and insertions was 160% and 127%. The overall mean was 143%. These numbers are despite the sticky trie being exact at $c = 0$ and BSi having false positives. They are also despite the sticky trie being ordered and the non-sticky trie data structures in our collection being unordered.

If BSi were excluded, then S+T's performance relative to the second best would be higher, ranging from 137% to 236%.

Relative to F+T, S+T's insertion and lookup performance ranged between 151% and 252%. And relative to TTG, S+T's insertion and lookup performance ranged between 137% and 249%. While F+T may not be as effective as S+T, it still can produce wins—e.g., F+T's insertion performance on synth relative to cn and TTG was up to 162% and 143%. Only synth provides fully-filled page opportunities. Not atrack and ctrack, because any two distinct tracked locations in them are at least 16 bytes apart.

On moving from left to right on a row, the cn, TTG, F+T and S+T curves move up in most cases. Consider insertion. At $c = 0$, cn was always below BSi for all benchmarks. But at $c = 2$, it was always above BSi. Increasing c improves memory usage because more keys are covered by a single card. Therefore, an inexact sticky trie is generally better performance-wise than an exact sticky trie.

By computing the ratio of the TTG curve to the cn curve, we find that the performance of TTG relative to cn ranged from 99% to 121% at $c = 0$, and from 97% to 117% at $c = 2$.

7.4.1 Performance Relative to an Ideal Trap-Based SSB

The first three graphs in Figure 7 show how the single-thread recording time of a trap-based reset SSB (i.e., $\tau^*(i)$ in Section 6.2) varies with block size. The block size, sans guard page, was increased from eight pages to 1024 pages. A dark curve for a benchmark corresponds to the block size with the smallest *mean* insertion time. For example, the atrack curve corresponding to 64 pages had the smallest mean insertion time; in this specific case, it also had the smallest individual times for nearly all insertions.

Therefore, from each of the first three graphs, we can determine the smallest time for i insertions into a trap-based reset SSB for a benchmark. This, by definition, is the time for i insertions into an ideal trap-based SSB for that benchmark. The fourth graph plots the ratio of this time to the time for i insertions with S+T at $c = 0$. The x-axis uses a log scale to accommodate all three input ranges. Only insertion performance was compared because an ideal trap-based SSB does not support lookup (block contents are ignored).

From the fourth graph, S+T's insertion performance relative to ITSSB was always better on ctrack, and sometimes better on atrack. For instance, it was always over 146% on ctrack, and up to 195% and 119% on ctrack and atrack. Its mean on ctrack and atrack was 163% and 104%. Hence, on these two, the insertion performance of an exact sticky trie that uses TTG and SLMLite could exceed that of any real trap-based SSB.

INSERTITSSB(k,s):
```
101 mov  (%rsi),%rax
102 lea  0x8(%rax),%rdx
103 mov  %rdx,(%rsi)
*104 mov  %rdi,(%rax)
105 retq
```

INSERTT(k,s) (when $\theta = 1, c = 0$):
```
201 mov  %rdi,%rax
202 and  $0x3ffffff,%edi
203 shr  $0x1a,%rax
204 mov  (%rsi,%rax,8),%rsi
*205 cmpb $0x1,(%rsi,%rdi,1)
206 je   208
207 movb $0x1,(%rsi,%rdi,1)
208 repz retq
```

Figure 9. x86-64 gcc code. %rdi, %rsi correspond to k, s.

By appropriately multiplying curves in Figures 6 and 7, we note that the insertion performance of cn, TTG and F+T at $c = 0$ was always lower than that of ITSSB, even on atrack and ctrack.

Figure 9 shows the gcc-compiled insertion subroutines for ITSSB and S+T. Line 104 is starred because it could write to the guard page. Although INSERTITSSB is smaller by three instructions, it performs more memory writes per call. In particular, it does two memory writes and one memory read, all of 64-bit values. In contrast, INSERTT reads one 64-bit value and one byte from memory, and conditionally writes one byte to memory.

The free-slot pointer is (%rsi). The compiler is limited in what it can do with the free-slot pointer because of the trap handler's asynchronous actions. We therefore mark (%rsi) as volatile. Otherwise, the compiler could transform code involving the free-slot pointer in ways that have ill-defined outcomes.

7.5 Scalability

We studied multithread performance by using p-ctrack, which is an n-thread generalization of ctrack. Each thread performs the actions of ctrack but on possibly a different payload field. Specifically, Thread t's insertion workload is the sequence of low 48-bit virtual addresses of the payload field $f_{t'}$ accessed by a linear traversal of *cll*, where $t' = t \bmod 4$. Its lookup workload is the sequence of low 48-bit virtual addresses of $f_{t'}$ accessed by a linear traversal of *cll* after splicing. The atomic insertions and lookups are on a shared exact sticky trie. p-ctrack is ctrack when $n = 1$.

Even when different fields are accessed in parallel, the sticky-trie accesses contend in the data cache. This is because the sticky-trie leaf bytes for a *cll* node's fields map to the same cache line.

S+T was compared with BSy, which is the only non-sticky-trie data structure in our collection that can be concurrently used without locks and whose insertion and lookup subroutines are comparable to S+T's in size (Table 2). Figure 8 shows how their run times scaled with n. A $D : n$ curve is the insertion or lookup time of D with n threads, where $1 \le n \le 8$ and D is either S+T or BSy.

In the leftmost two graphs, we see that the S+T : n insertion curves are far less divergent than the BSy : n insertion curves, as n increases from 1 to 8. For instance, at two billion insertions, whereas S+T's run time ranged from 3.9s to 10.1s, BSy's run time ranged from 10.1s to 262.1s. Because the slopes of the BSy : n curves increase much more rapidly than those of the S+T : n curves, the slowdowns for BSy were much more. As an example, at $n = 2$, 4 and 8, the slowdown factors for S+T were 1.1, 1.4 and 2.6; those for BSy were 3.6, 12.9 and 26.1. Thus, the scaling of S+T on insertion was dramatically better than that of BSy. This is basically because, excluding the occasional actions of the trap handler, S+T only conditionally writes a byte on each insertion, whereas BSy *always* writes two bytes on each insertion.

In the rightmost two graphs, although the S+T : n lookup curves are more divergent than the S+T : n insertion curves, they are still appreciably lower than the BSy : n lookup curves. For instance, at two billion lookups and $n = 2$, 4 and 8, the run times for S+T were 5.8s, 7.6s and 14.1s; those for BSy were 10.7s, 12.8s and 26.2s.

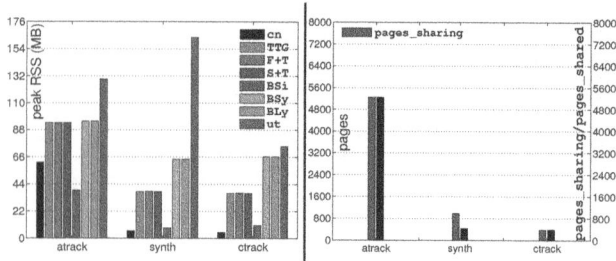

Figure 10. On the left is the peak RSS. On the right are KSM's `pages_sharing` and `pages_sharing/pages_shared` ratio.

7.6 Memory Usage

The left graph in Figure 10 shows the mean peak RSS for each data structure D on each benchmark. The shown sticky tries are all exact. (ITSSB is not shown because it does not support lookup.) The peak RSS was read from the VmHWM field in `/proc/self/status` at the end of a single-thread run. Each bar for a D in the left graph is the peak RSS averaged over all the runs of a benchmark with that D. For example, the mean peak RSS for atrack with BSi, TTG and ut was 39MB, 94MB and 129MB.

Overall, TTG's mean peak RSS relative to BSi, cn and ut was 347%, 523% and 48%. It was 71% relative to both BSy and BLy, which are the only non-sticky-trie data structures in our collection that can be concurrently used without synchronization.

Notice that TTG, F+T and S+T had about the same mean peak RSS. The /proc file system presently does not appear to reflect memory savings due to KSM. KSM maintains this information separately, in its `pages_shared` and `pages_sharing` files. They contain the number of pages in a shared pool and the number of sites using that pool [41]. A high `pages_sharing`-to-`pages_shared` ratio is indicative of good KSM efficiency [41]. The right graph in Figure 10 shows the mean `pages_sharing` value against the left axis and the mean `pages_sharing`-to-`pages_shared` ratio against the right axis. Individual values of `pages_sharing` and `pages_shared` were up to 7811 and 3.

8. Limitations

Our sticky-trie implementation, currently, has several limitations. First, the algorithm in Figure 5 is not starvation-free. It uses the asynchrony bit as a lock. So if a thread gains ownership of a branch-pointer slot *st* but indefinitely stalls before installing a normal pointer in *st*, every thread that attempts to grow the sticky trie through *st* will not make progress. Second, compression opportunities are limited to leaf pages. It would be beneficial to substitute identical nodes at every level by a single node at that level. Identical pages of pointers could then also be merged. Third, the design relies on sparsity and locality in the key distribution. It will likely perform poorly on key sequences that are highly variable in the high-order bits. In fact, an insertion sequence that creates a new leaf for each key can quickly exhaust the virtual-address space. This could be addressed by smaller leaves, and smaller nodes in general.

9. Other Related Work

A trie [18] can come in various forms, such as an LC-trie [3], burst trie [21], Judy array [22], and Ctrie [33]. All trie variants known to us incorporate deletion. And except for the Ctrie, none are designed for lockless concurrent usage. Also, a variety of techniques for reducing trie storage have been proposed, such as restructuring, dynamic programming, and variable-length encoding. However, as

far as we know, none attempt to reduce storage transparently in the manner that we do, by working off of the virtual-memory system.

There have been efforts on transparently reducing a program's primary-memory usage by using algorithms such as LZRW1, WKdm and LZO to compress page data—e.g., [17, 42, 45, 46]. These efforts, unlike ours, require a decompression step.

9.1 Some Trie Variants

The burst trie organizes a collection of "containers" into a standard trie structure. A container can be any data structure that is suitable for searching over small sets, such as a list or a binary search tree. The burst trie starts off as a single container. When a container is deemed to have become inefficient, it is "burst", which means replacing it by a trie node and child containers that, among them, partition the original container's contents [21]. Bursting has no trapping connotation. It is a logical action that is triggered by heuristics. Moreover, it grows the number of levels in the trie, incurring structural changes that are not transparent to the client and that also complicate a solution under concurrency.

A Judy array is similar to a regular array, except that it provides an "unbounded paradigm" [22], in the sense that its size is limited only by the primary memory available on a machine. Its underlying data structure is a hybrid trie in which each node's data structure is appropriate to the size of the population represented by that node.

The Masstree [28] is a wide-fanout trie whose nodes are B^+-trees. Its features include persistence and crash recovery. Some of the basic differences with a sticky trie are the inclusion of deletion and the possible splitting of nodes on insertion.

A leaf in our sticky trie is in essence a card table [37] with byte marks. But card tables in the past have been unconditionally updated—e.g., [7, 15, 23]. In light of Section 3.2.1, this can be deleterious to performance if multiple processors update the same card-table cache line. The problem is well-known and has been addressed by conditionally marking the bytes [16, 47].

Detlefs et al. [15] describe a scheme that uses two card tables, one coarse-grained and the other fine-grained. The latter is a regular card table. Each entry in the former corresponds to some number of entries in the latter. The tables are laid out so that they share a single base register [15]. They are grown neither incrementally nor on demand, and are neither conditionally updated nor compressed.

9.2 Techniques for Reducing Trie Storage

Tries have been pruned by restructuring. There have been two kinds of restructuring. The first is level compression, which recursively replaces the highest i complete levels in a binary trie by a single 2^i-degree node [3]. The second is path compression, which comes in two flavors. In one, branchless paths to a leaf are replaced by an edge [39]. In another, nodes with one child are merged with their child; this kind of compression occurs in a Patricia trie [30].

Maly's C-trie [27] represents a branch pointer by a single bit. The ensuing storage improvement comes at the expense of decreased flexibility and increased insertion time.

In the array-mapped trie (AMT) [6], an internal node may point to up to *wd* nodes, where *wd* is the size of a machine word. Rather than allocating an array of *wd* pointers, an AMT uses a machine-word bitmap to store only those among the *wd* pointers that are not null. Purdin [34] also uses bitmaps to eliminate null pointers.

Morimoto et al. [29] use two tries to separately represent front and rear key substrings. A trie shares common key prefixes; their double-trie approach seeks to also share common key suffixes.

Sahni and Kim [36] give dynamic programming formulations for constructing storage-optimal multibit tries of a specified height.

Germann et al. [20] use variable-length encoding to compact search keys. They represent the trie by a single byte array. In their setting, trie data is read from a file on disk. This file is mmap-ed so that the kernel manages the movement of data between primary memory and disk. There is no merging of pages.

Prokopec et al. [33] implemented the Ctrie in Java. Compression in their context refers to removing unneeded nodes after deletion.

9.3 Trapping Techniques

The self-pointing barrier [15] is an SSB variant in which blocks form a linked list. Slots except the last are initialized with normal pointers that point to themselves. The last slot ls is initialized with the null pointer. On handling the trap that is generated on the first dereference through ls, a block is added to the list by patching ls.

Brecht and Sandhu's Region Trap Library [11] allows for the creation of multiple objects with different protection levels on the same page. Only accesses to objects in the invalid state, or writes to objects in the read-only state, trap. They swizzle a pointer to kernel space when the targeted object transitions to the invalid state.

A multilevel page table is a trie that is also grown on demand by using traps [10]. But this trapping is at the granularity of physical pages and relies directly on hardware support.

10. Summary

We presented the sticky trie, a new trie variant for large key universes that achieves fast atomic insertions and lookups by precluding deletions. The absence of deletions enables the use of trapping and compression techniques to realize high performance. A possible extension is to allow bulk deletions at only certain points.

The TTG, FLM, SLM, and SLMLite techniques were described. TTG permits incremental and on-demand trie growth without incurring the overhead of checking on each insertion. The rest detect leaf parts that either cannot logically change or are identical. They then merge the physical storage of those parts in the background.

Implementations of the sticky trie were experimentally compared with each other, with Bloom filters, with the GNU C++ Library's `unordered_set` container, and with an ideal trap-based SSB. It was shown that among the techniques evaluated, a combination of TTG and SLMLite produces the best-performing sticky trie. It was also shown that this trie, performance-wise, could be superior to a Bloom filter and competitive with any trap-based SSB.

References

[1] ADVANCED MICRO DEVICES, INC. *AMD64 Architecture Programmer's Manual: System Programming (Vol. 2)*, Mar. 2012.

[2] AL-SUWAIYEL, M., AND HOROWITZ, E. Algorithms for Trie Compaction. *ACM Transactions on Database Systems 9*, 2 (June 1984), 243–263.

[3] ANDERSSON, A., AND NILSSON, S. Improved Behaviour of Tries by Adaptive Branching. *Information Processing Letters 46*, 6 (July 1993), 295–300.

[4] APPEL, A. W. Simple Generational Garbage Collection and Fast Allocation. *Software—Practice and Experience 19*, 2 (Feb. 1989), 171–183.

[5] ARCANGELI, A., EIDUS, I., AND WRIGHT, C. Increasing Memory Density by Using KSM. In *Proc. Linux Symposium* (July 2009), pp. 19–28.

[6] BAGWELL, P. Ideal Hash Trees. Research Report LAMP-REPORT-2001-001, École Polytechnique Fédérale de Lausanne, Oct. 2001.

[7] BLACKBURN, S. M., AND HOSKING, A. L. Barriers: Friend or Foe? In *Proc. International Symposium on Memory Management* (Oct. 2004), pp. 143–151.

[8] BLACKBURN, S. M., AND MCKINLEY, K. S. In or Out? Putting Write Barriers in Their Place. In *Proc. International Symposium on Memory Management* (June 2002), pp. 175–184.

[9] BLOOM, B. H. Space/Time Trade-offs in Hash Coding with Allowable Errors. *Communications of the ACM 13*, 7 (July 1970), 422–426.

[10] BOVET, D. P., AND CESATI, M. *Understanding the Linux Kernel*, third ed. O'Reilly Media, Inc., 2005.

[11] BRECHT, T., AND SANDHU, H. The Region Trap Library: Handling Traps on Application-Defined Regions of Memory. In *Proc. USENIX Annual Technical Conference* (June 1999), pp. 85–100.

[12] BRONEVETSKY, G., MARQUES, D., PINGALI, K., SZWED, P., AND SCHULZ, M. Application-Level Checkpointing for Shared Memory Programs. In *Proc. International Conference on Architectural Support for Programming Languages and Operating Systems* (Oct. 2004), pp. 235–247.

[13] CLÉMENT, J., FLAJOLET, P., AND VALLÉE, B. Dynamical Sources in Information Theory: A General Analysis of Trie Structures. *Algorithmica 29*, 1–2 (Feb. 2001), 307–369.

[14] CORMEN, T. H., LEISERSON, C. E., RIVEST, R. L., AND STEIN, C. *Introduction to Algorithms*, second ed. The MIT Press, 2007.

[15] DETLEFS, D., KNIPPEL, R., CLINGER, W. D., AND JACOB, M. Concurrent Remembered Set Refinement in Generational Garbage Collection. In *Proc. Java Virtual Machine Research and Technology Symposium* (Aug. 2002), pp. 13–26.

[16] DICE, D. False Sharing Induced by Card Table Marking. At https://blogs.oracle.com/dave/entry/false_sharing_induced_by_card, Feb. 2011.

[17] DOUGLIS, F. The Compression Cache: Using On-line Compression to Extend Physical Memory. In *Proc. USENIX Winter Technical Conference* (Jan. 1993), pp. 519–529.

[18] FREDKIN, E. Trie Memory. *Communications of the ACM 3*, 9 (Sept. 1960), 490–499.

[19] FREE SOFTWARE FOUNDATION. *The GNU C++ Library Manual*, 2011.

[20] GERMANN, U., JOANIS, E., AND LARKIN, S. Tightly Packed Tries: How to Fit Large Models into Memory, and Make them Load Fast, Too. In *Proc. Workshop on Software Engineering, Testing, and Quality Assurance for Natural Language Processing* (June 2009), pp. 31–39.

[21] HEINZ, S., ZOBEL, J., AND WILLIAMS, H. E. Burst Tries: A Fast, Efficient Data Structure for String Keys. *ACM Transactions on Information Systems 20*, 2 (Apr. 2002), 192–223.

[22] HEWLETT-PACKARD COMPANY. *Programming with Judy: C Language Judy Version 4.0*, June 2001. Part Number: B6841-90001.

[23] HOSKING, A. L., MOSS, E., AND STEFANOVIĆ, D. A Comparative Performance Evaluation of Write Barrier Implementations. In *Proc. Conference on Object-Oriented Programming, Systems, Languages and Applications* (Oct. 1992), pp. 92–109.

[24] HUDSON, R. L., AND DIWAN, A. Adaptive Garbage Collection for Modula-3 and Smalltalk. In *Addendum to OOPSLA/ECOOP'90 Proceedings* (Oct. 1990), E. Jul and N.-C. Juul, Eds.

[25] KIRSCH, A., AND MITZENMACHER, M. Less Hashing, Same Performance: Building a Better Bloom Filter. *Random Structures and Algorithms 33*, 2 (Sept. 2008), 187–218.

[26] KNUTH, D. E. *The Art of Computer Programming: Sorting and Searching*, second ed., vol. 3. Addison-Wesley, 2011.

[27] MALY, K. Compressed Tries. *Communications of the ACM 19*, 7 (July 1976), 409–415.

[28] MAO, Y., KOHLER, E., AND MORRIS, R. Cache Craftiness for Fast Multicore Key-Value Storage. In *Proc. European Conference on Computer Systems* (Apr. 2012), pp. 183–196.

[29] MORIMOTO, K., IRIGUCHI, H., AND AOE, J.-I. A Method of Compressing Trie Structures. *Software—Practice and Experience 24*, 3 (Mar. 1994), 265–288.

[30] MORRISON, D. R. PATRICIA—Practical Algorithm to Retrieve Information Coded in Alphanumeric. *Journal of the ACM 15*, 4 (Oct. 1968), 514–534.

[31] NEBEL, M. E. The Stack-Size of Combinatorial Tries Revisited. *Discrete Mathematics and Theoretical Computer Science 5*, 1 (2002), 1–16.

[32] PARK, G., HWANG, H.-K., NICODÈME, P., AND SZPANKOWSKI, W. Profiles of Tries. *SIAM Journal on Computing 38*, 5 (2009), 1821–1880.

[33] PROKOPEC, A., BRONSON, N. G., BAGWELL, P., AND ODERSKY, M. Concurrent Tries with Efficient Non-Blocking Snapshots. In *Proc. Symposium on Principles and Practices of Parallel Programming* (Feb. 2012), pp. 151–160.

[34] PURDIN, T. D. M. Compressing Tries for Storing Dictionaries. In *Proc. Symposium on Applied Computing* (Apr. 1990), pp. 336–340.

[35] RÉGNIER, M., AND JACQUET, P. New Results on the Size of Tries. *IEEE Transactions on Information Theory 35*, 1 (Jan. 1989), 203–205.

[36] SAHNI, S., AND KIM, K. S. Efficient Construction of Multibit Tries for IP Lookup. *IEEE/ACM Transactions on Networking 11*, 4 (Aug. 2003), 650–662.

[37] SOBALVARRO, P. G. A Lifetime-Based Garbage Collector for LISP Systems on General-Purpose Computers, 1988. BS thesis.

[38] SPRUGNOLI, R. Perfect Hashing Functions: A Single Probe Retrieving Method for Static Sets. *Communications of the ACM 20*, 11 (Nov. 1977), 841–850.

[39] SUSSENGUTH JR., E. H. Use of Tree Structures for Processing Files. *Communications of the ACM 6*, 5 (May 1963), 272–279.

[40] TARJAN, R. E., AND YAO, A. C.-C. Storing a Sparse Table. *Communications of the ACM 22*, 11 (Nov. 1979), 606–611.

[41] How to Use the Kernel Samepage Merging Feature. At https://www.kernel.org/doc/Documentation/vm/ksm.txt, 2009.

[42] TUDUCE, I. C., AND GROSS, T. Adaptive Main Memory Compression. In *Proc. USENIX Annual Technical Conference* (Apr. 2005), pp. 237–250.

[43] VOLOS, H., TACK, A. J., AND SWIFT, M. M. Mnemosyne: Lightweight Persistent Memory. In *Proc. International Conference on Architectural Support for Programming Languages and Operating Systems* (Mar. 2011), pp. 91–103.

[44] WHITE, S. J. *Pointer Swizzling Techniques for Object-Oriented Database Systems*. PhD thesis, University of Wisconsin-Madison, 1994.

[45] WILSON, P. R. Some Issues and Strategies in Heap Management and Memory Hierarchies. *ACM SIGPLAN Notices 26*, 3 (Mar. 1991), 45–52.

[46] YANG, L., LEKATSAS, H., AND DICK, R. P. High-Performance Operating System Controlled Memory Compression. In *Proc. Design Automation Conference* (July 2006), pp. 701–704.

[47] YANG, X., BLACKBURN, S. M., FRAMPTON, D., AND HOSKING, A. L. Barriers Reconsidered, Friendlier Still! In *Proc. International Symposium on Memory Management* (June 2012), pp. 37–47.

Concurrent, Parallel Garbage Collection in Linear Time

Steven R. Brandt

Center for Computation and Technology, School of Electrical Engineering and Computer Science, Louisiana State University, Baton Rouge, LA 70803, USA

sbrandt@cct.lsu.edu

Hari Krishnan

Center for Computation and Technology, School of Electrical Engineering and Computer Science, Louisiana State University, Baton Rouge, LA 70803, USA

hkrish4@tigers.lsu.edu

Gokarna Sharma

School of Electrical Engineering and Computer Science, Louisiana State University, Baton Rouge, LA 70803, USA

gokarna@csc.lsu.edu

Costas Busch

School of Electrical Engineering and Computer Science, Louisiana State University, Baton Rouge, LA 70803, USA

busch@csc.lsu.edu

Abstract

This paper presents a new concurrent garbage collection algorithm based on two types of reference, *strong* and *weak*, to link the graph of objects. Strong references connect the roots to all the nodes in the graph but do not contain cycles. Weak references may, however, contain cycles.

Advantages of this system include: (1) reduced processing, nontrivial garbage collection work is only required when the last strong reference is lost; (2) fewer memory traces to delete objects, a garbage cycle only needs to be traversed twice to be deleted; (3) fewer memory traces to retain objects, since the collector can often prove objects are reachable without fully tracing support cycles to which the objects belong; (4) concurrency, it can run in parallel with a live system without "stopping the world;" (5) parallel, because collection operations in different parts of the memory can proceed at the same time.

Previous variants of this technique required exponential cleanup time [27, 31], but our algorithm is linear in total time, i.e. any changes in the graph take only $\mathcal{O}(N)$ time steps, where N is the number of edges in the affected subgraph (e.g. the subgraph whose strong support is affected by the operations).

Categories and Subject Descriptors D.3.4 [*Programming Languages*]: Processors–Memory management (garbage collection)

General Terms Algorithms, Performance, Experimentation, Languages, Design, Termination

Keywords Garbage Collection, Parallel programming theory and models, Compilers and runtime systems, Software for productivity parallel programming, Parallel algorithms, Concurrent data structures

1. Introduction

Garbage collection is an important productivity feature in many languages, eliminating a thorny set of coding errors which can be created by explicit memory management [2, 3, 5, 10, 15, 23, 24].

ISMM'14, June 12, 2014, Edinburgh, United Kingdom.
Copyright © 2014 ACM 978-1-4503-2921-7/14/06...$15.00.
http://dx.doi.org/10.1145/2602988.2602990

Despite the many advances in garbage collection, there are problem areas which have difficulty benefiting, such as distributed or real-time systems; see [4, 28, 33]. Even in more mundane settings, a certain liveness in the cleanup of objects may be required by an application for which the garbage collector provides little help, e.g. managing a small pool of database connections.

The garbage collection system we propose is based on a scheme originally proposed by Brownbridge [8]. Brownbridge proposed the use of two types of pointers: *strong* and *weak*[1]. Strong pointers are required to connect from the *roots* (i.e. references from the stack or global memory) to all nodes in the graph, and contain no cycles. A path of strong links (i.e. pointers) from the roots guarantees that an object should be in memory. Weak pointers are available to close cycles and provide the ability to connect nodes in arbitrary ways.

Brownbridge's proposal was vulnerable to premature collection [31], and subsequent attempts to improve it introduced poor performance (at least exponential cleanup time in the worst-case) [27]; details in Section 1.1. Brownbridge's core idea, however, of using two types of reference counts was sound: maintaining this pair of reference counts allows the system to remember a set of acyclic paths through memory so that the system can minimize collection operations. For example, Roy et al. [30] used Brownbridge's idea to optimize scanning in databases. In this work we will show how the above problems with the Brownbridge collection scheme can be repaired by the inclusion of a third type of counter, which we call a *phantom count*. This modified system has a number of advantages.

Typical hybrid reference count and collection systems, e.g. [2, 3, 5, 19, 22], which use a reference counting collector combined with a tracing collector or cycle collector, must perform nontrivial work whenever a reference count is decreased and does not reach zero. The modified Brownbridge system, with three types of reference counts, must perform nontrivial work only when the strong reference count reaches zero and the weak reference count is still positive, a significant reduction [8, 15].

Many garbage collectors in the literature employ a generational technique, for example the generational collector proposed in [29], taking advantage of the observation that younger objects are more likely to need garbage collecting than older objects. Because the strong/weak reference system tends to make the links in long-lived paths through memory strong, old objects connected to these paths are unlikely to become the focus of the garbage collector's work.

In other conceptions of weak pointers, if a node is reachable by a strong pointer and a weak pointer and the strong pointer is removed,

---

[1] These references are unrelated to the weak, soft, and phantom reference objects available in Java under Reference class.

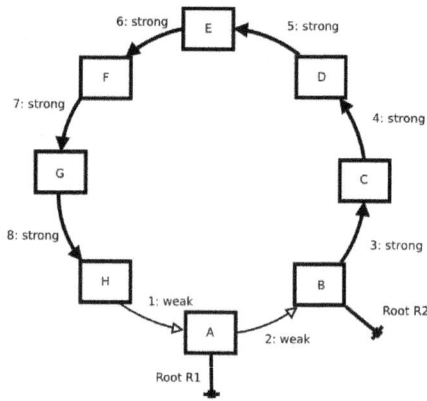

Figure 1. When root R1 is removed, the garbage collection algorithm only needs to trace link 2 to prove that object A does not need to be collected.

the node is garbage, and the node is deleted. In Brownbridge's conception of weak pointers, the weak pointer is turned into a strong pointer in an intelligent way.

In many situations, the collector can update the pointer types and prove an object is still live without tracing through memory cycles the object may participate in. For example, when root $R1$ is removed from the graph shown in Fig. 1, the collector only needs to convert link 1 to strong and examine link 2 to prove that object A does not need to be collected. What's more, because the strength of the pointer depends on a combination of states in the source and target, the transformation from strong to weak can be carried out without the need for back-pointers (i.e. links that can be followed from target to source as well as source to target).

This combination of effects, added to the fact that our collector can run in parallel with a live system, may prove useful in soft real-time systems, and may make the use of "finalizers" on objects more practical. These kinds of advantages should also be significant in a distributed setting, where traversal of links in the collector is a more expensive operation. Moreover, when a collection operation is local, it has the opportunity to remain local, and cleanup can proceed without any kind of global synchronization operation.

The contribution of this paper is threefold. Our algorithm never prematurely deletes any reachable object, operates in linear in time regardless of the structure (any deletion of edges and roots takes only $\mathcal{O}(N)$ time steps, where N is the number of edges in the affected subgraph), and works concurrently with the application, without the need for system-wide pauses, i.e. "stopping the world." This is in contrast to Brownbridge's original algorithm and its variants [8, 27, 31] which can not handle concurrency issues that arise in modern multiprocessor architectures [30].

Our algorithm does, however, add a third kind of pointer, a *phantom pointer*, which identifies a temporary state that is neither strong nor weak. The addition of the space overhead offsets the time overhead in Brownbridge's work.

1.1 Most Related Work: Premature Collection, Non-termination, and Exponential Cleanup Time

Before giving details of our algorithm in Section 2 – which in turn is a modification of Brownbridge's algorithm and its variants [8, 27, 31] – we first describe the problems with previous variants. In doing so, we follow the description given in the excellent garbage collection book due to Jones and Lins [15].

It was proven by McBeth [23] in early sixties that reference counting collectors were unable to handle cyclic structures; several attempts to fix this problem appeared subsequently, e.g. [7, 12, 22].

We give details in Section 1.2. In contrast to the approach followed in [7, 12, 22] and several others, Brownbridge [8] proposed, in 1985, a strong/weak pointer algorithm to tackle the problem of reclaiming cyclic data structures by distinguishing cycle closing pointers (weak pointers) from other references (strong pointers) [15]. This algorithm relied on maintaining two invariants: (a) there are no cycles in strong pointers and (b) all items in the graph must be strongly reachable from the roots.

Some years after the publication, Salkild [31] showed that Brownbridge's algorithm [8] could reclaim objects prematurely in some configurations, e.g. a double cycle. If the last strong pointer (or link) to an object in one cycle but not the other was lost, Brownbridge's method would incorrectly claim nodes from the cycle. Salkild [31] corrected this problem by proposing that if the last strong link was removed from an object which still had weak pointers, a collection process should re-start from that node. While this approach eliminated the premature deletion problem, it introduced a potential non-termination problem.

Subsequently, Pepels et al. [27] proposed a new algorithm based on Brownbridge-Salkild's algorithm and solved the problem of non-termination by using a marking scheme. In their algorithm, they used two kinds of mark: one to prevent an infinite number of searches, and the other to guarantee termination of each search. Although correct and terminating, Pepels et al.'s algorithm is far more complex than Brownbridge-Salkild's algorithm and in some cyclic structures the cleanup cost complexity becomes at least exponential in the worst-case [15]. This is due to the fact that when cycles occur, whole state space searches from each node in the cyclic graph must be initiated, possibly many times. After Pepels et al.'s algorithm, we are not aware of any other work on reducing the cleanup cost or complexity of the Brownbridge algorithm. Moreover, there is no concurrent collection technique using this approach which can be applicable for the garbage collection in modern multiprocessors.

The algorithm we present in this paper removes all the limitations described above. Our algorithm does not perform searches as such. Instead, whenever a node loses its last strong reference and still has weak references, it marks all affected links as phantom. When this process is complete for a subgraph, the system recovers the affected subgraph by converting phantom links to either strong or weak. Because this process is a transformation from weak or strong to phantom, and from phantom to weak or strong, it has at most two steps and is, therefore, manifestly linear in the number of links, i.e. it has a complexity of only $\mathcal{O}(N)$ time steps, where N is the number of edges in the affected subgraph. Moreover, in contrast to Brownbridge's algorithm, our algorithm is concurrent and is suitable for multiprocessors.

1.2 Other Related Work

Garbage collection is an automatic memory management technique which is considered to be an important tool for developing fast as well as reliable software. Garbage collection has been studied extensively in computer science for more than five decades, e.g., [2, 3, 5, 8, 15, 23, 27, 31]. Reference counting is a widely-used form of garbage collection whereby each object has a count of the number of references to it; garbage is identified by having a reference count of zero [2]. Reference counting approaches were first developed for LISP by Collins [10]. Improved variations were proposed in several subsequent papers, e.g. [12, 14, 15, 19, 22]. We direct readers to Shahriyar et al. [32] for the valuable overview of the current state of reference counting collectors.

It was noticed by McBeth [23] in early sixties that reference counting collectors were unable to handle cyclic structures. After that several reference counting collectors were developed, e.g. [7, 12, 20, 21]. The algorithm in Friedman [12] dealt with recovering cyclic data in immutable structures, whereas Bobrow's algorithm [7] can reclaim all cyclic structures but relies on the explicit information provided by the programmer. Trial deletion approach was studied by Christopher [9] which tries to collect cycles by identifying groups of self-sustaining objects. Lins [20] used a cyclic buffer to reduce repeated scanning of the same nodes in their mark-scan algorithm for cyclic reference counting. Moreover, in [21], Lins improved his algorithm from [20] by eliminating the scan operation through the use of a Jump-stack data structure.

With the advancement of multiprocessor architectures, reference counting garbage collectors have become popular because they do not require all application threads to be stopped before the garbage collection algorithm can run [19]. Recent work in reference counting algorithms, e.g. [2, 3, 5, 19], try to reduce concurrent operations and increase the efficiency of reference counting collectors. Since our collector is a reference counting collector, it can potentially benefit from the same types of optimizations discussed here. We leave that, however, to a future work.

However, as mentioned earlier, reference counting garbage collectors cannot collect cycles [23]. Therefore, concurrent reference counting collectors [2, 3, 5, 19, 22, 26] use other techniques, e.g. they supplement the reference counter with a tracing collector or a cycle detector, together with their concurrent reference counting algorithm. For example, the reference counting collector proposed in [26] combines the sliding view reference counting concurrent collector of [19] with the cycle collector of [2]. Our collector has some similarity with these, in that our *Phantomization* process may traverse many nodes. It should, however, trace fewer nodes and do so less frequently. Recently, Frampton provides a detailed study of cycle collection in his PhD thesis [11].

Herein we have tried to cover a sampling of garbage collectors that are most relevant to our work.

Apple's ARC memory management system makes a distinction between "strong" and "weak" pointers, similar to what we describe here. In the ARC memory system, however, the type of each pointer must be specifically designated by the programmer, and this type will not change during the program's execution. If the programmer gets the type wrong, it is possible for ARC to have strong cycles as well as prematurely deleted objects. With our system, the pointer type is automatic and can change during the execution. Our system protects against these possibilities, at the cost of lower efficiency.

There exist other concurrent techniques optimized for both uniprocessors as well as multiprocessors. Generational concurrent garbage collectors were also studied, e.g. [29]. Huelsbergen and Winterbottom [13] proposed an incremental algorithm for the concurrent garbage collection that is a variant of mark-and-sweep collection scheme first proposed in [24]. Furthermore, garbage collection is also considered for several other systems, namely real-time systems and asynchronous distributed systems, e.g. [28, 33].

Concurrent collectors are gaining popularity. The concurrent collector described in Bacon and Rajan [2] can be considered to be one of the more efficient reference counting concurrent collectors. The algorithm uses two counters per object, one for the actual reference count and other for the cyclic reference count. Apart from the number of the counters used, the cycle detection strategy requires a minimum of two traversals of cycle when the cycle is reachable and eleven cycle traversals when the cycle is garbage.

1.3 Paper Organization

The rest of the paper is organized as follows. We present our strong/weak/phantom pointer based concurrent garbage collector in Section 2 with some examples. In Section 4, we sketch proofs of its correctness and complexity properties. In Section 5, we give some experimental results. We conclude the paper with future research directions in Section 6 and a short discussion in Section 7. Detailed algorithms may be found in the appendix.

2. Algorithm

In this section, we present our concurrent garbage collection algorithm. Each object in the heap contains three reference counts: the first two are the strong and weak, the third is the phantom count. Each object also contains a bit named `which` (Brownbridge [8] called it the "strength-bit") to identify which of the first two counters is used to keep track of strong references, as well as a boolean called `phantomized` to keep track of whether the node is phantomized. Outgoing links (i.e., pointers) to other objects must also contain (1) a `which` bit to identify which reference counter on the target object they increment, and (2) a `phantom` boolean to identify whether they have been phantomized. This data structure for each object can be seen in the example given in Fig. 2.

Local creation of links only allows the creation of strong references when no cycle creation is possible. Consider the creation of a link from a source object S to a target object T. The link will be created strong if (i) the only strong links to S are from roots i.e. there is no object C with a strong link to S; (ii) object T has no outgoing links i.e. it is newly created and its outgoing links are not initialized; and (iii) object T is phantomized, and S is not. All self-references are weak. Any other link is created phantom or weak.

To create a strong link, the `which` bit on the link must match the value of the `which` bit on the target object. A weak link is created by setting the `which` bit on the reference to the complement of the value of the `which` bit on the target.

When the strong reference count on any object reaches zero, the garbage collection process begins. If the object's weak reference count is zero, the object is immediately reclaimed. If the weak count is positive, then a a sequence of three phases is initiated: *Phantomization*, *Recovery*, and *CleanUp*. In *Phantomization*, the object toggles its `which` bit, turning its incoming weak reference counts to strong ones, and phantomizes its outgoing links.

Phantomizing a link transfers a reference count (either strong or weak), to the phantom count on the target object. If this causes the object to lose its last strong reference, then the object may also phantomize, i.e. toggle its `which` bit (if that will cause it to gain strong references), and phantomizes all its outgoing links. This process may spread to a large number of target objects.

All objects touched in the process of a phantomization that were able to recover their strong references by toggling their `which` bit are remembered and put in a "recovery list". When phantomization is finished, *Recovery* begins, starting with all objects in the recovery list.

To perform a recovery, the system looks at each object in the recovery list, checking to see whether it still has a positive strong reference count. If it does, it sets the `phantomized` boolean to false, and rebuilds its outgoing links, turning phantoms to strong or weak according to the rules above. If a phantom link is rebuilt and the target object regains its first strong reference as a result, the target object sets its `phantomized` boolean to false and attempts to recover its outgoing phantom links (if any). The recovery continues to rebuild outgoing links until it terminates.

Finally, after the recovery is complete, *CleanUp* begins. The recovery list is revisited a second time. Any objects that still have no strong references are deleted.

Note that all three of these phases, *Phantomization*, *Recovery*, and *CleanUp* are, by their definitions, linear in the number of links; we prove this formally in Theorem 4.2 in Section 4. Links can undergo only one state change in each of these phases: strong or weak to phantom during *Phantomization*, phantom to strong or weak during *Recovery*, and phantom to deleted in *CleanUp*.

We now present some examples to show how our algorithm performs collection in several real word scenarios.

2.1 Example: A Simple Cycle

In Fig. 2 we see a cyclic graph with three nodes. This figure shows the counters, bits, and boolean values in full detail to make it clear how these values are used within the algorithm. Objects are represented with circles, links have a pentagon with state information at their start and an arrow at their end.

In Step 0, the cycle is supported by a root, a reference from stack or global space. In Step 1, the root reference is removed, decrementing the strong reference by one, and beginning a *Phantomization*. Object C toggles its which pointer and phantomizes its outgoing links. Note that toggling the which pointer causes the link from A to C to become strong, but nothing needs to change on A to make this happen.

In Step 2, object B also toggles its which bit, and phantomizes its outgoing links. Likewise, in Step 3, object A phantomizes, and the *Phantomization* phase completes.

Recovery will attempt to unphantomize objects A, B, and C. None of them, however, have any strong support, and so none of them recover.

Cleanup happens next, and all objects are reclaimed.

2.2 Example: A Doubly-Linked List

The doubly linked list depicted in Fig. 3 is a classic example for garbage collection systems. The structure consists of 6 links, and the collector marks all the links as phantoms in 8 steps.

This figure contains much less detail than Fig. 2, which is necessary for a more complex figure.

2.3 Example: Rebalancing A Doubly-Linked List

Fig. 4 represents a worst case scenario for our algorithm. As a result of losing root $R1$, the strong links are pointing in exactly the wrong direction to provide support across an entire chain of double links. During *Phantomization*, each of the objects in the list must convert its links to phantoms, but nothing is deleted. *Phantomization* is complete in the third figure from the left, and *Recovery* begins. The fourth step in the figure, when link 6 is converted from phantom to weak marks the first phase of the recovery.

2.4 Example: Recovering Without Detecting a Cycle

In Fig. 1 we see the situation where the collector recovers from the loss of a strong link without searching the entire cycle. When root $R1$ is removed, node A becomes phantomized. It turns its incoming link (link 1) to strong, and phantomizes its outgoing link (link 2), but then the phantomization process ends. Recovery is successful, because A has strong support, and it rebuilds its outgoing link as weak. At this point, collection operations are finished.

Unlike the doubly-linked list example above, this case describes an optimal situation for our garbage collection system.

3. Concurrency Issues

This section provides details of the implementation.

3.1 The Single-Threaded Collector

There are several methods by which the collector may be allowed to interact concurrently with a live system. The first, and most straightforward implementation, is to use a single garbage collection thread to manage nontrivial collection operations. This technique has the advantage of limiting the amount of computational power the garbage collector may use to perform its work.

For the collection process to work, phantomization must run to completion before recovery is attempted, and recovery must run to completion before cleanup can occur. To preserve this ordering in a live system, whenever an operation would remove the last

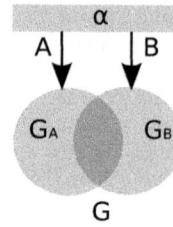

Figure 5. Graph model   **Figure 6.** Subgraph model

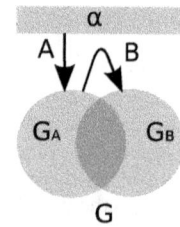

strong link to an object with weak or phantom references, the link is instead transferred to the collector, enabling it to perform phantomization at an appropriate time.

After the strong link is processed, the garbage collector needs to create a phantom link to hold onto the object while it performs its processing, to ensure the collector itself doesn't try to use a deleted object.

Another point of synchronization is the creation of new links. If the source of the link is a phantomized node, the link is created in the phantomized state.

With these relatively straightforward changes, the single-threaded garbage collector may interact freely with a live system.

3.2 The Multi-Threaded Collector

The second, and more difficult method, is to allow the collector to use multiple threads. In this method, independent collector threads can start and run in disjoint areas of memory. In order to prevent conflicts from their interaction, we use a simple technique: whenever a link connecting two collector threads is phantomized, or when a phantom link is created by the live system connecting subgraphs under analysis by different collector threads, the threads merge. A merge is accomplished by one thread transferring its remaining work to the other and exiting. To make this possible, each object needs to carry a reference to the collection threads and ensure that this reference is removed when collection operations are complete. While the addition of a pointer may appear to be a significant increase in memory overhead, it should be noted that the pointer need not point directly to the collector, but to an intermediate object which can carry the phantom counter, as well as other information if desired.

An implementation of this parallelization strategy is given in pseudocode in the appendix.

4. Correctness and Algorithm Complexity

The garbage collection problem can be modeled as a directed graph problem in which the graph has a special set of edges (i.e. links) called *roots* that come from nowhere. These edges determine if a node in the graph is reachable or not. A node X is said to be *reachable* if there is a path from any root to a node X directly or transitively. Thus, the garbage collection problem can be described as removing all nodes in the graph that are not reachable from any *roots*.

Our algorithm uses three phases to perform garbage collection. The three phases are *Phantomize*, *Recover* and *CleanUp*. The *Phantomization* phase is a kind of search that marks (i.e. phantomizes) nodes which have lost strong support. The *Recovery* phase unmarks the nodes, reconnecting the affected subgraph to strong links. If *Recovery* fails to rebuild links, the *CleanUp* phase deletes them. The algorithm progresses through all three phases in the order (1. *Phantomize*, 2. *Recover* and 3. *CleanUp*) and transitions only when there are no more operations left in the current phase. Our algorithm is concurrent because the garbage collection

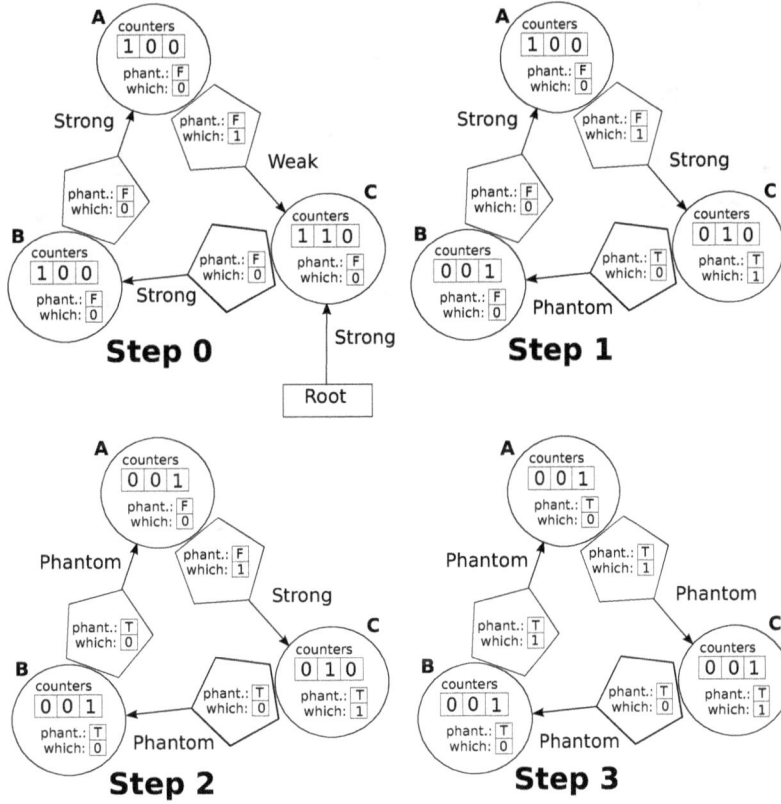

Figure 2. Reclaiming a cycle with three objects

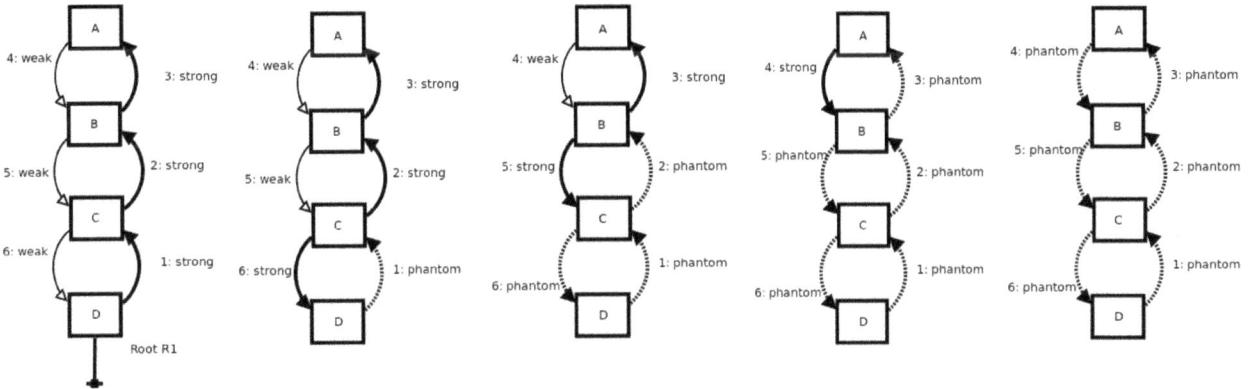

Figure 3. Doubly-linked list

on different subgraphs can proceed independently until, and unless they meet.

If G is the given graph and α is the root set prior to any deletions (see Fig. 5), $\alpha = \{A, B\}$, and $\alpha = \{A\}$ after deletions, then G will become G_A, the nodes reachable from A. Thus, $G = G_A \cup G_B$ initially, and the garbage due to the loss of B will be Γ_B.

$$\Gamma_B = G_B - (G_A \cap G_B).$$

During phantomization, all nodes in Γ_B and some nodes in $G_A \cap G_B$ will be marked. During recovery, the nodes in $G_A \cap G_B$ will all be unmarked. Hence, after the *Recovery* phase, all nodes

in $G_A \cap G_B$ will be strongly connected to A. The final phase *CleanUp* discards the marked memory, Γ_B.

The above discussion holds equally well if instead of being a root, B is the only strong link connecting subgraph G_A to subgraph G_B. See Fig. 6.

THEOREM 4.1 (Cycle Invariant). *No strong cycles are possible, and all cycles formed in the graph should have at least one weak or phantom edge in the cyclic path.*

Proof. (sketch) This invariant should be maintained through out the graph for any cycles for the algorithm. This property ensures the

51

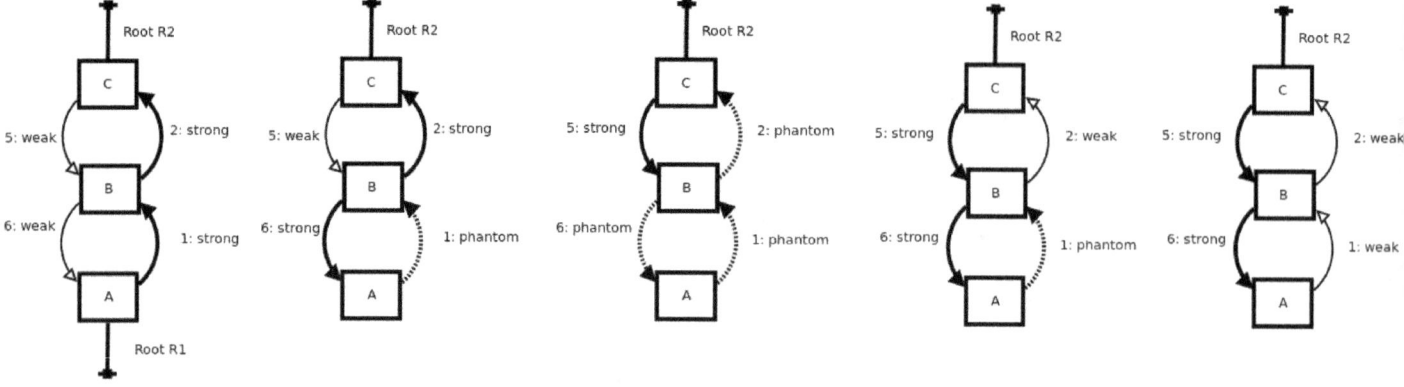

Figure 4. Rebalancing a doubly-linked list

correctness of the algorithm and the definition of the stable graph. In the rules below, the edge being created is E, the source node (if applicable) is called S, the target node is T. The edge creation rules state:

0. Roots always count as strong edges to nodes.

1. Edge E can be strong if S has no incoming strong edges from other nodes, i.e. if there is no node C with a strong edge to S, then E can be created strong. Thus, S is a source of strong edges.

2. A new edge E can be strong if node T has no outgoing non-phantom edges, and $S \neq T$. Thus, T is a terminus of strong edges.

3. A new edge E is strong if T is phantomized and S is not. Thus, T is a terminus of strong edges.

4. A new edge E is weak otherwise.

5. Edge E can only be converted to strong if T is phantomized.

6. A new edge E must be phantom if the node S is phantomized.

Any change described by the above rules regarding strong edges results in one of the nodes becoming a source or terminus of strong edges. Hence, no strong cycles are possible. □

THEOREM 4.2 (Termination). *Any mutations to a stable graph G will take $\mathcal{O}(N)$ time steps to form a new stable graph G', where N is number of edges in the affected subgraph.*

Proof. (sketch) By *stable graph* we mean a graph in which all nodes are strongly connected from the roots and no phantom links or phantomized nodes are present. Mutations which enlarge the graph, e.g. adding a root, or edge are constant time operations since they update the counters and outgoing edge list in a node. Mutations which diminish the graph, e.g. deleting roots, or edges potentially begin a process of *Phantomization*, which may spread to any number of nodes in G.

To prove the algorithm is linear we have to prove that each of the three phases in the algorithm is linear in time. Without loss of generality, consider the graph in Fig. 5 (or, equivalently, Fig. 6). In this graph there are two sets of root links A and B leading into graph G. The graph has three components $G_A, G_B, G_A \cap G_B$. So,

$$G_A \cap G_B \subset G_A$$

and

$$G_A \cap G_B \subset G_B,$$

where π_A and π_B are only reachable by A and B, such that

$$\pi_A = G_A - G_A \cap G_B,$$

$$\pi_B = G_B - G_A \cap G_B.$$

Phantomization starts when a node attempts to convert its weak links to strong, and marks a path along which strong links are lost. *Phantomization* stops when no additional nodes in the affected subgraph lose strong support. In Fig. 5 (or Fig. 6), the marking process will touch at least π_B, and at most, all of G_B. The marking step affects both nodes and edges in G_B and ensures that graph is not traversed twice. Thus, *Phantomization* will take at most $\mathcal{O}(N)$ steps to complete where N is the number of edges in G_B.

Recovery traverses all nodes in G_B identified during *Phantomization*. If the node is marked and has a strong count, it unmarks the node and rebuilds its outgoing edges, making them strong or weak according to the rules above. The nodes reached by outgoing links are, in turn, *Recovered* as well. Since *Recovery* involves the unmarking of nodes, it is attempted for every node and edge identified during phantomization, and can happen only once, and can take at most $\mathcal{O}(N)$ steps to complete.

Once the *Recovery* operations are over, then *CleanUp* traverses the nodes in the recovery list. For each node that is still marked as phantomized, the node's outgoing links are deleted. At the end of this process, all remaining nodes will have zero references and can be deleted. Because this operation is a single traversal of the remaining list, it too is manifestly linear. □

THEOREM 4.3 (Safety). *Every node collected by our algorithm is indeed garbage and no nodes reachable by roots are collected.*

Proof. (sketch) Garbage is defined as a graph not connected to any roots. If the garbage graph contains no cycles, then it must have at least one node with all zero reference counts. However, at the point it reached all zero reference counts, the node would have been collected, leaving a smaller acyclic garbage graph. Because the smaller garbage graph is also acyclic, it must lose yet another node. So acyclic graphs will be collected.

If a garbage graph contains cycles, it cannot contain strong cycles by Theorem 4.1. Thus, there must be a first node in the chain of strong links. However, at the point where a node lost its last strong link, it would have either been collected or phantomized, and so it can not endure. Since there no first link in the chain of strong links can endure, no chain of strong links can endure in a garbage graph. Likewise, any node having only weak incoming links will phantomize. Thus, all nodes in a garbage graph containing cycles must eventually be phantomized.

If such a state is realized, *Recovery* will occur and fail, and *Cleanup* will delete the garbage graph.

Alternatively, we show that an object reachable from the roots will not be collected. Suppose V^C is a node and there is an acyclic chain of nodes $Root \rightarrow ... \rightarrow V^A \rightarrow V^B \rightarrow ... \rightarrow V^C$. Let V^A be a node that is reachable from a root, either directly or by some chain of references. If one of the nodes in the chain, V^B, is connected to V^A and supported only by weak references, then at the moment V^B lost its last strong link it would have phantomized and converted any incoming weak link from V^B to strong. If V^B was connected by a phantom link from V^A, then V^B is on the recovery list and will be rebuilt in *Recovery*. This logic can be repeated for nodes from V^B onwards, and so V^C will eventually be reconnected by strong links, and will not be deleted. □

THEOREM 4.4 (Liveness). *For a graph of finite size, our algorithm eventually collects all unreachable nodes.*

Proof. (sketch) We say that a garbage collection algorithm is *live* if it eventually collects *all* unreachable objects, i.e. all unreachable objects are collected and never left in the memory.

The only stable state for the graph in our garbage collection is one in which all nodes are connected by strong links, because any time the last strong link is lost a chain of events is initiated which either recovers the links or deletes the garbage. Deletion of a last strong link can result in immediate collection or *Phantomization*. Once *Phantomization* begins, it will proceed to completion and be followed *Recovery* and *Cleanup*. These operations will either delete garbage, or rebuild the strong links. See Theorem 4.3. □

Note that the live system may create objects faster than the *Phantomization* phase can process. In this case, the *Phantomization* phase will not terminate. However, in Theorem 4.4 when we say the graph be "of finite size" we also count nodes that are unreachable but as yet uncollected, which enables us to bound the number of nodes that are being added while the *Phantomization* is in progress. On a practical level, it is possible for garbage to be created too rapidly to process and the application could terminate with an out-of-memory error.

5. Experimental Results

To verify our work, we modeled the graph problem described by our garbage collector in Java using fine-grained locks. Our implementation simulates the mutator and collector behavior that would occur in a production environment. Our mutator threads create, modify, and delete edges and nodes, and the collector threads react as necessary. This prototype shows how a real system should behave, and how it scales up with threads.

We also developed various test cases to verify the correctness of the garbage collector implementation. Our test cases involve a large cycle in which the root node is constantly moved to the next node in the chain (a "spinning wheel"), a doubly linked list with a root node that is constantly shifting, a clique structure, and various tests involving a sequence of hexagonal cycles connected in a chain.

In Fig. 7 we collected a large number of hexagonal rings in parallel. This operation should complete in time inversely proportional to the number of threads in use, as each ring is collected independently. The expected behavior is observed.

In Fig. 8 we performed the same test, but to a set of connected rings. The collection threads merge, but not immediately, so the collection time goes down with the number of threads used, but not proportionally because the collection threads only operate in parallel part of the time.

In Fig. 9, we perform tests to see whether our garbage collector is linear. We considered a clique, two different hexagonal cycles (one is interlinked and other separate), a doubly-linked list, and simple cycles, and measured the collection time per object by varying the size of the graph and fixing the collector threads to two all times. The results confirmed that our collector in indeed linear in time.

Our tests are performed on two 2.6 GHz 8-Core Sandy Bridge Xeon Processors (i.e. on 16 cores) running Redhat Linux 6 64-bit operating system.

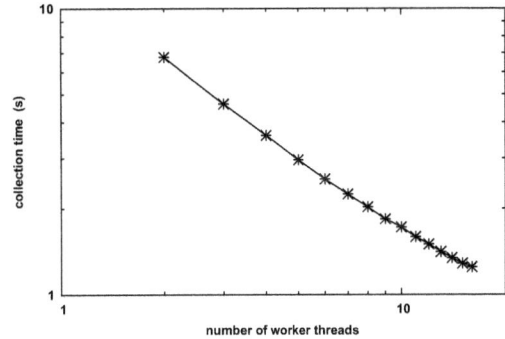

Figure 7. A large number of independent rings are collected by various number of worker threads. Collection speed drops linearly with the number of cores used.

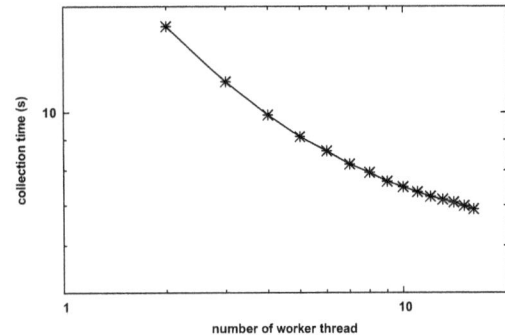

Figure 8. A chain of linked cycles is created in memory. The connections are severed, then the roots are removed. Multiple collector threads are created and operations partially overlap.

6. Future Work

There are numerous avenues to explore within this modified Brownbridge framework.

First there are the details of the concurrent operation. While we have explored the use of merging collector threads upon phantomization, we have not made use of parallelism within a single collection thread's operations. Doing so may or may not be desirable, depending on the requirements for liveness and the compute needs of the application.

Our implementation uses fine-grained locking, but an approach using atomic variables or atomic transactions should be possible.

Because the situations that lead to nontrivial work are algorithmic, it should be possible for compilers to optimize instructions to create or remove links to avoid work. Likewise, it should be possible to build profiling tools that identify garbage collection hot spots within a program, and give the programmer the option to take steps

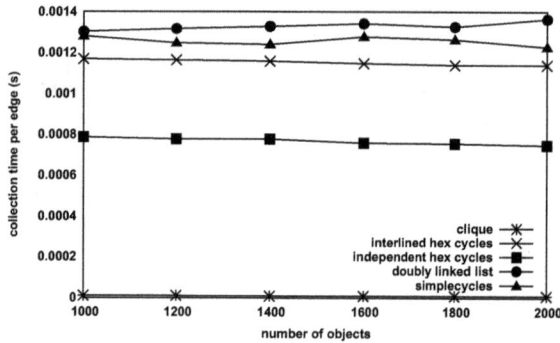

Figure 9. Graphs of different types are created at various sizes in memory, including cliques, chains of cycles, large cycles, and large doubly linked lists. Regardless of the type of object, collection time per object remains constant, verifying the linearity of the underlying collection mechanism.

(e.g. re-arrange link structure) to minimize the garbage collector's work.

We also intend to build a high performance distributed version in C++, for use in High Performance Computing (HPC) systems. HPC is entering a new phase in which more complex simulations are being carried out, covering multiple orders of time and space resolution, and merging the time evolution of multiple kinds of calculations within a single calculation. Parallelization of such systems is nontrivial, and increasingly researchers are moving to dynamic parallelism managed by task queues and active messages. Numerous frameworks exist, or are being constructed for this purpose (Charm++ [17], HPX [16], Swarm/ETI [18], UNITAH [6], The Global Arrays Toolkit [25], etc.)

Until this point, these systems have either required programmers to manage memory themselves, or use a form of simple reference counting. None of the systems above offer an option for global garbage collection capable of reclaiming cycles. Because garbage collection tends to be a complex, global operation which traces links throughout memory, it has not been considered viable in high performance computing to date. However, if the trend toward increasingly complex multi-scale multi-physics simulations continues, it may only be a time before garbage collection becomes a requirement.

7. Conclusion

We have described a garbage collector based on strong and weak reference counts, proven its validity, and illustrated its potential advantages over existing systems, including:

1. It can run at the same time as a live system, using multiple threads if that is desired, without needing to "stop the world."

2. It has a reduced need to operate on memory compared to collectors because it only performs nontrivial work when the last strong link is removed;

3. It has a reduced need to trace links in performing its operations, specifically:

   (a) When objects do not need to be collected, it is often able to prove this without completely tracing cycles to which they belong which have support;

   (b) It remembers stable paths through memory and thus avoids doing work on old objects, a benefit similar to that derived from generational collectors, e.g. [29]; deletions are occurring;

   (c) When objects do need to be collected, the collector only needs to trace the cycle twice;

   (d) The collector operation is local;

   (e) The collector does not need or use back-pointers;

These advantages should make our collector useful for distributed systems, where traces that cross node boundaries are likely to be extremely expensive.

Disadvantages include:

1. An increased memory overhead: three counters and a pointer are required for each object;

2. An additional cost of pointer creation/mutation;

3. The lack of a fault tolerance protocol;

4. Little effort has, as yet, been devoted to optimization of any implementation. Further reduction of memory and computational overheads may yet be achieved with variations on this algorithm.

While there are undoubtedly cases for which the increased overheads are unacceptable, there are just as undoubtedly cases where the potential performance gains make it acceptable.

For distributed applications, a fault tolerance protocol may be of high importance, depending especially on the reliability of the application components. We expect, however, that variants of this protocol and synchronization strategies associated with it may be discovered to assist with these problems.

In short, we feel that collectors based on a system of strong and weak references like the one we have described here have many potential advantages over existing systems and should provide a fertile ground for future research and language development.

Acknowledgments

We acknowledge the support of the following grants: The DoE XPRESS proposal (DE-SC0008714), and the NSF PXGL (1160602). We thank Frank Löffler and Hartmut Kaiser for helpful conversations.

References

[1] URL https://github.com/stevenrbrandt/MultiThreadBrownbridge.

[2] D. F. Bacon and V. T. Rajan. Concurrent cycle collection in reference counted systems. In *ECOOP*, pages 207–235, 2001.

[3] D. F. Bacon, C. R. Attanasio, H. B. Lee, V. T. Rajan, and S. Smith. Java without the coffee breaks: a nonintrusive multiprocessor garbage collector. *SIGPLAN Not.*, 36(5):92–103, 2001.

[4] D. F. Bacon, P. Cheng, and V. T. Rajan. A real-time garbage collector with low overhead and consistent utilization. *SIGPLAN Not.*, 38(1):285–298, 2003.

[5] K. Barabash, O. Ben-Yitzhak, I. Goft, E. K. Kolodner, V. Leikehman, Y. Ossia, A. Owshanko, and E. Petrank. A parallel, incremental, mostly concurrent garbage collector for servers. *ACM Trans. Program. Lang. Syst.*, 27(6):1097–1146, 2005.

[6] M. Berzins, J. Luitjens, Q. Meng, T. Harman, C. A. Wight, and J. R. Peterson. Uintah: a scalable framework for hazard analysis. In *TG*, pages 3.1–3.8, 2010.

[7] D. G. Bobrow. Managing reentrant structures using reference counts. *ACM Trans. Program. Lang. Syst.*, 2(3):269–273, 1980.

[8] D. Brownbridge. Cyclic reference counting for combinator machines. In J.-P. Jouannaud, editor, *Functional Programming Languages and Computer Architecture*, volume 201 of *Lecture Notes in Computer Science*, pages 273–288. 1985.

[9] T. W. Christopher. Reference count garbage collection. *Software: Practice and Experience*, 14(6):503–507, 1984.

[10] G. E. Collins. A method for overlapping and erasure of lists. *Commun. ACM*, 3(12):655–657, 1960.

[11] D. Frampton. *Garbage Collection and the Case for High-level Low-level Programming*. PhD thesis, Australian National University, June 2010.

[12] D. P. Friedman and D. S. Wise. Reference counting can manage the circular environments of mutual recursion. *Inf. Process. Lett.*, 8(1): 41–45, 1979.

[13] L. Huelsbergen and P. Winterbottom. Very concurrent mark-&-sweep garbage collection without fine-grain synchronization. *SIGPLAN Not.*, 34(3):166–175, 1998.

[14] R. Hughes. Managing reduction graphs with reference counts. Departmental Research Report CSC/87/R2, March 1987.

[15] R. Jones and R. Lins. *Garbage collection: algorithms for automatic dynamic memory management*. John Wiley & Sons, Inc., New York, NY, USA, 1996. ISBN 0-471-94148-4.

[16] H. Kaiser, M. Brodowicz, and T. Sterling. Parallex an advanced parallel execution model for scaling-impaired applications. In *ICPPW*, pages 394–401, 2009.

[17] L. V. Kale and S. Krishnan. *CHARM++: a portable concurrent object oriented system based on C++*, volume 28. 1993.

[18] C. Lauderdale and R. Khan. Towards a codelet-based runtime for exascale computing: position paper. In *EXADAPT*, pages 21–26, 2012.

[19] Y. Levanoni and E. Petrank. An on-the-fly reference-counting garbage collector for java. *ACM Trans. Program. Lang. Syst.*, 28(1):1–69, 2006.

[20] R. D. Lins. Cyclic reference counting with lazy mark-scan. *Inf. Process. Lett.*, 44(4):215–220, 1992.

[21] R. D. Lins. An efficient algorithm for cyclic reference counting. *Inf. Process. Lett.*, 83(3):145–150, 2002.

[22] R. D. Lins. Cyclic reference counting. *Inf. Process. Lett.*, 109(1):71–78, 2008.

[23] J. H. McBeth. Letters to the editor: on the reference counter method. *Commun. ACM*, 6(9):575, 1963.

[24] J. McCarthy. Recursive functions of symbolic expressions and their computation by machine, part i. *Commun. ACM*, 3(4):184–195, 1960.

[25] J. Nieplocha, R. J. Harrison, and R. J. Littlefield. Global arrays: A portable shared-memory programming model for distributed memory computers. In *SC*, pages 340–349, 1994.

[26] H. Paz, D. F. Bacon, E. K. Kolodner, E. Petrank, and V. T. Rajan. An efficient on-the-fly cycle collection. *ACM Trans. Program. Lang. Syst.*, 29(4), 2007.

[27] E. Pepels, M. Plasmeijer, C. van Eekelen, and M. Eekelen. *A Cyclic Reference Counting Algorithm and Its Proof*. Internal report 88-10. Department of Informatics, Faculty of Science, University of Nijmegen, 1988.

[28] F. Pizlo, E. Petrank, and B. Steensgaard. A study of concurrent real-time garbage collectors. *SIGPLAN Not.*, 43(6):33–44, 2008.

[29] T. Printezis and D. Detlefs. A generational mostly-concurrent garbage collector. *SIGPLAN Not.*, 36(1):143–154, 2000.

[30] P. Roy, S. Seshadri, A. Silberschatz, S. Sudarshan, and S. Ashwin. Garbage collection in object-oriented databases using transactional cyclic reference counting. *The VLDB Journal*, 7(3):179–193, 1998.

[31] J. Salkild. Implementation and analysis of two reference counting algorithms. Master thesis, University College, London, 1987.

[32] R. Shahriyar, S. M. Blackburn, and D. Frampton. Down for the count? getting reference counting back in the ring. In *ISMM*, pages 73–84, 2012.

[33] L. Veiga and P. Ferreira. Asynchronous complete distributed garbage collection. In *IPDPS*, pages 24.1–24.10, 2005.

A. Appendix

A.1 Multi-Threaded Collector

Note that in the following sections, locks are always obtained in canonical order that avoids deadlocks. Unlock methods unlock the last set of items that were locked.

The lists on the collectors are thread-safe.

The collector object is itself managed by a simple reference count. Code for incrementing and decrementing this count is not explicitly present in the code below.

A reference implementation is also provided [1].

Algorithm 1: LinkSet

```
   // LinkSet creates a new link, and decides the type
      of the link to create.
 1 LinkSet(link,node):
 2    lock (link.Source,node)
 3    if node == NULL then
 4       LinkFree(link)
 5       link.Target = NULL
 6    EndIf
 7    if link.Target == node then
 8       Return
 9    EndIf
10    oldLink = copy(link)
11    link.Target = node
12    If link.Source.Phantomized then
13       MergeCollectors(link.Source, link.Target)
14       link.PhantomCount++
15       link.Phantomized = True
16    ElseIf link.Source == node then
17       link.Which = 1 - node.Which
18       node.Count[link.Which]++
19    ElseIf node.Links not initialized then
20       node.Count[link.Which]++
21       link.Which = node.Which
22    Else
23       link.which = 1 - node.Which
24       node.Count[link.Which]++
25    EndIf
26    If oldLink != NULL
27       LinkFree(oldLink)
28    unlock()
```

Algorithm 2: LinkFree

```
    // Freeing a link is usually just the decrement of a
       reference count, but if it is the last strong
       count, this could potentially start a
       Phantomization process.
 1  LinkFree(link):
 2    lock(link.Source,link.Target)
 3    If link.Target == NULL then
 4      Return
 5    EndIf
 6    If link.Phantomized then
 7      DecPhantom(link.Target)
 8    Else
 9      link.Target.Count[link.Which]--
10      If link.Target.Count[link.Which] == 0 And
11         link.Target.Which == link.Which then
12        If link.Target.Count[1-link.Target.Which] == 0 And
13           link.Target.PhantomCount == 0 then
14          Delete(node)
15          link.Target = NULL
16        Else
17          If link.Target.Collector == NULL then
18            link.Target.Collector = new Collector()
19          EndIf
20          AddToCollector(link.Target)
21        EndIf
22      EndIf
23    EndIf
24    unlock()
```

Algorithm 3: AddToCollector

```
    // Adding an object to the collector puts back the
       strong count, effectively transferring the source
       of the strong link to the collector. It also adds
       a phantom count, which helps prevent the clearing
       of the Collector field.
 1  AddToCollector(node):
 2    While True
 3      lock(node,node.Collector)
 4      If node.Collector.Forward != NULL then
 5        node.Collector = node.Collector.Forward
 6      Else
 7        node.Count[node.Which]++
 8        node.PhantomCount++
 9        node.Collector.CollectionList.append(node)
10        Break
11      EndIf
12      unlock()
13    EndWhile
```

Algorithm 4: PhantomizeNode

```
    // The collector takes away the strong link it made
       in AddToCollector().
 1  PhantomizeNode(node,collector):
 2    lock(node)
 3    While collector.Forward != NULL
 4      collector = collector.Forward
 5    EndWhile
 6    node.Collector = collector
 7    node.Count[node.Which]--
 8    // Prevent deletion while the
 9    // node is managed by the Collector
10    Let phantomize = False
11    If node.Count[node.Which] > 0 then
12      Return
13    Else
14      If node.Count[1-node.Which] > 0 then
15        node.Which = 1-node.Which
16      EndIf
17      If Not node.Phantomized then
18        node.Phantomized = True
19        node.PhantomizationComplete = False
20        phantomize = True
21      EndIf
22    EndIf
23    Let links = NULL
24    If phantomize then
25      links = copy(node.Links)
26    EndIf
27    unlock()
28    ForEach outgoing link in links
29      PhantomizeLink(link)
30    EndFor
31    lock(node)
32    node.PhantomizationComplete = True
33    unlock()
```

Algorithm 5: Collector.Main

```
   // This method describes the work to be carried out
      by a garbage collection thread. Live objects
      pointing to this collector, or Forward pointers
      from other collectors contribute to the RefCount
      field on the Collector.
1  Collector.Main():
2     While True
3        WaitFor(Collector.RefCount == 0 Or Work to do)
4        If Collector.RefCount == 0 And No work to do then
5           Break
6        EndIf
7        While Collector.MergedList.size() > 0
8           Let node = Collector.MergedList.pop()
9           Collector.RecoveryList.append(node)
10       EndWhile
11       While Collector.CollectionList.size() > 0
12          Let node = Collector.CollectionList.pop()
13          PhantomizeNode(node,Collector)
14          Collector.RecoveryList.append(node)
15       EndWhile
16       While Collector.RecoveryList.size() > 0
17          Let node = Collector.RecoveryList.pop()
18          RecoverNode(node)
19          Collector.CleanList.append(node)
20       EndWhile
21       While Collector.RebuildList.size() > 0
22          Let node = Collector.RebuildList.pop()
23          RecoverNode(node)
24       EndWhile
25       While Collector.CleanList.size() > 0
26          Let node = Collector.CleanList.pop()
27          CleanNode(node)
28       EndWhile
29    EndWhile
```

Algorithm 6: PhantomizeLink

```
1  PhantomizeLink(link):
2     lock(link.Source,link.Target)
3     If link.Target == NULL then
4        unlock()
5        Return
6     EndIf
7     If link.Phantomized then
8        unlock()
9        Return
10    EndIf
11    link.Target.PhantomCount++
12    link.Phantomized = True
13    linkFree(link)
14    MergeCollectors(link.Source, link.Target)
15    unlock()
```

Algorithm 7: DecPhantom

```
   // DecPhantom is responsible for removing any
      reference to the collector.
1  DecPhantom(node):
2     lock(node)
3     node.PhantomCount- -
4     If node.PhantomCount == 0 then
5        If node.Count[node.Which]== 0 And
6           node.Count[1-node.Which] == 0 then
7           Delete(node)
8        Else
9           node.Collector = NULL
10       EndIf
11    EndIf
12    unlock()
```

Algorithm 8: RecoverNode

```
1  RecoverNode(node):
2     lock(node)
3     Let links = NULL
4     If node.Count[node.Which] > 0 then
5        WaitFor(node.PhantomizationComplete == True)
6        node.Phantomized = False
7        links = copy(node.Links)
8     EndIf
9     unlock()
10    ForEach link in links
11       Rebuild(link)
12    EndFor
```

Algorithm 9: Rebuild

```
1  Rebuild(link):
2     lock(link.Source,link.Target)
3     If link.Phantomized then
4        If link.Target == link.Source then
5           link.Which = 1- link.Target.Which
6        ElseIf link.Target.Phantomized then
7           link.Which = link.Target.Which
8        ElseIf count(link.Target.Links) == 0 then
9           link.Which = link.Target.Which
10       Else
11          link.Which = 1-link.Target.Which
12       EndIf
13       link.Target.Count[link.Which]++
14       link.Target.PhantomCount- -
15       If link.Target.PhantomCount == 0 then
16          link.Target.Collector = NULL
17       EndIf
18       link.Phantomized = False
19       Add link.Target to Collector.RecoveryList
20    EndIf
21    unlock()
```

Algorithm 10: CleanNode

// After deleting all the outgoing links, decrement
the phantom count by one (i.e. the reference held
by the collector itself). When the last phantom
count is gone, the object is cleaned up.

```
1  CleanNode(node):
2      lock(node)
3      Let die = False
4      If node.Count[node.Which]== 0 And
5          node.Count[1-node.Which]== 0 then
6          die = True
7      EndIf
8      unlock()
9      If die then
10         ForEach link in node
11             LinkFree(link)
12         EndFor
13     EndIf
14     DecPhantom(node)
```

Algorithm 11: Delete

```
1  Delete(node):
2      ForEach link in node
3          LinkFree(link)
4      EndFor
5      freeMem(node)
```

Algorithm 12: MergeCollectors

// When two collector threads realize they are
managing a common subset of objects, one defers
to the other. The arguments, source and target,
are both nodes.

```
1  MergeCollectors(source,target):
2      Let s = source.Collector
3      Let t = target.Collector
4      Let done = False
5      If s == NULL And t != NULL then
6          lock(source)
7          source.Collector = t
8          unlock()
9          Return
10     EndIf
11     If s != NULL And t == NULL then
12         lock(target)
13         target.Collector = s
14         unlock()
15         Return
16     EndIf
17     If s == NULL Or s == NULL then
18         Return
19     EndIf
20     While Not done
21         lock(s,t,target,source)
22         If s.Forward == t and t.Forward == NULL then
23             target.Collector = s
24             source.Collector = s
25             done = True
26         ElseIf t.Forward == s and s.Forward == NULL then
27             target.Collector = t
28             source.Collector = t
29             done = True
30         ElseIf t.Forward != NULL then
31             t = t.Forward
32         ElseIf s.Forward != NULL then
33             s = s.Forward
34         Else
35             Transfer s.CollectionList to t.CollectionList
36             Transfer s.MergedList to t.MergedList
37             Transfer s.RecoveryList to t.MergedList
38             Transfer s.RebuildList to t.RebuildList
39             Transfer s.CleanList to t.MergedList
40             target.Collector = t
41             source.Collector = t
42             done = True
43         EndIf
44         unlock()
45     EndWhile
```

Reference Object Processing in On-The-Fly Garbage Collection

Tomoharu Ugawa

Kochi University of Technology

ugawa.tomoharu@kochi-tech.ac.jp

Richard E. Jones   Carl G. Ritson

University of Kent

R.E.Jones@kent.ac.uk   C.G.Ritson@kent.ac.uk

Abstract

Most proposals for on-the-fly garbage collection ignore the question of Java's weak and other reference types. However, we show that reference types are heavily used in DaCapo benchmarks. Of the few collectors that do address this issue, most block mutators, either globally or individually, while processing reference types. We introduce a new framework for processing reference types on-the-fly in Jikes RVM. Our framework supports both insertion and deletion write barriers. We have model checked our algorithm and incorporated it in our new implementation of the Sapphire on-the-fly collector. Using a deletion barrier, we process references *while mutators are running* in less than three times the time that previous approaches take *while mutators are halted*; our overall execution times are no worse, and often better.

Categories and Subject Descriptors   D.3.4 [*Programing Languages*]: Processors—Memory management (garbage collection)

General Terms   Algorithms, Languages

Keywords   Garbage Collection; Real-time processing; Java; Weak Pointers; Jikes RVM

1. Introduction

The last decade has seen significant changes to the environments in which software is deployed. Developers have turned to managed languages and runtimes for easier deployment and increased security and multi-core processors are ubiquitous. Many applications are sensitive to response time: any pauses may be undesirable or unacceptable. Interactive applications need to respond crisply. Enterprise applications with highly concurrent workloads cannot afford to pause transactions, because delays may lead to either a backlog of re-tried transactions or direct financial loss. Embedded systems may have hard real-time requirements: all operations must complete with a fixed time. Stopping all *mutators* (user threads) in order to reclaim memory (*stop-the-world* or STW) garbage collection (GC) is likely to lead to unacceptable pauses. Even though STW techniques such as generational GC can reduce average pause times, they do not solve the problem of worst-case pause times when the entire heap must be collected.

Incremental GC, which interleaves mutator and collector actions, or *concurrent* GC, which allows mutator and collector

ISMM'14, June 12, 2014, Edinburgh, United Kingdom.
Copyright is held by the owner/author(s). Publication rights licensed to ACM.
ACM 978-1-4503-2921-7/14/06...$15.00.
http://dx.doi.org/10.1145/2602988.2602991

threads to run concurrently, address this problem. However, these strategies require careful synchronisation between mutators and collectors for safety (i.e. not reclaiming live objects). Thus, mutators emit *read* or *write barriers* as they access object fields in order to provide the collector with a coherent view of live objects in the heap. Correct termination of a GC cycle is also tricky: the simplest and most widely adopted strategy is to stop all mutator threads briefly to scan their stacks. *On-the-fly* (OTF) collectors, on the other hand, attempt never to stop more than one thread at a time (although even they may have to fall back to STW termination in the face of pathological mutator behaviour).

Problem solved? Unfortunately not. Java provides *reference type* objects — soft, weak and phantom — which can be used for a variety of purposes such as constructing caches, whose contents the collector can reclaim when the system is under memory pressure, or creating canonicalised mappings. Although barriers allow the collector gradually to build up a coherent (if conservative) view of the live objects in the heap, the Java specification requires reference type objects to be dealt with *atomically* by the collector. The simplest solution would be to stop the world while the collector processes reference type objects in the termination phase, but this is unacceptable for a truly on-the-fly collector. Another solution might be to block only those mutators that try to access reference type objects during the GC termination phase; we consider this equally unacceptable.

In this paper, we explore the issues faced by OTF reference type processing, and provide algorithms which we have model-checked and added to our new implementation of the Sapphire OTF copying collector. We find that reference type objects are (possibly surprisingly) heavily used in the DaCapo suite of Java benchmarks [5], although there is substantial variation between programs. Processing reference type objects while mutator threads are halted adds significantly to the time required to terminate a GC cycle. We then show how to process Java's reference type objects in a fully OTF collector. In summary, our contributions are:

- A study of the usage of reference type objects in DaCapo.
- A formalisation of reference type processing in Java.
- A novel algorithm for OTF processing of reference type objects.
- Verification of our algorithm using the SPIN model checker.
- Implementation of the algorithm for the Sapphire OTF copying collector [12] in the Jikes RVM virtual machine.
- Experimental evaluation of both blocking and OTF reference processing methods.

2. Reference Objects

`java.lang.ref` provides *reference object* classes, which support some interaction with the GC. Reference objects may be, in decreasing order of strength, *soft*, *weak* or *phantom*. Soft references are typically used to build caches that the GC can reclaim when

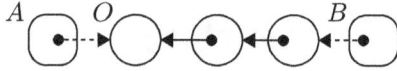

Figure 1: Soft references to be cleared; A and B are soft reference objects. They are assumed to be strongly reachable.

it comes under memory pressure, weak references to implement canonicalised mappings that do not prevent the GC from reclaiming their keys or values, and phantom references for scheduling cleanup actions more flexibly than is possible with finalisation.

The usual Java *strong reference* is created with the `new` operator. Other references are created with the `SoftReference`, `WeakReference` and `PhantomReference` constructors. For instance, the fragment below creates a strong reference o to an `Object` (which we call O) and a weak reference wo to the same object. Internally, a reference class has a field `referent` that holds a (strong) reference to the reference object's target, i.e. `wo.referent=o`:

```
Object o = new Object(); // call this object O
WeakReference wo = new WeakReference(o);
Object maybeNull = wo.get();
...
o = null;
maybeNull = wo.get();
```

O will be preserved by the GC as long as it is reachable by some thread by following a chain of strong references. If O is reachable, `wo.get()` will return a strong reference to O. However, at the second call to `wo.get()`, O may or may not have been reclaimed by the GC, depending on what the elided code marked ... does. Thus, `wo.get()` may return either a reference to O or `null`.

2.1 Reachability and referent clearing

The different levels of reachability are defined operationally in the `java.lang.ref` package [17].

- An object is *strongly reachable* if it can be reached by some thread without traversing any reference objects. A newly-created object is strongly reachable by its creator thread.

- An object is *softly reachable* if it is not strongly reachable but can be reached by traversing a soft reference.

- An object is *weakly reachable* if it is neither strongly nor softly reachable but can be reached by traversing a weak reference. When the weak references to a weakly-reachable object are cleared, the object becomes eligible for finalization.

- An object is *phantom reachable* if it is neither strongly, softly nor weakly reachable, it has been finalized, and some phantom reference refers to it.

- Otherwise an object is unreachable.

The GC will reclaim any weakly reachable object, and may decide at its discretion to reclaim any softly reachable object. In either case, it must clear the referent field of the reference type.

2.2 The challenge for OTF collection

In a concurrent GC, there may be a race between the collector clearing the reference and a mutator strengthening the reachability of its target by calling `get()`. For this reason, the semantics of reference classes require that, at the time that the GC decides to reclaim a softly reachable object (O in Fig. 1, for example), it must also clear *atomically*

1. *all* soft references to that object (reference from A in Fig. 1), and

2. *all* soft references to other softly-reachable objects from which that object is reachable through a chain of strong references (reference from B in Fig. 1).

At the same time as it clears references or at some later time, the GC may enqueue the reference onto a `ReferenceQueue`; the intention of this mechanism is to notify the program of changes in reachability. Similar semantics apply to weak references / chains of strong and soft references. In contrast, the `get` method of a phantom reference always returns `null`.

Thus, the challenge for OTF processing of soft (resp. weak) references is how to clear not only all soft (weak) references to a softly (weakly) reachable object but also all other soft (weak) soft references to any other softly (weakly)-reachable objects from which that object is reachable through a chain of strong (strong or soft) references in a way that appears atomic to all mutator threads.

3. Related Work

There is a considerable body of work on low pause-time garbage collection, much of it related to real-time systems [1–4, 6–8, 10, 12, 13, 15, 16, 19–24]. Most papers do not address the question of processing reference types.

Azul Systems' Pauseless GC [6] takes the most straightforward approach to avoiding races between mutator and collector threads on reference types: at the end of its marking phase, it stops all mutator threads and does "(in parallel but not concurrent) soft ref processing, weak ref processing, and finalization." Click et al. suggest that they could process references concurrently by having the GC and mutators race to set a value for referent field with a CAS operation if the referent is "not-marked-through". They suggest that if the mutator succeeds the target's reachability is strengthened and the collector knows it, whereas if the GC succeeds the mutator will see the `null`. However, this seems insufficient for correct behaviour as the GC may win one race but lose another, thereby failing to clear atomically all soft references to an object and all soft references to any other softly-reachable objects from which that object is reachable. Reference types are not discussed for other Azul collectors [13, 24]. The Staccato parallel and concurrent real-time compacting collector for multiprocessors [16] also stops the world to process soft, weak and phantom references.

A less intrusive option is to block only those mutators that attempt to call `get()` on reference types. Domani et al. extended the Doliguez-Leroy-Gonthier collector [7] for Java by adding support for finalisation and reference types [8]. They add a read barrier to `get()` that records the referent when called during the marking trace and before weak references have been processed. After the GC has completed its mark phase, it acquires a mutual exclusion lock to prevent any mutator turning a weakly reachable object into a strongly reachable one. Note that having acquired the lock, the GC must check again that marking is complete (since a mutator may have called `get()`) before it clears all reference types with unmarked referents.

The original version of the Metronome real-time collector was incremental, designed for use on a uniprocessor [4]; it did not handle reference types. IBM's first production JVM based on Metronome [1] dealt properly with reference types but was also incremental rather than concurrent.[1] Metronome-TS ("Tax and Spend") [2] is incremental, concurrent and parallel. However, although we believe that it may handle reference types properly in an OTF manner,[2] the paper is reticent on details, stating only: "the

---

[1] David Grove, personal communication.

[2] David Bacon, personal communication.

full Java language has constructs, such as finalization, weak and soft references, and string interning, which interact in complex ways with memory management. These constructs add phases to the collection cycle: for example, reference clearing can only be considered once marking is over and it is known which objects are reachable."

4. Formal Definition

The semantics of Java's reference types are not described in the Java Language Specification 1.7 [17], which instead refers (section 12.6.2) to the documentation for the package `java.lang.ref`; this package includes the classes `Reference`, `SoftReference`, `Weak-Reference`, `PhantomReference` and `ReferenceQueue`. Unsurprisingly, the English language descriptions of different levels of reachability given in `java.lang.ref` are unclear and ambiguous.

4.1 Reachability

In this section, we formalise definitions of reachability and, in the next, the actions required when the collector clears reference types. First, let R be a relation on the sets of objects in the heap, `Objects`, and slots in the roots, `Roots`, to objects in the heap,

$$R \subseteq \mathbb{P}((\texttt{Objects} \cup \texttt{Roots}) \times \texttt{Objects})$$

Let $TC(x, R)$ be the transitive closure of a relation R from an object or a slot in the roots, x,

$$TC(x, R) = \{o \in \texttt{Objects} | x R^* o\}$$

and expand TC pointwise:

$$TC(X, R) = \{o \in \texttt{Objects} | \exists x \in X . x R^* o\}$$

We can now define the sets of objects that are strongly, softly, weakly and phantom reachable, given the strong, soft, weak and phantom reference relations $StrR$, $SoftR$, $WeakR$ and $PhantR$. The definition of the set of strongly reachable objects, $StrongReachable$, is straightforward. Objects in this set must be preserved by the GC.

$$StrongReachable = TC(\texttt{Roots}, StrR)$$

However, we believe the `java.lang.ref` definition of 'softly reachable' is misleading: "An object is softly reachable if it is not strongly reachable but can be reached by traversing a soft reference." It does not specify how many soft references we can traverse and when but, worse, it does not require that there be no weak or phantom references in the chain. Without clarifying the kinds of reference that chains may *not* contain, the definitions in the API are inconsistent. We believe the correct specification is,

$$
\begin{aligned}
SoftReachable &= TC(\texttt{Roots}, StrR \cup SoftR) \\
&- StrongReachable
\end{aligned}
$$

The API definition of 'weakly reachable' is similarly unsatisfactory. Instead, we define

$$
\begin{aligned}
WeakReachable &= TC(\texttt{Roots}, StrR \cup SoftR \cup WeakR) \\
&- StrongReachable - SoftReachable
\end{aligned}
$$

Finally, we define the set of phantom reachable objects. To be phantom reachable, an object must have been finalised, so we assume a set of objects that have been finalised, $Finalised$.

$$
\begin{aligned}
PhantomReachable &= \\
(TC(\texttt{Roots}, StrR \cup SoftR \cup WeakR \cup PhantR) &\cap Finalised) \\
- StrongReachable - SoftReachable &- WeakReachable
\end{aligned}
$$

4.2 Clearing references

The GC clears all references to a weakly reachable object, and can elect to clear references to a softly reachable object. If it decides to do so, it must clear atomically *all* soft (resp. weak) references to the object and *all* soft (weak) references to any other softly (weakly) reachable objects from which that object is reachable through a chain of strong (soft and strong) references. At the same time it will declare all of the formerly weakly-reachable objects to be finalizable and, at that time or later, enqueue those newly-cleared references that are registered with reference queues.

Thus, if the GC decides to clear a soft reference to a softly reachable object o, it must also clear all soft references to the set

$$softToClear(o) = \{w \in SoftReachable | w \, StrR^* \, o\}$$

In Fig. 1, $softToClear(O)$ is the set of all the normal objects.

The API encourages the GC to preserve some set P of recently created or used soft references. To accommodate this, we modify the definition of $StrongReachable$ used to calculate $SoftReachable$ in order to retain objects in P:

$$StrongReachable' = TC(\texttt{Roots} \cup P, StrR)$$

Thus, $SoftReachable'$ represents the set of softly-reachable objects that are referents of soft references we have to clear atomically.

In the case of weak references, the GC must clear all weak references to the set

$$
\begin{aligned}
weakToClear(o) = \{w \in WeakReachable | \\
w \, (StrR \cup SoftR)^* \, o\}
\end{aligned}
$$

`PhantomReference.get()` always returns `null` so there is no need to clear phantom references.

5. On-the-fly Reference Processing

In this section, we describe our design and implementation of OTF processing of reference types. Java provides three types of reference objects, and the GC must take care to process these in the correct order, but we do not discuss that here. The focus of our work is how to have an OTF GC deal with reference type objects — determining reachability, clearing referents atomically — without blocking the mutators. For simplicity of exposition, we concentrate on how we treat weak references, but our implementation deals properly with all types of reference object.

5.1 Concurrent GC

Concurrent GC algorithms require mutator and GC threads to share a consistent view of the heap. This is typically achieved through *read* or, more commonly, *write barriers*, which impose a small overhead on mutator operations [25]. The synchronisation between mutator and GC is best described through the well-known tricolour abstraction [18]. In this abstraction, every object is assigned one of three colours. *White* objects are unknown to the GC; *grey* objects are known the GC but need to be visited again (e.g. to trace their children); and *black* objects are known to the GC but need not be visited again. Tracing live objects is complete as soon as the heap contains no grey objects: at this point, all strongly reachable objects have been marked black and, furthermore, *if we were to ignore reference types*, any white object can be reclaimed by the GC.

Write barriers can be used to ensure consistency between mutators and collectors by colouring objects. *Insertion* (or 'incremental update') barriers[3] shade grey a white target Dijkstra-style (or the source, Steele-style) of a reference write, thus preserving the strong tricolour invariant:

"There are no pointers from black objects to white objects."

---

[3] We use the terminology of [14].

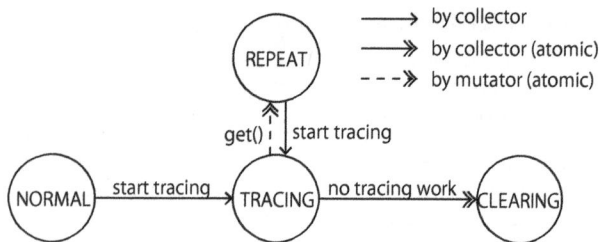

Figure 2: Global reference state transitions.

Deletion (or 'snapshot-at-the-beginning') barriers shade grey the old white target of a deleted reference, preserving the weak tri-colour invariant:

> "All white objects pointed to by a black object are reachable from some grey object, either directly or through a chain of white objects."

Colours can be extended to mutators. The roots of a *grey mutator* may refer to objects of any colour. Thus, the GC must rescan its roots in order to terminate tracing. In an OTF setting, the GC may have to stop a grey mutator repeatedly to scan its roots until is has succeeded in scanning all mutator threads without having discovered a new grey object. In contrast, once the roots of a *black mutator* have been scanned by the collector, they do not need to be scanned again. Insertion barriers preserve the strong invariant for grey mutators but cannot support black mutators [18]. Instead, a black mutator must use a deletion barrier.

5.2 Reference types and termination

The approaches described above are sufficient to ensure safe termination of a GC cycle in the absence of reference types. At the conclusion of the trace, they guarantee that no mutator can reach an unmarked, i.e. white, object through any path of strong references. This is an essential requirement for the safe reclamation of white objects. Note that the GC has traced only strong references at this point; it does not trace the referents of other reference types. However, reference types introduce a wrinkle: a mutator can acquire a strong reference to a weakly reachable object by calling get() on a weak reference that has yet to be cleared. There are several known solutions to this problem in a concurrent collector, all of which block mutators to one degree or another.

The simplest [1] is to stop the world while the collector traces again in order to identify the *weakToClear(o)* set defined in Sec. 4.1; weakly reachable white objects other than this set and its transitive closure under the strong reference relation are marked black. A global flag is then set to indicate that the references have been cleared logically, and the mutators are resumed. Once the flag is set and while the GC is concurrently and physically clearing selected weak references, WeakReference.get() returns null if the referent is white. Domani et al. [8] relax the requirement to stop the world by having the GC acquire a lock that blocks until the end of the reference processing phase any mutator that calls get() while the GC is processing reference types.

However, in a fully OTF collector, we do not want to stop any mutator, other than briefly to scan its roots. We describe our solutions for (a) insertion barriers and (b) deletion barriers next.

5.3 Insertion barrier solution

Our insertion barrier solution is a natural extension to the GC's incremental update termination loop: we repeatedly scan roots and trace until our work queue is empty. We add to the GC a global flag that can take one of four states: NORMAL, TRACING, CLEANING and

```
collection() {
  insertionBarrier ← ON;
  transitiveClosureFromRoot();
  while(true) {
    refState ← TRACING;
    handshake();
    transitiveClosureNoRootScan();
    scanRoot();
    if(workQueue.empty() &&
       CAS(refState, TRACING, CLEANING))
      break;
  }
  insertionBarrier ← OFF;
  clearReference();
  refState ← NORMAL;
  handshake();
  reclaim();
}
```

Figure 3: Insertion barrier: collector

```
get() {
  while(true) {
    switch(refState) {
    case NORMAL: case REPEAT:
      return referent;
    case TRACING:
      if (referent=null || COLOR(referent)≠WHITE)
        return referent;
      CAS(refState, TRACING, REPEAT);
      break; /* retry */
    case CLEANING:
      if (referent=null || COLOR(referent)≠WHITE)
        return referent;
      return null;
    }
  }
}
```

Figure 4: Insertion barrier: WeakReference.get()

REPEAT. The state transition diagram for this flag is shown in Fig. 2, and pseudocode for the collector and for the WeakReference.get method is shown in Figs. 3 and 4.

The system is in the NORMAL state when GC is not running. To start a new GC cycle, the collector turns on the insertion barrier[4] and traces strong references in the usual way before starting the insertion barrier termination loop. The task of the termination loop is to establish a consistent view, shared between mutators and collectors, of the reachability of objects while the mutators are running and possibly calling get().

The loop starts by setting the tracing state to TRACING and handshaking with mutators to ensure that they have all observed this transition. The collector then traces from the work queue of grey objects (transitiveClosureNoRootScan) and scans the roots again. If the work queue is empty, the GC attempts to set the tracing state to CLEANING using an atomic compare and swap operation (CAS). If this succeeds, tracing has terminated and the

---

[4] We do not discuss here the subtleties on initiating a GC cycle for an OTF collector; see [14] for details.

```
collection() {
  insertionBarrier ← ON;
  transitiveClosureFromRoot();
  deletionBarrier ← ON;
  handshake();
  scanRoot();
  insertionBarrier ← OFF;
  while(true)
    refState ← TRACING;
    handshake();
    transitiveClosureNoRootScan();
    if(workQueue.empty() &&
        CAS(refState, TRACING, CLEANING))
      break;
  }
  deletionBarrier ← OFF;
  clearReferences();
  refState ← NORMAL;
  handshake();
  reclaim();
}
```

Figure 5: Deletion barrier: collector

```
get() {
  while(true) {
    switch(refState) {
    case NORMAL:
      return referent;
    case REPEAT:
      if (referent=null || COLOR(referent)≠WHITE)
        return referent;
      COLOR(referent) ← GREY;
      return referent;
    case TRACING:
      if (referent=null || COLOR(referent)≠WHITE)
        return referent;
      if (CAS(refState, TRACING, REPEAT)) {
        COLOR(referent) ← GREY;
        return referent;
      }
      break; /* retry */
    case CLEANING:
      if (referent=null || COLOR(referent)≠WHITE)
        return referent;
      return null;
    }
  }
}
```

Figure 6: Deletion barrier: WeakReference.get()

collector can proceed to clearing weak objects' referents. At this point, we know precisely which objects to preserve and which weak reference objects' get methods should return null.

However, while the GC is TRACING, a mutator may call get() on a weak reference object whose referent is white. In this case, the mutator needs to force the collector to iterate its termination loop again. We do so by adding a read barrier to get that atomically sets the GC's state to REPEAT; to avoid a race condition, the mutator must also retry get's loop. While the GC is not TRACING or has to REPEAT, or if the referent is not white, get() simply returns the referent. The read barrier does not need to shade the target of the referent as we can defer this to the next root scan. However, once the GC has transitioned to the CLEANING state, get() must return null for any non-white, i.e. black, referent. In this way, it appears to the mutator that all weak reference objects selected for clearing are cleared atomically. Once the weak references have been cleared, the GC resets its state to NORMAL, handshakes with the mutators and then reclaims any garbage.

5.4 Deletion barrier solution

Measurements of reference processing with an insertion barrier (Sec. 7) showed that the GC sometimes takes a long time to complete due to the frequent use of WeakReference.get(). Perhaps this is not surprising since insertion barrier mutators are grey and so may need to be scanned several times to terminate, even in the absence of reference types. In contrast, a black mutator supported by a deletion barrier needs its stack to be scanned only once.

Our deletion barrier variant for reference object processing is shown in Fig. 5 and 6. We run the Sapphire OTF collector with its insertion barrier on as usual during the initial marking phase. However, before we start to process reference types, we switch on a deletion barrier, handshake with the mutators to ensure that they notice, and scan the roots. Note that an OTF collector requires both insertion and deletion barriers to be on while thread stacks are scanned to blacken the mutators [7]. Once the roots have been scanned, we can turn the insertion barrier off.

As with the insertion barrier, our deletion barrier scheme also requires a termination loop but does not need to rescan mutator roots. Instead, the get read barrier must shade the referent in both

the REPEAT and the TRACING states as we cannot rely on a future root scan to discover it.

5.5 Soft and Phantom references

Phantom reference objects are straightforward to process in an OTF manner since there is no interaction between collector and mutator: PantomReference.get() always returns null. However, the API encourages the GC to retain recently allocated or used soft reference objects. We treat these by marking them and their strong transitive closures black. We treat any other soft reference objects in the same way as weak reference objects.

6. Model Checking

We verified our framework for OTF reference processing using the SPIN model checker [11]. SPIN exhaustively checks all possible interleavings of processes. Since we deal with soft references as if they are strong or weak references depending on memory pressure, we focused on weak references. We verified the following properties:

P1 (Safety) A mutator will never see a reclaimed object.

P2 (Consistency) Once a get() method called on a reference object returns null, a mutator will never see the referent of that object.

These properties are from the mutator's view because there can be a variety of implementations of 'clearing'. In our implementation, logically cleared references appeared cleared to mutator. Property **P1** is required regardless of the existence of reference objects. But **P1** also requires that, if a mutator loads a referent of a reference object, the referent has not been reclaimed. Property **P2** implies the atomicity that the API definition requires. Assume that a weak reference to an object o is cleared in spite of retaining another weak reference to an object $w \in weakToClear(o)$. Since the weak reference is cleared, a mutator may see that get() returns null. But,

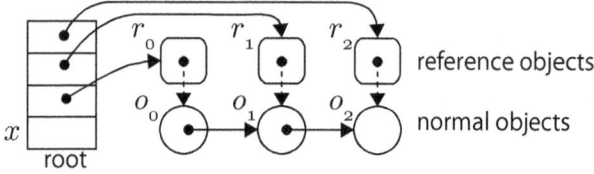

Figure 7: The model

```
while(true) {
  int i = random.nextInt(5);
  switch (i) {
    case 0: x = vr_0.get(); break;
    case 1: x = vr_1.get(); break;
    case 2: x = vr_2.get(); break;
    case 3: if (x != null) x = x.next; break;
    case 4: x = null; break;
  }
}
```

Figure 8: Simple mutator

since o is weakly-reachable through w, the mutator may also see o, contrary to **P2**.□

Since bounded model checking does not deal with infinite state, we checked the properties for the limited model shown in Fig. 7. This model has three pairs of reference and normal objects, namely r_0, r_1, r_2 for references and o_0, o_1, o_2 for the corresponding normal objects. These normal objects are linked in a list, but there are no other strong references to them. We assumed that all reference objects remain directly strongly reachable from the root and that the mutator can always call get() methods on them.

Fig. 8 shows the mutator's pseudocode: vr_i is a local variable whose value is a reference object r_i, and x is another local variable. The mutator repeatedly and arbitrarily calls a get() method to load the referent to x, loads the 'next' object of x, or clears x. Since we focus on the behaviour of references, the mutator does not write to any object. Thus, our model does not have write barriers.

Fig. 9 shows the model of the get() method on the reference object r_i, for a collector using an insertion barrier. This model is faithful to Fig. 4. The return value is passed to the caller through the parameter ret. mark[i] and CLEARED[i] represent the colour of o_i and whether r_i has been cleared or not, respectively. When get() returns o_i, it sets i to ret. In order to check **P2**, the model also puts i and ret in global variables getRef_arg and getRef_ret.

For the collector side, our model is faithful to the pseudocode in Fig. 3 and 5. At the end of a cycle, the collector reclaims white objects by calling reclaim(): we introduce a fourth object state RECLAIMED. Our model of reclaim() reclaims white objects and reverts the black objects to white. **P1** and **P2** can be interpreted as:

P1 $\quad \square((x \neq \text{NULL}) \implies (\text{mark}[x] \neq \text{RECLAIMED}))$

P2 $\quad \square(\text{RETNULL}_i \implies \neg\Diamond(x = i)) \ (i = 1, 2, 3)$

where $\text{RETNULL}_i \equiv (\text{getRef\_arg} = i) \wedge (\text{getRef\_ret} = \text{NULL})$.

We have model checked these properties with models both for collectors with an insertion barrier and a deletion barrier. We also tried to model check the termination property.

P3 (Termination) GC eventually terminates.

```
inline getRef(i, ret) {
  do::(refState == NORMAL ||
       refState == REPEAT) ->
      if::CLEARED[i] -> ret = NULL
        ::else        -> ret = i
      fi;
      break
    ::(refState == TRACING) ->
      if::(!CLEARED[i] && (mark[i] == WHITE)) ->
          CAS(refState, TRACING, REPEAT)
          /* continue */
        ::(!CLEARED[i] && (mark[i] != WHITE)) ->
          ret = i;
          break
        ::else ->
          ret = NULL;
          break
      fi
    ::(refState == CLEANING) ->
      if::(!CLEARED[i] && (mark[i] == WHITE)) ->
          ret = NULL
        ::(!CLEARED[i] && (mark[i] != WHITE)) ->
          ret = i
        ::else -> ret = NULL
      fi;
      break
  od;
  d_step { /* d_step is an atomic action */
    getRef_arg = i;
    getRef_ret = ret
  };
}
```

Figure 9: Promela model of a `Reference.get()` method with an insertion barrier

However, we found that, with an insertion barrier, the mutator can continually prevent the collector from breaking out of the termination loop, even if we assume weakly fair scheduling. The reason for this is that, while the collector is tracing or checking if the work queue is empty, a mutator has a chance to load a white referent to a local variable x and then clear x. The mutator changes $refState$ to REPEAT when it loads a reference with get(), thus forcing the collector to trace again. However, if the mutator has cleared x, the collector will not find, and hence shade, a new white referent: the number of white objects is not reduced and so no progress is made. Fortunately, the deletion barrier version *does* make progress, since get() shades white objects grey.

7. Evaluation

We built our OTF reference processing framework in Jikes RVM and evaluated it with our new implementation of the Sapphire collector [12], running DaCapo benchmarks that would run (10 from the 2006 and 6 from the 2009 suite). All measurements were performed on a 4-core, 3.4 GHz Intel Core i7-4770 CPU running Ubuntu Linux 12.04.4.

7.1 Reference Type Usage

To understand the behaviour of the benchmarks, we measured how often reference types were used. Fig. 10 shows the number of calls of a get() method per second in each 10 ms time window; the x-axis is the normalised elapsed time of the program.

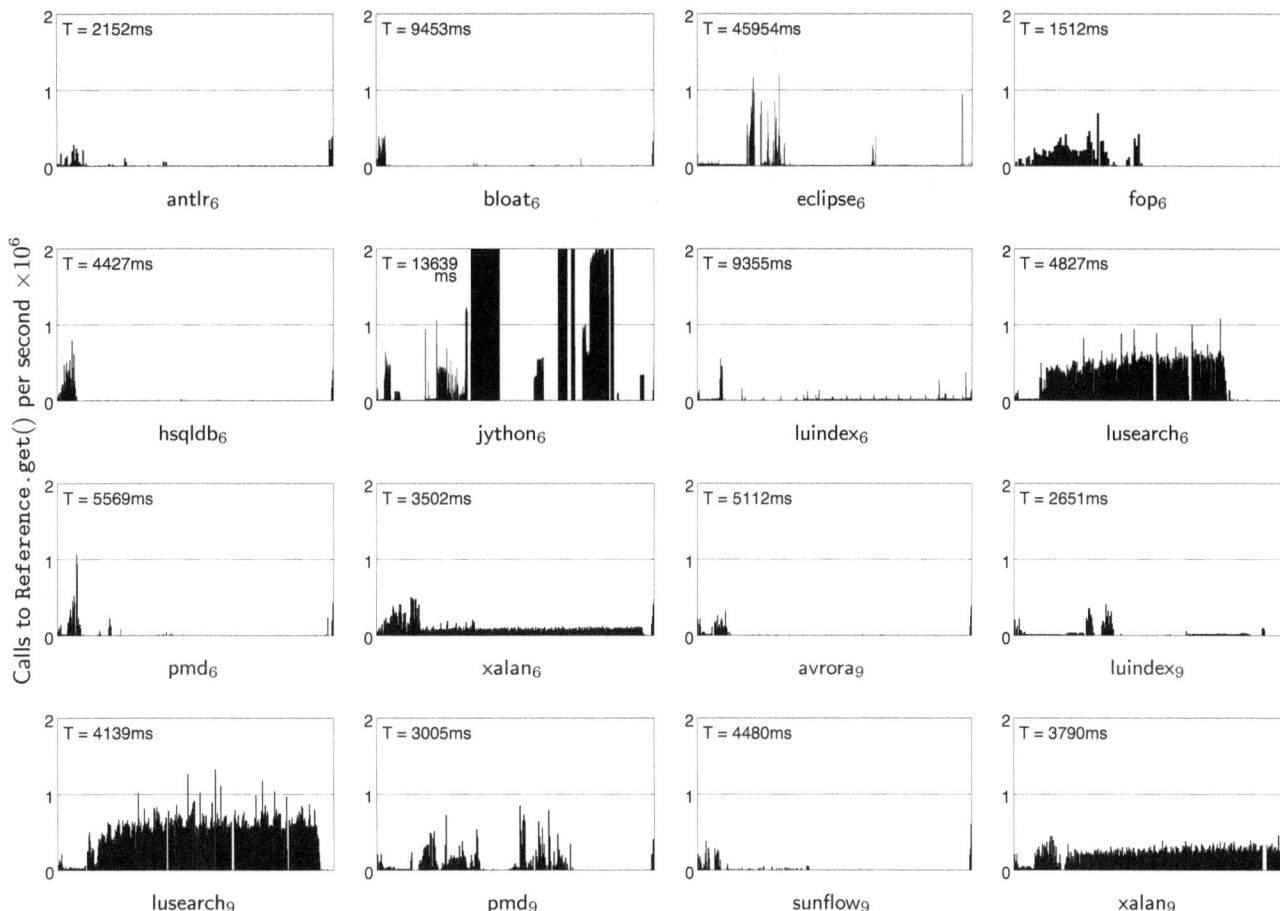

Figure 10: Frequency of calls to get() in DaCapo (10 ms quanta); the x-axis is the normalised entire execution time, T.

Contrary to our expectations, some programs used reference types heavily (more than 1 million times per second), but this varies between programs. Most showed a small peak at the beginning of execution; we found that these were due to the Jikes RVM class loader. Often programs made little further use of reference types but jython_6 made heavy use of them in particular phases. In contrast, lusearch_6, lusearch_9, xalan_6 and xalan_9 made substantial use of reference types for much of their execution. We conclude that

LESSON 1. *An OTF GC must not ignore reference types.*

7.2 Reference Processing Time: blocking schemes

Some implementations block mutator threads during reference type processing. To measure how long a mutator thread would be blocked if reference types were not handled OTF, we implemented two additional variants of reference type processing.

STW The collector stops all mutators during reference processing (tracing to determine reachability and clearing references).

lock The collector acquires a lock to block any mutator that calls get() during reference processing. For this variant, we experimented with both insertion and deletion barriers.

To stress the reference type processing mechanisms, we configured Sapphire to perform back-to-back collection cycles, initiating the next as soon as the previous one had completed, using two collector threads. To avoid having any GC cycle fall back from OTF to

stop-the-world collection because a mutator is starved of memory, we ran each benchmark in a 1 GB heap. We do not pretend that this is a suitable configuration for normal use. Despite this, we observed starvation in an execution of lusearch_6 and lusearch_9 due to their high allocation rate. We ignored any pauses not due to reference processing.

Fig. 11 shows frequency distribution histograms of reference processing pauses, using 3 ms bins, in jython_6 and DaCapo 2009 benchmarks (luindex_9, whose result was similar to avrora_9, is omitted to save space), using 'compiler replay' (methods pre-compiled based on an off-line profile [9], measurements started on benchmark rather than VM startup); each benchmark was executed three times (there was little variation between executions). Note that the **STW** histogram shows the distribution of times taken *to complete the entire reference processing phase*, whereas the **lock** histograms show the distribution of times *for which a mutator was blocked* because it called get() in a reference processing phase.

Unsurprisingly, stop-the-world reference processing consistently stopped mutators for only a limited time. Most pauses were less than 6 ms (maximum 9 ms). In contrast, the locking approach sometimes stopped mutators for up to 12 ms in lusearch_9 and xalan_9, regardless of the barrier used. We also measured reference processing time without compiler replay and taking VM startup into account. Broadly, the distributions were similar, although pauses taking VM startup into account were longer, up to 24 ms in xalan_9 (Fig. 12).

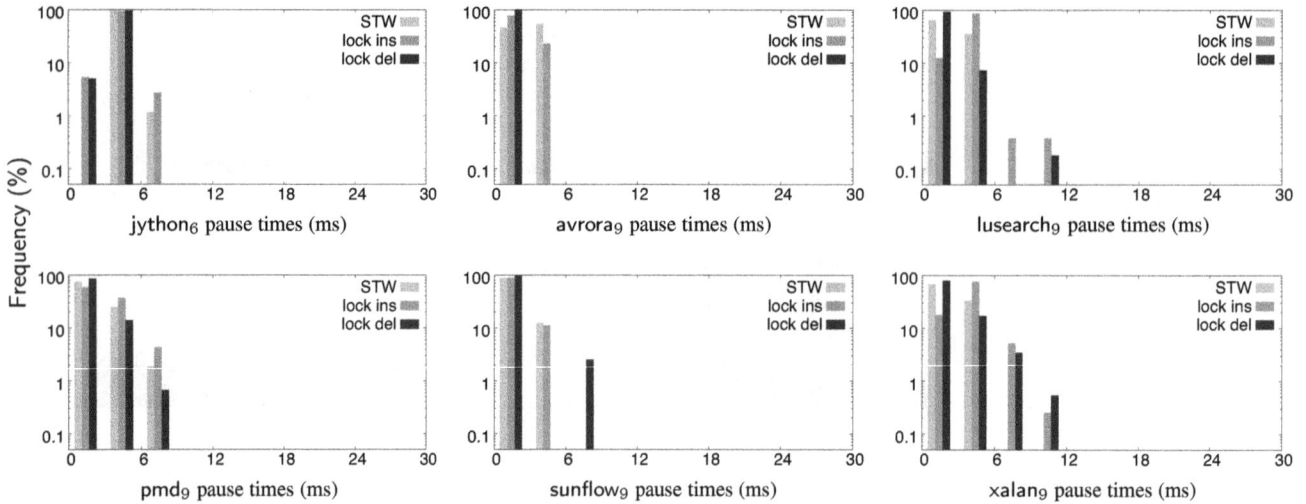

Figure 11: Frequency of pause times (3 ms bins) in jython$_6$ and DaCapo 2009 (compiler replay, measurement starts with benchmark). Note that the y-axis is logarithmic.

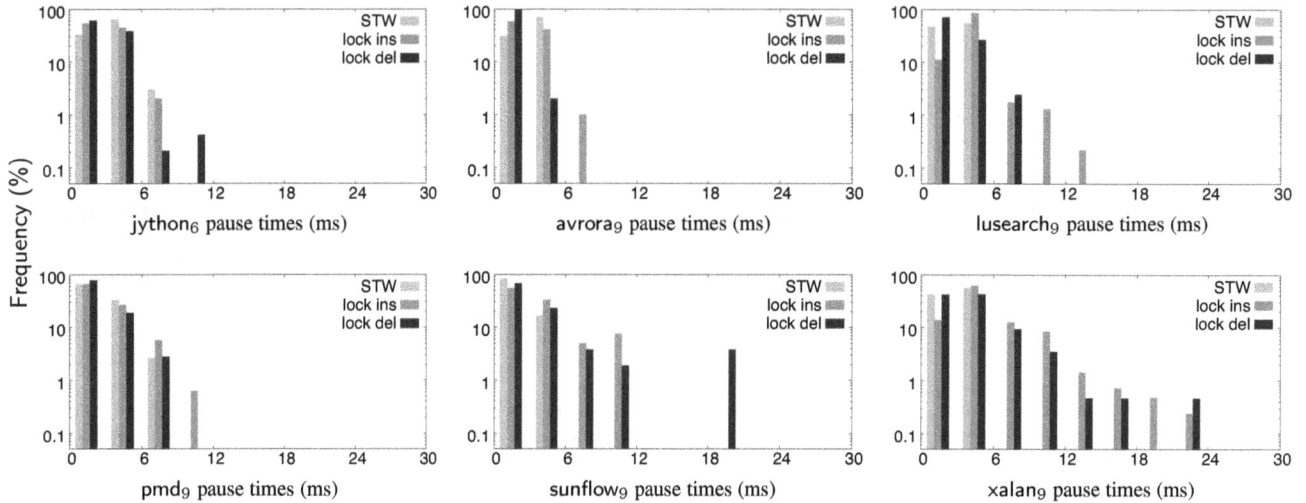

Figure 12: Frequency of pause times (3 ms bins) in jython$_6$ and DaCapo 2009 (without compiler replay, measurement starts with VM). Note that the y-axis is logarithmic.

By processing references in stop-the-world manner, the collector can use all resources available, and so reference processing completes promptly. In contrast, if we allow mutators to run as long as they do not use references, the collector may run more slowly. Handshakes with the mutators will also delay the collectors. Furthermore, write barriers may potentially force collectors to trace again though we did not observe this. All of this extends reference processing time. Thus, the locking approach may block mutators for longer than the stop-the-world approach. In contrast, our OTF reference processing framework does not pause mutators other than to scan an individual mutator's roots.

7.3 OTF Reference Processing Time

Mutator calls to `get()` may force an OTF collector to trace again several times, potentially endlessly (Sec. 6). However, in practice reference processing terminates in a short time. Tab. 1 shows how many times the GC was forced to re-trace, for our different variants of reference processing, using compiler replay. In our measurements, we never observed more than one iteration for the **STW** and **lock** approaches, although this is theoretically possible.

With **OTF**, we observed multiple re-tracings, particularly and unsurprisingly using an insertion barrier. Most benchmarks need to re-trace more than 10 times and lusearch$_9$, which has many mutator threads that allocate at a high rate, needed 62 iterations. One reason for this behaviour is that insertion barrier collectors scan all the mutators even though there may be only few objects to be traced. Scanning mutators takes long time, which increases the chance of mutators forcing the collectors to trace again. In contrast, processing with deletion barriers tended to converge in at most 3 iterations.

Fig. 13 shows the distribution of times for OTF reference processing phases (using compiler replay); the times for **STW** are

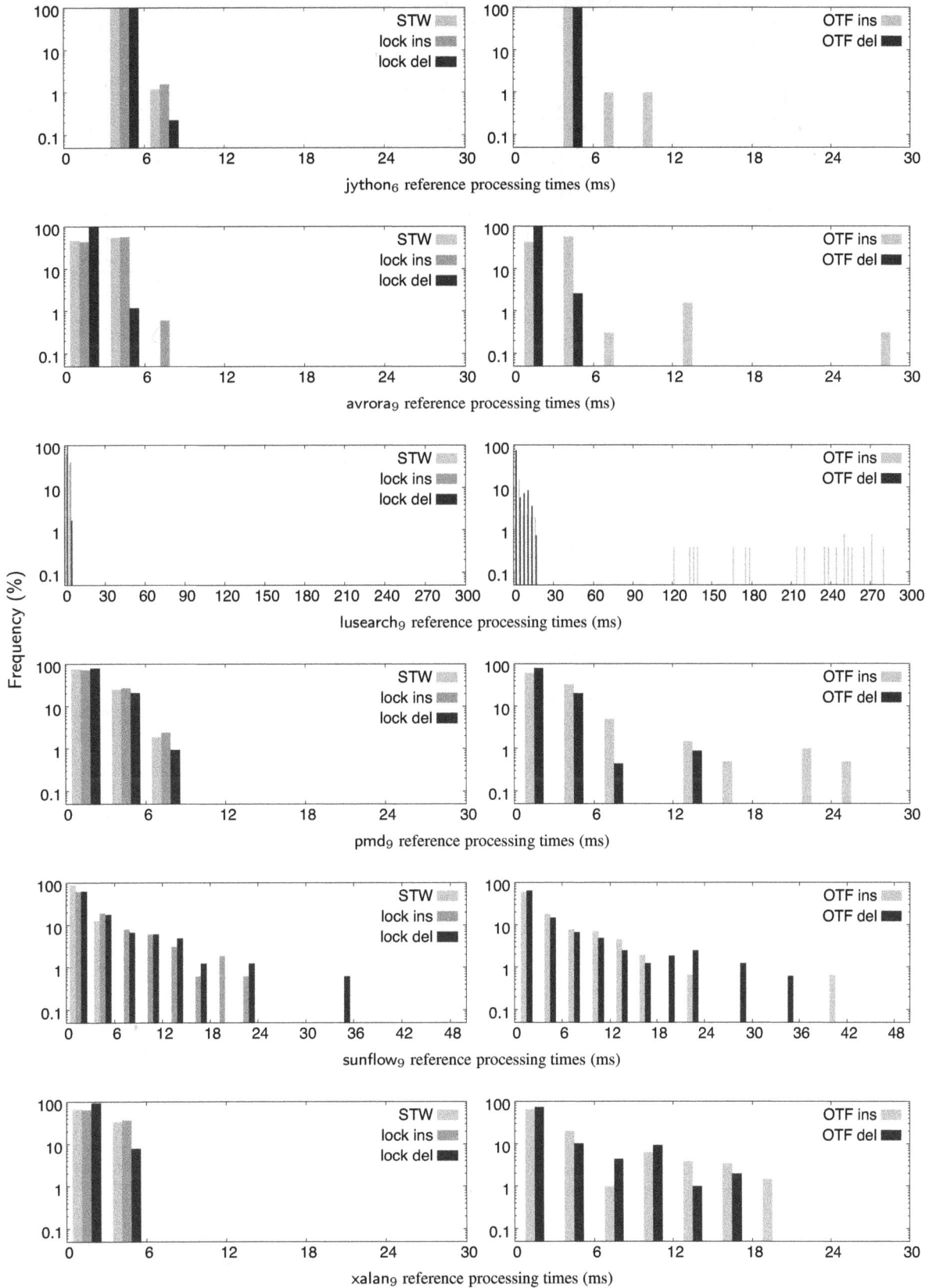

Figure 13: Reference processing time (3 ms bins) in jython$_6$ and DaCapo 2009 (compiler replay, measurement starts with benchmark)

Table 1: Maximum iteration counts (it.) for termination, benchmark execution times (mean t ms. and standard deviation σ over 10 runs, best in bold), number of threads that could be runnable without the reference lock (act) and number of threads blocked by the lock (blk) using compiler replay (measurement starts with benchmark).

	STW			lock ins					lock del					OTF ins			OTF del		
	it	t	σ	it	t	σ	act	blk	it	t	σ	act	blk	it	t	σ	it	t	σ
jython$_6$	1	7775	70	1	7334	50	1.98	0.37	1	9881	63	1.98	0.34	2	7159	71	1	**7047**	66
avrora$_9$	1	5642	199	1	5253	81	3.74	0.23	1	**5238**	56	3.79	0.19	12	5311	54	2	5314	45
luindex$_9$	1	2404	50	1	2343	58	2.00	0.60	1	2372	155	2.00	0.53	13	**2209**	47	1	2270	37
lusearch$_9$	1	4933	46	1	4869	32	3.42	2.06	1	4891	49	3.41	2.00	62	5328	71	2	**4658**	103
pmd$_9$	1	4417	69	1	**4216**	146	3.35	0.91	1	4333	50	3.34	0.79	13	4281	66	3	4581	63
sunflow$_9$	1	5270	246	1	4968	354	5.31	0.26	1	4793	39	5.26	0.22	3	4889	341	1	**4782**	85
xalan$_9$	1	5164	48	1	5039	42	3.29	1.88	1	4850	37	3.19	1.71	2	4877	50	1	**4746**	59

those of Fig. 11. The processing times reflect the number of time the GC has to re-trace; reference processing with insertion barriers shows long tails especially for lusearch$_9$. In contrast, reference processing with deletion barriers finished in under 20 ms except for a small fraction of collections in sunflow$_9$; total reference processing time was always within three times that of the **lock** approach.

LESSON 2. *OTF reference processing phases are longer in the worst case, but with deletion barriers, not by much.*

Even with insertion barriers, they are likely to be acceptable. With OTF processing, mutators continue to run, provided they do not exhaust memory (admittedly this risk is increased with a longer reference processing time), in sharp contrast to the other approaches. Tab. 1 shows the overall execution time in milliseconds (arithmetic mean and standard deviation) of each benchmark. We note that in five out of seven cases OTF reference processing led to the shortest execution times, though often the difference was small. The locking approach blocks only those mutators that call `get()` during the reference processing phase. For this approach, Tab. 1 also shows the average number of active (runnable) threads including those blocked on the reference lock ('act'), and the average number of threads blocked on this lock ('blk'). Of course, all the benchmarks have more threads than 'act' but some of these are blocked for other reasons. Because we have four cores (eight hardware threads) and two GC threads, we note that if $act - blk < 2(6)$ then some cores (hardware threads) would be idle.

LESSON 3. *Overall execution time is not increased significantly by processing references OTF, and is often reduced.*

However, Sapphire executes other GC phases OTF, trading pause time for increased overall execution time. The differences due to the way reference types are processed are small in comparison.

8. Conclusion

Reference types are frequently used in a significant number of programs. Our novel reference processing framework for fully OTF collectors works most efficiently with deletion barriers, but also supports with insertion barriers. We process reference types OTF while mutators are running in less than three times the time that previous approaches take while mutators are blocked. Furthermore, OTF reference processing typically reduces overall execution time.

Acknowledgments

We are grateful to Rick Hudson and Intel for a license to implement Sapphire in Jikes RVM, and Laurence Hellyer for his work on Sapphire. We are also grateful for the support of the JSPS KAKENHI Grant Number 25330080, the EPSRC through grant EP/H026975/1 and Google's Summer of Code.

References

[1] J. Auerbach, D. F. Bacon, B. Blainey, P. Cheng, M. Dawson, M. Fulton, D. Grove, D. Hart, and M. Stoodley. Design and implementation of a comprehensive real-time Java virtual machine. In *7th ACM & IEEE International Conference on Embedded Software*, pages 249–258, Salzburg, Austria, Sept. 2007. ACM Press.

[2] J. Auerbach, D. F. Bacon, P. Cheng, D. Grove, B. Biron, C. Gracie, B. McCloskey, A. Micic, and R. Sciampacone. Tax-and-spend: Democratic scheduling for real-time garbage collection. In *8th ACM International Conference on Embedded Software*, pages 245–254, Atlanta, GA, 2008. ACM Press.

[3] H. Azatchi, Y. Levanoni, H. Paz, and E. Petrank. An on-the-fly mark and sweep garbage collector based on sliding views. In *ACM SIGPLAN Conference on Object-Oriented Programming, Systems, Languages, and Applications*, ACM SIGPLAN Notices 38(11), pages 269–281, Anaheim, CA, Nov. 2003. ACM Press.

[4] D. F. Bacon, P. Cheng, and V. Rajan. A real-time garbage collector with low overhead and consistent utilization. In *30th Annual ACM Symposium on Principles of Programming Languages*, ACM SIGPLAN Notices 38(1), pages 285–298, New Orleans, LA, Jan. 2003. ACM Press.

[5] S. M. Blackburn, R. Garner, C. Hoffman, A. M. Khan, K. S. McKinley, R. Bentzur, A. Diwan, D. Feinberg, D. Frampton, S. Z. Guyer, M. Hirzel, A. Hosking, M. Jump, H. Lee, J. E. B. Moss, A. Phansalkar, D. Stefanović, T. VanDrunen, D. von Dincklage, and B. Wiedermann. The DaCapo benchmarks: Java benchmarking development and analysis. In *ACM SIGPLAN Conference on Object-Oriented Programming, Systems, Languages, and Applications*, ACM SIGPLAN Notices 41(10), pages 169–190, Portland, OR, Oct. 2006. ACM Press.

[6] C. Click, G. Tene, and M. Wolf. The Pauseless GC algorithm. In M. Hind and J. Vitek, editors, *1st ACM SIGPLAN/SIGOPS International Conference on Virtual Execution Environments*, pages 46–56, Chicago, IL, June 2005. ACM Press.

[7] D. Doligez and G. Gonthier. Portable, unobtrusive garbage collection for multiprocessor systems. In *21st Annual ACM Symposium on Principles of Programming Languages*, pages 70–83, Portland, OR, Jan. 1994. ACM Press.

[8] T. Domani, E. K. Kolodner, E. Lewis, E. E. Salant, K. Barabash, I. Lahan, E. Petrank, I. Yanover, and Y. Levanoni. Implementing an on-the-fly garbage collector for Java. In C. Chambers and A. L. Hosking, editors, *2nd International Symposium on Memory Management*, ACM SIGPLAN Notices 36(1), pages 155–166, Minneapolis, MN, Oct. 2000. ACM Press.

[9] A. Georges, L. Eeckhout, and D. Buytaert. Java performance evaluation through rigorous replay compilation. In *ACM SIGPLAN Conference on Object-Oriented Programming, Systems, Languages, and Applications*, ACM SIGPLAN Notices 43(10), pages 367–384, Nashville, TN, Oct. 2008. ACM Press.

[10] R. Henriksson. *Scheduling Garbage Collection in Embedded Systems*. PhD thesis, Lund Institute of Technology, July 1998.

[11] G. J. Holzmann. *The SPIN Model Checker: Primer and Reference Manual*. Addison-Wesley, 2004.

[12] R. L. Hudson and J. E. B. Moss. Sapphire: Copying garbage collection without stopping the world. *Concurrency and Computation: Practice and Experience*, 15(3–5):223–261, 2003.

[13] B. Iyengar, G. Tene, M. Wolf, and E. Gehringer. The Collie: a wait-free compacting collector. In McKinley and Vechev, editors, *11th International Symposium on Memory Management*, pages 85–96, China, June 2012. ACM Press.

[14] R. Jones, A. Hosking, and E. Moss. *The Garbage Collection Handbook: The Art of Automatic Memory Management*. CRC Applied Algorithms and Data Structures. Chapman & Hall, Aug. 2012.

[15] T. Kalibera. Replicating real-time garbage collector for Java. In *7th International Workshop on Java Technologies for Real-time and Embedded Systems (JTRES)*, pages 100–109, Madrid, Spain, Sept. 2009. ACM Press.

[16] B. McCloskey, D. F. Bacon, P. Cheng, and D. Grove. Staccato: A parallel and concurrent real-time compacting garbage collector for multiprocessors. IBM Research Report RC24505, IBM Research, 2008.

[17] Oracle Corp. *Java Platform, Standard Edition 7: API Specification*, 2013.

[18] P. P. Pirinen. Barrier techniques for incremental tracing. In S. L. Peyton Jones and R. Jones, editors, *1st International Symposium on Memory Management*, ACM SIGPLAN Notices 34(3), pages 20–25, Vancouver, Canada, Oct. 1998. ACM Press.

[19] F. Pizlo, D. Frampton, E. Petrank, and B. Steensgard. Stopless: A real-time garbage collector for multiprocessors. In G. Morrisett and M. Sagiv, editors, *6th International Symposium on Memory Management*, pages 159–172, Montréal, Canada, Oct. 2007. ACM Press.

[20] F. Pizlo, A. L. Hosking, and J. Vitek. Hierarchical real-time garbage collection. In *ACM SIGPLAN/SIGBED Conference on Languages, Compilers, and Tools for Embedded Systems*, ACM SIGPLAN Notices 42(7), pages 123–133, San Diego, CA, June 2007. ACM Press.

[21] F. Pizlo, E. Petrank, and B. Steensgaard. A study of concurrent real-time garbage collectors. In R. Gupta and S. P. Amarasinghe, editors, *ACM SIGPLAN Conference on Programming Language Design and Implementation*, ACM SIGPLAN Notices 43(6), pages 33–44, Tucson, AZ, June 2008. ACM Press.

[22] F. Pizlo, L. Ziarek, P. Maj, A. L. Hosking, E. Blanton, and J. Vitek. Schism: Fragmentation-tolerant real-time garbage collection. In *ACM SIGPLAN Conference on Programming Language Design and Implementation*, ACM SIGPLAN Notices 45(6), pages 146–159, Toronto, Canada, June 2010. ACM Press.

[23] M. Schoeberl and W. Puffitsch. Non-blocking object copy for real-time garbage collection. In *6th International Workshop on Java Technologies for Real-time and Embedded Systems (JTRES)*, pages 77–84, Santa Clara, CA, Sept. 2008. ACM Press.

[24] G. Tene, B. Iyengar, and M. Wolf. C4: The continuously concurrent compacting collector. In H. Boehm and D. Bacon, editors, *10th International Symposium on Memory Management*, pages 79–88, San Jose, CA, June 2011. ACM Press.

[25] X. Yang, S. M. Blackburn, D. Frampton, and A. L. Hosking. Barriers reconsidered, friendlier still! In McKinley and Vechev, editors, *11th International Symposium on Memory Management*, pages 37–48, China, June 2012. ACM Press.

Modeling Heap Data Growth Using Average Liveness

Pengcheng Li, Chen Ding and Hao Luo

Department of Computer Science, University of Rochester, Rochester, NY14627, USA

{pli, cding, hluo}@cs.rochester.edu

Abstract

Most of today's programs make use of a sizable heap to store dynamic data. To characterize the heap dynamics, this paper presents a set of metrics to measure the average amount of data live and dead in a period of execution. They are collectively called average liveness. The paper defines these metrics of average liveness, gives linear-time algorithms for measurement, and discusses their use in finding the best heap size. The algorithms are implemented in a Java tracing system called Elephant Tracks and evaluated using the DaCapo benchmarks running on the Oracle HotSpot and IBM J9 Java virtual machines.

Categories and Subject Descriptors D.3.4 [*Processors*]: Memory management (garbage collection); D.2.8 [*Metrics*]: Performance measures

General Terms algorithms, performance, measurement

Keywords liveness; all-window statistics; GC frequency; heap data growth

1. Introduction

In a heap, an object is live if it is allocated and not yet freed. The amount of live data can be measured at each time point in an execution. The amount is known as the *population count*. Traditionally, heap dynamics is shown by plotting the population counts over the entire execution. However, we often want to characterize a heap for a shorter period, e.g. a second. A problem arises because the population dynamics differs depending on the time window, and any window we select may not be representative.

This paper generalizes the concept of population count and defines *window-based liveness*. An execution window is a consecutive series of time points. The set of the live data in a window is the union of the population at all its time points. The liveness of the window is the size of the union set.

The liveness differs depending on which window we count. To have a deterministic metric, we define *average liveness* $wl(k)$, which is the average liveness in all windows of length k. The symbol *wl* designates window-based liveness or *win-live* for short. For any sequence of memory allocation and free events, $wl(k)$ is uniquely defined.

Average liveness provides strictly more information than the traditional population count. Population count is defined for each time point. Average liveness is defined for every window, which includes all time points as unit-length windows. A population includes only the live data. Average liveness counts both live and dead objects. Mathematically there is a fundamental difference: the population count over time is not monotone, but average liveness over increasing window lengths is monotone.

Average liveness can be used to derive optimal heap sizes. First, it avoids a problem known as the measurement bias [19]. When the same program is run multiple times, the GC frequency changes because it depends on the initial condition of the heap. A different initial point can lead to a different GC frequency. Average liveness computes the average frequency, since it assumes that the initial point can be anywhere. Second, for full-heap GC, it computes the average GC frequency for all heap sizes, so the most effective size can be identified. Third, for generational GC, it computes the minimal mature heap growth, which can be used to choose the size for the nursery heap to minimize the amount of premature promotion.

Average liveness is a collection of metrics counting objects differently based on the following factors:

- *Liveness and death.* In a liveness metric, we count the objects that are (or have been) live in a window. In a death metric, we count the number of objects that become dead in the window.

- *Window local and global.* An object, live or dead, is considered local in a window if it is allocated inside the window; otherwise it is global.

- *Reachable and actual.* The death of an object may be precipitated immediately when it becomes unreachable or later when its memory is actually reclaimed. We call them the *reachable liveness/death* and the *actual liveness/death* respectively.

In this paper we present mainly three novel findings. First, we define seven metrics of average liveness, give the algorithms to compute them precisely in linear time, and show the inclusion relation as a full lattice. Then we use average liveness to find the best application-specific heap and nursery size. Finally, we evaluate the average liveness of DaCapo benchmarks running on two different Java virtual machines.

The study has a few limitations. The goal of the work is formulating a new type of heap metric not optimizing a program or a garbage collector. The treatment of garbage collectors is simplistic and ignores much of the diversity and complexity in a real design. The best GC parameters are derived after running a program (but can be derived for all heap sizes). Next we will show that the new metrics are novel, compact, deterministic, and can be measured efficiently.

ISMM'14, June 12, 2014, Edinburgh, UK.

Copyright © 2014 ACM 978-1-4503-2921-7/14/06. . . $15.00.

http://dx.doi.org/10.1145/2602988.2602997

2. Average Liveness

The metrics can be divided into three groups, each containing the metrics with similar characteristics. This section first introduces common symbols, then gives the definitions and measurement algorithms for each group and finally formalizes their relationship in the last section.

2.1 Notations

We use the function symbol wl to denote liveness metrics and wd death metrics. Each function has two subscripts. The first is either global g or local l. The second is either reachable r or actual a. For example, $wd_{l,r}(k)$ is the function for local reachable death. It counts the average number of objects that are allocated and become unreachable in length-k windows. We may use only the first subscript, e.g. wl_g, when there is no need to specify whether the liveness is for reachable or actual lifetimes.

The metrics are defined for each execution trace. The length (logical time) of the trace is n. The total number of objects is m. For each object i, the allocation time is s_i, and the death time is e_i.

2.2 Global Liveness

In a time window w, for global liveness we count the number of objects live in w. The average global liveness, $wl_g(k)$, is the average of all $n-k+1$ length k windows.

There are two metrics: *global reachable liveness*, $wl_{g,r}(k)$ and *global actual liveness* $wl_{g,a}(k)$. The algorithms to compute the two are identical except that the death time is by reachability in the former and by actual reclamation in the latter. We show the algorithm as one to compute wl_g.

It is too numerous to count window by window. Considering all window length k, the total number of windows is $\binom{n}{2}$ or $\frac{n(n+1)}{2}$. First, we transform the problem to make it solvable.

Instead of counting window by window, we count lifetime by lifetime. Take object i whose lifetime spans $<s_i, e_i>$. Consider how many k-length windows in which the object is live. Ignoring boundary conditions (i.e. $s_i \geq k$ and $e_i \leq n-k+1$), object i is live in every k-length window starting from time $s_i - k$ to time e_i. In other words, A contributes 1 to the live count in and only in $e_i - s_i + k$ windows. Hence the transformation of the counting problem: summing the liveness in all windows is the same as summing the contributions by all objects. More formally, the equivalence means:

$$wl_g(k) = \frac{\sum_{\text{all window } w}(\text{num live objects in } w)}{n-k+1}$$
$$= \frac{\sum_{\text{all object } A}\text{contribution}(A)}{n-k+1} \quad (1)$$

Counting the contributions is done in four cases, shown in Figure 1. For Object 1, $s_1 \geq k$ and $e_1 < n-k+1$. It is live in $e_1 - s_1 + k$ length-k windows. This is the steady-state case. Others are boundary cases, $s_2 < k$ for Object 2 and $e_2 \geq n-k+1$ for Object 3. The fourth case is $s_i < k$ and $e_i \geq n+k+1$ for Object 4. In all four cases, the correct count for the contribution is $min(e_i, n-k+1) - max(s_i, k) + k$. Therefore, we have

$$wl_g(k) = \frac{\sum_{i=1}^{m}(\min(n-k+1, e_i) - \max(k, s_i) + k)}{n-k+1}$$
$$= \frac{\sum_{i=1}^{m}\min(n-k+1, e_i) - \sum_{i=1}^{m}\max(k, s_i) + mk}{n-k+1} \quad (2)$$

Algorithmic Complexity The total time cost to compute $wl_g(k)$ for all k is $O(n)$, where n is the length of the trace. The space cost is also $O(n)$. The length of a window is between 1 and n. If we

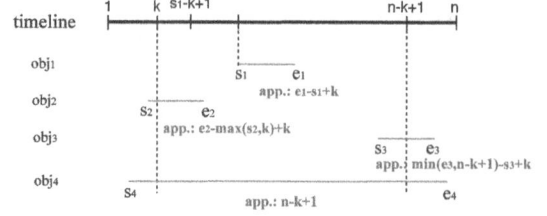

Figure 1: Four cases of an object lifetime. Object 1 is born after k and dies before $n-k+1$. Object 2 is born before k. Object 3 dies after $n-k+1$. Object 4 is born before k and dies after $n-k+1$. The contribution to liveness counts, i.e. the number of appearances in different windows, is given in "app."

consider a logarithmic rather than linear scale and let k range from 1 to $\log n$, the space cost is reduced to $O(\log n)$.

Monotonicity Average liveness in general and global liveness in particular is monotone. It shows the heap data growth for different window length k. When $k = 1$, $wl(1)$ is the average population (every time point is a length 1 window). When k increases, $wl(k)$ increases by including the live data in consecutive time points. When k is n the trace length, $wl(n)$ is the maximal object count, i.e. all allocated data.

Average Population Size A trivial use of global liveness is to compute the average population size, which is simply $wl_g(1)$. At each time point, the population size gives the minimal heap size. It shows the degree of cohabitation of objects. The same number of objects may be live at different times or at the same time. The average population size shows the average number of objects that are live at the same time.

Approximation Our earlier paper gives a simple formula to approximate the global liveness by ignoring the boundary conditions [16]. While the approximation is not used in this paper, the formulation may help to understand, for example, the relation between average liveness and the average rate of object allocation and death.

2.3 Local Liveness and Global Death

In the second group of metrics, just one end of the lifetime matters to the calculation. For local liveness, the significant event is the allocation at s_i. For global death, the significant event is the death at e_i. The event is significant because it affects the count in the windows that contain the event.

The formulas are given in Eq. 3 and 4. They are identical except where s_i is used in Eq. 3, e_i is used in Eq. 4.

$$wl_l(k) = \frac{\sum_{i=1}^{m}\min(s_i, k, n-s_i+1, n-k+1)}{n-k+1} \quad (3)$$

$$wd_g(k) = \frac{\sum_{i=1}^{m}\min(e_i, k, n-e_i+1, n-k+1)}{n-k+1} \quad (4)$$

The enumerators in the two equations are the sums of all object contributions: the total local live counts in Eq. 3 and the total death counts in Eq. 4. For each one, the contribution is the minimum of four numbers. The first three are cases ordered by the event time: earlier than k, between k and $n-k+1$, and after $n-k+1$ (provided $k \leq n/2$). The last number, $n-k+1$, is the maximal contribution, which means the object is counted in every window of length k.

For example, if the object is allocated before k ($s_i < k$), it appears in all windows whose starting time falls in the range between 1 and s_i. If $k \leq s_i \leq n-k+1$, it appears in all windows that start in

72

$s_i - k \ldots s_i$. If $s_i > n - k + 1$, it appears in all windows that start in $s_i - k \ldots n - k + 1$. The cases for the global death count are identical except that the event time is e_i instead of s_i.

We have just shown two nearly identical formulas to compute two seemingly different object counts: local live and global death. The reason is that both are counting "local" events in a window. In local liveness, it is an allocation happening inside a window. In global death, it is a death happening inside the window. Next we show the last metric, which depends on both ends of a lifetime.

2.4 Local Death

In a time window w, the local death count is the number of objects allocated in w and then dead in w. The average local death, $wd_l(k)$, is the average of all $n - k + 1$ length k windows.

The equation to compute the average local death $wd_l(k)$ is given in Eq. 5. The numerator counts the total local deaths in all windows. It uses a predicate function to select only the object lifetimes smaller than k. For each lifetime, the contribution is computed as the minimum of four cases. The four cases are similar to those discussed before: $s_i < k$, $s_i \geq k$, $e_i \leq n - k + 1$, $k - (e_i - s_i)$, and finally the total number of length k windows. For example, in the first case, the starting time $s_i < k$, so it may be local only in windows starting in the range $1 \ldots s_i$, that is, at most s_i windows. Considering all cases, we have

$$wd_l(k) = \frac{\sum_{i=1}^{m} I(v_i < k) \min(s_i, k - v_i, n - e_i + 1, n - k + 1)}{n - k + 1} \quad (5)$$

where $I(v_i < k)$ is a predicate function, which equals to 1 if the condition is true and 0 otherwise, and $v_i = e_i - s_i$.

2.5 Inclusion Lattice

The object counts presented in the preceding sections — global/local liveness/death — can be defined for either reachable or actual lifetimes, effectively doubling the number of metrics to 8. Two of them, local reachable liveness $wl_{l,r}$ and local actual liveness $wl_{l,a}$, are the same since both are concerned with only the allocation time. We denote it by wl_l without the second subscript. In total, we have seven new metrics.

The seven metrics are related by inclusion. For example, all the objects counted in local live are also counted in global live. To understand these relations, we show a set of example lifetimes in Figure 2. The graph shows four example objects whose lifetime overlaps with a given execution window. The global liveness counts all four objects, while the local liveness counts only the two that are allocated inside the window. The global death counts the two objects whose death time is inside the window, while local death counts the two that are allocated inside the window. The inclusion extends to reachable and actual liveness. In particular, global actual liveness includes global reachable liveness.

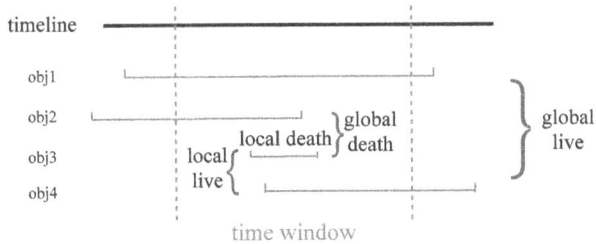

Figure 2: Illustration of the relations among four types of counts by showing how four example objects are counted differently in a given window.

The inclusion relations among the seven metrics are shown in Figure 3. Each inclusion relation is shown by a directed edge between the two metrics. If we view edges as a form of order, the relations form a partially ordered set. It has the greatest element, global actual liveness $wl_{g,a}$, and the smallest element, local actual death $wd_{l,a}$. Because of the maximum and minimum, the partially ordered set qualifies as a full lattice.[1] We call Figure 3 the *inclusion relation lattice*.

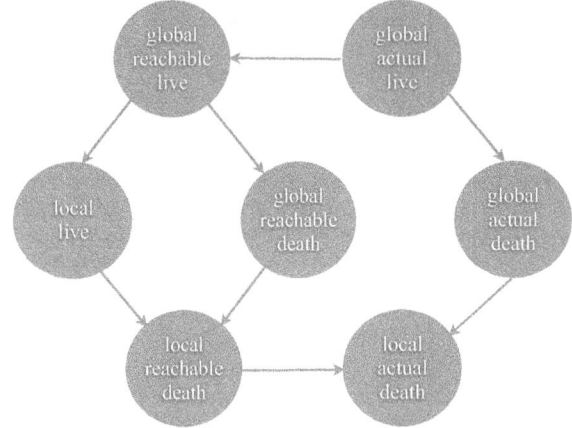

Figure 3: The inclusion relation lattice of the seven metrics. The object count at the source of an arrow includes the object count at the sink of the arrow.

Non-negative Differential We can compare among liveness metrics. Some are helpful to understand program behavior, for example, the difference between the liveness and death counts. Some are helpful to evaluate garbage collectors, for example, the different counts between the actual and the reachable objects in a heap. The inclusion relation lattice shows which pairs of metrics have always non-negative differences. These include all directly or indirectly connected pairs in the lattice. The maximum is the difference between the top and bottom metrics of the lattice. It shows the upper bound of the possible difference between any two metrics. In the evaluation section, we will show the non-negative difference between global actual liveness and global actual death.

3. Deriving Optimal Heap Sizes

In this section, we first explain the advantages of average liveness and then use its metrics to compute the data growth in a heap and analyzes the performance of garbage collectors.

3.1 Avoiding Measurement Bias

We define the *GC rate* as the GC frequency in a unit of time. The reciprocal is the *GC interval* or *inter-GC time*. The time here may be real or logical. A logical time may be the total number of allocated objects or the total amount of allocated memory.

Evaluating a garbage collector is tricky. After the first GC, the following GCs happen whenever the heap is full. However, the time of the first GC is not identical if we run the same program multiple times. It depends on initialization by the JVM, which varies from machine to machine and run to run. Mytkowicz et al. called such variation the measurement bias and showed that such bias is prevalent and significant in all systems [19]. For Java, the use

---

[1] In the lattice theory, a full lattice is one where upper-bound and lower-bound elements always exist for any set of lattice elements.

of a just-in-time (JIT) compiler further complicates the matter since the compiler may allocate a significant number of objects before and during a program execution.

Blackburn et al. gave the widely adopted solution known as the second-run methodology. The method forces initialization and JIT compilation to happen in the first run and then runs the program again to measure performance [7]. In this way, the result does not vary and can be reproduced.

The second-run solution ensures reproducible behavior, but it is not always the behavior seen by a user. This weakness does not necessarily invalidate the empirical conclusions drawn from second-run experiments. To characterize program behavior under all executions, the second-run result is incomplete.

Average liveness measures the expected behavior. It is the average count of all windows and therefore all possible GC windows. Window-based liveness does not evaluate garbage collectors as the second-run methodology does, but it evaluates the memory demand of a program in ways independent of specific GC windows, heap sizes, and initial conditions. In addition, the new metrics can be computed in a single pass. We may call average liveness a single-run solution to the problem of measurement bias.

3.2 Full Heap GC Frequency

We first consider mark-sweep GC. Let y be the heap size, i.e. the maximal size of data that the heap can store. The average GC interval $gci(y)$ can be computed using the global reachable liveness as follows:

$$gci(y) = wl_{g,r}^{-1}(y) \qquad (6)$$

The derivation is illustrated in Figure 4. The plot shows the average growth of live data in the heap. When it reaches the heap size y, GC is triggered. The window length t is then the average GC interval.

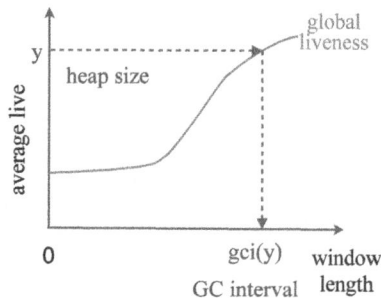

Figure 4: Computing the full-heap GC rate using the global reachable liveness

The computed interval is an average. It assumes that the GC window could be any window of the length of the interval. The computed interval is for all heap size y. The larger the heap size is, the longer the GC interval. If the heap size is infinite, the GC interval is also infinite.

Heap Size Selection The shape of the liveness curve shows the tradeoff between the heap size and the GC interval. Adding heap space reduces the GC frequency more effectively when the slope is steep than when it is flat. By examining the cost-effect, a user may choose the best heap size.

3.3 Minimal Mature Space Growth

Generational GC exploits the common case that most objects die young. In the basic form, generational GC divides the heap into two spaces: the nursery and the mature space. New objects are allocated in the nursery. When it is full, GC is incurred but only inside the nursery. A nursery GC is also called an incremental GC.

In this paper, we assume a simple design. Both the nursery and the mature space have a fixed size. After the nursery GC, the uncollected objects are moved (or "promoted") into the mature space. When the mature space is full, a full-heap GC is performed.

To compute the frequency of the nursery GC, we extend the previous formulation and make mainly two changes. The analysis is illustrated in Figure 5.

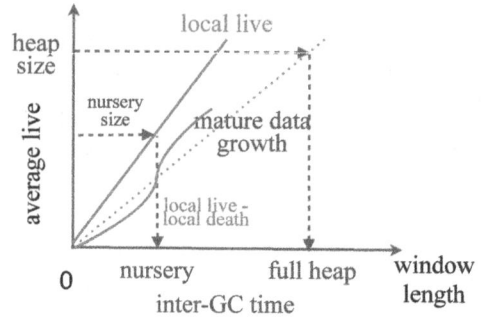

Figure 5: Computing the nursery and full-heap GC interval in generational GC. The local liveness is used to compute the nursery GC interval. The difference of local live and local reachable death gives the lower bound on the growth rate of the mature space.

First, we use the local liveness to model the nursery GC. Since only the objects allocated after the last collection occupy the space in the nursery, the inter-GC time for the nursery is simply the size of the nursery divided by the local liveness. Upon a nursery collection, the dead objects allocated after the last collection are collected.

Figure 5 shows the local liveness of a hypothetical program. The allocation starts from $y = 0$, because the nursery is initially empty. When the allocation fills the nursery, a nursery collection is triggered.

The second difference in generational GC is that the nursery heap is emptied after each GC, as the remaining objects are moved to the mature space. The process repeats when the emptied nursery is re-occupied by new allocation. The inter-GC time is still the size of nursery divided by the local liveness.

The mature space grows steadily as the uncollected objects are copied from the nursery. Figure 5 illustrates the growth curve of the mature space. The nursery acts as a filter to remove the objects that die young. An important metric is the *survival rate*, which is the average fraction of the nursery that survives the nursery GC.

The survivors include locally live objects, which can be counted by taking the local liveness and removing the local reachable death. The result is the minimal mature space growth *msg*:

$$msg(k) = wl_l(k) - wd_{l,r}(k) \qquad (7)$$

where k is the window length when $wl_l(k)$ equals to the nursery size, wl_l is local liveness and $wd_{l,r}$ local reachable death.

Not all survivors are live. In particular, they may be dead objects referenced by other dead objects in the mature space. Eq. 7 counts only the truly live survivors, so it gives the lower bound of the mature space growth.

Premature promotion is the chief weakness of the original generational GC. It is part of the fundamental tradeoff: the generational GC saves the collection time by granting immunity to the mature space, but it fails to collect dead mature objects or dead nursery objects pointed to by dead mature objects. The problem has been a focus of much of the past research, for example, the Beltway collector [6].

Without average liveness, it would be costly to measure the amount of premature promotion. We need a full-heap GC performed with every nursery GC. Even then, the result is specific to the specific execution, and the result changes when the initial GC time shifts (i.e. the measurement bias) and when the nursery size or the mature space size changes,

In evaluation, we will compute the lower bound growth for all heap sizes using Eq. 7. The difference between the actual survival and the minimal survival will show the average amount of premature promotion in an execution. It shows the efficiency of the generational GC in different heap configurations.

In future work, we plan to investigate a more direct method, which is to compute the average number of objects that are allocated and dead in a window but are pointed to by an object allocated outside the window. The extension would add a new type of average liveness in addition to global and local liveness.

4. Evaluation

In this section, we describe the experimental setup, the liveness result of DaCapo benchmarks, and the use of results in choosing the best heap size.

4.1 Experimental setup

Implementation using Merlin and Elephant Tracks We have implemented the new metrics using two existing systems, Merlin [13] by Hertz et al. and Elephant Tracks [20] by Ricci et al. Merlin [13] is the most precise technique for object lifetime profiling (OLP). It uses a forward pass to mark allocation times and potential death times for all objects and then a backward pass to (transitively) compute the exact death times. Using the precise object lifetimes measured by Merlin, we count reachable/unreachable objects.

Elephant Tracks [20] is a publicly available heap profiling tool. It captures a precise and complete record of object allocation, death and pointer updates. It monitors method entries and exits and uses the frequency as logical time. Elephant Tracks uses the standard JVMTI tool interface [18], so it can profile any JVM that has the interface, including Oracle HotSpot and IBM J9.

In more detail, the JVMTI interface [18] specifies a number of hooks for programmers to monitor JVM internal events. Elephant Tracks registers the hooks including *VMInit*, *VMDeath*, *GarbageCollectionStart*, *GarbageCollectionEnd*, *ObjAllocation*, *ObjDeath* and *PointerUpdates*. The Merlin reachability analysis is the backward pass in Merlin using the *VMDeath* hook inserted by Elephant Tracks. The liveness analysis primarily uses *VMInit*, *VMDeath*, *ObjAllocation* and *GarbageCollectionEnd* hooks. At a *VMInit* hook, we initialize the necessary data structure. At an *ObjAllocation* hook, we record the allocation time in a histogram. Similarly, we use another event to maintain a histogram of object death times. At a *GarbageCollectionEnd* hook, the GC time is recorded. All the object actual death times are estimated with the closest GC time after they become unreachable. Finally, at a *VMDeath* hook, the reachability analysis finishes, and the liveness analysis follows. Special operations such as exception handling and weak references are handled separately, in ways consistent with the solution in Elephant Tracks [20]. All our metrics are computed in a single pass in linear time.

Platform All experiments were conducted on an eight-core machine shipped with two Intel Xeon E5520 3.2GHz processors and running 2.6.34 Linux kernel. We tested two JVMs. On Oracle HotSpot OpenJDK7, we tested two garbage collectors: *ParallelGC* and *ConcMarkSweepGC*. The initial heap size and maximal heap

size were set to be same, 1000MB. For experiments that require explicit setting of the nursery size, we set the initial nursery size and the maximal nursery size the same. On IBM J9 1.6.0, we tested two garbage collectors: a full-heap GC called *optthruput* and a generational GC called *gencon*. For *optthruput*, the initial and maximum heap sizes were 4MB and 512MB. For *gencon*, the initial and maximum heap sizes were both set to 1000MB.

Cost of analysis On our machine platform, Elephant Tracks incurs over 500 times slowdown on average. Our liveness analysis is in linear time and the cost is negligible compared to the cost of instrumentation. Most of the space cost is due to object allocation time histograms and object death time histograms. Our liveness analysis is an online algorithm and does not store traces.

Test Programs For testing, we used the DaCapo benchmarks [7]. On Oracle HotSpot, we tested five DaCapo programs with two inputs, *default* and *small*. The programs are *luindex*, *pmd*, *sunflow*, *fop* and *avrora*. The five programs show a wide range of characteristics as we will see. The other seven programs are tested on IBM J9 using the *default* input and the *small* input except for the program *h2*, which uses only the *small* input.[2]

4.2 Liveness Trends

Figures 6 and 7 show the average liveness for the twelve DaCapo programs measured on HotSpot and J9. The x-axis is the window size from 1 to n, the length of the execution. Each window size has seven object counts. For easy viewing, we connect the points of the same metric and refer to a metric by its curve as a liveness and death curve. We shade the space between the top two liveness curves, which we will discuss later.

From top to bottom, we have at highest the curve of global actual live $wl_{g,a}$ and at lowest the curve of local reachable death $wd_{l,r}$. Since they are the top and the bottom metrics in the inclusion lattice, their counts are the upper and lower bounds for all liveness and death counts for all window sizes.

According to the inclusion lattice, there is a strict order for three liveness curves. It is possible for a death curve to be higher than two of the liveness curves. However, the liveness curves are the highest in all our results ("live before death").

Two liveness curves, global actual and global reachable, do not start from zero. They start from the average population count. The remaining five metrics, local liveness and the four death metrics all start from zero.

All curves end at the same point. When the window covers the entire execution, they converge to a single size, which is the size of all allocated data. At the maximal length, there is only one such window. It contains all allocations and reclamations. All data is freed when a program ends. There is no live data left afterwards. In this largest window, all seven object counts are equal (to the total number of objects).

In the graphs, the area between global actual live and global reachable live is shaded. We call the difference the GC penalty, because it includes the objects that could be freed but not freed by the garbage collector. The penalty is for every window length k. The shared area shows the average penalty. Consider $k = 1$. If we measure at each window (time point), the penalty is highest before GC and zero after GC. The difference $wl_{g,a} - wl_{g,r}$ is the average of all time points.

As the window size increases, both sides of the shaded area grow in parallel at the rate of new object allocation. The growth rate changes at a larger window size when GC frees data that are

---

[2] We did not finish testing the default input before the submission of the final paper.

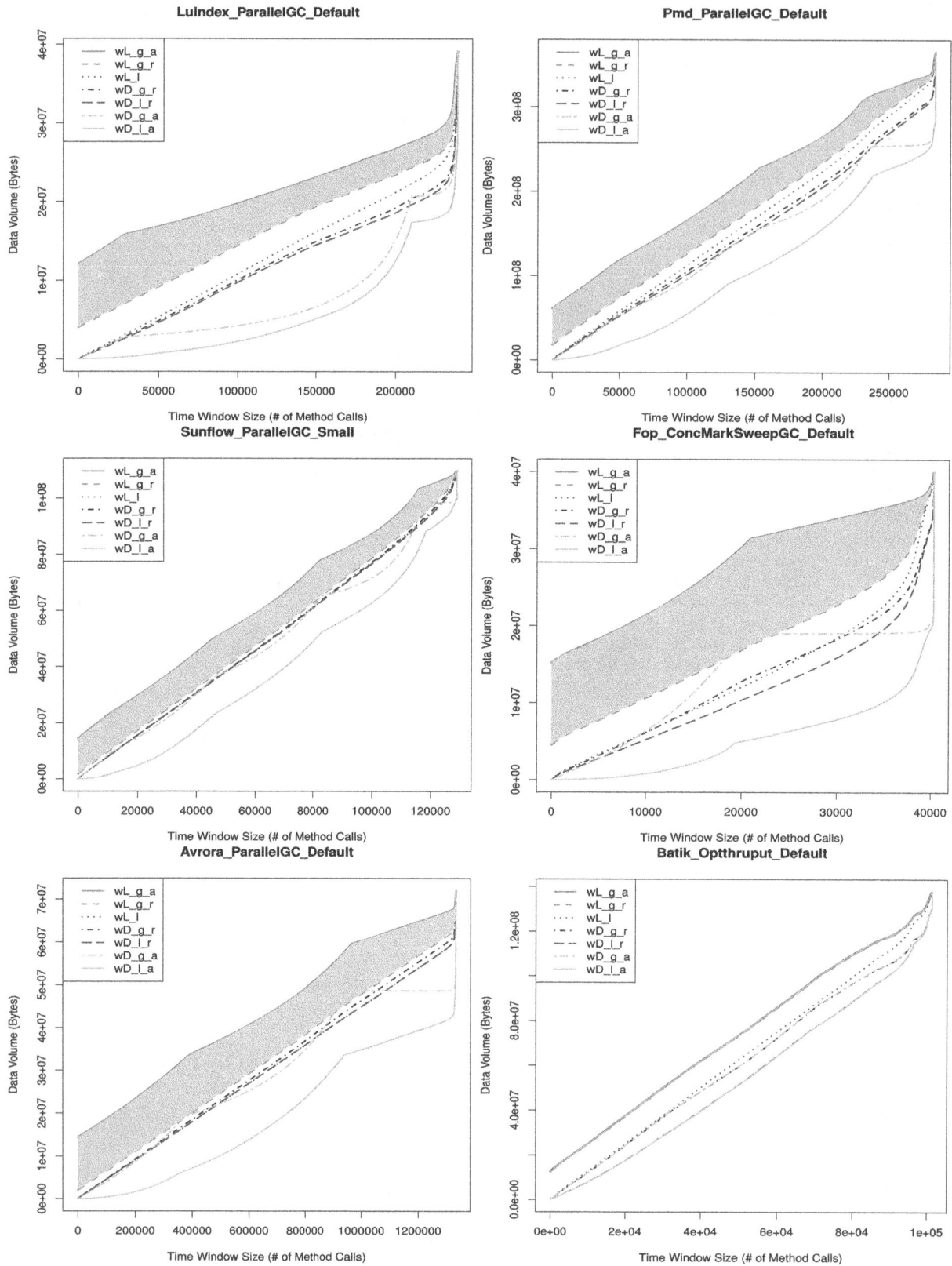

Figure 6: Average liveness metrics measured on HotSpot for *luindex, pmd, sunflow, fop, avrora* and on J9 for *batik*."wL_g_a" in the figures denotes $wl_{g,a}$.

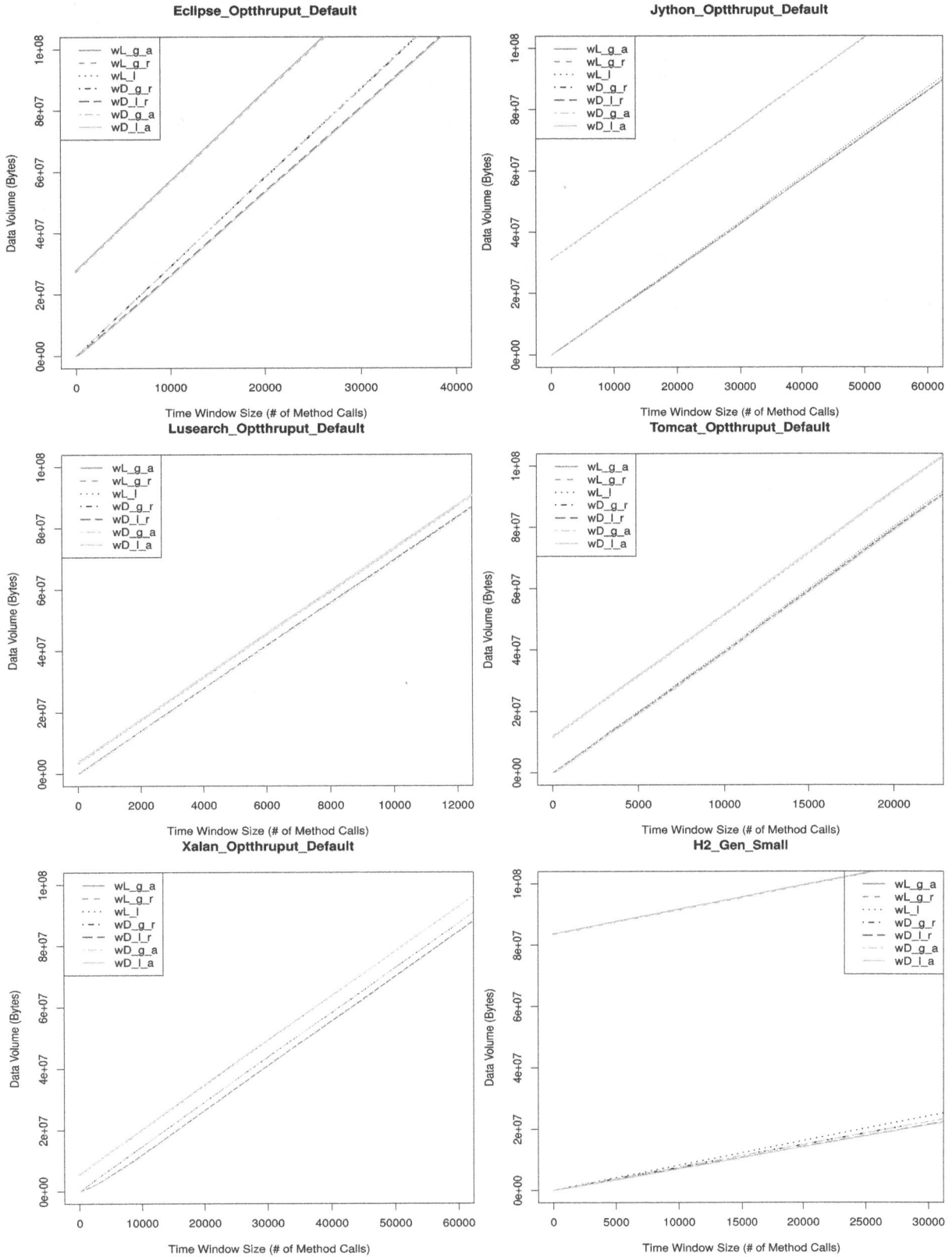

Figure 7: Average liveness measured on J9 for *eclipse, jython, lusearch, tomcat, xalan, h2*. "wL_g_a" in the figures denotes $wl_{g,a}$.

live at a smaller window size. This is shown when the shaded area narrows.

At the window length $k = n$, there is no penalty. The reason is more subtle, because the liveness count at larger k includes both live and dead objects. At $k = n$, it counts all objects, which are both live and dead in the window. The overlapping counting is also the reason that a liveness curve always keeps growing with the window size even though the size of live data is usually bounded.

In the experiments on HotSpot, we have tested two input sizes and each on two garbage collectors, for a total of four tests per program. In the figures, we choose to show one result for each program: the one that has striking shaded area. In the experiments on IBM J9, we found little or no variation between actual and reachable liveness. The reason is that J9 performs many garbage collections during an executions. The actual death time is computed from the closest GC time, which is very close to the reachable death time. Hence, the shaded area is small. The cause for this effect is still being investigated.

4.3 Finding Best Heap Size

First we consider full-heap GC. At each collection, a collector has to traverse all objects, so we we define the *effort* of a collection by the amount of the data in the heap at the time of the collection. The *GC effort* is the sum of the effort of all collections.

We use the GC effort to select the best heap size. In a small heap, GC is efficient but more frequent. It may take multiple GC passes for an object to become dead and collected. In a larger heap, each GC takes longer, but the collection of the same object may take just one pass. It depends on the frequency of the GC, which we can compute using average liveness, i.e., by Eq. 6 in Section 3.2. Then the GC effort is the heap size times the GC frequency.

As discussed in Section 3.1, if we naively test and find the best heap size, the result may be wrong because of measurement bias. Average liveness gives the best heap size *on average*, so the result is not biased.

Figure 8 shows the GC effort for all test programs on the default input (a,c) and the small input (b,d), except for *h2* in (d) which uses the small input. In these graphs, lower means less GC effort for the same mutator computation. The programs shown in (a,b) allocate a small amount of data. The total allocation is less than 70MB in all but two cases. When the heap size exceeds the total allocation, the effort is zero since no GC is needed.

The programs in (c,d) allocate more data. The GC effort is as high as 1.6GB. The effort decreases as the heap size increases. The change is not proportional. All programs have an inflection point, beyond which increasing the heap size no longer reduces the GC effort as much. In fact, in the majority of the cases, there is no benefit going beyond the inflection point. Before the inflection point, a larger heap means less GC effort. After the inflection point, a larger heap means the same GC effort.

To choose the best heap size, we need to compute the inflection point, which we can using average liveness. Figure 8 shows that the inflection point differs for different programs and inputs. However, at least two programs, *lusearch,eclipse*, have similar inflection points in their two inputs.

For these tests, the inflection point happens fairly early. Still, there are benefits in increasing the heap size beyond the inflection point. For *sunflow,eclipse*, the GC effort continues to drop for all heap sizes tested (up to 200MB).

4.4 Finding Best Nursery Size

We evaluate the (in)efficiency of a nursery size by the amount of premature promotion. Using average liveness (Section 3.3), we compute the minimal mature space growth. This is the ideal survival rate. There is no premature promotion. This is done through one-pass profiling. Then we test using different nursery sizes to measure the actual survival rate.[3] For lack of a better name, we call the difference the *zombie rate*. The zombie rate is the premature promotion, which we want to minimize.

Figure 9 shows the three results for all test programs. The default input is used for all except for *h2*. The programs are divided into two groups. The first group were tested on HotSpot, and the second on J9. The graphs show the nursery size on the *x*-axis. It increases from 4MB to 50MB for the programs running on HotSpot, and 3MB to 100MB for the programs running on IBM J9. The total heap size is 1000MB, partitioned between the nursery and the mature space.

When looking at the survival rate, there are no consistent trends for the five programs running on HotSpot. The rate ranges between 20% and 80%. As the nursery size increases, the rate may decrease or increase. The variation is large. The smallest is 20% (of the nursery size) in *fop*. The other four are over 35%. The relation between the survival rate and the nursery size defies analysis since the variation is large and unpredictable. However, there is consistent trends for most programs running on IBM J9, except *batik*.

When we divide the survival rate into two sub-components, we observe three fairly consistent trends. First, the minimal survival rate decreases as the nursery size increases, except for *luindex*. Second, the variation of the minimal survival rate is small, less than 5% for most programs except *luindex, batik, xalan* and less than 2% for *sunflow,avrora*. Finally, in most programs, zombies contribute to the majority of the survived data. In *sunflow* and *avrora*, the vast majority are zombies. The minimal survival rate is 1% or less, while the zombie survival rate is over 70% when the nursery size is between 15MB and 40MB. In *batik, python, eclipse, h2, tomcat*, as nursery size increases, zombie rate goes bigger. For best performance, we may choose the nursery size to be as small as possible while minimizing the zombie rate.

5. Related Work

In this section, we first discuss solutions to a similar problem in locality analysis and then review existing techniques for heap analysis.

All Window Analysis In locality analysis, a recent concept is the footprint, which is the average amount of data accessed in a time window. Like average liveness, footprint analysis needs to measure for all $O(n^2)$ execution windows. Xiang et al. gave two solutions. The first algorithm counts all windows efficiently and gives the distribution, including maximum and minimum, of footprints for each window length. It takes $O(n \log m)$ time, where n is the length of a trace and m the size of all data [10, 26]. The second solution takes linear time and computes the average footprint in all windows without having to enumerate the footprint in all windows [27]. A recent extension is an algorithm that measures the shared footprint in all execution windows [17]. These algorithms are very different from average liveness. For footprint, we count the number of distinct data accessed in a window. For liveness, we count the number of live data.

The footprint theory is for cache management [28]. Average liveness is for heap management. The two theories differ. In the former, there is a higher order relation between cache performance metrics. In this paper, there is the inclusion relation lattice. As a function, the footprint is not just monotone but concave. Average liveness is monotone.

Object Lifetime Profiling (OLP) Object lifetime is key to understand heap dynamics and evaluate heap efficiency. An early model

---

[3] The actual survival rate result is susceptible to the problem of measurement bias.

GC Efforts

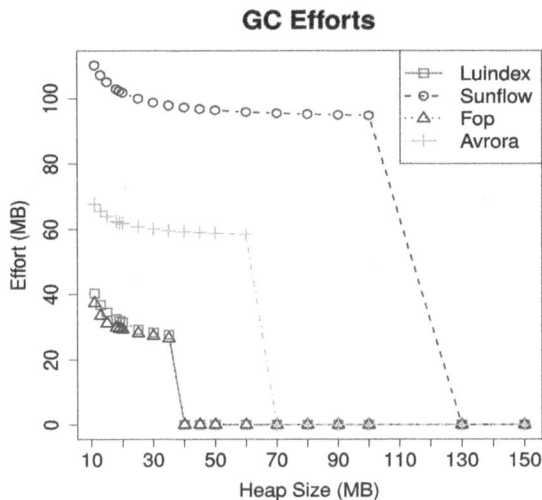

(a) The GC effort of *luindex, sunflow, fop* and *avrora* on default input

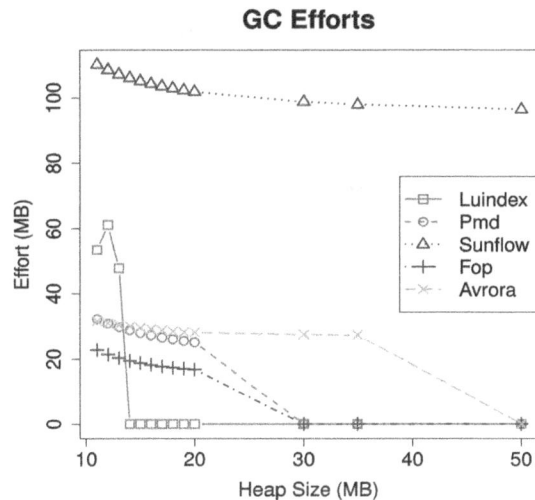

(b) The GC effort of *luindex, sunflow, fop, avrora* and *pmd* on small input

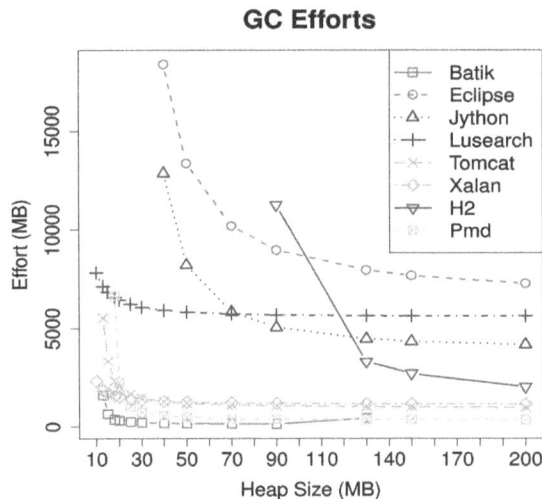

(c) The GC effort of the other eight programs on default input (except for *h2* on small input)

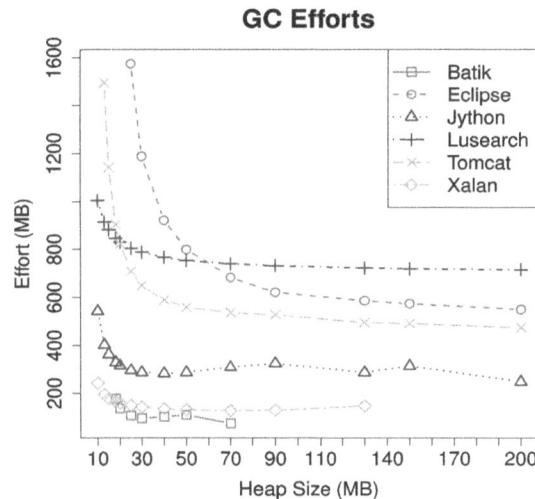

(d) The GC effort of the other seven programs on small input

Figure 8: The GC effort as a function of the heap size, measured for the test programs on the default input (a,c) and the small input (b,d).

by Röjemo and Runciman divides the lifetime and identifies the unnecessary parts as lag and drag [21]. Lifetime is defined by access. For garbage collected systems, lifetime is usually defined by reachability. Several techniques measure the lifetime using reference counting (RC) [4, 5]. While RC cannot detect death for objects involved in cycles, several variants [3, 24] use heuristics to detect dead cycles often by introducing periodic tracing collection or trial deletion. The solutions, however, do not guarantee precision. Merlin [13] uses a backward pass to compute transitive closure to find object death accurately. Although Merlin computes object lifetimes in linear time, it still incurs significant time and space overhead. Resurrector is a recent technique [29] to improve OLP performance. It identifies dead objects by timing method invocations on objects in conjunction with the use of reference counting. It does not detect dead cycles. Neither does it transitively discover the death times for objects that are pointed to by earlier dead objects. Other techniques such as [22, 25] proposed to use object lifetime profiles to improve GC performance. This paper uses Merlin

and extends the use of OLP to include the seven new metrics of average liveness.

Heap Performance Characterization It is desirable to have machine and VM independent metrics to characterize the memory demand of a program. To examine the efficiency of generational GC, Ungar evaluated the relation between the survival rate and nursery size [23]. The evaluation is specific to generational GC. Dufour et al. measured the memory usage by the amount of allocation per unit of time [11]. The allocation intensity is not a complete measure of memory usage since it does not consider memory reuse due to reclamation. Dieckmann and Holzle measured the size of live data by forcing a full-heap GC every 50KB of allocation [9]. They showed the result in a time series and found important facts about the SPEC JVM programs. For example, the maximal live data size is reachable relatively early in execution. Blackburn et al. used a similar strategy to evaluate DaCapo benchmarks and compare them with SPEC JVM [7]. In addition to time series, these and other studies measure the histogram of lifetimes, known as object

Actual Survival Rates

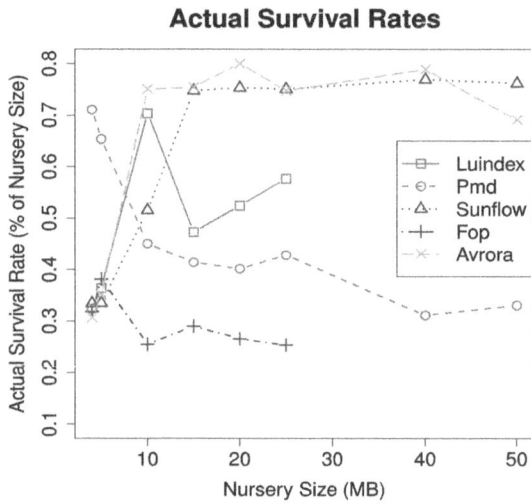

(a) Actual Survival Rate of *luindex, sunflow, fop, avrora* and *pmd*

Actual Survival Rates

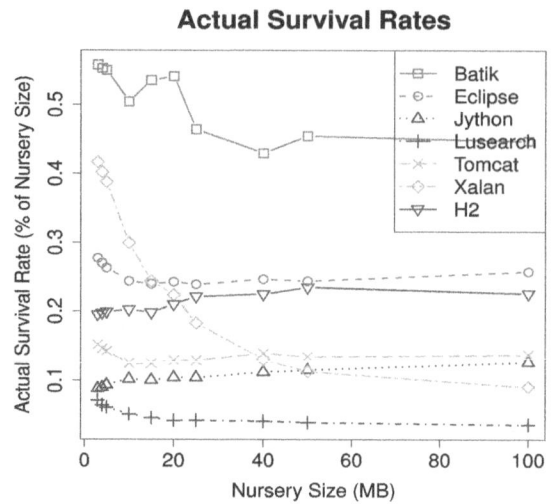

(b) Actual Survival Rate of the other seven programs

Minimal Survival Rates

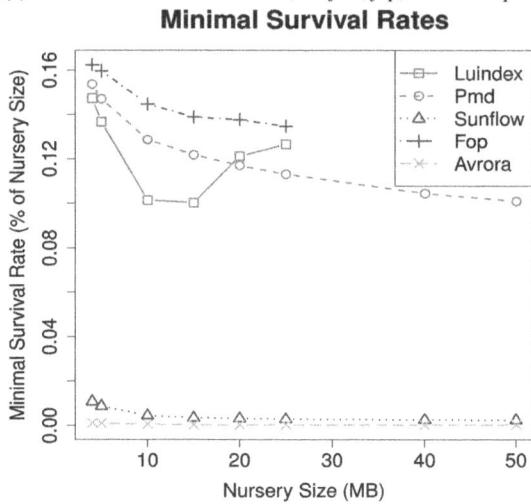

(c) Minimal Survival Rate of *luindex, sunflow, fop, avrora* and *pmd*

Minimal Survival Rates

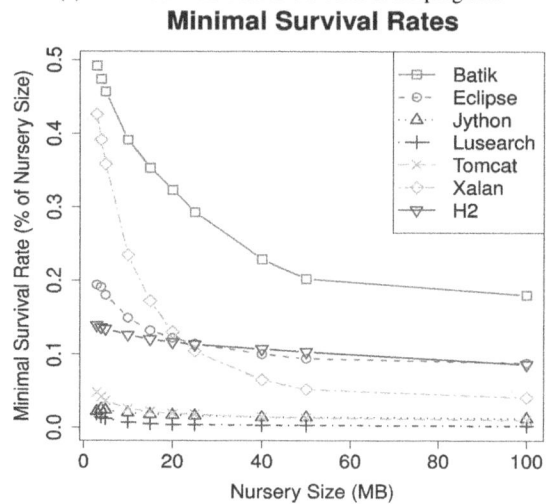

(d) Minimal Survival Rate of the other seven programs

Actual – Minimal

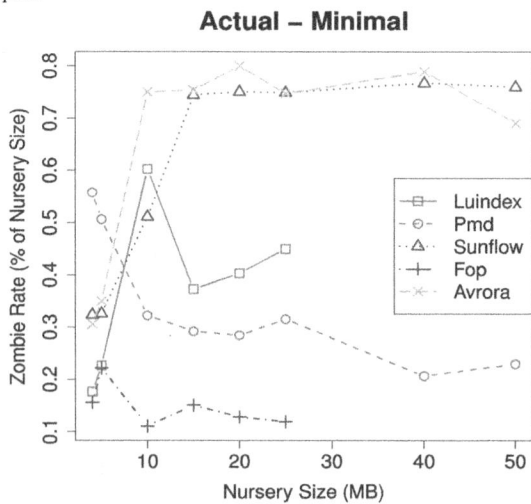

(e) Zombie Rate of *luindex, sunflow, fop, avrora* and *pmd*

Actual – Minimal

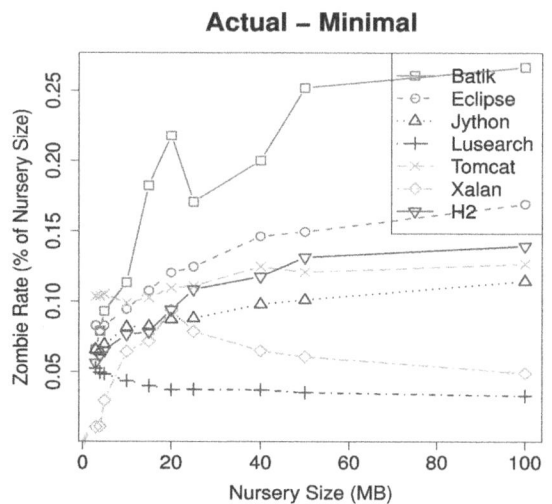

(f) Zombie Rate of the other seven programs

Figure 9: The efficiency of generational GC of different nursery sizes (in a 1000MB heap), measured by the actual survival rate (a), the minimal survival rate (b), and the difference, i.e. the zombie survival rate. The zombie is the portion of the dead objects survived due to premature promotion.

demographics [7, 14]. Others measured the connectivity in object graphs [12].

Kim and Hsu [15] studied the memory reference behavior of SPEC JVM applications by an exception-based tool. They observed that short-lived objects are more numerous in Java programs, small initial heap sizes are inefficient, and there exists an optimal heap size based on testing. In this paper we present the metrics for choosing the best heap size statistically. A set of papers [1, 2, 8] predicated heap memory requirements for garbage-collected languages. Braberman et al. [8] presents estimates based on program regions in particular methods. Their technique use static factors such as inputs and the program structure. In comparison, our metrics estimate the memory requirement in time windows. Albert et al. [1] describes an analysis to infer an accurate upper-bound on the peak heap usage. A later study [2] takes object lifetimes as parameters to give a conservative estimate of the memory requirement. If the estimated demand is met, a program should execute correctly.

6. Summary

In this paper, we have defined seven metrics: global actual live, global reachable live, local live, global reachable death, global actual death, local reachable death, and local actual death. They give the average count of live and dead objects in all execution windows in a program. They can be measured in linear time. They are monotone and have inclusion relations that form a complete lattice. The new metrics can be used to compute the average GC intervals for heaps of all sizes and the minimal mature space growth for nurseries of all sizes, without having to run a program multiple times. The result can be used to find the best heap size in mark-sweep GC and the best nursery size in generational GC. The evaluation shows these metrics and their uses using the DaCapo benchmarks.

Acknowledgments

We thank Matthew Hertz, Eliot Moss and Rathan Ricci for their help with the use of Merlin and Elephant Tracks. We also thank them and the reviewers of MSPC 2013 and ISMM 2014 for the review and critiques especially for improving the presentation of the theory and the evaluation.

References

[1] E. Albert, S. Genaim, and M. Gómez-Zamalloa Gil. Live heap space analysis for languages with garbage collection. In *ISMM*, pages 129–138, 2009.

[2] E. Albert, S. Genaim, and M. Gómez-Zamalloa. Parametric inference of memory requirements for garbage collected languages. In *ISMM*, pages 121–130, 2010.

[3] D. F. Bacon and V. T. Rajan. Concurrent cycle collection in reference counted systems. In *Proceedings of the 15th European Conference on Object-Oriented Programming*, pages 207–235, 2001.

[4] D. F. Bacon, C. R. Attanasio, H. B. Lee, V. T. Rajan, and S. Smith. Java without the coffee breaks: a nonintrusive multiprocessor garbage collector. *Proceedings of PLDI*, 36(5):92–103, 2001. ISSN 0362-1340. .

[5] D. F. Bacon, P. Cheng, and V. T. Rajan. A unified theory of garbage collection. In *Proceedings of OOPSLA*, pages 50–68, Vancouver, British Columbia, 2004.

[6] S. Blackburn, R. E. Jones, K. S. McKinley, and J. E. B. Moss. Beltway: Getting around garbage collection gridlock. In *Proceedings of PLDI*, pages 153–164, 2002.

[7] S. M. Blackburn et al. The DaCapo benchmarks: Java benchmarking development and analysis. In *Proceedings of OOPSLA*, 2006.

[8] V. Braberman, F. Fernández, D. Garbervetsky, and S. Yovine. Parametric prediction of heap memory requirements. In *ISMM*, pages 141–150, 2008.

[9] S. Dieckmann and U. Hölzle. A study of the allocation behavior of the specjvm98 java benchmark. In *ECOOP*, pages 92–115, 1999.

[10] C. Ding and T. Chilimbi. All-window profiling of concurrent executions. In *Proceedings of PPoPP*, 2008. *Poster paper*.

[11] B. Dufour, K. Driesen, L. Hendren, and C. Verbrugge. Dynamic metrics for java. In *Proceedings of OOPSLA*, pages 149–168, 2003.

[12] H. Eran and E. Petrank. A study of data structures with a deep heap shape. In *Proceedings of the ACM SIGPLAN Workshop on Memory System Performance and Correctness*, page 2, 2013.

[13] M. Hertz, S. M. Blackburn, K. S. McKinley, J. E. B. Moss, and D. Stefanovic. Generating object lifetime traces with Merlin. *ACM TOPLAS*, 28(3):476–516, 2006.

[14] R. E. Jones and C. Ryder. A study of java object demographics. In *ISMM*, pages 121–130, 2008.

[15] J.-S. Kim and Y. Hsu. Memory system behavior of java programs: Methodology and analysis. In *Proceedings of the 2000 ACM SIGMETRICS International Conference on Measurement and Modeling of Computer Systems*, pages 264–274, 2000.

[16] P. Li and C. Ding. All-window data liveness. In *Proceedings of the ACM SIGPLAN Workshop on Memory Systems Performance and Correctness*, 2013.

[17] H. Luo, X. Xiang, and C. Ding. Characterizing active data sharing in threaded applications using shared footprint. In *Proceedings of the The 11th International Workshop on Dynamic Analysis*, 2013.

[18] S. Microsystems. Jvm tool interface. In *http://java.sun.com/javase/6/docs/platform/jvmti/jvmti.html.*, 2004.

[19] T. Mytkowicz, A. Diwan, M. Hauswirth, and P. F. Sweeney. Producing wrong data without doing anything obviously wrong! In *Proceedings of ASPLOS*, pages 265–276, 2009.

[20] N. Ricci, S. Guyer, and E. Moss. Elephant tracks: Portable production of complete and precise GC traces. In *Proceedings of ISMM*, pages 109–118, 2013.

[21] N. Röjemo and C. Runciman. Lag, drag, void and use - heap profiling and space-efficient compilation revisited. In *Proceedings of ICFP*, pages 34–41, 1996.

[22] J. Singer, G. Brown, I. Watson, and J. Cavazos. Intelligent selection of application-specific garbage collectors. In *Proceedings of the International Symposium on Memory Management*, 2007.

[23] D. Ungar. Generation scavenging: A non-disruptive high performance storage reclamation algorithm. *SIGSOFT Softw. Eng. Notes*, 9(3):157–167, Apr. 1984. ISSN 0163-5948. . URL http://doi.acm.org/10.1145/390010.808261.

[24] S. C. Vestal. *Garbage collection: an exercise in distributed, fault-tolerant programming*. PhD thesis, 1987.

[25] F. Xian, W. Srisa-an, and H. Jiang. Allocation-phase aware thread scheduling policies to improve garbage collection performance. In *Proceedings of the 6th International Symposium on Memory Management*, 2007.

[26] X. Xiang, B. Bao, T. Bai, C. Ding, and T. M. Chilimbi. All-window profiling and composable models of cache sharing. In *Proceedings of PPoPP*, pages 91–102, 2011.

[27] X. Xiang, B. Bao, C. Ding, and Y. Gao. Linear-time modeling of program working set in shared cache. In *Proceedings of PACT*, pages 350–360, 2011.

[28] X. Xiang, C. Ding, H. Luo, and B. Bao. HOTL: a higher order theory of locality. In *Proceedings of ASPLOS*, pages 343–356, 2013.

[29] G. H. Xu. Resurrector: a tunable object lifetime profiling technique for optimizing real-world programs. In *Proceedings of OOPSLA*, pages 111–130, 2013.

A. Monotonicity Proof

Theorem A.1. Monotonicity of Global Liveness.
The global liveness $wl_g(k)$ is monotonically non-decreasing.

Proof. We show $wl_g(k+1) - wl_g(k) \geq 0$. For the left-hand side to be minimal, we should have $wl_g(k+1) - wl_g(k)$, $n-k+1 \leq e_i$ and $k \geq s_i$. Under these conditions, we have:

$$wl_g(k+1) - wl_g(k)$$

$$= \frac{\sum_{i=1}^m \min(n-k, e_i) - \sum_{i=1}^m \max(k+1, s_i) + mk + m}{n-k}$$
$$- \frac{\sum_{i=1}^m \min(n-k+1, e_i) - \sum_{i=1}^m \max(k, s_i) + mk}{n-k+1}$$

$$\geq \frac{\sum_{i=1}^m ((n-k) - (k+1)) + mk + m}{n-k}$$
$$- \frac{\sum_{i=1}^m ((n-k+1) - k) + mk}{n-k+1}$$

$$= \frac{mn - 2mk - m + mk + m}{n-k} - \frac{mn - 2mk + m + mk}{n-k+1}$$

$$= \frac{m(n-k)}{n-k} - \frac{m(n-k+1)}{n-k+1}$$

$$= m - m$$

$$= 0$$

$\square$

Theorem A.2. Monotonicity of Local Liveness.
The local liveness $wl_l(k)$ is monotonically non-decreasing.

Proof. We show $wl_l(k+1) - wl_l(k) \geq 0$, For $wl_l(k+1) - wl_l(k)$ to be minimal, we have $n-k+1 \leq s_i, n-s_i+1, k$ and the following inequality:

$$wl_l(k+1) - wl_l(k)$$

$$= \frac{\sum_{i=1}^m \min(s_i, k+1, n-s_i+1, n-k)}{n-k}$$
$$- \frac{\sum_{i=1}^m \min(s_i, k, n-s_i+1, n-k+1)}{n-k+1}$$

$$\geq \frac{\sum_{i=1}^m (n-k)}{n-k} - \frac{\sum_{i=1}^m (n-k+1)}{n-k+1}$$

$$= \frac{m(n-k)}{n-k} - \frac{m(n-k+1)}{n-k+1}$$

$$= m - m$$

$$= 0$$

$\square$

Theorem A.3. Monotonicity of Global Death.
The global death $wd_g(k)$ is monotonically non-decreasing.

Proof. We show $wd_g(k+1) - wd_g(k) \geq 0$. For $wd_g(k+1) - wd_g(k)$ to be minimal, we have $n-k+1 \leq e_i, n-e_i+1, k$ and the following:

$$wd_g(k+1) - wd_g(k)$$

$$= \frac{\sum_{i=1}^m \min(e_i, k+1, n-e_i+1, n-k)}{n-k}$$
$$- \frac{\sum_{i=1}^m \min(e_i, k, n-e_i+1, n-k+1)}{n-k+1}$$

$$\geq \frac{\sum_{i=1}^m (n-k)}{n-k} - \frac{\sum_{i=1}^m (n-k+1)}{n-k+1}$$

$$= \frac{m(n-k)}{n-k} - \frac{m(n-k+1)}{n-k+1}$$

$$= m - m$$

$$= 0$$

$\square$

Theorem A.4. Monotonicity of Local Death.
The local death $wd_l(k)$ is monotonically non-decreasing.

Proof. We show $wd_l(k+1) - wd_l(k) \geq 0$. In the following derivation, the first "$\geq$" is because $wd_l(k+1)$ contains more objects than $wd_l(k)$. For $wd_l(k+1) - wd_l(k)$ to be minimal, we have $n-k+1 \leq s_i, n-e_i+1, k-v_i$ and the second "$\geq$" relation shown below:

$$wd_l(k+1) - wd_l(k)$$

$$= \frac{\sum_{i=1}^m I(v_i < k+1) \min(s_i, k+1-v_i, n-e_i+1, n-k)}{n-k}$$
$$- \frac{\sum_{i=1}^m I(v_i < k) \min(s_i, k-v_i, n-e_i+1, n-k+1)}{n-k+1}$$

$$= \frac{\sum_{i=1}^m I(k \leq v_i < k+1) \min(s_i, k+1-v_i, n-e_i+1, n-k)}{n-k}$$
$$+ \frac{\sum_{i=1}^m I(v_i < k) \min(s_i, k+1-v_i, n-e_i+1, n-k)}{n-k}$$
$$- \frac{\sum_{i=1}^m I(v_i < k) \min(s_i, k-v_i, n-e_i+1, n-k+1)}{n-k+1}$$

$$\geq \frac{\sum_{i=1}^m I(v_i < k) \min(s_i, k+1-v_i, n-e_i+1, n-k)}{n-k}$$
$$- \frac{\sum_{i=1}^m I(v_i < k) \min(s_i, k-v_i, n-e_i+1, n-k+1)}{n-k+1}$$

$$\geq \frac{\sum_{i=1}^m I(v_i < k)(n-k)}{n-k}$$
$$- \frac{\sum_{i=1}^m I(v_i < k)(n-k+1)}{n-k+1}$$

$$= \sum_{i=1}^m I(v_i < k) - \sum_{i=1}^m I(v_i < k)$$

$$= 0$$

$\square$

JDMM: A Java Memory Model for
Non-Cache-Coherent Memory Architectures *

Foivos S. Zakkak

FORTH-ICS

zakkak@ics.forth.gr

Polyvios Pratikakis

FORTH-ICS

polyvios@ics.forth.gr

Abstract

As the number of cores continuously grows, processor designers are considering non coherent memories as more scalable and energy efficient alternatives to the current coherent ones. The Java Memory Model (JMM) requires that all cores can access the Java heap. It guarantees sequential consistency for data-race-free programs and no *out-of-thin-air* values for non data-race-free programs. To implement the Java Memory Model over non-cache-coherent and distributed architectures Java Virtual Machines (JVMs) are most likely to employ software caching.

In this work, *i)* we provide a formalization of the Java Memory Model for non-cache-coherent and distributed memory architectures, *ii)* prove the adherence of our model with the Java Memory Model and *iii)* evaluate, regarding its compliance to the Java Memory Model, a state-of-the-art Java Virtual Machine implementation on a non-cache-coherent architecture.

Categories and Subject Descriptors D.3.1 [*Programming Languages*]: Formal Definitions and Theory; F.3.2 [*Logics and Meanings of Programs*]: Operational Semantics; D.2.4 [*Software Engineering*]: Software/Program Verification

Keywords Java; Multithreading; Concurrency; Memory Model; Non Cache Coherent Memory; Software Cache; Virtual Machine

1. Introduction

As the number of cores in CMPs continuously grows, processor designers are trying to keep energy consumption low or even reduce it while improving the overall performance. Trends suggest that future manycore machines will have thousands of mid-range cores with very fast communication channels. At such high number of cores, memory management becomes a major issue. Implementing efficient cache coherency protocols over thousands of cores is not trivial. To make matters worse, previous work has shown that cache coherency protocols as we know them today are not going to scale in terms of energy consumption. Kaxiras et al. [13] show that directory coherence protocols does not scale in terms of power

---

ISMM'14, June 12, 2014, Edinburgh, UK.
Copyright is held by the owner/author(s). Publication rights licensed to ACM.
ACM 978-1-4503-2921-7/14/06... $15.00.
http://dx.doi.org/10.1145/2602988.2602999

and performance. Choi et al. [7] also argue that cache coherence protocols imply large performance and energy overhead.

To overcome this issue, hardware designs proposed by recent literature limit or do not implement hardware cache coherency. Intel has presented two examples: First, the Single-chip Cloud Computer (SCC) [10] is a homogeneous 48-core non-cache-coherent architecture. The SCC uses a full cache hierarchy per core, includes an on-chip buffer for core-to-core communication, and is programmed mainly using MPI or an alternative custom-tailored message passing programming model. Second, Runnemede [5] is a hierarchical non-cache-coherent many-core architecture design that can scale up to hundreds of cores. Runnemede has four levels of scratchpad memories and three levels of computational modules. Furthermore, in each execution engine, the finer computation module features a 32K software-managed non-coherent cache. All the scratchpads map to a unique address range from a global address space. Runnemede offers DMA-like transfers that can work on cache-line granularity. In related literature, Lyberis et al. [18, 19] introduce the Formic board and built the Formic-Cube, a 512-core prototype using 64 such boards. Each Formic-board features eight MicroBlaze-based, non-cache-coherent cores, while the prototype features DMA capabilities and full network-on-chip in a 3D-mesh topology. Runnemede and the Formic-Cube both propose using a task-based programming model as a higher-level abstraction to MPI, using task annotations to declare memory usage and a runtime system to schedule computations to data or set up all required data transfers among memories or caches in software.

In distributed or non-cache-coherent memory architectures like SCC, Runnemede and the Formic-Cube, the software needs to explicitly transfer data across nodes and make sure the transfers happen in the correct order to get the desired results. The Java Memory Model (JMM) [20] implies that each core in a manycore architecture has access to the whole Java heap (we further discuss the JMM in Sections 2 and 3). As a result, a Java Virtual Machine (JVM) implementation for these or similar architectures needs to explicitly move data across nodes to implement the JMM.

This work bridges the gap between the JMM and its implementation on non-cache-coherent and distributed architectures. Specifically, the contributions of this work are:

- A formalization of the Java Memory Model for non-cache-coherent and distributed architectures (Sections 4 and 5).

- The formalization's proof of equivalence with the Java Memory Model (Section 6).

- A case study, where we use our model to examine the correctness of Hera-JVM, a state-of-the-art JVM implementation on a non memory coherent architecture (Section 7).

The remainder of this paper presents the formalization of the Java Distributed Memory Model (JDMM). Specifically, Section 2 discusses the JMM; Section 3 presents a summary of the existing formalization of the JMM for shared memory systems; Section 4 presents a formalization of the memory model for non-cache-coherent memory systems; Section 5 presents several extensions of the formalization to take into account many additional parts of the Java language; Section 6 defines the property of equivalence between the JMM and JDMM and sketches the proof of equivalence; Section 7 discusses a case study of an existing JVM that adheres to the JMM and uses distributed non-cache-coherent memories; finally, Section 8 concludes.

2. The Java Memory Model

The JMM is a relaxed memory model, according to which, data-race free (DRF) programs are guaranteed to be sequentially consistent[1] and non DRF programs are guaranteed to be safe. In this context, safe means that a thread cannot observe an *out-of-thin-air* value. Every value, read by any thread, must have been previously written by some thread (that includes the initialization write).

The JMM abstracts program operations to *actions* (e.g., reads, writes, interrupts). These *actions* are grouped in *synchronization* actions and *external* actions. *Synchronization* actions, as their name implies, are responsible for inter-thread communication and synchronization. Without the use of *synchronization* actions, a write might never be seen by a different thread than the writer thread. However, this is by no means guaranteed, nor is the order in which such *leaked* writes are observed by other threads. *Synchronization* actions are further grouped in *acquire* and *release* actions. The JMM, based on these actions and their ordering, defines the possible values that each read may observe. In general, any writes visible to a thread executing a *release* action must become visible to the thread executing the corresponding *acquire* action. *External* actions are those observable out of the program (i.e., I/O). Section 3 presents the existing formalization of the above by the JMM.

Previous work on proving the JMM's DRF guarantee [3, 4, 11, 12, 17, 27, 28] has shown that the JMM is correct in the sense that any execution of a DRF program is sequentially consistent if the JMM rules are satisfied by the underlying JVM. However, there are still some counterexamples to the JMM regarding the *out-of-thin-air* guarantee [3, §5]. Specifically, the following transformations are allowed under the JMM, but might cause *out-of-thin-air* values to be seen under specific circumstances.

1. Reordering of Independent statements (also mentioned in [6, §7]).

2. Reordering of memory accesses with external actions.

3. Moving memory accesses into synchronized blocks. Also known as "roach motel" ordering [20, §3.5.1].

The JMM should also satisfy all the causality test cases [26]. Aspinall and Ševčík [3] show that the test cases 17-20 are not satisfied by the JMM. Torlak et al. [28] also show that the test cases 19 and 20 are not satisfied.

For the first group of transformations and the causality tests Ševčík and Aspinall [27] propose a change to the JMM that Lochbihler proves correct [17]. Furthermore, Lochbihler shows that the Java Language Specification (JLS) [9] and Java API define extra communication channels between Java threads than the JMM covers. In his work, Lochbihler, covers these communication channels as well as dynamic memory allocation, thread spawning

and joining, infinite executions, the wait-notify mechanism and interruption. Since that work provides a more complete and concise definition of the JMM properties, we use some of its definitions and formalization over the original definition of the JMM [20] for clarity. Moreover, there is an OpenJDK project in progress aiming to reformulate the base model of the JMM. We believe that any future changes to the JMM, to overcome the problems pointed out by Aspinall and Ševčík, Torlak et al. and Lochbihler, are orthogonal to our work and will not impact its correctness nor its contributions.

2.1 Implementing the JMM without cache coherency

In the x86 Total Store Order (x86-TSO) memory model [24], a memory fence is sufficient to make any writes in the write-buffer and/or registers visible to any subsequent action. However, in the context of non-cache-coherent architectures, a memory fence is not enough. The result of a memory fence in such architectures is observable only on the local node. For the writes to become visible to all nodes, at *release* actions, any writes must be committed to the main memory. To achieve this, the JVM needs to explicitly transfer data from the local node's scratchpad to the main memory. Then, the corresponding *acquire* action also needs to perform explicit data transfers to get the data from the main memory.

To implement the JMM in architectures like Runnemede, the Java Virtual Machine (JVM) needs to explicitly move data across nodes. Unfortunately, moving data across nodes for each remote memory access is prohibiting, due to its overhead. There is a lot of existing work on implementing a JVM over non-cache-coherent machines and distributed computer systems [1, 2, 8, 23, 29–32]. Most implementations are older than the JMM and they are based on the second edition of the Java Language Specification (without the updates introduced by JSR-133). These implementations follow three different approaches, regarding how they access remote data. Aridor et al. [2] and Zigman et al. [32] avoid transferring data by using object proxies; instead of transferring data, the operations on the data are performed on the node having the corresponding object on its local heap-slice. Other implementations [1, 23] use a custom software cache and implement some form of a hardware cache coherence protocol or global directory in software. The rest [8, 29–32] use Software Distributed Shared Memory (SDSM). In this work, we focus on the SDSM and the custom software cache approaches. SDSM and custom software caches have two common properties: (i) to access an object, they need to create a local copy; and (ii) to make writes visible to other processors they need to write-back the data to the main memory and also make sure that any local copies are updated, if needed. We believe that custom software caches scale better than SDSM; hence we focus our study on them. Note, however, that SDSM systems also make use of software caches and thus this work is also applicable to them.

The SDSM approach is the simplest to implement, since the developers can design the JVM as they would do for a shared memory machine with cache coherency. SDSM is responsible to ensure that all nodes have a coherent, according to some coherence protocol, view of the shared data. SDSM systems, however, produce more traffic than needed by the JMM. The JMM is a relaxed memory model, while SDSMs usually implement more strict coherence protocols. The model we propose in this work can help future JVM implementers to choose the more relaxed available coherence protocol for their SDSM based implementation.

The use of custom software caches, on the other hand, enables the JVM developers to improve performance by moving data, only when that is mandatory to comply with the JMM. Unfortunately, the efficient implementation of the custom software cache as well as the data movement mechanisms is a tedious and error prone process. Furthermore, it requires good understanding of the JMM to minimize the data movement while preserving the JMM's proper-

---

[1] Sequential consistency was first defined by Lamport in [15] as "the result of any execution is the same as if the operations of all the processors were executed in some sequential order, and the operations of each individual processor appear in this sequence in the order specified by its program."

ties. We believe that this work demystifies the JMM and the ways it can be implemented using software data caches.

Another software cache design is introduced by Puffitch [25]; it describes a software cache implementation for the Java Optimized Processor (JOP), a custom Java processor for embedded real-time systems. The software cache is a blocking write-through cache. As a result, at any *release* action all data written before it are already written to the main memory. However, they are not guaranteed to be visible by every core. To achieve the latter, the runtime invalidates the local cache at all *acquire* actions. As a result, any following reads will re-fetch the data from the main memory, making the latest writes visible to the executing core.

This design may decrease efficiency in architectures like Runnemede and the Formic-Cube that support asynchronous DMA-like transfers. Under the JMM there is no need for a blocking policy. Waiting for every write to be written-through results in expensive writes not only in distributed memory systems, but also on cache-coherent NUMA architectures, where the remote location may require several hops to be reached. Making writes non blocking usually improves the performance of applications. However, it often also increases the network traffic, since each core can have more than one outstanding data transfers. In memory intensive applications, memory bandwidth usually becomes a bottleneck on shared memory architectures, as having too many outstanding data transfers on the network does not scale well. A design where write-backs happen only when necessary —or, at least, not at every write— can be employed to reduce the number of outstanding data transfers.

Almost always, the design of a software cache (i.e., object caching, block caching, etc.) is heavily connected to the underlying design of the actual memory hierarchy. We aim to abstract over the actual memory architecture as much as possible, while targeting distributed memory or non-cache-coherent memory systems. To do that, we keep a simplified model of a non-cache-coherent memory, where software caches copy remote data to and from a local scratchpad memory. Such a design improves performance by reducing network on chip (NoC) traffic and access latency. We assume three actions that the memory system can take to change the state of a software cache:

- **fetch**: copies remote data to the software cache
- **write-back**: writes back *dirty* data. *Dirty* are any data that have been written in a software cache and not yet written-back.
- **invalidate**: invalidates cached data

We believe these actions are abstract enough to capture the behavior of a wide range of systems, including existing coherence protocols (i.e., MESI, MSI, MOESI). We believe these actions could not be more abstract without hiding the communication or more concrete without supposing a specific memory hierarchy or messaging protocol.

3. The formalization of the JMM

This section presents a summary of the formal definition of the JMM as introduced by Manson [20] and Lochbihler [17] that we use in the rest of this paper, since our memory model builds on the existing JMM formalization. Note that the formal definitions presented in this section have no modifications over the original definitions, introduced be Manson and Lochbihler, except for renaming of variables for clarity. Intuitively, the JMM defines the legal executions of a program P as set A of *actions*, restricting the order in which actions can become visible, or *committed* during the execution. In the following definitions, unless explicitly specified otherwise, when referring to actions x and y, we mean $\forall x, y \in A$.

Execution: The JMM defines an execution E as a tuple

$$E = \langle P, A, \leq_{po}, \leq_{so}, W, V, \leq_{sw}, \leq_{hb} \rangle$$

where the program P is a set of instructions; A is a set of actions; the program order $\leq_{po}$ is a relation on A defining the order of actions in A within each thread; the synchronization order $\leq_{so}$ is a relation on A defining a global ordering among all synchronization actions in A; the function W on A returns the write action seen by every read action in A; the function V on A returns the value written by every write action in A; the synchronizes-with order $\leq_{sw}$ is a relation on A defining which actions in A synchronize; and the happens-before order $\leq_{hb}$ is a relation on A that defines a partial order among actions in A.

Variable: According to the JMM [21, §4.1] a variable can be: a static variable of a loaded class, a field of an allocated object, or an element of an allocated array. In general, a variable is a memory location in the Java heap. Variables can be references to objects or primitive types. As a result, their size depends on the JVM implementation and the underlying system.

Actions: The JMM abstracts thread operations as actions [20, §5.1]. An action is a tuple $\langle t, k, v, u \rangle$, where t is the thread performing the action; k is the kind of action; v is the (runtime) variable, monitor, or thread, involved in the action; and u is a unique, among the actions, identifier.

We use similar abbreviations to [16, §1.1] to describe all possible kinds of actions:

- R for read, W for write, and In for initialization of a heap-based variable
- Vr for read and Vw for write of a volatile variable
- L for the lock and U for the unlock of a monitor
- S for the start and Fi for the end of a thread
- Ir for the interruption of a thread and Ird for detecting such an interruption by another thread
- Sp for spawning (`Thread.start()`) and J for joining a thread or detecting that it terminated
- E for external actions, i.e., I/O operations

Synchronization Actions: Any actions with kind In, Ir, Ird, Vr, Vw, L, U, S, Fi, Sp, or J are *synchronization actions*, which form the only communication mechanism between threads. Lochbihler shows that there are more *synchronization actions*, or "covert communication channels" in [17, §2.2]. The `java.util.concurrent` library, also introduces some more that we chose to omit in this work for the sake of readability. We use $x \in SA(A)$ to show that x is a synchronization action in A:

$$SA(A) = \{x \in A : x.k \in \{In, Ir, Ird, Vr, Vw, L, U, S, Fi, Sp, J\}\}$$

Program Order: The partial order $\leq_{po}$ among actions A of an execution that defines a total order over all the actions executed by any single thread t is a *program order*. We use $x \leq_{po} y$ to show that x comes before y according to the program order within a thread. Every pair of actions executed by a single thread t are ordered by the program order:

$$((x \neq y) \wedge (x.t = y.t)) \Leftrightarrow ((x \leq_{po} y) \vee (y \leq_{po} x))$$

Synchronization Order: A total order over all the synchronization actions of a program execution. Note that the JMM considers only synchronization orders consistent with the program order to preserve intra-thread semantics. We use $x \leq_{so} y$ to show that x comes before y according to the synchronization order. Every pair of synchronization actions are ordered by synchronization order.

$$x.k, y.k \in \mathrm{SA}(A) \Leftrightarrow \big((x \leq_{so} y) \vee (y \leq_{so} x)\big)$$

Synchronizes-With: We use $x \leq_{sw} y$ to show that x synchronizes-with y. Note that $x \leq_{sw} y \Rightarrow x \leq_{so} y$. An action x synchronizes-with an action y, written $x \leq_{sw} y$, when:

- x is the initialization of variable v and y is the first action of any thread: $\big((x.k = In) \wedge (y.k = S)\big)$

- y is a subsequent read of the volatile variable written by x: $(x.k = Vw) \wedge (y.k = Vr) \wedge (x \leq_{so} y)$

- y is a subsequent lock of the monitor that x unlocked: $(x.k = U) \wedge (y.k = L) \wedge (x.v = y.v) \wedge (x \leq_{so} y)$

- y is the start action of thread t and x is the spawn of t: $(x.k = Sp) \wedge (y.k = S) \wedge (x.v = y.t)$

- y is a call to `Thread.join()` or `Thread.isAlive()` and x is the finish action of this thread: $(x.k = Fi) \wedge (y.k = J) \wedge (x.t = y.v)$

- y is an action detecting if a thread has been interrupted and x is an interrupt to that thread: $(x.k = Ir) \wedge (y.k = Ird) \wedge (x.v = y.v)$

- y is the implicit read of a reference to the object being finalized and x is the end of the constructor of this object.

In the synchronizes-with examples above, when comparing the variable v of one action with the thread t of the other (i.e., $x.t = y.v$) means that y acts on thread $x.t$. The x action is a *release* action and y is an *acquire* action. A *release* action must make all writes, visible to the executing thread, visible to the actions following (according to any of the orders defined till now) the *acquire* action.

Happens-Before Order: The happens-before notion is the one introduced by Lamport in [14]. In the context of the JMM this is the transitive closure of the program order and the synchronizes-with order. We use $x \leq_{hb} y$ to show that x happens-before y.

Write-seen Function: The write-seen function W for every read action r returns the write action seen by r. As a result, $W(r).v = r.v$.

Value-written Function: The value-written function V returns the value written for every write action w; every read r reads the value $V\big(W(r)\big)$.

Conflicting Accesses: If one of two accesses to the same variable is a write then these two accesses are *conflicting*.

Data-Race: A data-race occurs when two conflicting accesses may happen in parallel. That is, they are not ordered by happens-before.

Correctly Synchronized or Data-Race-Free Program: A program is correctly synchronized or DRF if and only if all sequentially consistent executions are free of data-races.

Well-Formed Executions: The JMM considers only well formed executions. According to the JMM, an execution

$$E = \langle P, A, \leq_{po}, \leq_{so}, W, V, \leq_{sw}, \leq_{hb} \rangle$$

is well-formed under the following conditions (refer to [20, §5.3] for a more detailed description):

WF-1: Each read of a variable v sees a write to v:

$$\forall x \in A : (x.k = R) \Rightarrow \exists y \in A : \big(W(r) = y\big)$$

WF-2: All reads and writes of volatile variables are volatile actions:

$$\forall x \in A : x.k \in \{ Vw, Vr \} \Rightarrow$$
$$\nexists y \in A : (y.k \in \{R, W\}) \wedge (x.v = y.v)$$

WF-3: The number of synchronization actions preceding another synchronization action y is finite:

$$\forall y \in \mathrm{SA}(A) : \#\{x \in \mathrm{SA}(A) : x \leq_{so} y\} < \infty$$

WF-4: Synchronization order is consistent with program order:

$$\forall x, y, z \in A : \big((x.t = z.t) \wedge (x \leq_{so} y \leq_{so} z)\big) \Rightarrow (x \leq_{po} z)$$

WF-5: Lock operations are consistent with mutual exclusion. The number of lock actions performed by any thread t' before, according to the synchronization order, the lock action l performed by thread t on the monitor m must be equal to the number of unlock actions performed by thread t' before l on the monitor m:

$$\forall x \in A : \forall t \in T : (x.k = L) \wedge (x.t \neq t) \Rightarrow$$
$$\#\{y \in A : (y.t = t) \wedge (y.k = L) \wedge$$
$$(y.v = x.v) \wedge (y \leq_{so} x)\} =$$
$$\#\{z \in A : (z.t = t) \wedge (z.k = U) \wedge (z.v = x.v) \wedge (y \leq_{so} x)\}$$

where T is the set of all the execution threads:
$$T = \{t : (\exists x \in A : t = x.t)\}$$

WF-6: The execution obeys intra-thread consistency.

WF-7: The execution obeys synchronization-order consistency:

$$\forall r \in A : (r.k = Vr) \Rightarrow$$
$$\Big(\neg\big(r \leq_{so} W(r)\big) \wedge \nexists w' \in A : (w'.k = Vw) \wedge$$
$$(w'.v = r.v) \wedge \big(W(r) \leq_{so} w' \leq_{so} r\big)\Big)$$

WF-8: The execution obeys happens-before consistency:

$$\forall r \in A : \Big(\neg\big(r \leq_{hb} W(r)\big) \wedge \nexists w' \in A : (w'.v = r.v) \wedge$$
$$\big(W(r) \leq_{hb} w' \leq_{hb} r\big)\Big)$$

Lochbihler in [17, §2.4.3] additionally requires that:

WF-9: Every thread's start action happens-before its other actions except for initialization actions:

$$\forall x, y, z \in A : \big((z.k \notin \{S, I\}) \wedge (x.k = I) \wedge$$
$$(y.k = S)\big) \Rightarrow (x \leq_{hb} y \leq_{hb} z)$$

Intuitively, an execution of a Java program can be visualized as a graph, where the actions are nodes connected by synchronizes-with and program order edges, as in Figure 1. An action x happens-before an action y if and only if there is a path in the graph that connects x and y. Figure 1 visualizes program order edges using solid arrows and synchronizes-with edges using dashed arrows. As implied by the program order, actions in the same row are executed by a single thread. To maintain the JMM properties, any code optimization must preserve all the synchronizes-with edges, the happens-before edges and the *intra-thread* consistency of the program.

4. The Distributed Model

This section extends the formalization of the JMM to present the Java Distributed Memory Model (JDMM). We follow a similar approach to the x86 Total Store Order definition [24]. We first define an abstract machine model and then use it to define well-formed executions for the JDMM.

4.1 The JDMM's Abstract Machine Memory Model

As stated in Section 1, larger numbers of cores lead processor designers towards using non coherent memory. This approach sim-

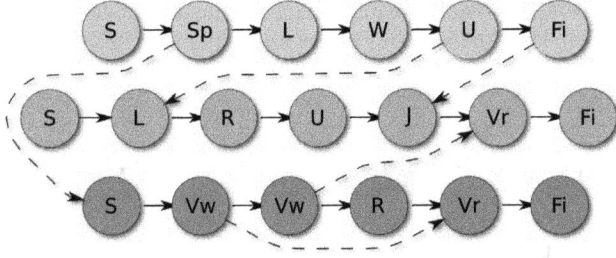

Figure 1. Actions ordering visualization

plifies the processor's design and verification, and improves performance and energy footprint. On the other hand, it renders the application responsible for keeping the memory consistent. With the latter being a tedious and error prone process; especially in hierarchical architectures, featuring multiple levels of scratchpad memories, like SCC, Runnemede and the Formic-Cube.

In our abstract machine memory model we assume a single level of scratchpad memories for simplicity. Although simpler, this abstract machine model maintains the same properties as a machine with multiple levels of scratchpad memories regarding consistency. Multiple levels of scratchpad memories are mainly used to improve performance with reasonable cost. The low level scratchpad memories are faster and more expensive per byte while the higher level ones are slower and the cost per byte is lower. Note that we chose to omit hardware data caches from our abstract machine memory model. Hardware caches in non coherent architectures are usually software managed. As a result, we can treat them like software data caches. In the rest of this paper when we refer to caches we mean both hardware and software data caches.

Figure 2 shows an example abstract machine. On the left are several computation blocks with four hardware threads in each of them. Each computation block connects directly to its local scratchpad memory. We slice the scratchpad memory into a local and a global slice. In this model, each local slice connects with every other global slice in the system, but not with any local slice. The connections are bi-directional: a core can copy data from a remote global slice to the local cache to improve performance; after finishing the job it can transfer back the new data.

In this abstract machine the state of the memory, marked as a light gray rectangle with dashed surrounding, is driven by the computation units. The only way to modify the state of the abstract machine's memory is by committing fetch, write-back and invalidate actions as described in Section 2.1.

Although the local slice is used for caching of remote objects to increase efficiency and reduce data-transfers, it can also be used for all the local data (i.e., Java stacks). Overall, the Java Heap is split and stored across all global slices, so that a total —virtual— Java Heap consists of all the contents of all global slices, similarly to Partitioned Global Address Space (PGAS) models.

4.2 The Java Distributed Memory Model

To simplify the definition of the JDMM and the reasoning about its correctness, we assume that all accesses to heap-based locations go through the cache, even when they reside in the local heap-slice. This is a safe assumption, since not caching these locations does not break our model (see Section 5). As in hardware caches, when accessing a variable, it is either present in the cache or not cached. In the first case the cache immediately returns cached data, whereas in the second it initiates a data transfer from a remote memory to the cache, before it can reply with the requested value.

Our JDMM definition and formalization extends the definition of the JMM discussed in Section 3. We extend the notion of an

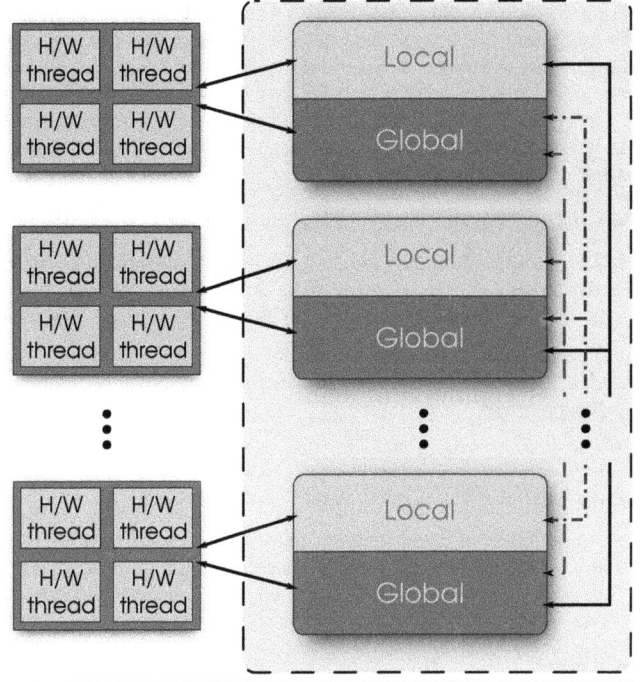

Figure 2. The abstract machine

action with additional kinds that capture the extra functionality of the abstract machine described in Section 4.1, and extend the definition of an execution with additional constructs that capture relations between these additional actions.

In the rest of this Section we refer to hardware threads as *cores* and to Java threads as *threads*. Furthermore, unless explicitly specified otherwise, we use variable t for threads, v for variables, r for (volatile) read actions, w for (volatile) write actions, i for initialization actions, s for thread start actions, f for fetch actions, p for invalidation actions, b for write-back actions, and x, y, z to name actions of any kind.

To define the JDMM we extend the JMM with the following definitions.

Cache Actions: We extend the available action kinds defined in Section 3 by adding the three new action kinds that can change the cache state (Section 2.1):

- F for fetch from heap-based variables,
- B for write-backs of heap-based variables,
- I for invalidations of cached variables.

Actions with kind F or B are also synchronization actions, since they implement a communication channel between threads, so we adapt the definition of the set SA accordingly. We denote the set of all actions in an execution of the JDMM as A_D.

Distributed Execution: A distributed execution E_D is a tuple

$$E_D = \langle P, A_D, \leq_{po}^d, \leq_{so}^d, W, V, Cs, Bf, Ab, Ai, \leq_{sw}^d, \leq_{hb}^d \rangle$$

where the program P is a set of instructions; A_D is a set of actions (including actions of the new kinds); the program order $\leq_{po}^d$ is a relation on A_D defining the order of actions in A_D; the synchronization order $\leq_{so}^d$ is a relation on A_D defining a global ordering among all synchronization actions in A_D; the function W on A_D returns the write action seen by every read action in A_D; the function V on A_D returns the value written by every write action in A_D; the function Cs is a cache-action-seen function; the function Bf is a write-back-fetched function; the function Ab is an action-written-back function; the function Ai is an action-invalidated function; the distributed synchronizes-with order $\leq_{sw}^d$ is a relation on A_D defining which actions in A_D synchronize; and the happens-before order $\leq_{hb}^d$ is a relation on A_D that defines a partial order among actions in A_D.

Functions: We introduce four functions, similar to V and W:

- The *cache-action-seen* function Cs, which for each read r in A_D, gives $Cs(r)$, the fetch or write action, that cached $r.v$, seen by r. Note that $Cs(r) \leq_{po}^d r$ and $Cs(r).k \in \{W, F\}$.

- The *write-back-fetched* function Bf, which for each fetch f in A_D, gives $Bf(f)$, the write-back action whose data f fetches. Note that $Bf(f) \leq_{sw}^d f$.

- The *action-written-back* function Ab, which for each write-back b in A_D, gives $Ab(b)$, the action that b writes-back. Note that $Ab(b) \leq_{po}^d b$ and $Ab(b).k \in \{In, W, Vw\}$.

- An action-invalidated function Ai, which for each invalidation p in A_D, gives $Ai(p)$, the write or fetch action that cached the data that p invalidates. Note that $Ai(p) \leq_{po}^d p$ and $Ai(p).k \in \{W, F\}$.

Note also that for each function f above, $f(x).v = x.v$ where x is an action in A_D.

Distributed Synchronizes-With: We use $x \leq_{sw}^d y$ to show that x synchronizes-with y in a distributed execution. $\leq_{sw}^d$ is similar to the $\leq_{sw}$ relation defined in Section 3, with two extensions. An action x of A_D synchronizes-with an action y of A_D when:

- x is the write-back of a variable's initialization and y is the first action of any thread: $\big((Ab(x).k = In) \wedge (y.k = S)\big)$

- x is the write-back of a variable and y is a subsequent fetch of that variable:
$\big((x.k = B) \wedge (y.k = F) \wedge (x.v = y.v) \wedge (x \leq_{so}^d y)\big)$

Well-Formed Distributed Execution: JDMM defines well-formed executions similarly to the JMM. The additional properties we present are derived from the abstract machine memory model discussed above. For brevity, in our formal definitions we use A_D instead of $E_D.A_D$ to denote a distributed execution's set of actions. Specifically, a distributed execution E_D is well-formed when:

WF-1 – WF-9: It satisfies conditions **WF-1** through **WF-9** defined in Section 3, for the new definitions of action set A_D, functions W, V, and relations $\leq_{po}^d$, $\leq_{so}^d$, $\leq_{sw}^d$ and $\leq_{hb}^d$ over A_D.

WF-10: Every read is preceded by a write or fetch action, acting on the same variable as the read. As we stated above, in our model all reads of heap-based variables see cached values. Formally:
$\forall r \in A_D :$
$$\Big((W(r) \leq_{po}^d r) \vee \exists f \in A_D : \big((f.v = r.v) \wedge (f \leq_{po}^d r)\big)\Big)$$

WF-11: There is no invalidation, update, or overwrite of a variable's cached value between the action that cached it and the read that sees it. Formally:
$\forall r \in A_D : \nexists x \in A_D :$
$$\Big((x.k \in \{I, F, W\}) \wedge \big(Cs(r) \leq_{po}^d x \leq_{po}^d r\big)\Big)$$

WF-12: Fetch actions are preceded by at least one write-back of the corresponding variable. For a value to be fetched, it must first be written to the main memory. The only way to write to the main memory, by definition, is through a write-back. Formally:
$\forall f \in A_D, \exists b \in A_D : \big(b = Bf(f)\big)$

WF-13: Write-back actions are preceded by at least one write to the corresponding variable. For a variable to be written-back, it must be dirty in some cache; a cached copy becomes dirty only when written. Formally:
$\forall b \in A_D, \exists w \in A_D : \big(w = Ab(b)\big)$

WF-14: There are no other writes to the same variable between a write and its write-back. Formally:
$\forall b \in A_D :$
$$\Big(\nexists w` \in A_D : \big((w'.v = b.v) \wedge (Ab(b) \leq_{po}^d w' \leq_{po}^d b)\big)\Big)$$

WF-15: Only cached variables are invalidated. Invalid cached data cannot be invalidated. Formally:
$\forall p \in A_D : \nexists p' \in A_D :$
$$\Big(\big(Ai(p) = Ai(p')\big) \wedge \big(Ai(p) \leq_{po}^d p' \leq_{po}^d p\big)\Big)$$

WF-16: Reads that see writes performed by other threads are preceded by a fetch action that fetches the write-back of the corresponding write and there is no other write-back of the corresponding variable happening between the write-back and the fetch. Since all writes go through the cache, for a write to be seen by a read on a different thread, there must exist a write-back action and a subsequent fetch action for it. Formally:
$\forall r \in A_D : \big(W(r).t \neq r.t\big) \Rightarrow \exists b, f \in A_D :$
$$\Big(\big(Ab(b) = W(r)\big) \wedge \big(Bf(f) = b\big) \wedge$$
$$\big(W(r) \leq_{po}^d b \leq_{sw}^d f \leq_{po}^d r\big) \wedge$$
$$\big(\nexists b' : (b'.v = b.v) \wedge (b \leq_{hb} b' \leq_{hb} r)\big)\Big)$$

WF-17: Volatile writes are immediately written back. Allowing other actions between a volatile write and its write-back may result in other threads observing these actions as if they were executed before the volatile write. This is similar to moving these actions before the volatile write, which is an invalid reordering according to the JMM. Formally:
$\forall w \in A_D : (w.k = Vw) \Rightarrow \exists b \in A_D :$
$$\big((w \leq_{po}^d b) \wedge (w.v = b.v) \wedge \nexists x \in A_D : (w \leq_{po}^d x \leq_{po}^d b)\big)$$

WF-18: A fetch of the corresponding variable happens immediately before each volatile read. Allowing other actions between a volatile read and its fetch may result in other threads observing these actions as if they were executed after the volatile read. This is similar to moving these actions after the volatile read, which is an invalid reordering according to the JMM. Formally:
$\forall r \in A_D : (r.k = Vr) \Rightarrow \exists f \in A_D :$
$$\Big((f \leq_{po}^d r) \wedge \big(f = Cs(r)\big) \wedge \nexists x \in A_D : (f \leq_{po}^d x \leq_{po}^d r)\Big)$$

WF-19: Initializations are immediately written-back and their write-backs are completed before the start of any thread.

WF-20: The happens-before order between two writes is consistent with the happens-before order of their write-backs. If, for two writes w and w', w happens-before w', then the corresponding write-backs, b for w and b' for w', must also be ordered, so that $b \leq_{hb} b'$ and vice versa. Formally:
$\forall b, b' \in A_D : \big(Ab(b) \leq_{hb} Ab(b')\big) \Leftrightarrow \big(b \leq_{hb} b'\big)$

4.3 Short discussion

As described in [20, §5.4], the JMM, validates well-formed executions by *committing* actions from A. If all actions can be committed then the execution is valid. The use of caches and the introduction of the new actions does not change the validation process. As a result, we do not introduce any extensions to the causality requirements for executions.

Note that in well-formedness constraints **WF-17** and **WF-18**, we chose not to embed the write-back and fetch actions in the corresponding synchronization actions. This way, the model remains simple and as non intrusive as possible to the JMM. However, the JDMM requires that the write-backs of volatile writes and the fetches of volatile reads are executed immediately after and before the corresponding volatile action, respectively.

In our memory model we are reasoning about cached data invalidations, while there is no obvious use of them in the JMM. In an ideal machine with infinite caches, invalidations would be redundant. However, in real machines the cache size is limited. At some point the cache becomes full and to fetch a variable it is obligatory to invalidate another cached variable. If invalidations were left out of the memory model we would not be able to reason about its correctness, especially when such evictions and invalidations are not implemented in hardware, but are rather part of the JVM.

We have omitted final fields from the formalization. In that, we follow the JMM presentation that does not include final fields in the core model. The JMM extensions for final fields apply to the JDMM without requiring any additional modification.

Up to this point we did not mention the case where a thread needs to fetch a variable which is already cached and dirty. A thread needs to fetch a variable to read it, if it is not cached (see condition **WF-2**). If a variable is dirty then it is already cached, so this is not the case. A thread also needs to fetch a volatile variable for every volatile read (see condition **WF-18**). However, volatile variables are only written through volatile writes, which immediately write-back the corresponding variable (see condition **WF-17**). As a result, a volatile variable cannot be observed as dirty by any action. Finally, when a write happens-before a read that sees the value written from a different thread ($W(r) \leq_{hb} r$ and $W(r).t \neq r.t$), the reading thread might need to re-fetch the variable v, if already cached. In this case, if $r.v$ is dirty, then there exists a write w' to it from the same thread ($w'.t = r.t$) that happens-before r. Under DRF programs w' and $W(r)$ are ordered through happens-before and since t needs to re-fetch $r.v$ then w' happens-before $W(r)$ and $V(w')$ can be dropped. For non-DRF programs, the JMM guarantees only no *out-of-thin-air* values; there is no guarantee that all writes will be seen by some read, so dropping dirty data is acceptable. As a result, we can unconditionally fetch variables when needed and overwrite any cached data.

5. Extensions and Optimization

This section discusses extensions to the memory model to support garbage collection, context switching and thread migration. Furthermore, we argue that not caching data residing into the local heap-slice does not impact the correctness of the JVM, allowing implementers to reduce the access latency to the local-heap slice.

5.1 Garbage Collection

The use of caches introduces some extra overhead to copying garbage collectors. The JMM requires that the relocation of a variable or its reuse is not observable by the semantics. To achieve this, any relocated and garbage collected addresses must be invalidated. If a cache does not invalidate these objects reads might see *out-of-thin-air* values. The following example demonstrates such a case.

Class Definition	Thread *T1*	Thread *T2*
1 class A {	// ...	// ...
2 public int v;	a = new A(1);	e = a.v;
3 A(int i) { v = i; }	a = null;	f = b.v;
4 }	b = new A(4);	

e == f == 1 is unacceptable

To simplify our reasoning we assume that the compiler does not optimize the code. The possible values of a and b are a valid memory address or null. As a result, one would expect this program to throw a NullPointerException or have one of the following states at the end of the run (e=1, f=4), (e=1, f=0) and (e=0, f=0). The zero values can be observed if the constructor's store does not commit before the corresponding access from *T2*. Note that this is acceptable since this is not a DRF program and according to the JMM there is no ordering between the *construction* of an object and its accesses. However, e == f == 1 is not acceptable. f can only take values zero and four. Zero is the default value of b.v while four is the value that b.v gets from the constructor. That said, any other value (i.e., one) is *out-of-thin-air*.

If a garbage collection happens after executing *T1*'s line 3 (e.g., by a reference counting garbage collector), the memory address previously referenced by a can be garbage collected and reused in *T1*'s line 4. If this address is cached in *T2*'s cache, which means that e = a.v in *T2* happened before the garbage collection and the cache is not invalidated, then the execution of f = b.v will hit the cache and read a bogus value, leftover from a. As a result, f is assigned the value one.

5.2 Context switching and thread migration

Context switching and thread migration can also affect an execution and the writes seen by reads. Context switching is the process where a thread stops running to allow another thread to run on the same core. On the other hand, thread migration occurs when a thread is moved to another core to continue its execution. To the best of our knowledge, in all available systems caches are shared between the different threads of an application. As a result, we expect JVM implementers to also allow their caches to be shared between Java threads of the same application. However, a problem may arise by context switching when a thread stops executing right after fetching a variable and continues its execution right after another thread has invalidated this variable; or under thread migration, when the thread continues its execution on a *different* core, whose cache does not contain that variable. In these cases an immediate read of this variable may return an *out-of-thin-air* value for non cache coherent systems. In cache coherent shared memory systems this issue is implicitly resolved by producing a cache miss and fetching the variable. We present a solution to this issue below, which addresses an additional issue caused by thread migration.

A context switch can cause a thread to see the data of another thread. The JMM allows threads to see writes performed by other threads even when they are not ordered by happens-before. The only case where this can cause a problem, is when a thread t' changes the write that a different thread t would otherwise observe. There are three ways to cause this; a) t' writes the variable in question (e.g., v), and t sees this write; b) t' invalidates v and t fetches it from the main memory, where its value is different from the old cached value; c) t' fetches v from the main memory, where again its value is different from the old cached value. Note that all three scenarios are only possible under non-DRF programs. In the first scenario, t sees the value written by t'. The corresponding write in t' and read in t are conflicting accesses. If the data-race does not occur, then t' happens-before t and t sees t' write anyway (assuming there are no other threads running). The second and third scenarios, produce the same behavior, they both update the cached value. If t sees a different value from the one it would see if there was no context switch, then there is a write w that does not happen-before the read r performed by t. This implies a data race between w and r. Under non-DRF programs the only guarantee that should hold, is the *out-of-thin-air* guarantee. Since, under well formed executions, initialization actions happen-before the first action of any thread context switching cannot result in *out-of-thin-air* values.

Similarly for thread migration, there are three scenarios that can cause the behavior described above; a) t accesses a dirty cached variable at its *new* core; b) t does not find the variable cached and fetches it from the main memory, with a different value from the one cached at its *old* core; c) t finds another value cached to its *new* core than the one cached at its *old* one. In the first scenario, t sees the value written by another thread t'. This is exactly the same scenario discussed above for context switching. The second scenario again produces the same behavior with scenarios b and c discussed above for context switching. The third scenario, however, is different. In the case of thread migration, t can see an older value than the one cached at its *old* core. This may result in executions inconsistent to the happens-before order and is possible under both DRF and non-DRF programs. As a result, migrating threads, to preserve the happens-before order, need to re-fetch all variables before their first access, after the migration. To express this formally we need to introduce a new (synthetic) action kind, M, that denotes the migration of a thread. Note that $M.v$ is the migrating thread. We extend the well-formedness conditions to allow migration as follows.

WFE-1: There is a corresponding fetch action between thread migration and every read action. Formally:

$$\forall m, r \in A_D : \big((m.k = M) \wedge (m \leq_{po}^d r) \big) \Rightarrow$$
$$\big(\exists f \in A_D : (m \leq_{po}^d f \leq_{po}^d r) \big)$$

WFE-2: Additionally, to make sure the fetched value is the latest according to the happens-before order, any dirty data on the *old* core need to be written-back. Formally:

$$\forall m, w \in A : \Big((m.k = M) \wedge \big(w \leq_{po} B(w) \leq_{po} m \big) \Big)$$

Given these extensions of the JDMM, our model allows context switching without violating the JMM. Context switching enables multiple threads to share the same core and the same cache. As a result, a cache can be shared by multiple cores having the same access time to it. This way, memory can be better utilized, by reducing the number of variable replicas across the system.

5.3 No Local Caching Optimization

In Section 4.2, we assume that all accesses to heap-based locations go through the cache. However, caching data for the local heap-slice increases the memory traffic of the system and slows down the application. We argue that JMM implementers can avoid data caching for data that reside in a core's local heap-slice. For writes, it is straightforward to show that not using a cache will have the same behavior. Assume a write-through and blocking cache, under this configuration, writes are immediately written to the local heap-slice as they would do if they were not cached. Regarding reads, not caching data from the local-heap slice is identical to fetching the data before every read. This behavior is similar to having a tiny cache that results in the invalidation of the cached data at every fetch. As a result, not caching data from the local heap-slice does not impact the JMM's properties and JVM implementers could follow this approach when more efficient.

It is important to note that the above reasoning is valid even if we choose not to cache data residing in a remote heap-slice. This enables the JVM implementer to have a hybrid system where some cores use data caches while others do not. Such a hybrid JVM would be a perfect fit for heterogeneous architectures where some cores have access to coherent hardware caches while others do not.

6. Proof of adherence to the JMM

We sketch a proof of equivalence to show that the JDMM still adheres to the JMM, while allowing a more detailed modeling of non cache coherent or distributed memory implementations. The proof consists of a construction of a shared memory well-formed execution from a given distributed memory well-formed execution.

Assume the well-formed JDMM execution

$$E_D = \langle P, A_D, \leq_{po}^d, \leq_{so}^d, W_D, V_D, \text{Cs}, \text{Bf}, \text{Ab}, \text{Ai}, \leq_{sw}^d, \leq_{hb}^d \rangle$$

such that $\text{WF}_D(E_D)$. We define the set A to be the set of actions in A_D excluding all actions x with kind F, B, or I:

$$A = \{x \in A_D : x.k \notin \{F, B, I\}\}$$

In the same fashion, we define the relations $\leq_{po}, \leq_{so}, \leq_{sw}$ and $\leq_{hb}$ to be the projections of $\leq_{po}^d, \leq_{so}^d, \leq_{sw}^d$ and $\leq_{hb}^d$, respectively, that only refer to actions in A. To prove the adherence of JDMM to the JMM, we construct a JMM execution

$$E = \langle P, A, \leq_{po}, \leq_{so}, W, V, \leq_{sw}, \leq_{hb}' \rangle$$

where $\leq_{hb}'$ is the transitive closure of $\leq_{po}$ and $\leq_{sw}$ and show that $\leq_{hb}' \subseteq \leq_{hb}$ and $\text{WF}(E)$.

To do that, it suffices to show (i) the well-formedness conditions **WF-1 – WF-9** as defined in Section 3, and also show that (ii) the $\leq_{hb}$ relation resulting from the projection of $\leq_{hb}^d$ to A is the transitive closure of the corresponding relations $\leq_{po}$ and $\leq_{sw}$. From assumption $\text{WF}_D(E_D)$ we have that conditions **WF-1 – WF-9** hold for A_D, $\leq_{po}^d$, $\leq_{so}^d$, W_D, V_D, $\leq_{sw}^d$ and $\leq_{hb}^d$. As no constraints refer to actions with kinds F, B or I, functions W and V are the same as W_D and V_D for all actions in A, and relations $\leq_{po}^d \leq_{so}^d$ and $\leq_{sw}^d$ are supersets of $\leq_{po}, \leq_{so}$ and $\leq_{sw}$, so none of the actions removed from A_D to A cause any of the conditions **WF-1 – WF-9** to be broken. Less intuitively, the happens-before relation $\leq_{hb}'$ will not always be equal to the relation $\leq_{hb}'$ resulting from the projection of $\leq_{hb}^d$ over A. The reason is that $\leq_{hb}^d$ is the transitive closure of $\leq_{sw}^d$, which includes all synchronization edges involving fetch and write-back actions. The projection to A will remove these actions but will not remove all transitive edges added to $\leq_{hb}^d$ among unrelated actions, because of the additional $\leq_{sw}^d$ edges. Conversely, the relation $\leq_{hb}'$ is included in $\leq_{hb}$, as it only contains the transitive closure of $\leq_{po}$ and $\leq_{sw}$, which are included in $\leq_{po}^d$ and $\leq_{sw}^d$. Thus, the JDMM may incur additional happens-before relations than are observable in the JMM, because memory-to-memory communication is explicit in JDMM, whereas JMM abstracts it away, as it is implemented by the hardware in all cache-coherent shared-memory systems.

6.1 Code optimization: Reordering

Manson et al. have proved that reordering two independent statements, when it does not affect the happens-before relation of any other actions, is legal under the JMM [20, §6.2.1]. Specifically, [20, THEOREM 1] shows that two adjacent statements s_x and s_y, where x and y are the corresponding actions of the statements, can be reordered as long as:

1. their reordering does not eliminate any transitive happens-before edges in any valid execution

2. they are not conflicting accesses

3. they are not both synchronization or external actions

4. their reordering does not move an action before an infinite loop

5. their reordering preserves the intra-thread consistency

We argue that the reorderings allowed by [20, THEOREM 1] under the JMM are the same as the ones allowed under JDMM. In JDMM, there are four newly introduced (synthetic) actions, fetch, write-back, invalidate and migrate. These actions do not map to statements and may appear between the corresponding actions of adjacent statements. As a result, the reordering of two independent statements might also require the reordering of some synthetic actions. Consider the case $x \leq_{po} f \leq_{po} r$, where x and r are independent and r sees the value fetched by f. If s_x and s_r are reordered, so that $r \leq_{po} x \leq_{po} f$, then $f \leq_{hb} r$ is eliminated and r may see another value. Disallowing such reorderings would make our model more strict than the JMM. To avoid this, we relax the definition of allowed reorderings to also allow change in the happens-before relation for any cache (synthetic) actions between the actions of the reordered statements to get moved, except those referring to the same variable as one of the two actions. For the latter, we need to preserve the program order.

In the special case of a migration happening between the two adjacent statements, $x \leq_{po} m \leq_{po} y$, we need to satisfy Equations **WFE-1** and **WFE-2**. Additionally, changing the order of m can affect the program's performance. As a result, we cannot enforce a single ordering for every case. In the case where m is moved before both statements, any write-backs happening before m, must preserve this ordering, except the write-back of x (if any) and if x is a read action, then we also need to add a fetch action f, such that $m \leq_{po} f \leq_{po} x$. In the case where m is moved after both statements, any fetches happening after m, must preserve this ordering, except the fetch of y (if any) and if y is a write, it must be written-back before m. Finally, in the case where m is kept between y and x; if x is a read, a fetch f for $x.v$ needs to be added so that $m \leq_{po} f \leq_{po} x$; if x is a write that gets written-back before m, its write-back must be moved after x.

Our model allows the same reorderings as the JMM, as long as some synthetic actions are also reordered as described above.

6.2 The DRF guarantee

Similarly, we show that our model guarantees sequential consistency to DRF programs. J. Manson has already proved that, under DRF programs, reads can only see writes that happen-before them and that when each read sees a write that happens-before it, then the execution's behavior is sequentially consistent [20, §6.2.2].

Given a JDMM well-formed execution, conditions **WF-20**, **WFE-1**, and **WFE-2** hold. From these it follows that all reads see writes that happen-before them. As a result, according to [20, THEOREM 3], the executions of DRF programs are guaranteed to be sequentially consistent.

7. Case Study

In this section we use our memory model to verify the correctness of existing JVMs regarding their compliance to the JMM. To select the JVMs to examine, we went through all publications citing [21], [22] or [20], looking for JVM implementations on non memory coherent architectures that comply with the JMM. We also searched for open-source JVMs targeting non coherent architectures. We narrowed our search only to open-source projects, since proprietary JVMs are not accompanied with enough details to extract how they implement the JMM. Surprisingly we found only one JVM claiming that it fully complies with the JMM (as defined by JSR-133 in the current Java Language Specification) and targets non-cache-coherent architectures.

Hera-JVM [23] targets the IBM's Cell B.E. processor. Cell B.E. is a heterogeneous multiprocessor featuring one POWER Processing Unit (PPU) and eight Synergistic Processing Units (SPUs). The cores can access each other's memory through DMA transfers and there is no cache coherency. Hera-JVM uses a software cache for heap-based variables, which caches whole objects or array blocks of 1KB. In the case of a cache miss, the JVM fetches a whole object or a 1KB block of an array. To do that, Hera-JVM initiates a DMA transfer to fetch the data and blocks the execution of the Java thread until the DMA is complete. The cache uses a write through policy: Whenever a thread writes to a cached ad-

dress, Hera-JVM initiates a non-blocking DMA, copying the new data to the main memory. To conform to the JMM, a Java thread blocks until all DMAs complete before releasing a lock, writing to a volatile variable, context switching or migrating to another core. Furthermore, Hera-JVM purges (invalidates) the caches before every monitor-enter (acquire lock) or volatile read, causing any future reads to fetch the data from the main memory.

Examining the text in [23] we were able to verify that most of the JDMM constraints are satisfied by Hera-JVM. Hera-JVM appears to handle caches properly as far as it concerns context switching, synchronized blocks and volatile variables. We were unable, however, to verify that thread migration is properly handled. Specifically, Hera-JVM claims that it writes-back all dirty data before a thread migrates off an SPE core, but does not explicitly state that the cache is invalidated. Section 5.2 describes a scenario where this is not enough and may result in executions that are not consistent to the happens-before order. In short, consider a thread that migrates to another core and attempts to read a variable, which happens to be already cached on that core.

To verify that Hera-JVM fully adheres to the JMM we had to examine its source code and contact the authors. We found that the source code does not explicitly invalidate the cache. Note, however, that in Hera-JVM the context switching and the thread migration mechanisms are written in Java and rely on synchronized methods. This implicitly satisfies **WFE-1** and **WFE-2**, since the runtime synchronized method call for the context switch or thread migration will invalidate the cache contents. Note here that Hera-JVM also invalidates the caches for context switches, that as we show in Section 5.2 is not mandatory and may result in additional energy and performance overheads.

8. Conclusions

This paper extends the Java Memory Model by modeling cache and memory transfers, to target emerging non-cache-coherent or distributed memory multicore architectures. To the best of our knowledge JDMM is the first formalization of the JMM for non-cache-coherent and distributed memories. JDMM is a pure extension of the JMM, which means that all properties of the JMM are also properties of JDMM's and all valid JMM reorderings are also valid JDMM reorderings. JDMM aims to help future JVM developers better understand when it is mandatory to transfer data across nodes and verify that their implementation is JMM compatible. Using JDMM, we were able to verify that Hera-JVM, a JVM implementation for a distributed memory architecture, adheres to the JMM. We were also able to detect a redundant invalidation of the software cache in the case of context switching, which could potentially have a negative impact on the performance, as well as, the energy consumption of Hera-JVM. This result increases our confidence that JDMM can benefit JVM designers and developers in the future.

Acknowledgments

We would like to thank Prof. Panagiota Fatourou, Prof. Manolis Katevenis, Dr. Vassilis Papaefstathiou and Dr. Spyros Lyberis for their insightful comments and discussion. We would also like to thank the anonymous reviewers for their constructive feedback.

This work was supported by the *GreenVM* project on Energy-Efficient Runtimes for Scalable Multicore Architectures (project #1643), which is being implemented under the *ARISTEIA* Action of the "Operational Programme on Education and Lifelong Learning", co-funded by the European Social Fund (ESF) and Greek National Resources.

References

[1] G. Antoniu, L. Bougé, P. J. Hatcher, M. MacBeth, K. McGuigan, and R. Namyst. The Hyperion system: Compiling multithreaded Java bytecode for distributed execution. *Parallel Computing*, 27(10):1279–1297, 2001.

[2] Y. Aridor, M. Factor, and A. Teperman. cJVM: A Single System Image of a JVM on a Cluster. In *Proceedings of the 1999 International Conference on Parallel Processing*, ICPP, pages 4–11. IEEE Computer Society, 1999.

[3] D. Aspinall and J. Ševčík. Java Memory Model Examples: Good, Bad and Ugly. In *1st International Workshop on Verification and Analysis of Multi-threaded Java-like Programs*, VAMP, 2007.

[4] D. Aspinall and J. Ševčík. Formalising Java's Data Race Free Guarantee. In *Proceedings of the 20th International Conference on Theorem Proving in Higher Order Logics*, TPHOLs, pages 22–37. Springer Berlin Heidelberg, 2007.

[5] N. P. Carter, A. Agrawal, S. Borkar, R. Cledat, H. David, D. Dunning, J. B. Fryman, I. Ganev, R. A. Golliver, R. C. Knauerhase, R. Lethin, B. Meister, A. K. Mishra, W. R. Pinfold, J. Teller, J. Torrellas, N. Vasilache, G. Venkatesh, and J. Xu. Runnemede: An architecture for Ubiquitous High-Performance Computing. In *Proceedings of the 19th IEEE International Symposium on High Performance Computer Architecture*, HPCA, pages 198–209. IEEE Computer Society, 2013.

[6] P. Cenciarelli, A. Knapp, and E. Sibilio. The Java Memory Model: Operationally, Denotationally, Axiomatically. In *Proceedings of the 16th European Symposium on Programming*, ESOP, pages 331–346. Springer Berlin Heidelberg, 2007.

[7] B. Choi, R. Komuravelli, H. Sung, R. Smolinski, N. Honarmand, S. V. Adve, V. S. Adve, N. P. Carter, and C.-T. Chou. DeNovo: Rethinking the Memory Hierarchy for Disciplined Parallelism. In *Proceedings of the 12th International Conference on Parallel Architectures and Compilation Techniques*, PACT, pages 155–166, 2011.

[8] M. Factor, A. Schuster, and K. Shagin. JavaSplit: a runtime for execution of monolithic Java programs on heterogenous collections of commodity workstations. In *Proceedings of the International Conference on Cluster Computing*, CLUSTER, pages 110–117, 2003.

[9] J. Gosling, B. Joy, G. Steele, and G. Bracha. *Java(TM) Language Specification, 3rd Edition*. Addison-Wesley Professional, 2005.

[10] J. Howard, S. Dighe, Y. Hoskote, S. Vangal, D. Finan, G. Ruhl, D. Jenkins, H. Wilson, N. Borkar, G. Schrom, F. Pailet, S. Jain, T. Jacob, S. Yada, S. Marella, P. Salihundam, V. Erraguntla, M. Konow, M. Riepen, G. Droege, J. Lindemann, M. Gries, T. Apel, K. Henriss, T. Lund-Larsen, S. Steibl, S. Borkar, V. De, R. Van der Wijngaart, and T. Mattson. A 48-Core IA-32 message-passing processor with DVFS in 45nm CMOS. In *Proceedings of the International Solid-State Circuits Conference*, ISSCC, pages 108–109, 2010.

[11] M. Huisman and G. Petri. The Java Memory Model: a Formal Explanation. In *1st International Workshop on Verification and Analysis of Multi-threaded Java-like Programs*, VAMP, pages 81–96, 2007.

[12] R. Jagadeesan, C. Pitcher, and J. Riely. Generative operational semantics for relaxed memory models. In *Proceedings of the 19th European Symposium on Programming*, ESOP, pages 307–326. Springer, 2010.

[13] S. Kaxiras and G. Keramidas. SARC Coherence: Scaling Directory Cache Coherence in Performance and Power. *Micro, IEEE*, 30(5):54–65, 2010.

[14] L. Lamport. Time, clocks, and the ordering of events in a distributed system. *Commun. ACM*, 21(7):558–565, 1978.

[15] L. Lamport. How to make a multiprocessor computer that correctly executes multiprocess programs. *Computers, IEEE Transactions on*, C-28(9):690–691, 1979.

[16] A. Lochbihler. Java and the Java Memory Model — A Unified, Machine-Checked Formalisation. In *Proceedings of the 21th European Symposium on Programming*, ESOP, pages 497–517. Springer Berlin Heidelberg, 2012.

[17] A. Lochbihler. Making the java memory model safe. *ACM Transactions on Programming Languages and Systems*, 35(4):1–65, 2014.

[18] S. Lyberis. *Myrmics: A Scalable Runtime System for Global Address Spaces*. PhD thesis, 2013.

[19] S. Lyberis, G. Kalokerinos, M. Lygerakis, V. Papaefstathiou, D. Tsaliagkos, M. Katevenis, D. Pnevmatikatos, and D. Nikolopoulos. Formic: Cost-efficient and scalable prototyping of manycore architectures. In *Proceedings of the 20th Annual International Symposium on Field-Programmable Custom Computing Machines*, FCCM, pages 61–64, 2012.

[20] J. Manson. *The Java Memory Model*. PhD thesis, 2004.

[21] J. Manson, W. Pugh, and S. V. Adve. The Java Memory Model. In *Proceedings of the 32nd ACM SIGPLAN-SIGACT Symposium on Principles of Programming Languages*, POPL, pages 378–391, 2005.

[22] J. Manson, W. Pugh, and S. V. Adve. The Java Memory Model, 2005. SPECIAL POPL ISSUE Submission.

[23] R. McIlroy and J. Sventek. Hera-JVM: A Runtime System for Heterogeneous Multi-core Architectures. In *Proceedings of the 25th Annual ACM SIGPLAN Conference on Object-Oriented Programming, Systems, Languages, and Applications*, OOPSLA, pages 205–222, 2010.

[24] S. Owens, S. Sarkar, and P. Sewell. A Better x86 Memory Model: x86-TSO. In *Proceedings of the 22th International Conference on Theorem Proving in Higher Order Logics*, TPHOLs, pages 391–407. Springer Berlin Heidelberg, 2009.

[25] W. Puffitsch. Data Caching, Garbage Collection, and the Java Memory Model. In *Proceedings of the 7th International Workshop on Java Technologies for Real-Time and Embedded Systems*, JTRES, pages 90–99. ACM, 2009.

[26] W. Pugh and J. Manson. Java Memory Model Causality Test Cases, 2004. On http://www.cs.umd.edu/ as ~pugh/java/memoryModel/-CausalityTestCases.html.

[27] J. Ševčík and D. Aspinall. On Validity of Program Transformations in the Java Memory Model. In *Proceedings of the 22nd European Conference on Object-Oriented Programming*, ECOOP, pages 27–51. Springer, 2008.

[28] E. Torlak, M. Vaziri, and J. Dolby. MemSAT: Checking Axiomatic Specifications of Memory Models. In *Proceedings of the ACM SIGPLAN Conference on Programming Language Design and Implementation*, PLDI, pages 341–350. ACM, 2010.

[29] R. Veldema, R. Bhoedjang, and H. Bal. Distributed Shared Memory Management for Java. In *Proceedings of the 6th Annual Conference of the Advanced School for Computing and Imaging*, ASCI, pages 256–264, 1999.

[30] W. Yu and A. Cox. Java/DSM: A platform for heterogeneous computing. *Concurrency: Practice and Experience*, 9:1213–1224, 1997.

[31] W. Zhu, C.-L. Wang, and F. C. M. Lau. JESSICA2: A Distributed Java Virtual Machine with Transparent Thread Migration Support. In *Proceedings of the IEEE International Conference on Cluster Computing*, CLUSTER, pages 381–388. IEEE Computer Society, 2002.

[32] J. N. Zigman and R. Sankaranarayana. Designing a Distributed JVM on a Cluster. In *Proceedings of the 17th High Performance and Large Scale Computing Conference*, HP&LSC, 2002.

Massive Atomics for Massive Parallelism on GPUs

Ian Egielski

Rutgers University

egielski@eden.rutgers.edu

Jesse Huang

Rutgers University

jh3141@gmail.com

Eddy Z. Zhang

Rutgers University

eddy.zhengzhang@cs.rutgers.edu

Abstract

One important type of parallelism exploited in many applications is *reduction type* parallelism. In these applications, the order of the read-modify-write updates to one shared data object can be arbitrary as long as there is an imposed order for the read-modify-write updates. The typical way to parallelize these types of applications is to first let every individual thread perform local computation and save the results in thread-private data objects, and then merge the results from all worker threads in the *reduction* stage. All applications that fit into the *map reduce* framework belong to this category. Additionally, the *machine learning*, *data mining*, *numerical analysis* and *scientific simulation* applications may also benefit from *reduction type* parallelism. However, the parallelization scheme via the usage of thread-private data objects may not be viable in massively parallel GPU applications. Because the number of concurrent threads is extremely large (at least tens of thousands of), thread-private data object creation may lead to memory space explosion problems.

In this paper, we propose a novel approach to deal with shared data object management for *reduction type* parallelism on GPUs. Our approach exploits fine-grained parallelism while at the same time maintaining good programmability. It is based on the usage of intrinsic hardware atomic instructions. Atomic operation may appear to be expensive since it causes thread serialization when multiple threads atomically update the same memory object at the same time. However, we discovered that, with appropriate atomic collision reduction techniques, the atomic implementation can outperform the non-atomics implementation, even for benchmarks known to have high performance non-atomics GPU implementations. In the meantime, the usage of atomics can greatly reduce coding complexity as neither thread-private object management or explicit thread-communication (for the shared data objects protected by atomic operations) is necessary.

Categories and Subject Descriptors D.3.4 [*Programming Languages*]: Processors—code generation, compilers, optimization

General Terms Performance, Management

Keywords GPU; Atomics; Parallelism; Concurrency

ISMM'14, June 12, 2014, Edinburgh, UK.
Copyright © 2014 ACM 978-1-4503-2921-7/14/06... $15.00.
http://dx.doi.org/10.1145/2602988.2602993

1. Introduction

Parallel applications need to manage shared data object updates efficiently. In many important parallel applications, operations on shared memory objects are commutative and thus the execution order of these operations can be arbitrary [8]. These applications include *map reduce* applications, *machine learning*, *numerical analysis* and *scientific simulation* applications. Parallelism in these applications is typically exploited via the usage of thread-private data structures to hold local computation results. Eventually, a final *reduction* step merges results from all worker threads. In this way, a large task can be split into multiple independent small subtasks that can be executed in parallel. However, this approach may incur large memory space overhead when there are many concurrent threads. This is typically the case in GPU applications, where a kernel function may easily invoke millions of threads.

An alternative parallelization approach is to partition the workload in a way such that the write updates to every data object is at most from one thread. In certain cases, communication among individual threads can be completely eliminated. For instance, in a sparse matrix vector multiplication kernel, the dot product between one entire row in the input matrix and the input column vector results in a single write to one entry in the result vector. Every dot product can be performed by one and at most one thread. However this approach may suffer from the load-unbalancing issue. It is challenging to maintain a balanced workload across all threads when the number of threads is large. In the sparse matrix, the number of non-zero entries in every row may vary a lot. Therefore, if one thread is assigned only one dot product, the amount of multiplication steps (equivalent to the number of non-zero elements in a row) for every thread may vary a lot. It is relatively easier to balance the workload in multi-core architectures that exploit coarse-grained parallelism. This is because we can use a much smaller number of threads and assign multiple dot products to one thread for load balancing. However, the GPU applications exploit fine-grained parallelism and thus it is difficult to achieve load balancing if inter-thread communication is eliminated.

Due to the space explosion and load-unbalancing issues, some prior studies have explored the use of atomic operations in combination with shared data objects with for specific applications [13] [4] [18] or specific memory layer (scratch-pad memory) [6]. The atomic operations help ensure the atomicity of the read, modify and write steps. Therefore, managing the commutative memory updates is purely automatic, requiring no extra algorithmic complexity. The GPU hardware atomic support has also been improved from time to time. For instance, the atomic memory objects can be cached in NVIDIA Fermi GPUs and the L2 cache hit bandwidth is enhanced significantly in NVIDIA Kepler GPUs [3] (for instance by 73% in Geforce GTX680). However, there is a lack of systematic exploration in the application of native atomics to general commutative computations operations. The challenge mainly comes from atomic collision – if multiple concurrent threads attempt to read-modify-write the same memory location at the same time, then these threads need to be serialized, forfeiting the potential massive parallelism in GPU architectures. It remains unclear whether atomics implementation can be profitable for a more general class of parallel GPU applications, i.e., the applications that already have highly optimized non-atomics implementations. If it is potentially profitable, we need to address the atomic collision challenge.

In this work, we conducted a systematic exploration in the usage of atomic operations for a general class of applications that are abundant in *reduction type* parallelism. We studied the impact of atomic collisions and proposed efficient atomic collision reduction techniques based on two principles. The first principle is to scatter atomic updates to the same memory location at different time intervals to avoid thread serialization. The second principle is to convert atomic collision to parallel computation so that atomic updates can be performed by a few leader threads that do not conflict with each other. In contrast to the traditional perception that atomic operations should mainly be used as synchronization primitives (locks and barriers), our study shows that using atomics for general purpose computation can actually be profitable, in terms of both programmability and efficiency, if used appropriately. We summarize our contributions as follows:

- We discovered that atomic operation can be profitable in parallelizing applications with abundant *reduction type* parallelism, even for parallel GPU applications that already have highly optimized non-atomics implementations, including sparse matrix vector multiplication and parallel summation (reduction).

- We identified two principles for efficient reduction of atomic collisions. Based on these two principles, we designed a set of reduced-collision atomic algorithms. We presented the complexity of our algorithms and discussed the applicability of these algorithms in different scenarios. We built a statistical learning model to choose over the non-atomics, naive atomics and reduced-collision atomics implementations given different atomic collision levels.

- We built a library that implemented these atomic collision reduction algorithms. The functions in this library have simple interfaces. In most cases, programmers can call these functions in a way similar to calling regular native atomic functions .

The rest of the paper is organized as follows. In Section 2 we give the background on GPU programming and present a motivation example. In Section 3, we discuss the performance aspect of generally using atomic operations in computation. We present detailed algorithms for eliminating atomic collision. In Section 4, we present evaluation results. We describe related work in Section 5 and conclude in Section 6.

2.   Motivation

Background   Throughout this paper we use NVIDIA CUDA terminology to describe the GPU architecture and programming model. A GPU is made up of multiple Streaming Multiprocessors (SMs). An SM is a Single Instruction Multiple Data (SIMD) like processor in which a group of threads execute the same instructions on multiple data elements. A GPU program includes both CPU code and GPU code. The function that runs on the GPU is called a kernel function. A kernel function is typically launched by more than thousands of threads. These threads are divided into small groups to be executed and scheduled on different SMs. Each group is called a thread warp. There is implicit synchronization within a thread warp – in which threads execute in lockstep.

There are two major types of memory on a GPU – on-chip memory and off-chip memory. On-chip memory includes registers, cache, and shared memory. Scratch-pad memory is nearly as fast as cache memory though it has to be explicitly managed by the programmer. Scratch-pad memory is called *shared memory* in NVIDIA terminology. The off-chip memory of an NVIDIA GPU is partitioned into *global memory* for heap objects, *local memory* for local variables, *constant memory* for constant objects and, *texture memory* for multi-dimensional read-only data objects. We primarily use *shared memory* and *global memory* for our atomics study.

We define *atomic collision* as the event of multiple threads attempting to update the same data object at the same time. These memory updates must be serialized due to the atomicity property of atomic operations. The shared memory atomic instruction is implemented as a loop that atomically updates unique unlocked memory locations at each iteration until one thread warp's requested atomic memory updates are complete. The number of iterations for a warp is the number of times the most frequent memory location is accessed by threads in the whole thread warp. Common atomic operations include atomicAdd, atomicOr, atomicAnd, atomicMin, etc. We focus on the commutative atomic operations.

Sparse Matrix Vector Multiplication Example   As a motivation example, we first show the atomics-based implementation of a real application. We then compare the performance between the traditional non-atomics implementation and the atomics-based implementation. We use a highly optimized sparse matrix vector multiplication kernel from CUSP [5], which is an open source C++ library of generic parallel algorithms for sparse linear algebra and graph computations on GPUs. We show the main computation code in the left half of Fig. 1. In this implementation, a thread warp iterates over one or multiple consecutive rows in the input sparse matrix represented by $V[ ]$ (at line 1), multiplies every non-zero element by the corresponding element in the input column vector (at line 4), performs segment reduction on the multiplication results and updates the output column vector correspondingly (at lines 5-20). If the last thread in a thread warp at previous iteration obtains the multiplication value to be added to the same output vector entry, then the value is carried into the current iteration (lines 7-8). Otherwise the value from the last iteration needs to be added to the corresponding output vector entry (at lines 9-10). The control flow is relatively complex here since the thread warps may cross input matrix row boundaries.

In the right half of Fig. 1, we show the atomics-based implementation. The multiplication code is exactly the same (at line 4). The difference begins from line 5. We atomically add the multiplication result into the corresponding output vector entry $y[row]$. There is no thread divergence in the code and the total number of lines of code is significantly reduced. Although not included in the code snippet, note that the non-atomics version uses shared memory to hold intermediate reduction results. The *rows[]* and *vals[]* arrays are shared memory arrays. However, our naive atomics implementation does not use *shared memory*.

In Fig. 2, we show the performance comparison results. The experiment is performed on an NVIDIA GTX 680, which is an NVIDIA Kepler card, we denote as kepler, and a NVIDIA Tesla C2075, which is a NVIDIA Fermi card, we denote as Fermi. We use the non-atomics implementation as baseline and the y axis represents are speedup. If the speedup is greater than 1, *atomics* version is faster, otherwise the *non-atomics* version is faster. Every bar in this graph corresponds to an input matrix. We use the sparse matrix input from matrix market [2] – the standard pool of sparse matrix in real world applications which is typically used for benchmarking sparse matrix programs. In Fig. 2, we can see that, surprisingly, the *naive* atomics implementation is faster for some case(s) on both Fermi and Kepler despite the atomic collisions. For Fermi, in most cases, the atomics version runs slower than the non-atomics version. One reason is that the original non-atomics version used shared memory to store intermediate results, while the naive *atom-*

Non-atomics Implementation

```
1: for(IndexType n = interval_begin + thread_lane; n < interval_end; n += WARP_SIZE)
2: {
3:     IndexType row = I[n];                          // row index (i)
4:     ValueType val = V[n] * fetch_x<UseCache>(J[n], x);   // A(i,j) * x(j)

5:     if (thread_lane == 0)
6:     {
7:         if(row == rows[idx + 31])
8:             val += vals[threadIdx.x + 31];          // row continues
9:         else
10:             y[rows[idx + 31]] += vals[threadIdx.x + 31]; // row terminated
11:     }

12:     rows[idx]      = row;
13:     vals[threadIdx.x] = val;

14:     if(row == rows[idx - 1]) { vals[threadIdx.x] = val = val + vals[threadIdx.x - 1]; }
15:     if(row == rows[idx - 2]) { vals[threadIdx.x] = val = val + vals[threadIdx.x - 2]; }
16:     if(row == rows[idx - 4]) { vals[threadIdx.x] = val = val + vals[threadIdx.x - 4]; }
17:     if(row == rows[idx - 8]) { vals[threadIdx.x] = val = val + vals[threadIdx.x - 8]; }
18:     if(row == rows[idx - 16]) { vals[threadIdx.x] = val = val + vals[threadIdx.x - 16]; }

19:     if(thread_lane < 31 && row != rows[idx + 1])
20:         y[row] += vals[threadIdx.x];               // row terminated
21: }
```

Atomics Implementation

```
1: for(IndexType n = interval_begin + thread_lane; n < interval_end; n += WARP_SIZE)
2: {
3:     IndexType row = I[n];                          // row index (i)
4:     ValueType val = V[n] * fetch_x<UseCache>(J[n], x);   // A(i,j) * x(j)

5:     atomicAdd(y+row, val);

6: }
```

One line of code in atomics version.
16 lines of code in the non-atomics versions.

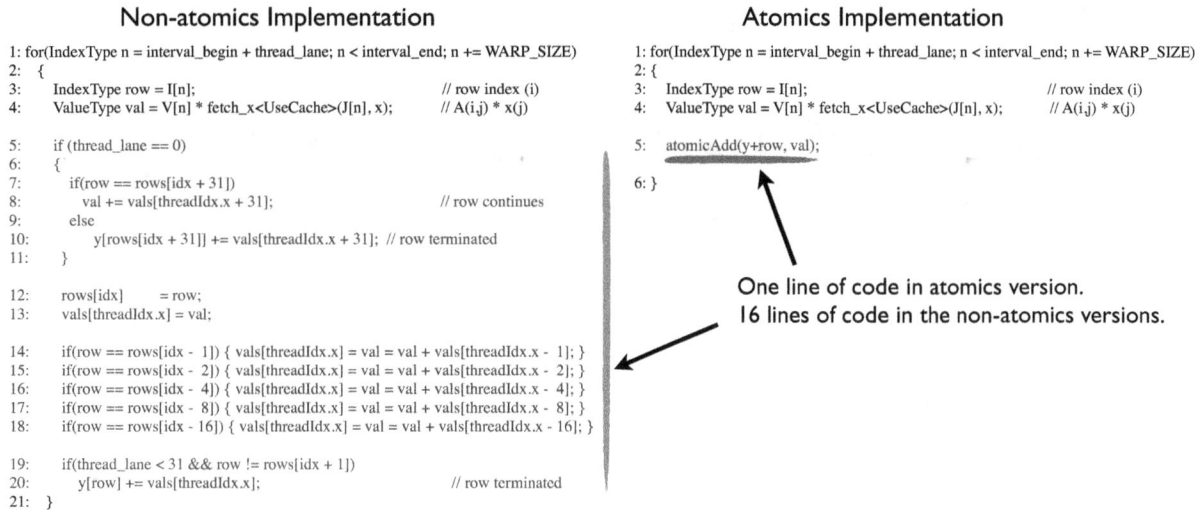

Figure 1. Atomics based SPMV implementation v.s. non-atomics based SPMV implementation

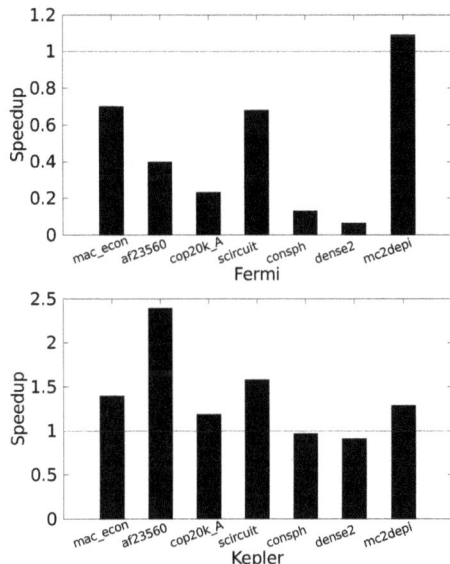

Figure 2. Performance of naive atomics implementation on Kepler and Fermi

ics implementation illustrated in Fig. 1 uses global memory, which is much slower. The other reason is the atomic collision incurred by threads operation on elements at the same row of the matrix. For the Kepler card, we already saw performance improvement for most benchmark matrices. Only two of them have performance slowdown. The atomics hardware support on Kepler has been improved significantly compared to the Fermi generation (especially for multiple atomic updates to single memory locations [3]). Further, the thread divergence is significantly eliminated in the naive atomics version, which also contributes to the performance improvement [19]. The experiment results demonstrated the potential of using atomic operations for programs with abundant *reduction type* parallelism even without applying any atomic collision elimination techniques. In the following Section 3, we show that with appropriate collision-removal techniques, the already atomics-based implementation can be further improved.

3. Performance

In this section, we discuss the performance aspect of applying atomic operations extensively for computing purposes. Atomic collision may degrade atomic performance significantly. We describe our approaches that reduce atomic collisions. There are two major types of approaches. The first type of approach is based on converting atomic collision into computation. This approach leverages local parallel reduction and reduces atomic memory operations. The second type of approach is based on re-scheduling atomic memory operations so that we can scatter potential atomically conflicted accesses over different time intervals. The basic idea is that if the atomic updates of the same memory addresses from different threads are scheduled at the same time, they collide with each other; however, if these threads are scheduled to run at different time intervals, they do not collide with each other. GPU programs typically launch a lot more threads than the number of physical GPU cores for maximal concurrency. Therefore, there is great potential to schedule threads for minimal atomic collisions. We name the first type of approach as *atomic-collision-to-computation*, and the second as *atomic-collision-to-scatter*. We describe the first approach in Section 3.1 and the second one in Section 3.2.

3.1 Convert Atomic Collision To Computation

With the *atomic-collision-to-computation* approach, we first perform local parallel reduction for the threads that atomically access the same memory location. We then let one thread perform atomic updates to every unique memory address based on the local reduction result. We present the design of the *atomic-collision-to-computation* algorithm in two scenarios: (1). the threads that access the same address are placed next to each other as illustrated in Fig. 3 (a), which happens frequently in kernels with structured parallelism such as matrix/vector computation in linear algebra libraries [12] ; (2) the threads that access the same memory locations are not placed next to each other as illustrated in Fig. 3 (b), which is the case for kernels with unstructured parallelism such as graph traversal kernels. We refer to the first scenario as the *clustered-collision* case and the second one as the *non-clustered-collision* case.

Clustered-collision Case: One of the major difficulties of the atomic-collision-to-computation approach is that the number of threads accessing every unique memory address may not be uni-

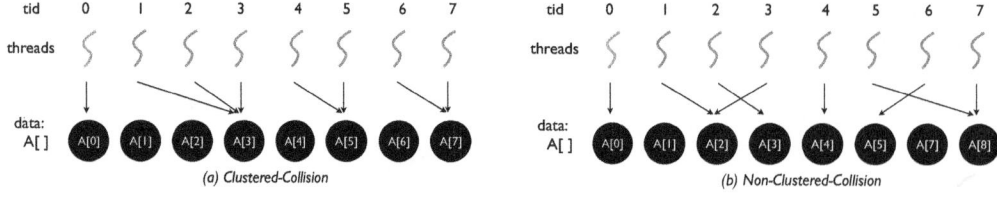

Figure 3. Atomic Collision Pattern

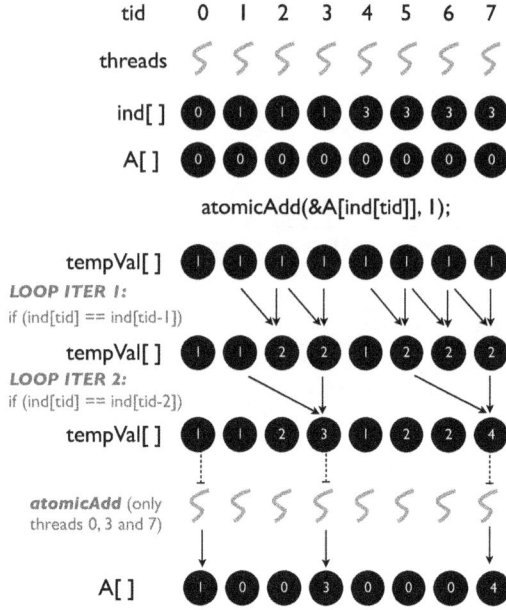

Figure 4. An example of atomic scan and reduce approach

form. Thus the number of local parallel reduction steps for every unique memory address may also vary significantly. Further, the thread boundary for local parallel reduction, the first and the last thread for one unique memory address, is usually not determined during static time. An example is the *sparse matrix vector multiplication* kernel we discussed in Section 2, in which the threads that process the non-zero elements at the same input matrix row may span across different thread warps and blocks. In a word, it is challenging to detect the size and boundary of every thread group that performs local parallel reduction for an unique memory address.

We propose an algorithm for the *clustered-collision* case that can perform the minimal number of local parallel reduction steps and can detect thread boundaries for unique memory addresses at the same time. In this algorithm, within every thread, we check the current thread and the thread with a logical id that is smaller than the current thread by a power of 2. If the two threads' memory addresses are the same, then we perform partial reduction on these two threads, and store the result in the current thread's temporary storage. If the two threads' memory addresses are different, we do not perform any action since we have already crossed the boundary of the thread region corresponding to the same unique memory address. Start from the thread distance of 2^0, we repeat this process and double the distance at every iteration until we have finished local parallel reduction for the largest thread region.

We describe the detailed algorithm in algorithm 1. We illustrate the algorithm with atomic addition operations, which applies to

---

Algorithm 1 Atomic scan and reduce algorithm

```
1:  procedure ATOMICADDSR(A[], idx, val, N)
2:      // Naive atomic version: atomicAdd(&A[idx],val)
3:      // Allocate temporary storage for addresses and values
4:      alloc tempVal[]; // One value per thread
5:      alloc tempIdx[]; // One integer per thread
6:      alloc tempMask[]; // One integer per thread warp
7:      tempIdx[tid] = idx;
8:      tempVal[tid] = val;
9:      sync(); // Barrier at a given thread scope
10:     tempMask[warpid] =
            __ballot(tempIdx[tid]==tempIdx[tid-thresh]);
11:     if (tempMask[1:lastWarpid] == 0) then
12:         // If all masks are 0s, use naive atomic and return
13:         atomicAdd(&A[idx], val);
14:         return ;
15:     end if
16:     for i = 1 to log₂ N do
17:         if (tempIdx[tid] == tempIdx[tid-2ⁱ] && tid ≥ 2ⁱ) then
18:             tempVal[tid] += tempVal[tid-2ⁱ];
19:             sync();
20:         else
21:             sync();
22:             break;
23:         end if
24:     end for
25:     if (tempIdx[tid] ≠ tempIdx[tid+1] && tid ≤ N-2) then
26:         atomicAdd(&A[idx], tempVal[tid]);
27:     end if
28:     sync();
29: end procedure
```

other commutative atomic operations as well. Programmers who want to convert atomic collision to computation can simply replace the original atomic add function *atomicAdd* with this *atomicAddSR* function. The parameters of *atomicAddSR* include the array pointer A, the index *idx* and the value *val*, which means the array cell *A[idx]* needs to be atomically increased by *val*. The parameter N is the number of threads on which local parallel reductions need to be performed. Note there might be more than one local parallel reduction thread regions within the N threads. This function is executed by every individual thread. In this algorithm, we synchronize after every local (partial) parallel reduction step to make sure the memory updates are visible to all threads within the N threads (at line 19 and 21). If local parallel reduction is performed within every thread warp, the barrier synchronization statement is not necessary since thread warp level synchronization is implicit. We ensure that local parallel reduction is only performed by threads that access the same unique memory address by the condition check at line 17. This can be nicely integrated with the local parallel reduction steps as the number of condition checks is also logarithmic. If the two threads do not pass the condition check at line 17, then we know we crossed the boundary of the thread region corresponding to the same memory location, we break out of the loop at lines 20-22. Henceforth, the number of local parallel reduction steps for every unique memory address is logarithmic with respect to the thread group size. When all local parallel reduction operations are done, we break out of the loop from line 16 to 24. Therefore we ensure the minimal number of computation steps with this approach. Note that we only perform local parallel reduction if there are at least *thresh* threads which access the same memory location. It is performed with the help of a voting function at lines 10-15. We will describe the selection of the *thresh* variable in *Performance Guarantee* discussion in this section. We will discuss the voting function in more detail at the *Non-Clustered-Collision Case* scenario.

We illustrate the use of our algorithm in Fig. 4. In this example, every thread tries to atomically add an value 1 to a cell in array A with the index of ind[tid]. The *tid* variable represents the thread index. Every cell in $A[]$ array is 0 initially as illustrated in Fig. 4. We also show the values of every cell in array *ind[]*, which corresponds to the location of the array cell every thread needs to access. Assume there are 8 threads. According to ind[], the first thread needs to increment $A[0]$ by 1, the second to the fourth thread need to atomically increment $A[1]$ by 1, and the fifth to the eighth thread need to increment $A[3]$ by 1. The optimal case is to perform 2 local reduction steps for threads *2-4* and threads *5-8*, and no reduction for thread *1*. We achieve this by using the condition at line 17 in Alg. 1. At *loop iteration 1* in Fig. 4, we only perform addition if the current thread and its precedent thread have exactly the same memory access. Then we save the partial reduction result in temporary array cell *tempVal[tid]* for each thread. At *loop iteration 2*, we perform the same check and partial reduction operations except that we check the current thread and the thread that has a tid smaller than the current thread by 2. After two loop iterations, we get the summation results for every element and the elements to its left that correspond to the same memory in array *tempVal[]*. In the last step, we perform atomic add only with thread 0, thread 3 and thread 7 to $A[0]$, $A[1]$ and $A[3]$ and array $A[]$ is completely atomically updated. Our algorithm eliminates atomic collision completely and needs the minimal number of local parallel reduction steps.

Non-Clustered-collision Case: In this case, not only is the amount of atomic collision irregular, but also how it is distributed among threads is irregular – the threads that access the memory address are not necessarily placed next to each other, which makes local parallel reduction boundary even more challenging. We propose an algorithm that identifies the most frequently accessed memory locations with the maximum likelihood. Then we obtain the frequency of these memory addresses in one pass or log(Nwarp) passes, with Nwarp being the number of thread warps. Based on this, we determine if it is necessary to perform local reduction and if so how many local reduction steps is necessary. We name this approach as *atomic vote and reduce*.

We describe the *atomic vote and reduce* algorithm in Alg. 2. Given a local reduction scope (whether it is within every thread warp or every thread block or among all the threads), we first randomly pick a thread and obtain the thread's memory access location (lines 10-11). Then, we let all threads vote to find out which threads access the same memory address (line 12). Thus, we get the thread access frequency of this memory address. If it is above a threshold (the *thresh* variable in Alg. 2), we perform a local reduction on the corresponding threads and let one leader thread write the local reduction result back atomically (lines 14-17). Otherwise, we use the naive atomic operations (lines 21-22). Similarly, this approach not only applies to atomic addition but also other commutative atomic operations. The barrier synchronization instruction at line 9 is not necessary if we perform atomic vote and reduce at thread warp level as synchronization within a thread

---

Algorithm 2 Atomic vote and reduce algorithm

```
 1: procedure ATOMICADDVR1(A[], idx, val)
 2:     // Naive atomic version: atomicAdd(&A[idx],val)
 3:     // Allocate temporary storage for addresses and values
 4:     alloc tempVal[]; // One value per thread
 5:     alloc tempIdx[]; // One integer per thread
 6:     alloc tempMask[]; // One mask per thread warp
 7:     tempIdx[tid] = idx;
 8:     tempVal[tid] = val;
 9:     sync(); // Thread barrier at a given thread scope
10:     rid = rand[(scopeid + kbase)% rand_cycle]; //randomly
        selected thread id
11:     sampleIdx = tempIdx[rid];
12:     tempMask[warpid] = __ballot(idx == sampleIdx);
13:     if (freq(tempMask[1:lastWarpid]) ≥ thresh)  then
14:         lsum = localReduce(); // Local parallel reduction
15:         if (scopeTid == 0) then
16:             atomicAdd(&A[sampleIdx], lsum);
17:         end if
18:         if (idx ≠ sampleIdx ) then
19:             atomicAdd(&A[idx], val);
20:         end if
21:     else
22:         atomicAdd(&A[idx], val);
23:     end if
24: end procedure
```

---

warp is implicit. In Alg. 2, we illustrated the *atomic vote and reduce* algorithm with the case where we want to pick the most frequently accessed memory address and perform local reduction. We name it as *atomicVR1()*. We also extend it to the case where we want to pick top m most frequently accessed memory addresses. We use a loop to sample the top m most frequent addresses. The local reductions of these m unique addresses happen in parallel. In practice, we find *atomicVR1()* at the thread warp level is most helpful. If the amount of atomic collision is excessive at thread block level or among all running threads, then the non-atomics code version usually outperforms the atomic version (even the reduced atomic collision version). We use a regression tree model described in Section 3.3 to identify different atomic collision level.

We use the random sampling and voting based collision detection approach for the following reason. Given a set of memory addresses accessed by one thread group (group is the scope we mentioned above), the more frequent a memory address appears, the more likely the thread that accesses it will be selected if we draw one thread from this thread group with uniform probability distribution. As the number of thread groups and the number of sampling points increase, the most frequent memory address can be obtained with maximum likelihood according to the *large number theorem*. The number of threads launched by a GPU kernel is typically large which ensures the efficiency of the random sampling and voting based approach. For random number generation, we do not directly use a random number generator during runtime. Instead, we generate a large sequence of random numbers with a full cycle random number generator. We save the sequence in memory. Whenever a kernel is invoked, we pick a location in the sequence randomly as the seed position. The thread groups then use the random number sequence in a round robin fashion. The first thread group in the GPU kernel uses the random number in the seed position. The second thread group uses the number immediately after the seed position. The following thread groups get their random number in a similar fashion and when they hit the end of the sequence, the first random number in the sequence is selected. This process is described at line 10. The *kbase* is the seed position determined when the kernel is invoked. We use the system time mod the random number cycle to obtain the seed position in the random sequence. Every time the kernel runs, it starts with a different seed position. Therefore the randomness across all thread groups is ensured in a lightweight fashion (no dynamic random number generation is necessary).

Performance Guarantee We choose the **thresh** variable in Alg. 1 and Alg. 2 in a way that guarantees no performance degradation if compared to the naive atomic implementation. Assume the total number of threads in the thread group is N, the maximal number of threads that access the same memory location is x, and the initial setup overhead is s (the voting, boundary checking and counting in Alg. 1 and Alg. 2). We determine the threshold value by finding the minimal of x in the following inequalities:

$$log_2 x + s \leq x (atomic\ scan\ and\ reduce) \quad (1)$$
$$(N - x) + log_2 x + s \leq x (atomic\ vote\ and\ reduce) \quad (2)$$

In the above inequalities, the left-hand side estimates the total number of computation steps needed if we perform the local reduction, and the right-hand side represents total number of computation steps if we use the naive atomic implementation. For atomicVR, in the left-hand side, the $N - x$ component represents, after local parallel reduction on the set of threads that access the most frequently accessed address, the number of extra atomic computation steps needed in the worst scenario (assuming all other threads collide at the same memory address). For both *atomicVR* and *atomicSR*, the $log_2 x$ component represents the number of computation steps needed for local parallel reduction. The s component represents initial set up overhead. We first change the $\leq$ to $=$ and solve this nonlinear equation for x. Then we set the threshold variable **thresh** as the x value we solved. Following this inequality, we guarantee that our transformed atomics code does not run any slower than the naive atomics code. We obtain the overhead s by checking number of binary instructions that are needed to implement the initial setup and normalize it with respect to the latency of the binary instructions needed to perform every step of local reduction.

3.2 Atomic Collision to Scatter

In the *atomic-collision-to-computation* approach, we perform local reduction operations before we perform any atomic updates. In this section, we present an approach that does not use extra local reduction steps. The basic idea is that two different threads accessing the same unique memory address do not collide atomically if they are scheduled to run at different points in time. Since GPU programs typically launch a lot more threads than physical GPU cores, we can schedule these threads to scatter the potentially conflicting atomic operations over time.

We propose an algorithm that achieves the scattering of potentially conflicting atomic accesses through thread layout transformation. The essential idea is to separate the threads that have conflicting memory accesses from each other as far as possible. The logical thread layout implies the thread co-running pattern; for instance, every thread in a thread warp or a thread block runs at the same time at one SM. The threads from different thread blocks may run at different time intervals, as the GPU hardware only support a limited number of active thread warps at one time. The thread warps are divided into batches, with the size of each batch being the maximal number of active thread warps the GPU can support. These thread batches run sequentially [1]. To enable scattering, we first group threads by the memory addresses they access. We construct one set of threads for every unique memory address. We then reorder threads based on these sets and create a new thread layout. Starting from the first set of threads, we take out one thread

and place it as the first thread in the new thread layout. Next we pick a thread from the second set and place it as the second thread in the new thread layout. We repeat this step and keep appending threads to the new thread layout. If we reach the last set of threads, we restart from the first set. The process stops until we remove all threads from the sets. Finally, we obtain a new order of logical threads. For clustered-collision case, since the threads have already been grouped according to their memory access addresses the set creation step is omitted. For non clustered-collision case, both the set creation step and the reordering step are necessary. If the scattering overhead is non-trivial, we run the scattering algorithm on CPUs. We can overlap the actual computation on GPU with the scattering process on CPU. If necessary, we use the kernel spilling technique described in [19] to enable the overlapping and overcome dependence. Further, we can regroup and reorder thread warps instead of threads. For non-clustered collision cases, we obtain the most frequently accessed address in one warp using the random sampling approach described in Alg. 2 and we label the thread warp with this address. For the clustered case, we associate every thread warp with its first thread's address since threads are already grouped. These two overhead reduction techniques help us achieve performance improvement or at least no performance degradation by making the thread layout transformation overhead transparent. The algorithm for scattering is illustrated with pseudo-code in Alg. 3.

Algorithm 3 Atomic scatter algorithm

```
 1: procedure ATOMICSS(tAddr[], newLayout[], tNum)
 2:     //Obtain sets of threads that access unique addresses
 3:     wSets = groupThreads(tAddr[]);
 4:     i = 0;
 5:     while (i < tNum) do
 6:         for each set ∈ wSets do // In address ascending order
 7:             if ( set.size ≠ 0 ) then
 8:                 tId = set.pop();
 9:                 newLayout[i] = tId;
10:                 i++;
11:             end if
12:         end for
13:     end while
14:     return newLayout[];
15: end procedure
```

3.3 Atomic Collision Sampling

Eliminating atomic collision incurs overhead. If there is little atomic collision, there is little benefit in eliminating atomic collision. We should use naive atomics directly in these cases as the overhead for detecting and eliminating collision is non-trivial. If there is too much atomic collision, we should use the non-atomics code version or the reduced-collision atomics. We need to determine for every given program input: (1) whether the atomics code version should be used; (2) if so, whether the reduced atomic collision version or the naive atomics version should be used. Although we can perform a dynamic collision check with the voting approach described in Section 3.1, the check overhead s in inequalities 1 and 2 needs to be incurred regardless of the fact whether atomic collision needs to be reduced or not. We propose statistical learning techniques to model the relationship between the collision statistics and the decision on whether and which atomic code version should be used. Specifically, we use regression tree model [10] for its simplicity and good interpretability. We use three major collision parameters: (1). intra-warp collision level (2) intra-block collision level (3) all-thread collision level. We first define the *maximal collision factor* as the ratio between the maximal access frequency of

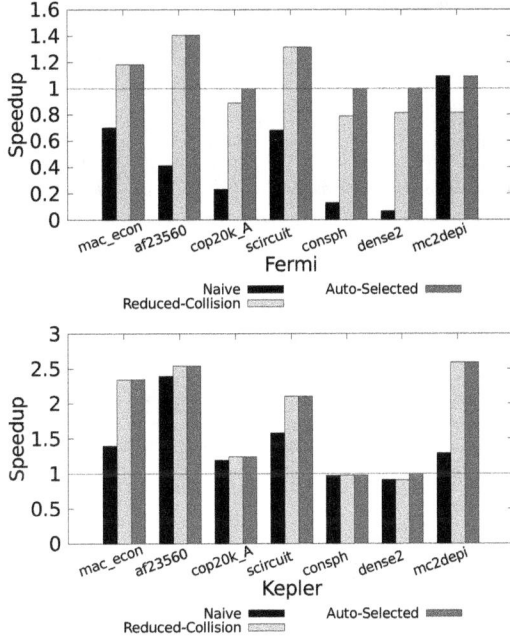

Figure 5. Performance results of sparse matrix vector multiplication after eliminating atomic collision

every unique memory address in a warp/block and the total number of threads in a warp/block. The maximal collision factor can be obtained using the voting step we discussed in Alg. 2. It is lightweight as the process can be easily parallelized by many threads. We define the intra-warp/intra-block collision level as the average of all thread warps'/blocks' maximal collision factors. We choose maximal collision factor because it is the minimal amount of time the whole thread warp/block needs to finish all atomic updates. The all-thread collision level is the average access frequency of all unique memory addresses. We use a training set of inputs, calibrate a database that stores tuples mainly consisting of the three collision parameters and the corresponding best code version (naive atomics or reduced-collision atomics or no atomics), and build the regression tree model. Given the collision stats of a new program input, we feed it as input to the statistical learning model and outputs the code version to be used. We may also use other factor of a program to build the regression tree model such as the scale of a program. If a program runs a small number of threads such that the running time is trivial, it may not be necessary to perform any optimization.

Discussion The atomicSR, atomicVR and atomicSS algorithms can be applied at different scenarios. For the programs that have inherent clustered-collision pattern such as sparse matrix multiplication, we should always use atomicSR. For the programs that have inherent non-clustered-collision pattern such as image histogramming or graph traversal, we should use the atomicVR algorithm. Both atomicSR and atomicVR algorithms has less complexity than the atomicSS algorithm since it needs to scatter conflicted atomic memory addresses. Also the atomicSS algorithm might incur larger transformation overhead, however it also has greatest potential to improve performance since no extra local reduction needs to take place. Overall, the combination of atomicSR+atomicSS can achieve relatively low overhead and satisfactory performance improvement. The atomicVR is best not to be used in combination with atomicSS since the atomic memory access is likely randomly distributed for non-clustered collision case unless the distribution

of collision statistics is degenerate (which can be detected through the statistical learning model).

We present the performance results of the sparse matrix multiplication example used in Section 2 after we apply the optimization techniques in this section. The sparse matrix vector multiplication program has an inherent clustered collision pattern. Therefore, we apply a combination of the atomic scan/reduce algorithm (atomicSR) and the atomic scattering algorithm (atomicSS). In Fig. 5, we show the naive atomics version, the atomicSR+atomicSS and the final selected version based on the statistical learning model for both Fermi and Kepler. The left bar in every group represents the performance of naive atomics. The middle bar represents the performance after we reduce atomic collisions. The right bar represents the selected version with the statistical learning model. The baseline is the original non-atomics implementation. The graph shows that these techniques improved performance significantly. For Kepler, though naive atomics version is already fast compared to the non-atomic version for a number of benchmarks, reduced-collision atomics version can make them even faster. The *mac_econ*, *scircuit* and *mc2depi* matrices have up to 60% improvement. For Fermi, since its intrinsic atomic speed is slower than Kepler [3], the reduced-collision atomic implementation make a big performance difference when compared to the naive atomics implementation almost for every benchmark. Comparing the reduced-collision atomic implementation to the non-atomic implementation, four out of seven cases are better. Three others are slightly worse. That is because these three benchmarks *cop20k_A*, *dense2* and *consph* are relatively denser matrices. The final version selected by the statistical learning model for these matrices is the non-atomics version (with the speedup as 1 in these bars).

4. Evaluation

In this section we evaluate the performance of our atomic algorithms described in section 3 with various important and practical kernels. We conduct our experiments on two GPUs with different hardware atomic instruction latencies. One is an NVIDIA Kepler GPU card – GTX680 with CUDA computing capability 3.0. It has 8 streaming multiprocessors with 192 cores on each of them. There are 65536 registers and 48KB shared memory on each SM. The other one is an NVIDIA Fermi GPU card – Tesla C2075 with CUDA computing capability 2.0. It has 14 streaming multiprocessors (SM) with 32 cores on each of them. Each SM has 32768 registers and 48KB of shared memory. The hardware atomics speed in Kepler card is improved over the Fermi card [3]. Both host machines run 64-bit Linux with kernel version 3.1.10 and CUDA 5.5.

For each benchmark, we have collected data for the original non-atomics implementation, the naive atomics implementation and the reduced-collision atomics implementation. We denote our atomic-collision-to-computation function for clustered-collision case – the "atomic scan and reduce" function as *atomicSR*, and the atomic-collision-to-computation function for non-clustered-collision case – the "atomic vote and reduce" function as *atomicVR*. They are abbreviated as *SR* and *VR* respectively in figures. We denote our atomic-collision-to-scatter function "atomic set scatter" as *atomicSS*, abbreviated as *SS*. The default naive atomic implementation is denoted as *AA*.

As of benchmark applications, we use five important kernels that are commonly used in various applications. They are histogramming [13], merge-sort [14], page-view-count [11], parallel summation [14], and sparse matrix vector multiplication [5]. All benchmarks are highly optimized GPU kernels. They are obtained either from the CUDA linear algebra library for sparse matrices (CUSP) [5], the CUDA SDK [14], or published papers [11]. We describe the features of these five benchmarks as follows:

- **Image Histogramming** Image processing applications extensively use the *histogram* kernel, which counts the frequency of each color for all pixels taken from an input image. We used the image histogramming benchmark optimized by the authors in [13]. The authors provided a warp-private histogram implementation which uses warp-private histograms to store local histogramming results, and a thread-private histogram implementation which does not use any atomics. We extended this benchmark by adding a block-private histogram and a global histogram implementation (which uses no private histogram) in order to test atomic-collision reduction techniques at different memory levels. Both block-private and warp-private histograms are stored in shared memory. The no-private implementation uses a global histogram in device memory for all threads.

- **SPMV** Sparse matrix vector multiplication is from the CUSP [5] library, an open source C++ library of parallel algorithms for sparse linear algebra and graph computations on GPUs. This kernel uses shared memory to enhance performance. Its GPU implementation is much faster than the CPU implementation. In our naive atomics implementation mentioned in Section 2, each thread warp operates on an interval of nonzero elements in the input matrix. The threads fetch the row index, column index, and value of the non-zero input matrix elements. Each thread multiplies the non-zero input matrix element with the corresponding input vector element, and atomically adds the multiplication result to the output vector.

- **Merge Sort** We use *merge sort* from CUDA Thrust library (*Thrust is a parallel algorithms library which resembles the C++ Standard Template Library (STL)*) as the baseline *nonatomic* implementation. Similarly, this kernel is highly optimized. It iteratively performs local sorting and then merges the partially sorted results at different levels until the entire array is sorted. At every local sort stage, it is typically common that multiple elements have the same value. Sorting these duplicated elements causes increased sorting overhead. Our atomic implementation eliminates redundancy at the end of every local sorting stage so that the following sorting stage sort only unique values from every local sorted group. We use atomic add to count the frequency of each element. Every element is associated with a frequency attribute and it is propagated across all levels of sorting. The frequency information helps restore the array to the original length after the multi-level sorting of all locally unique elements is completed.

- **Page View Count** Page View Count is a *map-reduce* application used to track the number of unique visitors for a given web page. It is from the GPU *map-reduce* benchmark suite Mars [11]. The authors implemented Page View Count by using two invocations of Map Reduce. The first invocation eliminates duplicate page views by mapping each entry to a unique value, globally sorting these values, and then eliminating adjacent duplicates. The second iteration counts the number of remaining unique views for each web page. Our naive atomic implementation extends this benchmark by using atomic reduction between the map and reduce phases of the first iteration of Page View Count in order to eliminate all duplicate entries within each block prior to global sorting. Our block-level atomic redundancy elimination invokes relatively very little overhead and vastly improves the performance of global sorting which is by far the most constricting bottleneck of Mars as the authors themselves mentioned in [11].

- **Summation** The parallel summation kernel is taken from the CUDA computing SDK 5.0 (the reduction kernel), which is carefully optimized with respect to different factors such as shared memory bank conflicts, loop unrolling, etc. The original

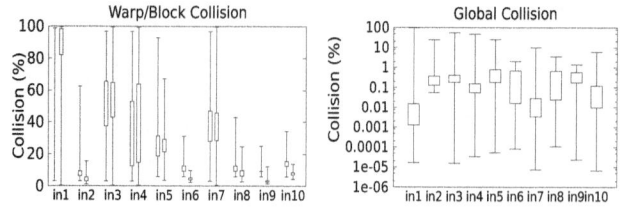

Figure 6. Histogram input statistics

Method	Minimum	Maximum	Average	% Off Opt.
Block P.	0.91	14.74	3.90	9.41%
Warp P.	0.58	6.98	2.03	12.80%
No P.	0.99	6.87	2.30	0.04%

Table 1. Histogramming kernel speedup with regression tree model (kepler)

Method	Minimum	Maximum	Average	% Off Opt.
Block P.	0.68	9.51	3.08	7.82%
Warp P.	0.65	7.61	2.39	8.21%
No P.	0.99	15.40	4.28	0.10%

Table 2. Histogramming kernel speedup with regression tree model (fermi)

version computes a local sum at the block-level at each iteration. It then saves the partial sum for every block in the output array buffer, which becomes the input array for the next iteration of local sum computation. Instead of writing to the block-private data objects, we allow threads to atomically add results to a compacted output array. We vary the level of atomic collision by changing the size of the compacted output array. The program run-time is taken as the total time of all the kernel invocations that are necessary to perform complete summation of a large array.

For the benchmarks that have inherent clustered-collision pattern such as sparse matrix vector multiplication, we use atomicSR within the thread warp scope and atomicSS at the thread warp level. For the benchmarks that have inherent non-clustered-collision pattern such as image histogramming, we use the atomicVR and atomicSS versions at the thread warp level. In our experiments, we found that atomicSS in non-clustered-collision benchmarks do not help as much as it does in clustered-collision benchmarks. Therefore, we do not present the results of atomicSS for non-clustered-collision cases.

We first present the detailed analysis results of two benchmarks. One benchmark has non-clustered-collision pattern. It is the image histogramming kernel. The other benchmark has clustered-collision. It is the sparse matrix vector multiplication kernel. We show the collision statistics for ten representative inputs of every benchmark. And we discuss performance results of various atomic collision reduction techniques.

In the image histogramming kernel, atomic operations are utilized in both the block-private, warp-private, and no-private implementations. We tested the atomic performance on 37 different images with varying degrees of atomic collision levels. We choose to present the results for 10 representative input images. Fig. 6 shows the warp, block, and global collision statistics. In the *Warp/Block Collision* graph, we use box plot to represent the distribution of the maximal collision factors in thread warps/blocks. The bottom of the box correspond to the first quartile and the top of the box

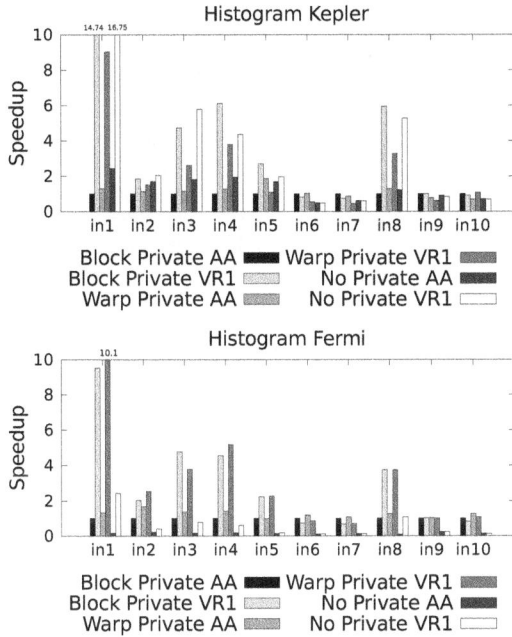

Figure 7. Histogram speedup

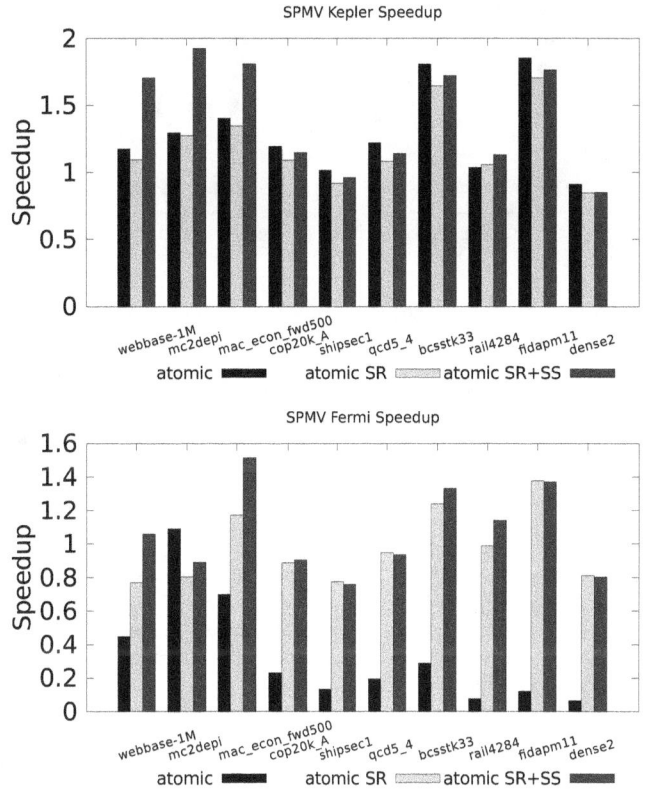

Figure 8. SPMV speedup

Arch.	Minimum	Maximum	Mean	% Off Opt.
Kepler	0.99	1.35	2.46	4.68%
Fermi	0.70	1.04	1.51	8.55%

Table 3. SPMV method prediction speedup and optimality

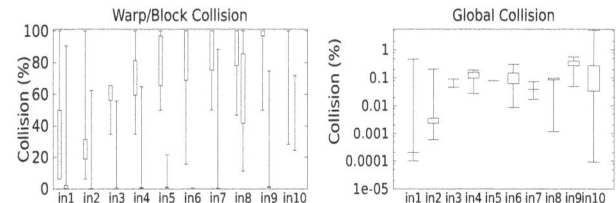

Figure 9. SPMV input statistics

correspond to the third quartile. The top bar corresponds to the 100 percentile (the largest max collision factor) and the bottom bar corresponds to the 0 percentile (the smallest max collision factor). The left box plot in every group corresponds to the warp and the right box plot corresponds to the block. The *global collision* graph shows the box plot for the access frequency of unique memory addresses. As can be seen from Fig. 6, the collision statistics vary heavily from image to image. Tables 1 and 2 show the minimum, maximum, and average speedup of the predicted implementation with our statistical learning model (the non-atomic implementation is the baseline). The columns of "% Off Opt." shows on average how much slower the predicted implementation is compared to the optimal implementation. As both tables show, the average slowdown is extremely small. Even when the predicted code version is suboptimal, in most cases, the performance difference between these two is negligible. Figure 7 shows the speedup of all implementations with respect to the block-private naive atomics implementation. We did not use the original non-atomics as baseline because it is typically much slower even than the naive atomics version [13]. We observe significant speedup in cases with heavy collision and non-trivial speedup even in cases with relatively light collision. Note that on Kepler, the naive no-private version that does not use shared memory is sometimes faster than the block-private and warp-private versions that use shared memory. It is because the Kepler hardware atomic updates are automatically cached and the Kepler's L2 cache hit bandwidth is much larger. However, after applying our atomic collision reduction techniques, the atomicVR version still performs better in block-private and warp-private versions. The implication is that atomic collision reduction is necessary even when the intrinsic hardware atomic operations are faster. Note that, the number of concurrent threads that are interleaved to execute may also have an impact on the atomics performance. The higher the concurrency level, the more atomics collision overhead can be hidden. The image *in8* has relatively high intra-warp collision level as shown in Fig. 6, however, the collision reduction did not help much on either Fermi or Kepler architecture. That is because image *in8* is the largest and requires a larger number of threads to be launched,

which enables maximal concurrency level. Therefore, the difference between naive atomics and reduced-collision atomics is not that large.

For the sparse matrix vector multiplication kernel, we ran the benchmark on 18 different matrices with different sparsities, sizes, and degrees of atomic collision levels. The result of the benchmarks for 10 representative matrices is shown in Figure 8. The speedups in this chart are relative to the non-atomics kernel. We also present the atomic collision level statistics for each matrix in Figure 9 as a box plot. Similarly, the chart on the left displays the collision levels for thread warps and blocks. The left box plot in every group corresponds to thread warp, and the right box plot corresponds thread block. As usual, this plot shows the min, first

101

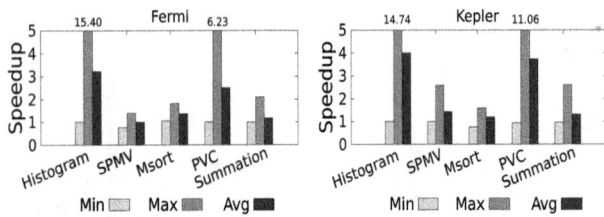

Figure 10. Benchmark speedup summary

quartile, third quartile, and max collision percentage over the set of collisions per warp and block. The right chart shows a box plot for the global collisions level. Overall, we observe that the Kepler architecture has improved atomic addition performance compared to Fermi, which is expected due to an improved L2 cache bandwidth [3]. We used leave-one-out cross validation for statistical learning model. Table 3 show statistics on the average slowdown of the kernel chosen by the decision tree with respect to the fastest implementation. For Fermi architecture, we observe that kernels which use our collision reduction techniques generally offer a significant improvement in performance over the naive atomics kernel. Despite the overall slow performance of naive atomic operations on Fermi, the optimized kernels can even outperform the non-atomic version for some matrices. For Kepler architecture, we observe that the reduced-collision atomic implementations either improved significantly or decreased slightly compared to the naive atomic implementation.

Finally, we present the performance summary for all benchmarks. In Fig 10 we present the minimum, maximum and average speedup across different inputs for each benchmark on both the Kepler and Fermi architectures. The speedup values are normalized with respect to the original code version. In most cases, the original code version is the non-atomic implementation except in the case of image histogramming, where the original code version is the block-private naive atomics version (histogramming already has fast naive atomics implementation published [13] [6]). Non-trivial average speedup is achieved in all benchmarks on both architectures. For most benchmarks, minimal speedup is around 1 (rare case has minimal speedup of 0.65) and about 1.5x-15x maximal speedup is achieved across all benchmarks. For some benchmarks, particularly image histogramming and PVC, we observe a very significant disparity between minimal and maximal speedup. The effectiveness of our atomic collision reduction techniques is obviously heavily dependent on the nature of the program input. Differing inputs may generate heavily contrasting levels of atomic collision. For the sake of fair comparison, our testing input sets have been chosen to represent a broad range of atomic collision from heavy collision to little to no collision on the extreme ends. Our data shows that while presented with a workload generating heavy atomic collision, our techniques improve potential performance tenfold or more (compared to the naive atomic case), and while presented with a workload generating light atomic collision, our techniques induce little to no slowdown (and potentially speedup over the non-atomics version) in most cases. In combination with our regression tree model, our collision reduction techniques have the potential to provide not only vastly simplified programmability but also incredible performance improvement with minimal performance degradation.

5. Related Work

One of the few relevant studies is the hardware extension for efficient atomic vector support [12], where the authors study atomics for SIMD processors in Chip Multi-processors (CMP). Another relevant hardware work is by Gottlieb and others [7], where the fetch-

and-add operation is implemented by an Omega-network for NYU ultracomputer such that memory latency for updates to the same address is logarithmic with respect to the number of cores. There are also limited relevant software studies that systematically explore the usage of atomics for *reduction type* parallelism abundant applications. Most existing software work focuses on application-specific atomic usage, including GPU-MCML[4] – a highly optimized Monte Carlo (MC) code package for simulating light transport, GPU histogramming [16] [15] [13] and GPU graph-cut [18]. Some software work studies atomic collision for a specific memory level, for instance, Gomez-Luna and others [6] optimize atomics operations for scratch-pad memory. To the best of our knowledge, this work is the first one that systematically studies the impact of extensive atomics usage, and explores a variety of atomics collision reduction techniques. The *atomic collision to scatter* approach is relevant to the job swapping idea used in control divergence and memory irregularity removal for GPU programs [19]. The local reduction in *atomicSR* algorithm is similar to the global reduction [9] approach, which does not need to detect boundaries and sizes of local reduction groups. The GPU voting used in *atomicVR* is studied extensively in [17], the techniques in which can help us speedup *atomicVR* even more.

6. Conclusion

In this paper, we proposed to use atomic operations extensively for computation rather than communication on many-core GPUs. We systematically studied the influence of atomic collision on GPU programs and investigated various solutions on the elimination of atomic collisions.

Acknowledgement

We thank Jos E. Moreira for his comments on the draft of this paper. We owe a debt to the anonymous reviewers for their invaluable comments. This material is based upon the work supported by Rutgers University Research Council Grant. Any opinions, findings, and conclusions or recommendations expressed in this material are those of the authors and do not necessarily reflect the views of our sponsors.

References

[1] "Cuda occupancy calculator." NVIDIA. [Online]. Available: http://developer.download.nvidia.com/compute/cuda/CUDA_Occupancy_calculator.xls

[2] "Matrix market." [Online]. Available: http://math.nist.gov/MatrixMarket/

[3] "Whitepaper - nvidia's next generation cuda compute architecture: Kepler gk110." [Online]. Available: http://www.nvidia.com/content/PDF/kepler/NVIDIA-Kepler-GK110-Architecture-Whitepaper.pdf

[4] E. Alerstam, W. C. Y. Lo, T. D. Han, J. Rose, S. Andersson-Engels, and L. Lilge, "Next-generation acceleration and code optimization for light transport in turbid media using GPUs," *Biomedical Optics Express*, vol. 1, no. 2, pp. 658–675, 2010.

[5] N. Bell and M. Garland, "Cusp: Generic parallel algorithms for sparse matrix and graph computations," 2012, version 0.3.0. [Online]. Available: http://cusp-library.googlecode.com

[6] J. Gomez-Luna, J. M. Gonzalez-Linares, J. I. B. Benitez, and N. G. Mata, "Performance modeling of atomic additions on gpu scratchpad memory," *IEEE Transactions on Parallel and Distributed Systems*, vol. 24, no. 11, pp. 2273–2282, 2013.

[7] A. Gottlieb, R. Grishman, C. P. Kruskal, K. P. McAuliffe, L. Rudolph, and M. Snir, "The nyu ultracomputer—designing a mimd, shared-memory parallel machine (extended abstract)," in *Proceedings of the 9th Annual Symposium on Computer Architecture*, ser. ISCA '82. Los Alamitos, CA, USA: IEEE

Computer Society Press, 1982, pp. 27–42. [Online]. Available: http://dl.acm.org/citation.cfm?id=800048.801711

[8] M. W. Hall, J. M. Anderson, S. P. Amarasinghe, B. R. Murphy, S.-W. Liao, E. Bugnion, and M. S. Lam, "Maximizing multiprocessor performance with the suif compiler," *Computer*, vol. 29, no. 12, pp. 84–89, Dec. 1996.

[9] M. Harris, "Optimizing parallel reduction in cuda," 2007, http://developer.download.nvidia.com/compute/cuda/1_1/Website/projects/reduction/doc/reduction.pdf.

[10] T. Hastie, R. Tibshirani, and J. Friedman, "The elements of statistical learning." Springer, 2001.

[11] B. He, W. Fang, Q. Luo, N. K. Govindaraju, and T. Wang, "Mars: a mapreduce framework on graphics processors," in *Proceedings of the 17th international conference on Parallel architectures and compilation techniques*, ser. PACT '08. New York, NY, USA: ACM, 2008, pp. 260–269.

[12] S. Kumar, D. Kim, M. Smelyanskiy, Y.-K. Chen, J. Chhugani, C. J. Hughes, C. Kim, V. W. Lee, and A. D. Nguyen, "Atomic vector operations on chip multiprocessors," in *Proceedings of the 35th Annual International Symposium on Computer Architecture*, ser. ISCA '08. Washington, DC, USA: IEEE Computer Society, 2008, pp. 441–452.

[13] C. Nugteren, G.-J. van den Braak, H. Corporaal, and B. Mesman, "High performance predictable histogramming on gpus: exploring and evaluating algorithm trade-offs," in *Proceedings of the Fourth Workshop on General Purpose Processing on Graphics Processing Units*, ser. GPGPU-4. New York, NY, USA: ACM, 2011, pp. 1:1–1:8.

[14] NVIDIA, "Gpu computing sdk." NVIDIA. [Online]. Available: https://developer.nvidia.com/gpu-computing-sdk

[15] V. Podlozhnyuk, "Histogram calculation in cuda," in *Technical Report*. NVIDIA, 2007.

[16] R. Shams and R. A. Kennedy, "Efficient histogram algorithms for NVIDIA CUDA compatible devices," in *Proc. Int. Conf. on Signal Processing and Communications Systems (ICSPCS)*, Gold Coast, Australia, Dec. 2007, pp. 418–422.

[17] G.-J. Van Den Braak, C. Nugteren, B. Mesman, and H. Corporaal, "Gpu-vote: A framework for accelerating voting algorithms on gpu," in *Proceedings of the 18th International Conference on Parallel Processing*, ser. Euro-Par'12. Berlin, Heidelberg: Springer-Verlag, 2012, pp. 945–956. [Online]. Available: http://dx.doi.org/10.1007/978-3-642-32820-6_92

[18] V. Vineet and P. Narayanan, "Cuda cuts: Fast graph cuts on the gpu," in *Proceedings of CVPR workshop on Visual Computer Visions on the GPUs*, 2008.

[19] E. Z. Zhang, Y. Jiang, Z. Guo, K. Tian, and X. Shen, "On-the-fly elimination of dynamic irregularities for gpu computing," in *Proceedings of the sixteenth international conference on Architectural support for programming languages and operating systems*, ser. ASPLOS '11. New York, NY, USA: ACM, 2011, pp. 369–380.

Exploring Garbage Collection with Haswell Hardware Transactional Memory

Carl G. Ritson

University of Kent

C.G.Ritson@kent.ac.uk

Tomoharu Ugawa

Kochi University of Technology

ugawa.tomoharu@kochi-tech.ac.jp

Richard E. Jones

University of Kent

R.E.Jones@kent.ac.uk

Abstract

Intel's latest processor microarchitecture, Haswell, adds support for a restricted form of transactional memory to the x86 programming model. We explore how this can be applied to three garbage collection scenarios in Jikes RVM: parallel copying, concurrent copying and bitmap marking. We demonstrate gains in concurrent copying speed over traditional synchronisation mechanisms of 48–101%. We also show how similar but portable performance gains can be achieved through software transactional memory techniques. We identify the architectural overhead of capturing sufficient work for transactional execution as a major stumbling block to the effective use of transactions in the other scenarios.

Categories and Subject Descriptors   D.3.4 [*Programing Languages*]: Processors—Memory management (garbage collection)

General Terms   Algorithms, Languages

Keywords   Garbage Collection; Transactional Memory; Java; Jikes RVM

1. Introduction

As physical and energy constraints have led to the end of Dennard scaling and ever increasing clock speeds, manufacturers have instead sought to increase performance by delivering increasingly parallel hardware. Garbage collection (GC) designers have taken advantage of parallel hardware in two ways. *Parallel collectors* use multiple collector threads for activities such as marking, sweeping or moving objects, although these collectors may still 'stop the world' (halt all user threads, or mutators) while they work. *Concurrent collectors* allow mutator and collector threads to execute simultaneously, although they briefly stop the world, for example, to scan mutator threads. *On-the-fly* concurrent collectors, on the other hand, never stop the world, but may stop one mutator at a time to scan its roots.

All of these strategies require synchronisation. Parallel collectors require coordination between collector threads, and concurrent collectors between mutator and collector threads so that all threads share a consistent and correct view of the heap. Synchronisation is needed in parallel collectors to ensure that if two collector threads

attempt simultaneously to mark objects, e.g. by setting bits in a bitmap, the mark state is updated correctly and no marks are lost. Similarly, parallel copying collectors must ensure that if two collector threads attempt to move an object, precisely one succeeds. Concurrent copying collectors need to ensure that mutator updates are not lost if a collector attempts to move an object at the same time as a mutator is modifying its fields. All concurrent collectors need to ensure that mutator and collector threads share a consistent, if conservative, view of the liveness of objects in the heap.

Coordination between mutators and concurrent and incremental collectors is typically achieved by having the mutator use read and/or write barriers as it loads values from or stores values into object fields; often only pointer values need be barriered. Barrier actions may notify the collector of changes to the connectivity of objects, or may ensure that mutators only see the most up-to-date versions of objects. In many cases, coordination actions can be implemented cheaply using simple loads and stores [24]. However, in some cases, collector and/or mutator threads need be synchronised, for example by using atomic instructions [11]. However, not only are such instructions more expensive than simple loads and stores, but the instructions sequences required are hard to get right, especially in the face of modern processor memory models.

Recently, there has been considerable interest in *transactional memory* as a simpler yet efficient solution to the problem of writing concurrent software. Inspired by database systems, transactional memory allows a thread to execute a sequence of instructions as a transaction. If no other thread makes a conflicting access to the memory locations used by the first thread, the transaction commits. Otherwise, the transactions aborts and the state of the thread is rolled back to that before the transaction started.

Transactional memory can be implemented in software or hardware. Until recently, hardware transactions have not been available in commodity processors, but this has changed with the release of Transactional Synchronization Extensions in Intel's new Haswell family of processors. We explore whether transactional memory, implemented in hardware or software, can improve the performance of common GC actions. Our context is Jikes RVM [1], a widely used metacircular Java virtual machine. We identify, from an audit of its wide range of GCs, parallel semispace copying collection, concurrent replicating GC and parallel bitmap marking as candidates for transactional memory support. Our results show that:

- Both software and hardware transactional memory techniques can improve the concurrent object copying speeds in the Sapphire on-the-fly collector by 48–101%.

- Hardware transactional memory offers no benefit to parallel copying or bitmap-based mark-sweep collection.

- It is essential perform sufficient work to amortise the cost of a transaction, and to plan activities to do as much work as possible outside the transaction; we demonstrate how to do this.

2. Haswell

With the release of their latest processor microarchitecture, code-named Haswell, Intel added new *Transactional Synchronization Extensions* (TSX) to their processors' instruction set [12]. These extensions provide *Restricted Transactional Memory* (RTM). Transactional memory allows the atomic manipulation of arbitrary size units of memory. Without transactional memory the largest unit of memory that can be atomically manipulated on x86 architectures is two memory words, 64 bits or 128 bits, using for example a *compare-and-swap* (CAS) operation.[^1]

2.1 Programming Model

At an instruction level, Intel's RTM is simple to use. A transaction is initiated with an XBEGIN instruction. Computation proceeds normally: memory can be read and written with common instructions and other activities such as branching and arithmetic may also be used. At the end of the transaction an XEND instruction commits any changes to memory.

During the transaction, read and write sets are constructed. These sets have cache line granularity and are based on the memory addresses read or written by the transaction's body. If these sets conflict with memory being read or written by other hardware threads then the transaction is aborted. If a transaction is aborted, all changes to memory and registers are discarded and execution jumps to a *fallback handler* supplied to the initial XBEGIN instruction. Before invoking the fallback handler, status flags are set in the processor's EAX register. These flags allow the fallback handler to determine what caused the transaction to abort.

It is worth clarifying that read and write sets are specific to a given hardware thread (the smallest unit of parallel execution in a computer system). In Intel's Haswell architecture a computer may have multiple processors, each of which has multiple cores, each of which has multiple hardware threads. Hardware threads on the same core share components such as arithmetic units and cache, but have their own registers and instruction pointer.

2.2 Performance

Our early results suggest that the set-up and tear-down cost of a successful memory transaction on Haswell is at least three times the cost of a compare-and-swap [20]. This means that there is no benefit from simply replacing other synchronisation operations with transactions; rather, sufficient work must be available to merit the use of the transaction. Beyond set-up and tear-down costs, we found that reads within a transaction incur a performance penalty of up to 20%. We believe that this arises from the additional coherence constraints placed on reads. Writes normally incur this coherence penalty anyway and thus are not affected. This makes transactions most suited to write and update activity.

3. Methodology

All GC implementations presented in this paper were modifications of Jikes RVM. Performance was evaluated using the 2006 and 2009 DaCapo benchmark suites [3]. All results were obtained from a system with a 4-core Intel Core i7-4770 processor running at 3.4GHz, with 16GiB of RAM. Stock Ubuntu Linux 12.04.3 LTS was used with kernel 3.8.0-25-generic. The processor's Turbo Boost mode and CPU frequency scaling were disabled in the system's BIOS to allow for consistent results regardless of hardware temperature.

Unless otherwise stated, testing on Jikes RVM used 'compiler replay' [7]. For each selected DaCapo benchmark, an initial set of

[^1]: Compare-and-swap updates a memory location M with a new value Y iff its current value matches another value X, reporting the success or failure of the update.

ten warmup runs are used to allow the optimising compiler to reach a stable state. The state of the optimising compiler is then recorded. Results are collected from 20 independent runs in which classes are compiled and initialised using the previously recorded compiler state. A given benchmark run generates multiple data points (one per GC); these are aggregated from all runs and the geometric mean computed. Error bars presented represent the 95% confidence interval computed as per Kalibera and Jones [17].

As we are interested in the performance of individual collector actions (e.g. copying an object) rather than total time spent in GC, a single fixed heap size of 350MiB is used for all tests, rather than conducting experiments with a range of different heap sizes. For stop-the-world collection, the GC is triggered when the available heap is exhausted. For concurrent collection, the GC is triggered as soon as 32MiB have been allocated since the last GC.

We do not explore reattempting failed transactions. While retry of transactions is possible with all the algorithms presented here, if a transaction fails we revert to the defined fallback case. This is based on our earlier observation [20] that only a small percentage of transactions are suitable for the processor to retry. Hence we assume that only a small percentage of failing transactions would succeed if reattempted.

4. Parallel Copying Collection

Copying collection typically creates a copy of all live objects in a logically contiguous area of memory, the *to-space*, discarding the previously used *from-space* and thus de-fragmenting the heap. Copying is usually integrated with tracing of live objects. When an uncopied object is reached, the GC copies the object and updates with the object's new *to-space* address the field in the *to-space* object from which it reached this object. To preserve the topology of the object graph, this address is also installed as a *forwarding pointer* in the *from-space* object in case the trace should reach it again by following other pointers. As part of this trace, unmarked edges from the object are placed onto a work queue. By sharing this work queue between a number of collector threads, copying activity can be performed in parallel [15, 22].

Two or more threads may attempt to copy the same object simultaneously. If unmanaged, this could result in multiple divergent copies of an object in *to-space*. To avoid this, interactions on the same object must be synchronised. One solution is to reserve space *optimistically* for the copy, race to install the forwarding pointer with a compare-and-swap then, if successful, copy the object. Alternatively and more *conservatively*, a GC thread could acquire exclusive access to the object while it copies it. The disadvantage of this method is that any other tracing threads that reach the object must wait until the copy is complete. On the other hand, the disadvantage of optimistic copying is that it may be difficult to un-reserve space — for example, the GC thread may have had to acquire a fresh allocation buffer — if a thread loses the race to install the forwarding pointer.

Jikes RVM adopts the conservative approach, assigning objects three distinct monotonic states: *uncopied*, *copying* and *copied*. The designers' assumption was that contention by GC threads was likely to be rare. On reaching an uncopied object the collector threads race to transition the object from *uncopied* to *copying*, using a compare-and-swap operation on the object's header. The winning thread copies the object before installing the forwarding pointer and setting the object's state to *copied*. In the Jikes RVM *semispace* collector, waiting threads spin, testing a field in the object's header. This is potentially expensive as these threads make no progress tracing until the copying thread completes. There is also no protection for the case where the copying thread is context switched by the operating system: other threads may be left busy waiting until the copying thread is resumed.

4.1 Transactional Implementation

The obvious objective for a transactional implementation of this algorithm is to remove the intermediate *copying* state. Instead, an object should transition atomically from *uncopied* to *copied*. This transition should be possible for any collector thread irrespective of the state of the other collector threads in the system. In order to amortize the overhead of the atomic update, a number of these updates must be gathered into a single transaction.

To focus on the costs of transactional and non-transactional copying, we investigated Jikes RVM's simplest copying collector. We modified the Jikes RVM semispace collector to use an optimistic copying strategy. Each object is copied to *to-space* without updating the *from-space* object's state. On completion of the copy, the state of the *from-space* object is updated (and the forwarding pointer installed) using a compare-and-swap operation. If this operation fails then the object has already been copied by another collector thread. This process potentially creates redundant copies which are discarded, creating floating garbage. However, unlike the unsynchronised case, references to these copies are not used and hence the integrity of *to-space* is preserved.

It might be thought that it would be better for the GC thread to optimistically *reserve* space, and only to copy the object if it succeeded in installing the forwarding pointer in the *from-space* object. However, the structure of Jikes RVM makes this approach difficult, and we wanted to minimise the changes that had to be made. Furthermore, as we noted above, it may be difficult to un-reserve space if the thread loses the race to install the forwarding pointer. These difficulties are exacerbated if we try to deal with multiple objects in a transaction.

Multiple forwarding pointer installations can be combined within a transaction to reduce the overhead of the atomic operations. This is achieved by buffering forwarding pointer/state updates to *from-space* objects and flushing the buffer within a transaction. Any writes dependent on the final value of these updates must also be buffered in order to maintain heap integrity. These writes include updates to the fields in *to-space* from which the trace discovered the copied objects. If dependent writes are not delayed then *to-space* objects may prematurely become visible.

In Jikes RVM copying to *to-space* occurs while tracing objects. Edges are updated to point at *to-space* as they are traced. These updates depend on the final value of the *from-space* object state. Hence these updates cannot be made until *to-space* address of the object is committed. This preserves the integrity of the heap. Tracing of copied objects is also delayed until the buffer has been committed to avoid traversing cyclic subgraphs.

Within a transaction each buffer entry is processed as follows:

1. Load the buffer entry.

2. Load the state of the *from-space* object.

3. Update the *from-space* object state if it is still *uncopied*.

4. Commit writes dependent on the *to-space* value. If the *from-space* object was updated, this will be the address stored in the buffer entry. Otherwise it will be the forwarding pointer stored in the *from-space* object (by another collector thread).

Only *from-space* object state updates and dependent edge updates are buffered. This minimises the size of the transaction. In the worst case the transaction size is three cache lines per copy: the buffer entry, the *from-space* object state and the dependent write. Thus transactions of up to 85 updates are theoretically possible. However, there are also architectural reasons why some transactions may never be able to complete, such as page faults or insufficient associative space in cache or TLB entries.

When a hardware transaction fails a fallback is needed. In our case we fall back to using atomic compare-and-swap operations

to update *from-space* object state. The result of the compare-and-swap determines the value of its dependent writes. It is not possible to determine which memory access caused the transaction to fail, hence if the transaction fails we use this method to flush the entirety of the present transaction buffer.

4.2 Results

Figure 1 shows the copying speed of four copying methods for a selection of DaCapo benchmarks. Space limitations prevent showing all the DaCapo 2006 and 2009 benchmarks, but the results shown here are representative. Performance is derived from the geometric mean of GC times. Results are normalised against the copying speed of the unmodified semispace collector with a single collector thread to show speed up. Within the figure the *std* series represents the unmodified collector. The *opt* series represents the modified collector performing optimistic copying, but not buffering updates. The series *htm* and *cas* are the collector configured to buffer 16 object updates and commit these updates using hardware transactional or compare-and-swap (fallback) mechanisms respectively. A transaction size of 16 objects provides the largest transaction size where the mean rate of transaction failures is less than 0.5% (and 1.5% of objects are duplicated due to buffering).

There are three cases where the hardware transactional variant outperforms the unmodified collector: *hsqldb* 4-threads, *antlr* 8-threads and *pmd* 8-threads. Of these the optimistic variant has better performance in two cases. Hence there is no clear benefit from using hardware transactional memory in this scenario. Additionally, optimistic copy appears to provide no clear performance or scalability benefit and typically results in reduced performance.

Comparing the hardware transactional and compare-and-swap variants gives an indication of the performance gain from transactional memory as the infrastructure cost is the same. Here hardware transactional memory provides performance increases of up to 20% (e.g. *antlr* 1, 2 and 4 threads) and a mean performance increase of 2%, 5% or 4% for 1, 2 or 4 threads respectively. Using all hardware threads (8 collector threads) degrades hardware transactional performance (mean 2% performance drop); this is to be expected as the transaction buffer (L1 cache) is shared between hardware threads. Given that the performance of the transactional collector does not surpass that of the unmodified collector (with the noted exceptions), it is clear that the architectural cost of buffering updates to form transactions negates its associated performance gains.

5. Concurrent Copying Collection

Section 4 described a collection scenario in which only collector threads are executing during collection: *stop-the-world* collection. However, concurrent GC threads must also synchronise with mutator threads. In this section we investigate explore how transactional memory can be used to accelerate copying in an implementation of the Sapphire concurrent collector [11].

Garbage collection in Sapphire has three distinct phases of activity: *tracing*, *copying* and *flipping*. In the tracing phase all reachable objects in *from-space* are allocated a *to-space* 'shell'. This is similar to stop-the-world copying collection but the object contents are not copied in this phase. An allocation barrier ensures that any newly allocated objects are also allocated shells in *to-space*. Once all objects have been traced the copying phase begins.

During the copying phase the collector copies the fields of each *from-space* object to its *to-space* shell. Mutator threads use a write barrier to replicate updates to both *from-space* and *to-space* versions of the object. Collector thread writes to the *to-space* shells are performed using compare-and-swap operations to ensure that mutator updates will not be overwritten by the collector copying activity. Critically, copying is 'semantic': *to-space* copies point

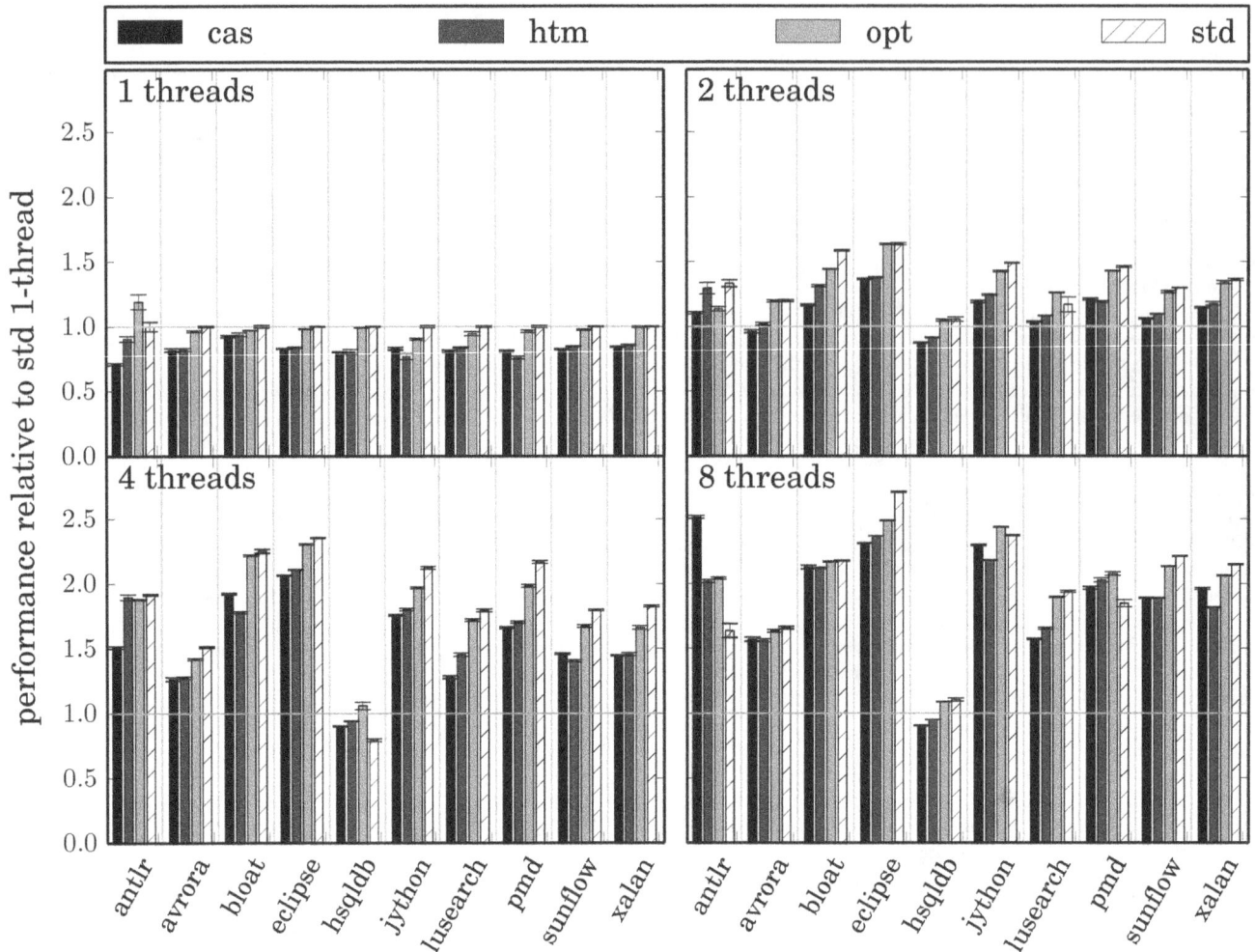

Figure 1: Performance (based on time per collection) of different copying methods. Results are normalised against the unmodified semispace collector (*std*) with one thread (higher is faster). The *opt* series shows optimistic copy, *htm* shows the hardware transactional method and *cas* the compare-and-swap fallback method of executing transactions.

only at *to-space* versions of objects. Once all objects have been copied the flip phase begins.

In the flip phase, references to *from-space* objects are replaced with references to their *to-space* versions, and mutator threads begin reading from *to-space* objects. Flipping is applied to roots and mutator stacks only: references in *to-space* already point at *to-space*. Collection is complete when all references to *from-space* have been flipped. Within the copying phase two significant overheads exist:

- semantic copying requires conditional copying of each field,
- compare-and-swap is significantly slower than simply writing to memory.

Semantic copying can be optimised by data structuring such that fields can be copied in linear word-by-word fashion. We modified Jikes RVM to ensure that reference maps are always ordered, allowing us to process object data word-by-word efficiently. Once all reference fields (and preceding data) have been semantically copied, any remaining data can be copied unconditionally word-by-word. This leaves the use of compare-and-swap as a good candidate for replacement with transactional memory instructions.

5.1 Hardware Transactional Method

The simplest approach is to copy a single object in each transaction. This method is implemented using a version of the semantic copy which does not rely on compare-and-swap. A transaction is started and this method is then invoked. If the transaction fails then we can fall back to the compare-and-swap version.

Object size is typically less than that of a single cache-line (64-bytes) [6]. This represents the expected write set of a transaction containing a single object. However, semantic copying requires the dereferencing of each reference field of the source object. On a 32-bit machine a single cache-line can hold 16 references, each of which may refer to a distinct object, hence a transaction's read-set may grow to 17 cache lines or 1088 bytes at most. In the best case the object has no reference fields and hence the read-set is only 64 bytes.

Our earlier work indicated that transactions up to 16KiB are possible on Haswell [20]. The estimates of transaction size above show there is scope for copying multiple objects within a transaction. Based on a read and write set total of 1152 bytes, 13 whole objects will fit in a transaction, disregarding other overheads.

Inline copying A multiple-object transaction can either be constructed inline with scanning of the heap, or planned by building a 'to-be-copied' list during the scan. Inline copying starts a transaction (*XBEGIN*) and scans the heap as normal. On visiting each object the scan checks if the object will fit in the transaction. If not, then the transaction is committed (*XEND*) and a new transaction is started. Otherwise the object is copied within the open transaction and its size added to the transaction size. Inline transaction construction has the disadvantage that scanning-related reads will be included in the transaction.

Planned copying removes the open transaction. Each object visited by the scan is added to a to-be-copied list. When the list reaches the desired size, a transaction is initiated and all objects are copied before committing the transaction. Planning removes scanning traffic from the transaction, but has a comparatively more heavy weight implementation and associated overheads. Various other activities may be performed as part of planning the transaction, for example looking up and caching object type information (so that associated reads do not inflate the transaction). In section 5.3 we evaluate different methods of constructing a transaction.

5.2 Software Transactional Method

In addition to a hardware transactional implementation we also tested a software transactional implementation. Rather than apply a general purpose transactional solution we constructed a minimal mechanism just for the copying phase of our Sapphire implementation. This is facilitated by the fact that the *to-space* replica of an object is not read until after the copying phase is complete and thus does not need to maintain consistency during the phase itself.

Our software transactional method comprises copying and verification steps which are performed for each object. The *copying step* semantically copies a *from-space* object to its *to-space* replica without using compare-and-swap. Any reference that has to be resolved as part of the semantic copy is stored in a buffer. A memory barrier (an *MFENCE* instruction on x86) is used to separate the copying step from the verification step. In the *verification step* the contents of a *to-space* replica are semantically compared to the *from-space* object; reference fields in the *from-space* object are compared against the buffer created during copying. If the two objects are consistent, the object has been successfully replicated. If at any point the objects are found to be inconsistent then the object is copied again using the fallback compare-and-swap method.

5.3 Results

To evaluate the performance of the different concurrent copying methods described in this section, we measured the speed of copying objects between *from-space* and *to-space*. We measured this by instrumenting Jikes RVM to record the time taken for the copy phase of collection and the number of bytes copied during this phase. These measurements are used to compute the copying speed of each copying phase independently. The geometric mean of these measurements is then computed from all measurements collected across all runs of a given DaCapo benchmark. Each benchmark may have a different copying speed due to variations in reference density; references will slow copying as they must be resolved. The measurement architecture was the same for all tests and thus any overhead was constant.

First we investigated the multi-object copying methods described in section 5.1 to determine the optimal transaction size for these. We parameterised these methods over the number of bytes written to *to-space* as a proxy for the overall transaction size. While computing the size of the transaction required to copy an object is possible at run time, the overhead incurred would be detrimental to performance. Due to semantic copying each word written to

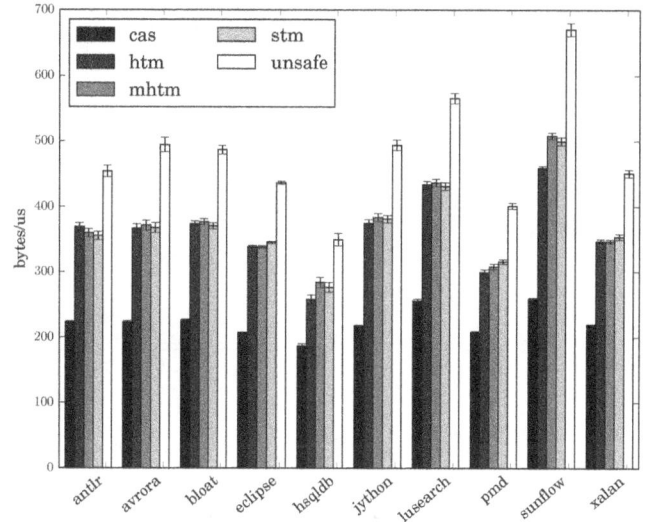

Figure 2: Speed of different copying methods in Sapphire with mutators stopped. The base compare-and-swap method is shown as *cas*. Hardware transactional copy is shown as *htm* and the planned multi-object variant with 256 byte transactions as *mhtm*. Software transactional copy is shown as *stm*. Unsynchronised copying, a method only safe when mutators are stopped, is shown as *unsafe*.

to-space can cause an additional cache line to be added to the transaction's read set. Hence the worst case transaction size required to copy and object is proportional to the *to-space* size of the object.

Figure 3 shows the performance of three different multi-object copying methods across a range of DaCapo benchmarks and transaction sizes. For these tests mutators are not active during the copying phase and hence results represent the *optimal* performance. The inline scanning method is shown as *mhtm inline*. Planned transactions are shown as *mhtm plan* and *mhtm full*. For *mhtm plan* the transaction plan consists of the *from-space* and *to-space* addresses of each object to be copied. With *mhtm full* the plan also includes two words of header information from the object's type information block (TIB) in order to further reduce the number of cache lines referenced during the transaction.

At small transaction sizes the performance of all three variants is very similar. As transaction size increases, a tipping point is reached, for the inline variant at around 128 bytes (approximately 2–3 objects). After this tipping point the performance of the inline variant rapidly degrades, presumably as a result of the read set size becoming too large for most transactions to complete.

Performance of both *mhtm plan* and *mhtm full* is stable once an optimal transaction size has been reached. Some gradual decline in performance can be seen, but a tipping point has clearly not been reached. The *full* variant is always marginally slower that the more basic *plan* variant. This suggests that the overhead of preloading the TIB data is not amortized by any performance gained by this optimisation. Based on these results we only evaluated the basic planning model *mhtm plan* with a transaction size of 256 bytes.

Figure 2 shows the copying speed of all methods across a selection of DaCapo benchmarks with a single collector thread. These tests represent the *optimal* case as mutator threads are stopped during the copying phase: no interference is present. The base case using compare-and-swap is represented by the *cas* series. The hardware transactional method is shown by *htm* and multi-object hardware transactional by the *mhtm* series. The software transactional

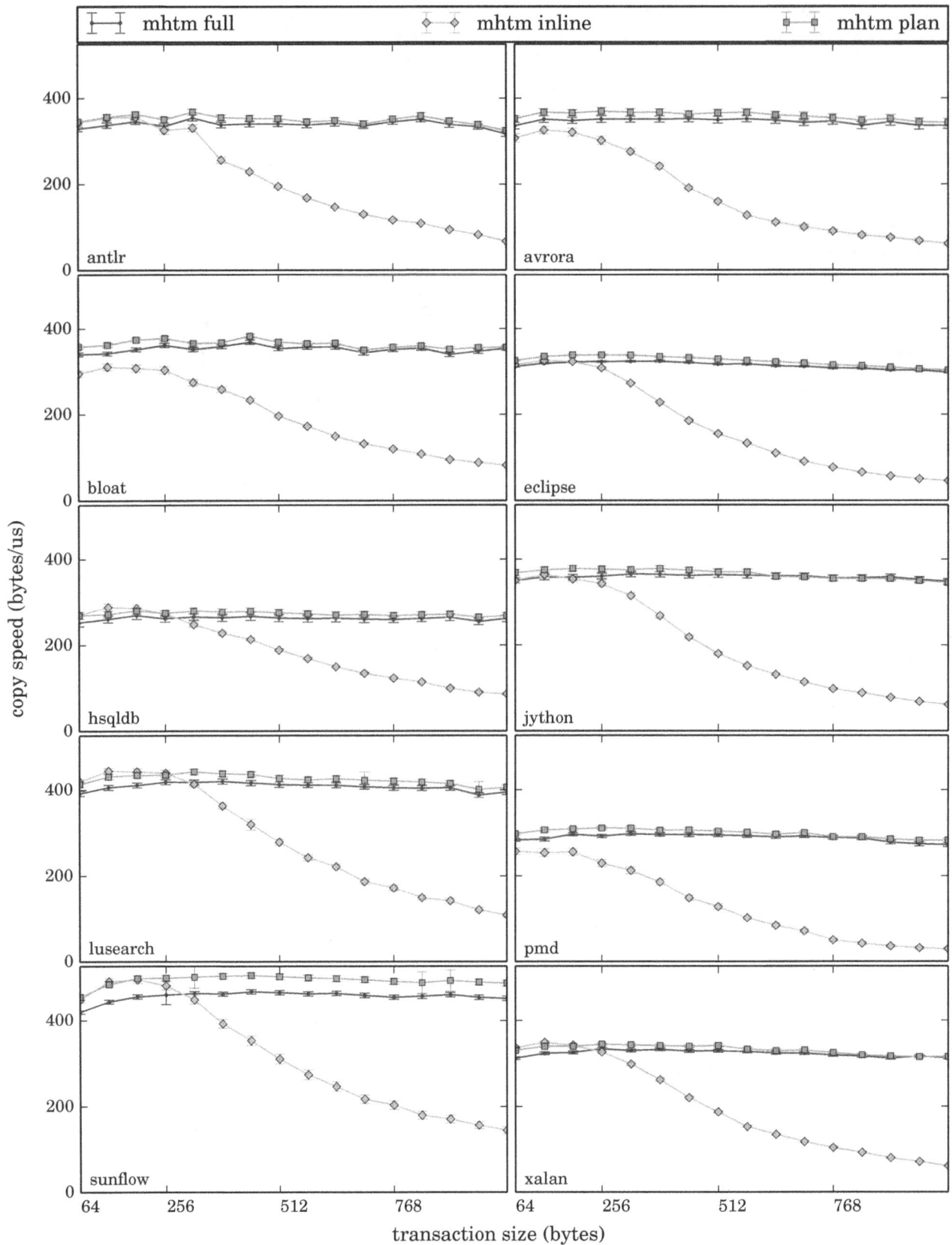

Figure 3: Speed of different transaction size transactions with multiple object copying. Inline transaction construction is shown as *mhtm inline*. Planned transaction construction is shown as *mhtm plan*. Planned transaction construction including TIB pre-loading is shown as *mhtm full*.

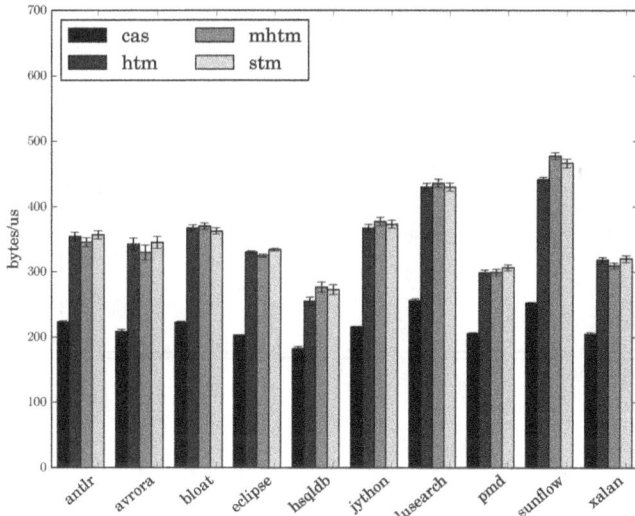

Figure 4: Speed of different copying methods in Sapphire with mutators running. Copying methods are the same as those shown in figure 2.

method corresponds to the *stm* series. As mutators are stopped it is also possible to use an unsynchronised method of copying: this is corresponds to the *unsafe* series. This series is unsafe because it does not prevent inconsistencies arising from concurrent mutator activity. Copying with transactional methods is 60-80% faster than the base *cas* variant. However, there is still a significant difference in copying speeds between synchronised variants and the unsynchronised case (*unsafe*). It is significant that *stm* and *htm* variants have comparable performance. This suggests that transactional performance gains can be made without hardware support.

Figure 4 reproduces the tests shown in figure 2 with results from the realistic configuration with mutator threads active during the copying phase. The transactional methods, both hardware and software, continue to show substantial performance improvements over the original method of copying objects using CAS instructions. Results for some benchmarks with many mutator threads, in particular *sunflow* and *xalan*, show some reduction in performance of the transactional methods. While the pattern of performance is broadly similar to the case with mutators stopped, there is a slight indication that the *mhtm* method is affected more by mutator contention.

Figure 5 shows the speed of different copying methods with increasing numbers of collector threads. While the processor used for testing has four cores, each of these cores has two hardware threads, so we explore scaling up to eight collector threads. For *cas*, *htm* and *stm*, peak performance is reached with six or seven collector threads. As most benchmarks are not heavily multi-threaded this may correspond to the case where there are one or two mutator threads executing in parallel with the collector threads. Adding further collector threads causes context switching with the mutator and hence does not yield any further gain in performance.

Significantly, the multi-object hardware transactional method (*mhtm*) does not scale as well as other methods. Haswell uses the processor's L1 cache to hold a transaction's read and write sets. Hardware threads on the same core share the L1 cache. As *mhtm* creates larger transactions there is greater contention on L1 cache, leading to more transaction failures with higher numbers of collector threads and reduced copying speeds. In particular *antlr* shows an oscillation in performance. This may correspond to the mapping of collector threads to hardware threads on the same or different cores; this requires further investigation.

6. Bitmap Marking

All tracing collectors need some mechanism to mark the objects that they have visited. Non-moving mark-sweep collectors do so by setting a mark either in the object's header or in a separate side table. In principle, a single bit is sufficient for the mark, and there is usually space for it in an existing header word. However, some collectors use a small number of bits so that the value of a mark used for the current collection is different from that used for the next collection. This removes the need for the sweep phase to clear the marks from live objects and hence reduces the number of objects modified in the cache.

The alternative to storing the mark bit in object headers is to use separate bitmaps. The size of the bitmap depends on two factors: the alignment of objects in the heap and the number of bits used to represent a mark. For example, a system that allocates objects on double-word boundaries will require a mark bitmap half the size of that required by a system that allocates on single-word boundaries.

The simplest design is a single bitmap to represent the entire heap. However, in a block-structured heap, a separate bitmap can be used for each block. The latter organisation has the advantage that no space is wasted if the heap is not contiguous. This organisation also permits varying alignment of objects per block, e.g. for 'big bag of pages' schemes, further increasing the density of bitmaps. Per-block bitmaps might be stored in the blocks. However, placing the bitmap at a fixed position in each block risks degrading performance as the bitmaps contend for the same sets in a set-associative cache. A solution is to vary the position of the bitmap in the block using some simple hash of the block's address to determine an offset for the bit map. Alternatively, the bitmap can be stored to the side, somehow indexed by the block, again perhaps by hashing [4].

Mark bitmaps have a number of potential advantages over mark bits in object headers. A bitmap stores marks more densely. Marking with a bitmap modifies only the bitmap, not objects; conservative collectors use bitmap marking for this reason: as they are not type accurate, they dare not modify data in the heap. Sweeping need neither read nor modify live objects. Moreover, given the tendency of objects to live and die in clusters [9, 16], use of a bitmap allows a sweeper to test the liveness of several objects at a time in the common case that every bit is set or every bit is clear. A corollary is that it is simple to determine from the bitmap whether a complete block is garbage. Overall, bitmap marking might be expected to dirty fewer cache lines than header marking.

However, bitmaps also have disadvantages. A collector with parallel marking threads must ensure that GC threads do not interfere with each other as they update a bit map word: the update must be indivisible. Either the bitmap must be updated with an atomic instruction or bytes rather than bits must be used for marks. In contrast, parallel collector threads can use plain stores to mark header words since the action of setting the mark bit(s) is idempotent. However, this may not be the case for a concurrent collector in which both mutator and collector threads are active simultaneously. If mark bits share the same header words as other runtime structures such as lock or hashcode bits, both mutator and collector operations must be synchronised.

In this section we ask, can transactional memory techniques reduce the synchronisation overheads required by bitmap marking in Jikes RVM on Intel's Haswell architecture?

6.1 Transactional Method

Updating a single mark in a bitmap is insufficient to amortize the cost of transaction setup and shutdown: a transaction must set multiple marks to be efficient. As with concurrent copying (section 5) there are two potential methods for constructing a transaction: *inline* and *planned*. We evaluated a method of constructing the transaction inline with heap tracing and found that transaction formation

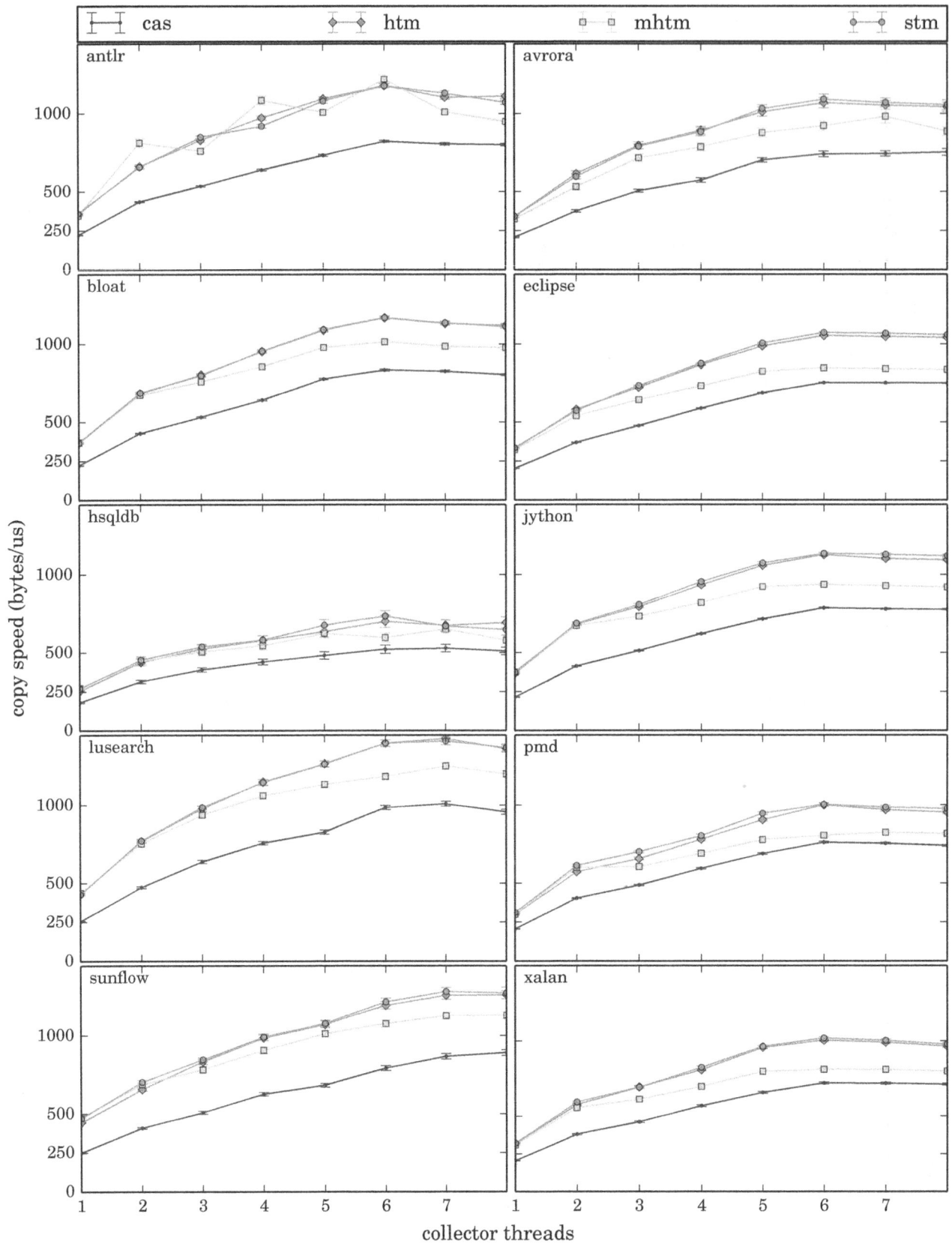

Figure 5: Speed of copying methods with increasing numbers of collector threads. The series are the same as figure 2.

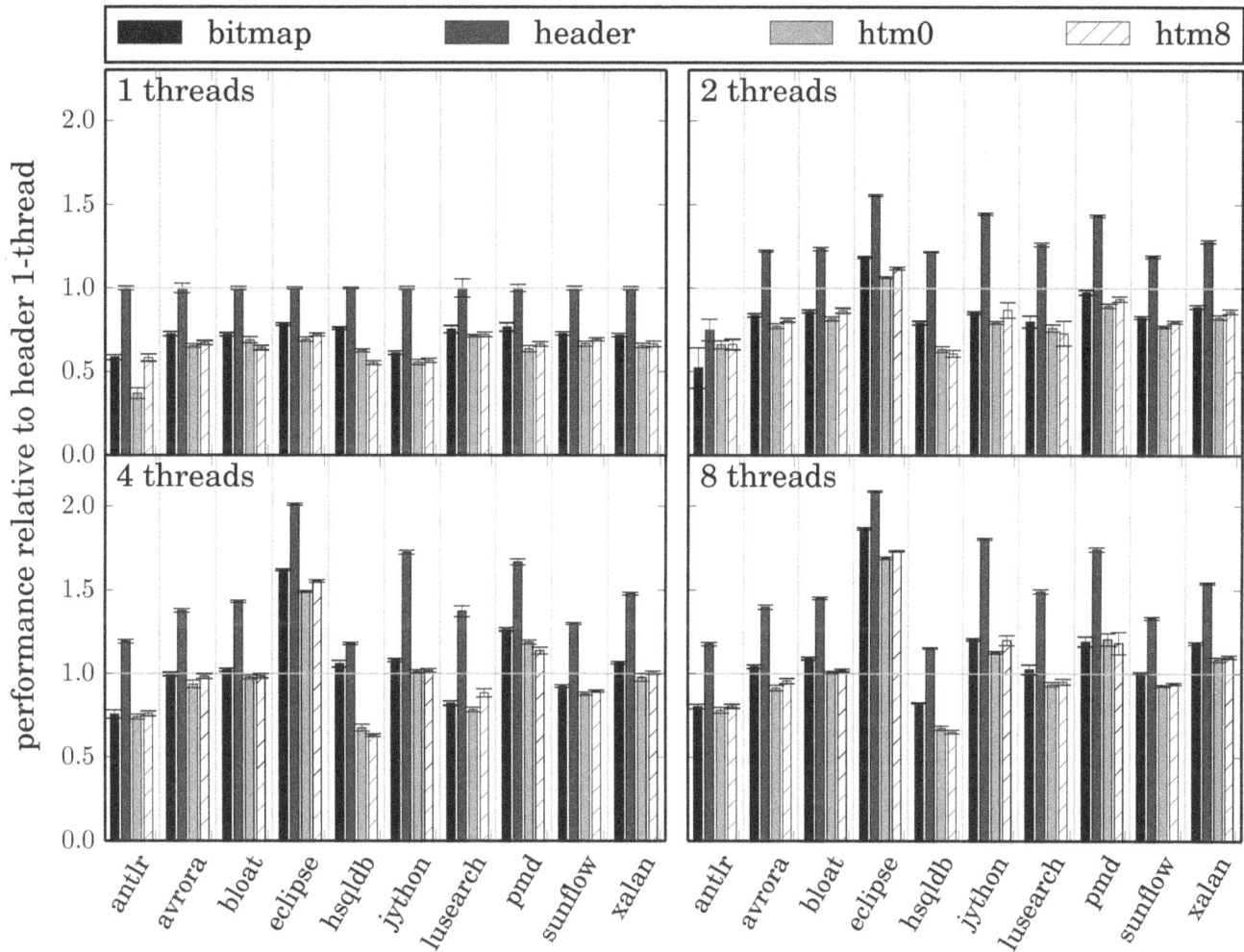

Figure 6: Performance (based on time per collection) of different marking methods. Results are normalised against the unmodified mark-sweep collector using header marking (*header*) and one thread. The *bitmap* series shows the same collector using bitmap marking. The hardware transactional architecture without using transactions is shown as *htm0*, and with transactions of eight marks as *htm8*.

and mark queue interaction interfered. Pushing and popping from a shared queue of gray objects requires thread synchronisation operations which cannot be performed within a transaction. These operations are non-trivial to remove so we abandoned an inline approach.

A planned transaction can be constructed by buffering updates to the marking bitmaps. During the trace when an object is to be marked, the bitmap is not updated; rather, the relevant bitmap address and mark bit are stored in a buffer. Once the buffer reaches a given size, it is flushed by writing the relevant bitmap words within a transaction. In the event of transaction failure the buffered updates are applied using compare-and-swap.

This planning scenario produces an almost ideal transaction as the read and write sets of the transaction need only contain the buffer and the bitmap words updated. However it is important to consider that each bitmap word updated by the transaction may lie on a different cache line. Hence the worst case transaction size is 64 bytes for each mark, plus 64 bytes buffer bytes per eight marks. We determined by testing (results not shown) that optimal performance was reached with transactions of eight marks.

6.2 Results

We tested the performance of transactional marking using Jikes RVM's mark-sweep collector. Figure 6 compares the performance of different marking methodologies. As with parallel copying in section 4, our performance metric is GC time.

The default configuration of the mark-sweep collector is to use header marking, rather than bitmap marking. Header marking (labelled *header*) does not require synchronisation and thus represents the unsynchronised case; we normalise results from other configurations against this base case. Standard bitmap marking with a CAS operation is represented by the *bitmap* series.

Results for the transactional method are shown by the *htm8* series. To evaluate the impact of the architectural changes required for transactional marking, we include results for the case where marks are captured during the trace, but are committed immediately using compare-and-swap (*htm0* series).

Clearly performance of bitmap marking is significantly lower than header marking (30–40% slower). Some of this performance decrease can be attributed to the need for synchronisation on bitmap marking; it is this that we hope to reclaim by using transactions.

Comparing *htm0* to *bitmap*, we see that introducing our architecture for buffering marking reduces performance by a further 10%. A key architectural cost of buffering marks is the introduction of branching and indirect call costs on each mark operation. Clearly these have a significant impact on the pipelining activity of the processor and thus overall performance.

Once margins of error have been considered there is no clear case where the transactional implementation (*htm8*) surpasses the performance of synchronised bitmap marking. This suggests that architectural costs have not been amortized by performance gains. Furthermore this performance margin is maintained with increased numbers of collector threads. Hence we can also conclude that the transactional method does not have any improved scaling behaviour. However, we did not explore different organisations and placements of the bitmaps in order to reduce the risk of contention or false sharing of cache lines.

7. Related Work

The earliest work on GC transactions discussed it in the context of transactional systems, such as reliable distributed systems [5], object-oriented databases [2] or persistent object stores [25]. Here the main issues were how to expose rollback mechanisms to the collector. in contrast, we are interested in using transactional memory to support GC.

Transactional memory was first proposed by Herlihy and Moss [10] as a hardware architecture intended to make lock-free synchronization as efficient (and easy to use) as conventional techniques based on mutual exclusion. Hardware transactional memory (HTM) has been provided by Sun Microsystems' Rock processor (although this was never released as a product), IBM's BlueGene/Q and Azul Systems Vega processors. In 2009 AMD proposed the Advanced Synchronization Facility (ASF), a set of x86 extensions to provide a limited form of hardware transactional memory, but has yet to announce whether it will be used in products.

However, Intel's Transactional Synchronization Extensions (TSX) have been implemented in some of its new Haswell commodity processors (2013). Ritson and Barnes evaluate in detail the performance of this restricted transactional memory on a Core i7-4770 processor and examine its potential application for the implementation of communicating process architectures [20].

The idea of implementing transactional memory in software alone (STM) is due to Shavit and Touitou [21]. Researchers have proposed exposing STM to the programmer through language extensions such as `atomic` blocks with `retry` actions [8].

7.1 Transactional memory for copying

To the best of our knowledge, the first use of software transactional memory to support GC was by McGachey et al. [18]. Their concurrent GC supported a version of Java extended with an `atomic` construct. Read and write barriers were used both for transactional code and to provide strong atomicity. Each object stores a transaction version number in its header, which is used by both the mutators and the GC. In contrast to (our transactional memory implementations of) the Sapphire on-the-fly copying GC which places no restrictions on mutators, McGachey et al. must put an object into exclusive mode before writing to it. The GC notes the version number before copying then object and checks that the number has not changed afterwards. If it has, the copy aborts and has to be retried. Only one object is copied in a transaction.

Collie [13] is an on-the-fly, concurrent collector that uses the HTM provided by Azul Systems Vega processors to provide wait-free compaction; again, to the best of our knowledge, it is the first GC to exploit HTM. Collie uses a hardware supported read barrier to ensure that mutators always access to-space replicas of objects, unlike Sapphire which uses from-space objects until its root-

flip phase. Collie is mostly compacting: an object that cannot be physically copied wait-free ("individually transplanted") is virtually copied by mapping its from-space page to the same physical memory as its mirrored to-space page. In order to provide wait-freedom, objects referenced from roots or accessed by mutators while Collie is trying to move them are not compacted. During its mark phase [23], Collie constructs conservative "referrer sets" of objects holding references to each object. During the compaction phase, read and write barriers mark objects as non-transportable, replacing references to them (including those in their referrer set) with references to their corresponding address on the mirrored to-space page. In contrast, our copying collectors never pin objects, although Jikes RVM does allocate some object in non-moving spaces. Like our implementations, Collie tries to reduce the size of transactional read and write sets. To transplant an individual object, Collie copies its contents before it starts a transaction. Inside the transaction, it checks the references in the referrer set: if any point to the mirrored to-space, the transaction (and the copy) is aborted. Otherwise the transaction commits.

8. Conclusion and Further Work

In this work we have explored the basic application of hardware transactional memory to GC. Our results show that transactional memory can provide performance gains if sufficient and concise work is available for embedding in a transaction. The work must be *sufficient* to amortize the cost of transaction setup and any other architectural costs, and *concise* enough not to inflate the work that must be performed within the transaction with dependent activity that could be performed outside it.

Our results also suggest that while appropriate work may be available for transactional execution, the architectural overheads of capturing this work within existing collectors may outweigh the benefits of using transactions (section 6.2). Further work is required to establish how collectors may be designed to produce packets of work suitable for transactional execution. From our work here transactional memory is most applicable to concurrent and on-the-fly collectors where synchronisation requirements are complex. Whilst we present results only for Jikes RVM on Intel's Haswell architecture, the requirements for sufficient and concise work make it unlikely that different conclusions could be drawn for other GCs or architectures.

While not fully explored in this work, software transactional approaches can be applied to all the algorithms presented here. Where tested, our software transactional approaches performed as well or better than hardware transactional memory, suggesting that many of the benefits of transactions can be obtained without hardware support. One reason is that we can weaken the requirements for consistency within a software transaction.

The existence of software transactional solutions to the algorithms explored here suggests that the full potential of hardware transactional memory is not being exploited. Hardware transactional memory has the potential to solve problems which cannot be overcome with traditional synchronisation mechanisms as it can provide strong consistency for reads and writes to distributed memory locations. We suggest further work to explore this design space for virtual machines and GC.

Acknowledgments

We are grateful to Rick Hudson and Intel for a license to implement Sapphire in Jikes RVM, and Laurence Hellyer for his work on Sapphire. We are also grateful for the support of the JSPS KAKENHI Grant Number 25330080, the EPSRC through grant EP/H026975/1, Google's Summer of Code and the University of Kent Sciences Faculty Research Fund.

References

[1] B. Alpern, C. R. Attanasio, A. Cocchi, D. Lieber, S. Smith, T. Ngo, J. J. Barton, S. F. Hummel, J. C. Sheperd, and M. Mergen. Implementing Jalapeño in Java. In *ACM SIGPLAN Conference on Object-Oriented Programming, Systems, Languages, and Applications*, ACM SIGPLAN Notices 34(10), pages 314–324, Denver, CO, Oct. 1999. ACM Press.

[2] L. Amsaleg, M. Franklin, and O. Gruber. Garbage collection for a client-server persistent object store. *ACM Transactions on Computer Systems*, 17(3):153–201, 1999.

[3] S. M. Blackburn, R. Garner, C. Hoffman, A. M. Khan, K. S. McKinley, R. Bentzur, A. Diwan, D. Feinberg, D. Frampton, S. Z. Guyer, M. Hirzel, A. Hosking, M. Jump, H. Lee, J. E. B. Moss, A. Phansalkar, D. Stefanović, T. VanDrunen, D. von Dincklage, and B. Wiedermann. The DaCapo benchmarks: Java benchmarking development and analysis. In *ACM SIGPLAN Conference on Object-Oriented Programming, Systems, Languages, and Applications*, ACM SIGPLAN Notices 41(10), pages 169–190, Portland, OR, Oct. 2006. ACM Press.

[4] H.-J. Boehm and M. Weiser. Garbage collection in an uncooperative environment. *Software: Practice and Experience*, 18(9):807–820, 1988.

[5] D. L. Detlefs. *Concurrent, Atomic Garbage Collection*. PhD thesis, Carnegie Mellon University, Pittsburgh, PA, 15213, Nov. 1991.

[6] S. Dieckmann and U. Hölzle. A study of the allocation behaviour of the SPECjvm98 Java benchmarks. In R. Guerraoui, editor, *13th European Conference on Object-Oriented Programming*, volume 1628 of *Lecture Notes in Computer Science*, pages 92–115, Lisbon, Portugal, July 1999. Springer-Verlag.

[7] A. Georges, L. Eeckhout, and D. Buytaert. Java performance evaluation through rigorous replay compilation. In *ACM SIGPLAN Conference on Object-Oriented Programming, Systems, Languages, and Applications*, ACM SIGPLAN Notices 43(10), pages 367–384, Nashville, TN, Oct. 2008. ACM Press.

[8] T. Harris and K. Fraser. Language support for lightweight transactions. In *ACM SIGPLAN Conference on Object-Oriented Programming, Systems, Languages, and Applications*, ACM SIGPLAN Notices 38(11), pages 388–402, Anaheim, CA, Nov. 2003. ACM Press.

[9] B. Hayes. Using key object opportunism to collect old objects. In *ACM SIGPLAN Conference on Object-Oriented Programming, Systems, Languages, and Applications*, ACM SIGPLAN Notices 26(11), pages 33–46, Phoenix, AZ, Nov. 1991. ACM Press.

[10] M. P. Herlihy and J. E. B. Moss. Transactional memory: Architectural support for lock-free data structures. In *20th Annual International Symposium on Computer Architecture*, pages 289–300, San Diego, CA, May 1993. IEEE Press.

[11] R. L. Hudson and J. E. B. Moss. Sapphire: Copying garbage collection without stopping the world. *Concurrency and Computation: Practice and Experience*, 15(3–5):223–261, 2003.

[12] Intel. *Intel® 64 and IA-32 Architectures Software Developer's Manual*, June 2013.

[13] B. Iyengar, G. Tene, M. Wolf, and E. Gehringer. The Collie: a wait-free compacting collector. In McKinley and Vechev [19], pages 85–96.

[14] R. Jones and S. Blackburn, editors. *7th International Symposium on Memory Management*, Tucson, AZ, June 2008. ACM Press.

[15] R. Jones, A. Hosking, and E. Moss. *The Garbage Collection Handbook: The Art of Automatic Memory Management*. CRC Applied Algorithms and Data Structures. Chapman & Hall, Aug. 2012.

[16] R. Jones and C. Ryder. A study of Java object demographics. In Jones and Blackburn [14], pages 121–130.

[17] T. Kalibera and R. Jones. Rigorous benchmarking in reasonable time. In E. Petrank and P. Cheng, editors, *12th International Symposium on Memory Management*, Seattle, WA, June 2013. ACM Press.

[18] P. McGachey, A.-R. Adl-Tabatabi, R. L. Hudson, V. Menon, B. Saha, and T. Shpeisman. Concurrent GC leveraging transactional memory. In *ACM SIGPLAN Symposium on Principles and Practice of Parallel Programming*, pages 217–226, Salt Lake City, UT, Feb. 2008. ACM Press.

[19] K. McKinley and M. Vechev, editors. *11th International Symposium on Memory Management*, Beijing, China, June 2012. ACM Press.

[20] C. G. Ritson and F. R. Barnes. An evaluation of Intels Restricted Transactional Memory for CPAs. In *Communicating Process Architectures*, 2013.

[21] N. Shavit and D. Touitou. Software transactional memory. In *Proceedings of the 14th ACM Symposium on Principles of Distributed Computing*, pages 204–213, Aug. 1995.

[22] F. Siebert. Limits of parallel marking collection. In Jones and Blackburn [14], pages 21–29.

[23] G. Tene, B. Iyengar, and M. Wolf. C4: The continuously concurrent compacting collector. In H. Boehm and D. Bacon, editors, *10th International Symposium on Memory Management*, pages 79–88, San Jose, CA, June 2011. ACM Press.

[24] X. Yang, S. M. Blackburn, D. Frampton, and A. L. Hosking. Barriers reconsidered, friendlier still! In McKinley and Vechev [19], pages 37–48.

[25] J. Zigman, S. M. Blackburn, and J. E. B. Moss. TMOS: a transactional garbage collector. In G. N. C. Kirby, A. Dearle, and D. I. K. Sjoberg, editors, *9th International Workshop on Persistent Object Systems (Sept., 2000)*, volume 2135 of *Lecture Notes in Computer Science*, pages 116–135, Lillehammer, Norway, 2001. Springer.

Parallel Real-time Garbage Collection of Multiple Heaps in Reconfigurable Hardware

David F. Bacon   Perry Cheng   Sunil Shukla

IBM Research
{dfb,perry,skshukla}@us.ibm.com

Abstract

Despite rapid increases in memory capacity, reconfigurable hardware is still programmed in a very low-level manner, generally without any dynamic allocation at all.

This limits productivity especially as the larger chips encourage more and more complex designs to be attempted.

Prior work has shown that it is possible to implement a real-time collector in hardware and achieve stall-free operation — but at the price of severe restrictions on object layouts. We present the first hardware garbage collector capable of collecting multiple inter-connected heaps, thereby allowing a rich set of object types.

We show that for a modest additional cost in logic and memory, we can support multiple heaps at a clock frequency competitive with monolithic, fixed-layout heaps. We evaluate the hardware design by synthesizing it for a Xilinx FPGA and using co-simulation to measure the run-time behavior over a set of four benchmarks. Even at high allocation and mutation rates the collector is able to sustain stall-free (100% minimum mutator utilization) operation with up to 4 inter-connected heaps, while only requiring between 1.1 and 1.7 times the maximum live memory of the application.

Categories and Subject Descriptors   B.5.1 [*Register-Transfer-Level Implementation*]: Memory design; B.7.1 [*Integrated Circuits*]: Gate arrays; C.3 [*Special-Purpose and Application-Based Systems*]: Real-time and embedded systems; D.3.3 [*Programming Languages*]: Language Constructs and Features;   D.3.4 [*Programming Languages*]: Memory management (garbage collection)

General Terms   Design, Languages, Experimentation, Performance

Keywords   Block RAM, FPGA, High Level Synthesis, Garbage Collection, Real Time

1. Introduction

With CPU clock frequencies stalled, the search for performance has turned to heterogeneous computing systems exploiting large amounts of parallelism. Most radically, one can generate custom hardware for a program, either as an ASIC or using reconfigurable hardware (FPGAs). Current FPGAs contain multiple megabytes of on-chip memory, configured in hundreds of individual banks which can be accessed in parallel with single-cycle latency.

As the size and complexity of FPGAs increases, garbage collection emerges as a plausible technique for improving programmability of the hardware and raising its level of abstraction.

In previous work [2] we demonstrated the first collector for on-chip memory in reconfigurable hardware, but it could only handle 2 pointers per object. We subsequently generalized and improved this design to allow an arbitrary—but fixed—number of pointers per object [3]. This allows the support of *general data types*. However, since real programs may use many data types, with potentially very different sizes and pointer densities, this system is still insufficient to provide garbage collection for *general programs*, and thus remains impractical.

There are essentially two ways to support diverse data types. The first is to make the heap itself more flexible, with variable object sizes, byte-addressability, and so on. However, such a design would sacrifice many of the fundamental desirable properties of these hardware garbage collectors: deterministic single-cycle access, support for parallel operations on fields, etc. Furthermore, placing all objects in a single heap eliminates the possibility of parallel access to different objects, which is also inimical to hardware implementation. Fundamentally, a traditional byte-oriented, variable object-size heap would be applying a software-oriented approach to hardware, and thereby sacrifice the fundamental advantages of the hardware itself.

The alternative is to support object heterogeneity by having multiple hardware heaps, each with different object layouts. This is roughly analogous to the "big bag of pages" approach to a software memory allocator, in which each page only contains one type of object, and the metadata for the objects is implicit in the page in which they reside [16].

In this work we investigate the latter style of solution. The challenges in such a design primarily lie in managing the coordination between the heaps, avoiding live-lock and deadlock, ensuring that single-cycle access is maintained, and devising a correct and efficient termination algorithm.

Superficially, having multiple independent heaps with inter-heap pointers seems like a form of distributed garbage collection. In some sense this is true, but as Abdullahi and Ringwood observe, the fundamental defining characteristic of distributed garbage collection is multiple orders of magnitude difference in local versus remote pointer access [1].

However, within a single FPGA chip, even with the interposition of queues for load balancing, the inter-heap delay is only be a few clock cycles. Therefore the approaches developed for distributed systems do not really apply.

It might seem as though collectors for many-core systems with fast on-chip networks (such as the collector of Zhou and Demsky for the 64-core Tilera chip[20]) might share some

ISMM'14, June 12, 2014, Edinburgh, UK.
Copyright © 2014 ACM 978-1-4503-2921-7/14/06. . . $15.00.
http://dx.doi.org/10.1145/2602988.2602996

features with our hardware collector. However, in such systems the dominant issues are maintaining locality between objects and the cores on which they are processed, and handling the complexities of distributed agreement given the variable latencies between cores.

In hardware, on the other hand, we can coordinate multiple heaps within one or two cycles, greatly simplifying distributed agreement. And the dominant concern is minimizing the number of wires and amount of multiplexing.

The contributions of this work are

- The first garbage collector for reconfigurable hardware that comprises multiple heterogeneous heaps, making hardware garbage collection practical for complex data structures;

- Quantitative comparison with previous, less general hardware garbage collectors showing that the cost for such generality is modest when applied to a single heap;

- Evaluation of the costs involved in wiring together multiple heaps and coordinating between them;

- Validation and characterization of dynamic properties of the system using co-simulation with several benchmarks, showing that they can achieve stall-free (100% minimum mutator utilization) real-time operation at multiples between 1.1 and 1.7 times the maximum live data of the program.

2. FPGA Basics

Field Programmable Gate Arrays (FPGAs) are programmable logic devices consisting of 4- or 6-input look-up tables (LUTs) which can be used to implement combinational logic, and flip-flops which can be used to implement sequential logic. On the Xilinx FPGAs which we use in this work, several LUTs and flip-flops are combined together to form a unit called a *slice*, which is the standard unit in which resource consumption is reported for FPGAs.

FPGAs also include a clock distribution network for propagating a globally synchronized clock to allow for the use of conventional clocked digital logic. Our collector takes advantage of this global clock in a number of ways, in particular to implement an efficient single-cycle atomic root snapshot.

The FPGA also contains a large amount of configurable routing resources for connecting the slices, based on the data flow in the hardware description language program. The routing resources are used by the place-and-route (PAR) tool during hardware synthesis.

2.1 Memory Structures on FPGAs

Particularly important to this work are the memories available on the FPGA. Block RAMs (BRAMs) are specialized memory structures embedded within the FPGA for resource-efficient implementation of large random- and sequential-access memories.

The Xilinx Virtex-5 LX330T [18] device that we use in this paper (one of the largest in that family) has a BRAM capacity of 1.5 MB; the latest generation of Xilinx devices, the Virtex-7, have as much as 8 MB of BRAM.

A single BRAM in a Virtex-5 FPGA can store up to 36 Kilobits (Kb) of memory. An important feature of BRAM is that it can be organized in various form factors (analogous to word sizes on a CPU). On the Virtex-5, form factors of 1, 2, 4, 9, 18, 36, 72, and so on are supported. A 36 Kb BRAM can also be used as two logically separate 18 Kb BRAMs. Moreover, a larger memory structure can be built by cascading multiple BRAMs horizontally, vertically or in a hybrid manner. Any memory structure in the design which is smaller than 18 Kb would lead to quantization (or, in memory system parlance, "fragmentation").

The quantization effect can be considerable depending on the logical memory structure in the design. A BRAM can be used as a true dual ported (TDP) RAM providing two fully independent read-write ports. Furthermore, each port supports either read, write, read-before-write, or read-after-write operations. Our collector makes significant use of read-before-write for things like the Yuasa-style write barrier [19].

BRAMs can also be configured for use as FIFO queues rather than as random access memories; we make use of this feature for implementing the mark queues in the tracing phase of the collector.

FPGAs are typically packaged on boards with dedicated off-chip DRAM and/or SRAM which can be accessed via a memory controller synthesized for the FPGA. Such memory could be used to implement much larger heap structures. However, we do not consider use of DRAM or SRAM in this paper because we are focusing on high-performance designs with highly deterministic (single cycle) behavior.

Apart from BRAM, group of LUTs can be used to implement memory structures too. Such memories in FPGA design are referred as *distributed RAM*. This is the most fine-grained type of memory on the FPGA. When the amount of memory in question is small, it is often the best choice: distributed RAM provided 0-latency memory access. We make limited use of distributed RAM for small queues.

2.2 Explicit Memory Management on the FPGA

To begin with, we describe the way in which objects with pointers in high-level programs are mapped to memory in the FPGA's block RAMs. There are of course many possible variations, but this one will form the basis of the garbage-collected memory managers in subsequent sections.

As shown in Figure 1, all objects of a given type are mapped to a group of BRAMs, one per object field — a "column-based" layout. In Figure 1, we show a heap for objects with two fields: a pointer and an integer, which would correspond to a type like

```
struct LinkedListNode {
  LinkedListNode next;
  int data;
}
```

There are a number of advantages to using one BRAM per field: (1) it allows simultaneous access to different fields in a single cycle, increasing parallelism; (2) field updates are atomic, and can therefore be performed in a single cycle, rather than using a 2-cycle read-modify-write operation; and (3) for larger memories where many physical BRAMs are cascaded to form a large logical BRAM, segregating the fields reduces the amount of cascading which increases the achievable clock frequency.

Thus for each field there is an input which is the address of the object (*Ptr Address* or *Data Address*), an input which is the new value when writing (*Ptr In* or *Data In*), and an output which is the value when reading (*Ptr Out* or *Data Out*).

Figure 1 shows a heap with 8 objects (with object 0 reserved for **null**). Therefore pointers are only 3 bits wide. In general, the ability to customize the pointer width using the variable word size of BRAMs can save considerable memory over a general-purpose CPU in which all pointers are the same size.

2.2.1 Allocation and De-allocation

The memory allocation and de-allocation is handled by using a separate BRAM as the **Free Stack**. At initialization time, all pointer values (except 0) are pushed onto the free stack. The *Stack Top* register points to the top of the stack.

An allocation is requested by setting the one-bit *Alloc* signal to 1 for one clock cycle. In this case, the *Stack Top* register is decremented, and the pointer at the top of the stack is returned via the *Addr Alloc'd* port.

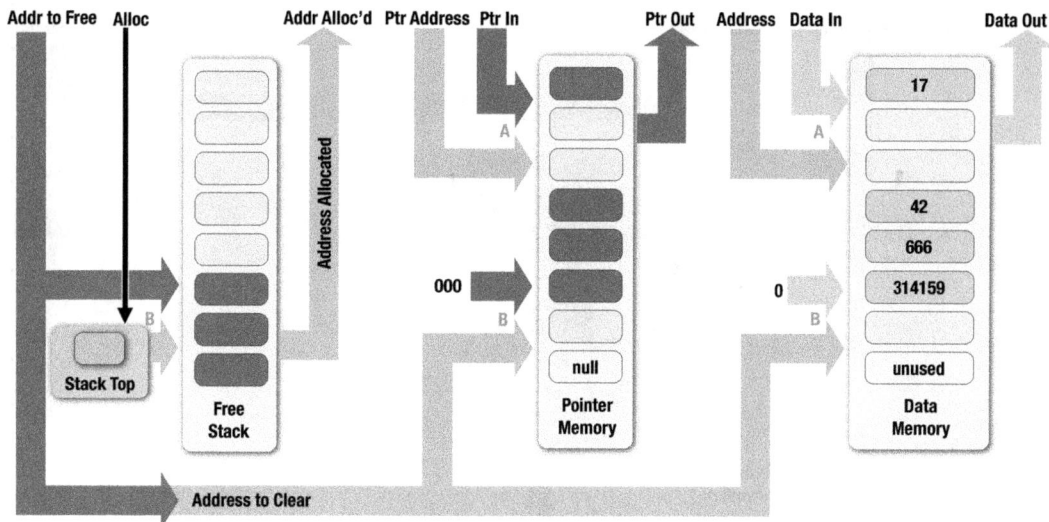

Figure 1. Memory Architecture with Malloc/Free Interface, showing a heap of 8 objects with two fields each: a pointer and an integer. Pointer values are shown in blue, data values in green, and nulls in white.

In fact, since we can "register" the top-of-stack value, an *Alloc* operation can be performed with a 0-cycle delay — that is, it can compute with the allocated address in the same cycle that it is allocated, and one object can be allocated in every clock cycle.

To de-allocate an object, its pointer is presented on the *Addr to Free* port. The address is stored into the **Free Stack** BRAM and the *Stack Top* is incremented. In addition, using port B of the BRAMs containing the object fields, the object is cleared using the *Addr to Free* on the address lines and an input value hard-wired to 0.

2.2.2 Increasing Memory Bandwidth

For simplicity, in the design we have shown, port B of the heap BRAMs is reserved for use by the memory manager when it needs to clear a freed object. However, port B can also be used by the application as long as it does not free an object in the same cycle.

Alternatively, the application can take responsibility for clearing the memory, in which case the memory manager never needs access to the data fields.

Note that by using a threaded free list within the pointer memory, we could eliminate the need for a separate BRAM to hold the free stack. However, this would mean that allocate and free operations could not proceed in parallel with pointer read/write operations.

3. Background: Single-Heap Collector

In this section we describe our prior work [3] in which we created a garbage collector for reconfigurable hardware that supports a single heap with a fixed layout (P pointer fields D data fields per object), with each field allocated to its own BRAM. This generalized the our first hardware collector [2] which only allowed two pointers per object.

The collector algorithm is based on Yuasa's snapshot algorithm [19]. The fundamental properties of Yuasa's algorithm are the fact that the amount of work required for marking is bounded by the size of the heap at snapshot time, and the simplicity of the collector invariants make for a much simpler and more deterministic termination protocol.

Our hardware collector comprises three components: snapshot support, a marking engine, and a sweeping engine. Since the complexity of multi-heap collection resides almost entirely in the mark-

ing phase, we will only briefly describe the snapshot and sweep phases, which we adopt almost unmodified from our prior work.

3.1 Root Snapshot

When available memory falls bellow a certain threshold, a *GC* signal is asserted which triggers a snapshot and begins the collection process.

For the snapshot, we use the design of Bacon et al. [2]. There are two cases: roots in registers and roots on a stack. For registers that contain pointers, we allocate a shadow register. When the *GC* signal goes high, the values in pointer registers are copied into the shadow registers (using read-before-write). These registers are then fed into the marking engine, one per cycle.

If there is a program stack, the pointers are read out and fed to the marking engine, one per cycle. This begins immediately, and since at most one value can be popped from the stack at a time, the process of collecting the roots can stay just ahead of the application.

3.2 The Mark Engine

The single-heap marking engine is shown in Figure 3 (not all aspects of the design can be shown; the diagram is intended to provide a high-level understanding of the design).

The external interface to the application consists of three inputs, *Pointer Select*, which selects which of the pointer BRAMs to access, *Address* and (used for write mode) *Pointer In*, and one output (used for read mode), *Pointer Out*. In addition, the roots of collection are supplied via the *Root* input.

Each pointer field is stored in its own BRAM (we do not show the data fields in the diagram, since they are irrelevant to the collector). For a heap of N objects with P pointers per object, there are P BRAMs of width $\log N$ bits (so that all N objects can be addressed). Figure 3 shows the case when $N = 8$ and $P = 3$.

The mark engine begins work when the first root pointer arrives on the *Root* input. The root has priority on MUX 1 and flows along the path labeled "Pointer to Trace".

The pointer is looked up in parallel in two maps, each containing one item per heap element: the **Mark Map** and the **Black Map**. The **Mark Map** tells us whether the object has been marked; the **Black Map** tells us whether the object has been allocated black (that is, allocated during collection, meaning that it must be treated as live). The reason for using two maps rather than one has to

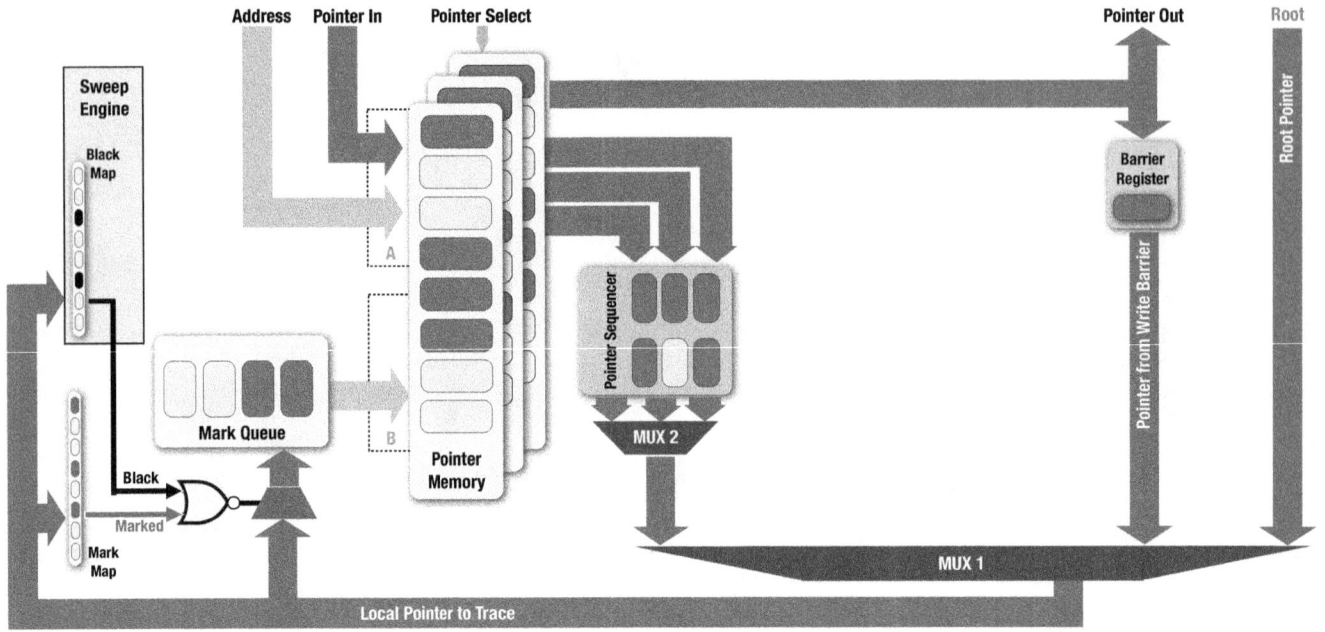

Figure 2. The Mark Engine of the Single-Heap Collector [3]

do with maximizing concurrency and avoiding stalls: the allocator only has to update the **Black Map**, so it does not pre-empt the mark phase.

An object must be traced if it is neither marked nor black. Thus the results of looking up the pointer in the **Mark Map** and **Black Map** are fed into the nor gate that controls the write-enable signal – when true, the "Pointer to Trace" is placed into the **Mark Queue**, a BRAM configured to act as a FIFO.

When the mark queue is non-empty and the mark pipeline is not exerting back-pressure, a pointer is dequeued and looked up in all of the pointer memories using port B (port A is reserved for the application). The result is P new pointers that need to be looked up in the mark map and (potentially) traced. These are fed into **Pointer Sequencer**, which is a queue that holds a few objects (determined by the overall pipeline depth; two are shown in the figure). When the free space in the **Pointer Sequencer** falls below the number of pipeline stages between the **Mark Queue** and the bramPointer Sequencer a back-pressure is applied and no more pointers are dequeued from the **Mark Queue** until the bramPointer Sequencer occupancy falls below the threshold.

Since a significant number of pointers may be null, a valid mask (not shown in the figure) is also calculated indicating which of the fields actually need to be processed.

When a set of pointers is dequeued from the **Pointer Sequencer**, the valid mask is used to extract the next non-null pointer which is then fed through MUX 2. This pointer is fed to the mark engine via MUX 1 as the next "Pointer to Trace", and the process repeats itself.

3.2.1 Paired Mark Queues

Since the mark map and black map are implemented with BRAMs which are dual-ported, we can in fact perform two lookups per cycle. The design takes advantage of this by processing two pointers at a time (this is not shown in the figure).

Therefore, the pointer sequencer actually generates two pointers to trace per cycle, which are fed to the A and B ports of the mark and black maps, respectively.

A second **Mark Queue** is needed to store the results of the second look-up. The two **Mark Queues** are sized to hold $N/2$ pointers each to ensure that overrun never happens. When a pointer is dequeued to look up in the pointer memory, it is taken from the fuller of the two queues.

3.2.2 Write Barrier

Meanwhile, if the application writes a pointer value using port A, the old pointer that it over-writes must be traced in order to maintain the snapshot property of garbage collection (otherwise, we might fail to traverse objects that were live in the snapshot).

Using read-before-write mode of BRAM, the old pointer is retrieved and placed in the **Barrier Register**.

Because we can mark two pointers in one cycle by using the paired mark queues, we wait until a second non-null write-barrier pointer arrives, at which point the *Pointer Sequencer* is pre-empted and the write barrier pointers are processed via the "Pointer to Trace" path.

3.2.3 Termination

One of the trickiest parts of any garbage collector is the termination algorithm for the mark phase: since the application continues to allocate objects and write to the heap, how can we guarantee that marking is done?

We implement termination as follows: when the **Mark Queue** is empty, we start a counter that is incremented in every clock cycle. If no new pointers are inserted into the **Mark Queue** after t cycles, then marking is complete.

The value we choose for t has to be sufficient to process any pointers in the last object that we dequeued, as well as any pointers in the write barrier buffer at that time. Since marking is a monotonic, idempotent process, once we process the last object and it results in no new objects, we know that we are done.

If the marking pipeline contains σ stages, and there are P pointers per object, then a sufficient bound on termination is $t = \sigma + P$.

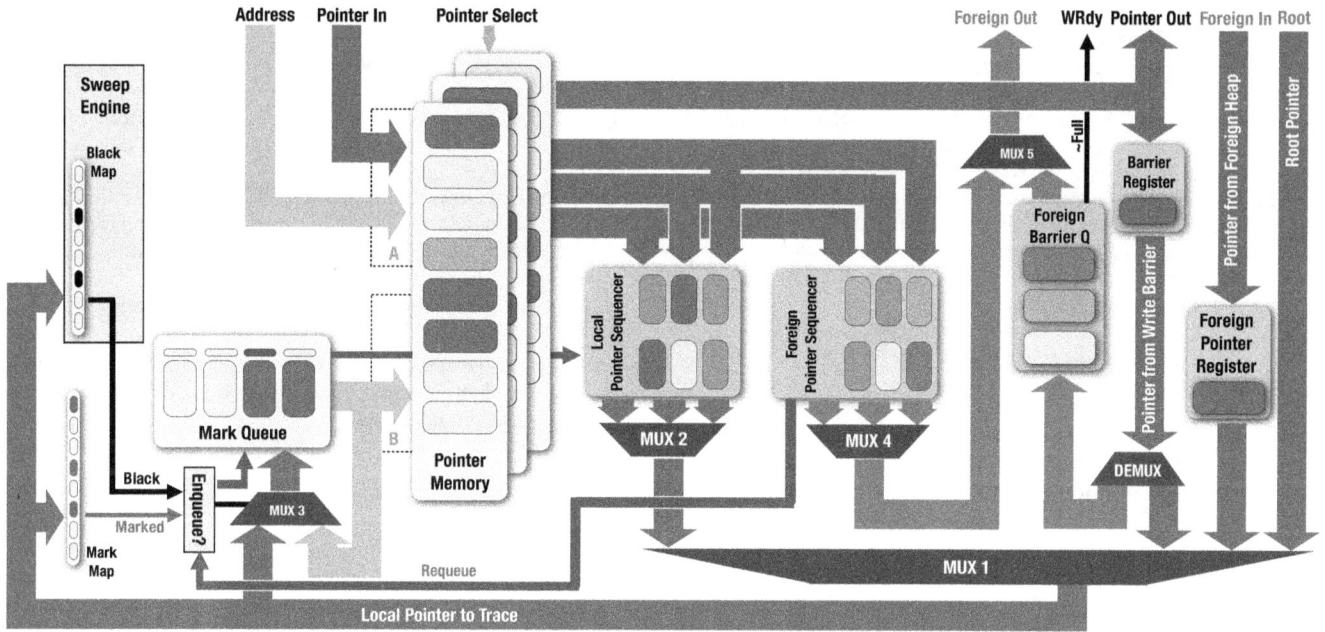

Figure 3. The Multi-Heap Mark Engine. Local pointers are shown in blue and foreign pointers are shown in red, green, and yellow. Null pointers are shown in white. Data paths that contain foreign pointers exclusively are shown in red.

3.3 Sweeping

Sweeping simply iterates over the objects in the heap, using the mark map and the black map to determine which objects can be freed. It is thus highly deterministic (taking just N cycles to scan the heap). For further details see our prior work [2, 3].

4. The Multi-Heap Collector

To implement a program with a variety of data types, of potentially drammatically different shape, we implement the memory system as several heaps of the kind described in Section 3. We denote the number of such heaps H.

With respect to any particular heap, we denote it as the *local heap* the other heaps as *foreign heaps*.

Pointers consist of a *heap index* and an *object index*. Since heaps are allowed to point to each other in arbitrary fashion, we use a uniform pointer type across all heaps. If there are H heaps each of which has N_i objects, then a pointer contains $\lceil \log_2 H \rceil$ bits for the heap index and $\lceil \log_2 \max_i N_i \rceil$ bits for the object index.

Other ways of representing pointers are possible, and may be optimized in conjunction with compiler knowledge of data types. In this section we present the system as we implemented and measured it.

4.1 The Snapshot and Sweep Phases

Handling multiple heaps is almost entirely a matter of the mark phase. Since we assume a statically typed language, we know statically which heap each register may point to. Therefore, once the snapshot has been taken, roots are simply sequenced to each individual heap to which they belong.

Sweeping, since it is essentially just a linear traversal of the mark map and the black map, is a purely heap-local operation. Once we determine that marking has (globally) terminated, we simply initiate sweeping in each of the individual heaps, which proceeds in parallel. Garbage collection terminates when all heaps have been swept.

4.2 The Multi-Heap Mark Engine

Supporting multiple heaps comprises two aspects: (1) extending the single-heap mark engine to handle pointers to and from foreign heaps, and (2) an interconnect to route pointers between the mark engines.

The extended mark engine design is shown in Figure 3. The heap can now hold both local pointers and foreign pointers. However, each heap takes care of marking only its local pointers.

The two fundamental changes to the interface of the heap are the *Foreign In* and *Foreign Out* ports. These are not user-visible, but are used to connect the local heap to its foreign heaps. Fundamentally, when the mark engine encounters a foreign pointer, it must be routed to the correct foreign heap.

The routing itself is handled by a central component external to the mark engine, called the *Mark Router*, which is described in Section 4.5. The responsibility of the mark engine is simply to accept and provide foreign pointers to the Mark Router.

As with the single-heap collector of Section 3, marking begins with the arrival of the first root on the *Root* interface. This is guaranteed to be a local pointer. The root pointer flows through MUX 1 and is looked up in the mark and black maps. Since it is the first root, it will be unmarked; assuming it was not allocated in the last few cycles (since the collection was triggered) it will also not be black. Therefore it should be added to the mark queue.

Because of foreign pointers, the enqueueing logic is more complex, as represented by the "Enqueue?" module and MUX 3. The mark queue also contains an additional bit for each entry, the "foreign bit", which will initially be 0. We will describe all of these details shortly once we have shown how foreign pointers are handled.

4.2.1 Handling Foreign Pointers in Local Objects

The mark queue can only contain local pointers but the objects it references may contain a mixture of local and foreign pointers. The local pointers are handled in the local mark engine whereas the foreign pointers have to be routed to their respective mark engines. We handle this by having two sequencers, a *Local Pointer Sequencer* and a *Foreign Pointer Sequencer*. The pointer fields of each object are fed into both sequencers.

The *Local Pointer Sequencer* performs the same function as the *Pointer Sequencer* in the single-heap design (Section 3.2). However, any foreign pointers are simply treated as if they are nulls). The local pointers now flow through MUX 2 and then MUX 1 and the local marking process continues.

The *Foreign Pointer Sequencer*, on the other hand, masks out the local pointers. When it processes an object, it successively selects the next non-null foreign pointer field via MUX 4. Thence it is routed to the *Foreign Out* port via MUX 5.

However, these pointers have lower priority than foreign pointers from the write barrier, as described below in Section 4.3. The write barrier must be given priority to avoid pre-empting the mutator.

At some point in the future, when the **Foreign Barrier Queue** is empty and the Mark Router is able to send the pointer to its heap, the pointer will be sent to the foreign heap via the *Foreign Out* interface.

On the incoming side, each mark engine gives priority first to local write barrier pointers, second to roots (not present during most of marking), third to pointers arriving on the *Foreign In* port, and finally to the local pointer sequencer.

4.2.2 Deadlock Avoidance: Requeuing Objects

When the foreign pointer sequencer emits a foreign pointer, it could be send to the foreign heap as soon as the next cycle. But it may also be pre-empted for some time by the foreign barrier queue. Even then, it is possible that all $H - 1$ heaps will come across a foreign pointer to heap H_k in the same cycle. In this case, there may be a considerable delay.

So what happens when the *Foreign Pointer Sequencer* is full, and another object is being processed which contains foreign pointers? Fundamentally, there are three options: (1) we could block the mark engine until more pointers are sent to the foreign heap, making space in the sequencer; (2) we could increase the buffering of foreign pointers by increasing the size of the queue inside the sequencer; or (3) we could re-enqueue the object in the local mark queue and re-process it later, when there will hopefully be bandwidth available to the foreign heap(s).

In fact, we do the latter, but first it is worth explaining why we rejected the other two options.

Blocking the mark engine is dangerous because it is possible that the global marking operation could deadlock, with heaps waiting on each other. With a clever design of the Mark Router and careful analysis, it might be possible to design a system that is free of deadlock. But it would still be subject to long delays. The local marking process could be slowed down by orders of magnitude.

This problem could be ameliorated by having a substantial queue inside the foreign pointer sequencer, instead of just a few objects. But this simply delays the inevitable, and large queues must be synthesized as BRAMs, effectively increasing the memory cost of garbage collection relative to manual memory management, so we view this as a last resort.

Thus when we encounter an object with foreign pointers and the foreign pointer sequencer is full, we assert the *Requeue* signal, which causes the original object pointer to be selected from MUX 3 and stored in the mark queue. When this happens, the "foreign bit" of that mark queue entry is also set. This has no effect on the Local Pointer Sequencer, so all local pointers in the object will be marked and traced (if needed).

This guarantees that local heaps always make progress tracing their local pointers. As a result, they will eventually have spare

cycles to accept pointers from foreign heaps, and global progress is assured.

When a pointer is dequeued from the Mark Queue and its foreign bit is set, the Local Pointer Sequencer simply discards the contents of its fields, so they are not re-traced. The Foreign Pointer Sequencer, on the other hand, processes the fields just as it normally would.

Note that when we re-process a pointer with its foreign bit set, the pointer values in the object it points to might have changed. However, if they have, they would have been caught by the write barrier. So we will not violate the snapshot invariant.

4.3 Write Barriers

Handling write barriers turns out to be one of the most challenging aspects of the multi-heap collector. Since we use a Yuasa barrier, the barrier must record the old value of the field, which could be a foreign pointer. So even though each heap individually can handle one write barrier pointer per cycle (if they are all local pointers), it is once again possible that in a single cycle, all pointers that are over-written will be to the same heap H_k.

While we were willing to accept delays to the marking process when a foreign pointer could not be sent to the foreign heap, delaying the mutator is a last resort.

When an overwritten pointer in the *Barrier Register* needs to be processed, it flows through the DEMUX which routes it through MUX 1 if it is a local pointer. However, if it is a foreign pointer, we enqueue it in the *Foreign Barrier Queue*. As discussed above, this queue has priority over the *Foreign Pointer Sequencer*, since we prefer to throttle the collector rather than the mutator.

The presence of the barrier queue makes it possible to absorb short-term bursts in the mutation rate when those mutations all have to be routed to the same heap. Ultimately, however, this queue will fill up.

Thus in the worst case the mutation rate of the application might have to be throttled. However, in many cases the compiler will have knowledge of data types and be able to determine statically that the number of possible foreign write barriers is below the limit. An algorithm akin to VLIW scheduling [8] , where there are a fixed number of functional units that can be used in a cycle, could be applied.

As a last resort, we provide a "write ready" signal (*WRdy*), which is true so long as the barrier queue is not full. When the barrier queue is full, the mutator may not write to this heap if there is any possibility that such a write will over-write a foreign pointer. In such a case, the compiler can generate a dynamic schedule that takes account of the *WRdy* signal.

In practice, we believe this is unlikely to be a problem. This restriction applies only to pointers (data field access is unrestricted), and then only to writes, and only to fields that may point to other heaps. Given the natural serialization that pointer-based data structures impose, it seems unlikely that a real program could generate a sustained foreign-pointer write rate of many per cycle (bursts are not a problem since the barrier queue can absorb them).

4.4 Termination

Because we use a snapshot-based algorithm, the work that the collector must perform is bounded and termination can take advantage of this monotonicity property.

The termination algorithm is as follows:

- Each heap maintains a *ready to terminate* signal which is the *and* of the empty signals from the mark queues and the local and foreign pointer sequencers;

- When all heaps assert *ready to terminate*, a *start terminate* signal is asserted to all heaps (if at any point in the termination

122

algorithm any of the *ready to terminate* signals become false, the entire termination protocol is aborted). When all heaps are ready to terminate, they snapshot the state of their foreign barrier queue by recording its occupancy in a termination counter register;

- Every time a pointer is removed from the foreign barrier queue, its termination counter register is decremented; when it reaches 0 it asserts a *foreign barriers complete* signal;

- Once all heaps assert *foreign barrier complete*, a termination counter register is initialized to some value δ, which must be greater than the maximum delay in cycles from any foreign barrier queue to the pipeline stage in which pointers are enqueued into the mark queue. In our design we conservatively set $\delta = 16$.

- The termination counter is decremented in every cycle. If it reaches zero and all heaps are still asserting the *ready to terminate* signal, then the mark phase has finished.

4.5 Inter-Heap Routing

When there are exactly two heaps (which we expect will not be an uncommon case), the *Foreign Out* port of one heap is connected directly to the *Foreign In* port of the other heap, and vice-versa.

When there are more than two heaps, we connect them in a "crossbar" pattern: each heap is connected to every other heap. Before the *Foreign In* port, there is a MUX that selects from the available foreign pointers from the other heaps. This MUX uses an eager round-robin discipline, to ensure that each heap is able to make progress in dispatching foreign pointers.

5. Experimental Methodology

The memory management unit is implemented in Verilog, a hardware description language (HDL). To evaluate the generated hardware for the collector, we synthesize the design to an FPGA and report the consumption of logic and memory resources, as well as the resulting clock frequency. The latter is critical to achieving high performance.

We used the Xilinx Virtex-5 LX330T [18] FPGA for our experiments which is the largest LXT device in the Virtex-5 family. Given that the motivation to use dynamic memory management will go up with complexity, and complexity will go up with larger chips, we believe that this is a good representative device. The LX330T has 51,840 slices and 648 (18Kb)BRAMs amounting to 1.4 MB of storage.

We used Xilinx ISE 14.5 tool for synthesis. For each design point, we do a *clock search* which involves running full synthesis including place-and-route iteratively. We begin by synthesizing the design with an arbitrary clock frequency constraint of 180 MHz. Based on the synthesis result we change the constraint by a small delta either in upward or downward direction. We exit when multiple successive synthesis runs fail to yield an improvement.

We adopt this strategy because the Xilinx synthesis tool is very sensitive to the clock constraint and both an under- and over-specified clock constraint generally returns worse result than a realistic clock constraint.

5.1 Co-Simulation

Eventually, we intend to connect the garbage collector to a compiler for a high-level, synthesizable, garbage-collected language. But before we do such integration we need to fully understand the trade-offs, and tying the design to a particular compiler would allow limitations in the generated code of the compiler to mask problems in the collector.

Prior work on hardware garbage collection has used benchmarks hand-coded in Verilog. However, writing these benchmarks is extremely time-consuming, and they are quite inflexible.

In order to evaluate the multi-heap collector, we needed to be able to experiment with a large variety of configurations and data structure connectivities. Therefore, a more flexible methodology is required.

Our approach is to use *co-simulation*. We write or adapt programs written in Java so that each allocation, read, or write is performed both in the JVM and also in the hardware collector running in a cycle-accurate simulator. The Java program maintains all pointers at both the Java level and the hardware collector level, and all reads are validated for consistency.

As a result, we can very easily modify the programs to allocate objects in different hardware heaps, and simulate varying mutation and allocation rates. Because the hardware simulator is *only* performing the heap pointer operations, the rest of the calculations take zero time. In actual compiled code the pointer operations would be slowed to some extent by the rest of the computation. But with this method, we can put maximum stress on the collector.

We implemented two micro-benchmarks: *SortedList* maintains a sorted linked list of objects; *TreeSearch* maintains a tree and performs insert, delete, and lookup operations.

We also adapted two of the JOlden benchmarks: *TSP* (travelling salesman) and *EM3D* (3-dimensional electro-magnetic wave propagation).

These four benchmarks require 1, 2, 4, and 24 pointers per object, respectively. This lets us test various heap geometries, which can raise different issues in the design.

In order to evaluate the effect of multiple heaps in a systematic way, we artificially partition objects between several identical heaps. While this is artificial, a more realistic approach (such as putting different data types in different heaps) would only be applicable to a particular number of heaps, and not allow us to vary them for study.

6. Experimental Evaluation

6.1 Multi-Heap Overhead with a Single Heap

To begin with, we wish to understand what extra costs are introduced by the design shown in Figure 3, relative to previous designs which do not support inter-connection of heaps. Therefore, we synthesize a single heap instance of our multi-heap collector, without any inter-heap routing. Subsequent measurements will show the separate effect of scaling the number of heaps.

Figure 4 compares a single instance of our multi-heap collector with a simple Malloc ("Malloc") design, our original hardware collector which only supports 2 pointers per object ("2-ptr Heap"), our subsequent work which supports arbitrary number of pointers per heap ("General Heap"), and the collector described in this paper ("Multi-Heap"). In all cases, we configure the heap to contain 2 pointers so that direct comparisons can be made.

Figure 4(a) shows that our design consumes considerably more logic resources (in relative terms). However, even at 32K objects we use less than 1% of the logic resources of the chip. In addition, as the heap size increases, the relative additional cost of multi-heap support goes down.

Figure 4(b) shows the memory consumption in Block RAMs. All of the collectors pay a noticeable overhead relative to Malloc, but the multi-heap support consumes negligible additional memory.

Figure 4(c) shows the synthesized clock frequency achieved by the different designs. It is here that Malloc has the clearest advantage over garbage collection, although that advantage shrinks considerably as the memory size increases.

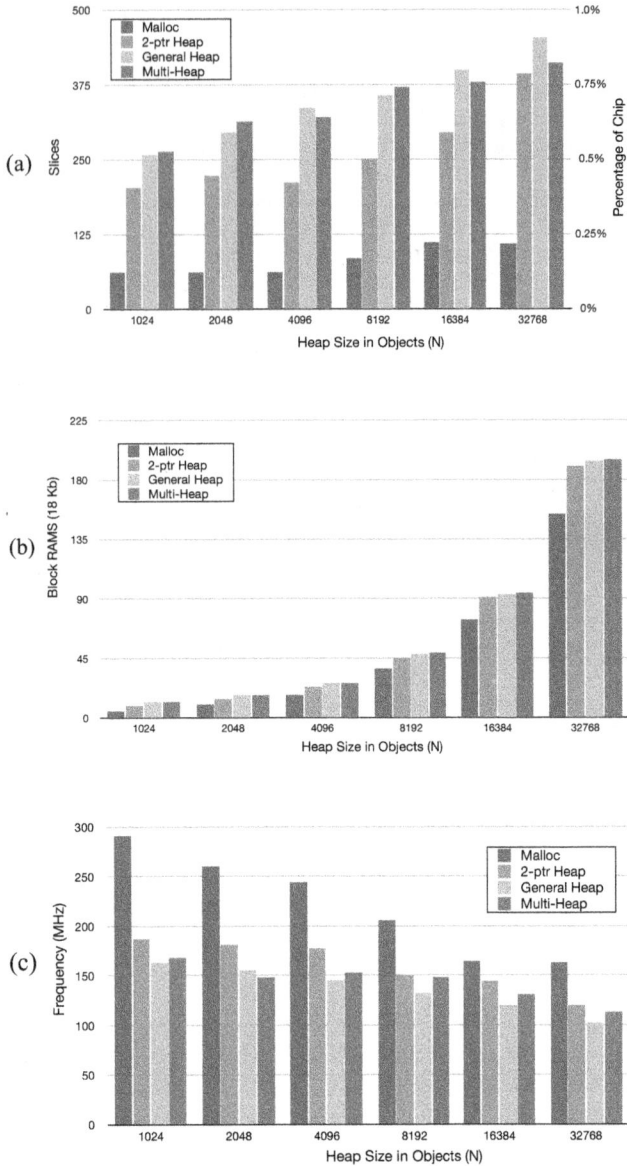

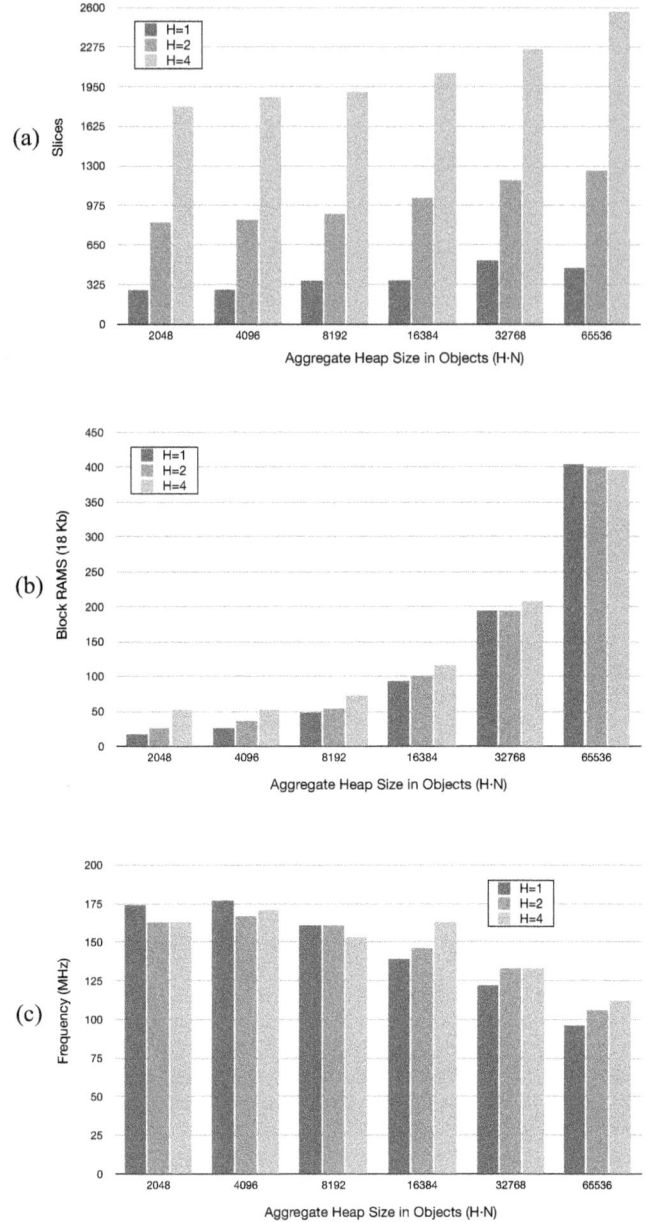

Figure 4. The cost of generality: for a heap with 2 pointers per object, comparison of Malloc, a specialized 2-pointer-only heap, a generalized heap supporting arbitrary pointers per object, and a single instance of a heap supporting multiple interconnected heaps. Slices (a), BRAMs (b), and synthesized clock frequency (c).

Figure 5. Slice count (a), BRAM consumption (b), and synthesized clock frequency (c) of our design for different numbers of heaps H and different total heap sizes (the amount of total heap memory is constant at each x-axis data point).

The General Heap design pays some performance cost relative to the 2-ptr Heap, and the Multi-Heap design performance falls in the middle, almost on a par with the 2-ptr design.

While this seems counter-intuitive, it is because we made a decision to more aggressively pipeline the mark engine of the multi-heap design (using 7 stages compared to 6 in the General Heap design). This can have a negative effect on worst-case performance pathologies, but yields better overall performance in their absence. Considerable further experience will be required before we can say definitively which is the better option.

6.2 Static Effects of Multiple Heaps

Figure 5 presents data that shows the effects of connecting multiple heaps. At each x-axis value, we fix the *total* amount of memory,

which is then spread evenly across 1, 2, or 4 heaps. Recall that in the case of two heaps, we avoid the general inter-connection network and simply wire them together directly.

In Figure 5(a) we see that the number of slices (logic resources) scales roughly linearly with the number of heaps. The routing network between the heaps when $H = 4$ does not consume significant additional resources, which had been a concern.

Figure 5(b) shows the Block RAM usage. At small heap sizes, $H = 4$ consumes considerably more memory. Part of this is accounted for by overheads associated with multiple collectors: 4 mark maps, 8 mark queues, and so on. However, the main culprit is quantization effects: At 2K with $H = 4$, each heap only contains 512 objects. These are insufficient to fill even a single BRAM;

Benchmark	Heaps	Min Heap	GC Count	Max GC	Avg GC	Avg Mark	Mark Stalled	Avg ReQ's	Avg Sweep	Mutation Rate	Alloc. Rate	Foreign Ptrs	Barrier Q Max
SortedList	1	1.094	199	2037	1360	1076	77.0%	—	280	0.084	0.044	0.0%	—
	2	1.125	205	2101	1290	1142	89.1%	0	144	0.080	0.041	51.0%	1
	4	1.219	214	2063	1292	1210	94.8%	0	78	0.080	0.042	76.4%	1
SearchTree	1	1.031	316	583	549	281	15.7%	—	264	0.032	0.034	0.0%	—
	2	1.094	411	370	336	192	37.5%	1	140	0.032	0.034	52.1%	1
	4	1.219	440	315	271	189	67.2%	1	78	0.030	0.032	73.9%	1
EM3D	1	1.062	359	1512	1173	794	76.3%	—	272	0.495	0.245	0.0%	—
	2	1.094	359	933	741	497	69.4%	57	140	0.473	0.238	44.6%	1
	4	1.156	399	706	537	351	42.7%	155	74	0.387	0.194	65.2%	1
TSP	1	1.500	14	785	710	320	33.8%	—	384	0.395	0.063	0.0%	—
	2	1.500	14	444	383	186	43.5%	2	192	0.395	0.063	24.3%	0
	4	1.656	27	278	251	138	51.4%	1	106	0.395	0.063	25.5%	1

Table 1. Dynamic measurements of the four benchmarks running on 1, 2, and 4 heaps. The measurements are taken with the heaps configured at the smallest size still capable of providing stall-free (100% MMU) operation.

therefore, much of the space is wasted. In practice, one would always want to round heap sizes up so that they took advantage of these quantization effects to provide the largest heap possible.

At the heap size 64K, there is an inversion in the memory trade-off. This is because with multiple heaps, the number of bits required to address the local heap is smaller. This does *not* affect the width of the **Pointer Memory**, which must be able to refer to foreign heaps. But it *does* affect the width of the **Mark Queue** and the **Free Stack**, and therefore in some cases (when a BRAM quantization boundary is crossed), the total BRAM consumption decreases.

Figure 5(c) shows the effect on frequency of partitioning memory into multiple heaps. Generally speaking the frequency is similar, or (at larger sizes) increases with the number of heaps. As we saw in Figure 4(c), smaller heaps can sustain higher clock frequencies, which explains this phenomenon – since the total space is now split into several smaller heaps. However, we had hoped for a larger improvement.

The culprit appears to be in the long wires and complex multiplexing required by the inter-connection of the heaps. We have performed some registering and pipelining optimizations, but the improvements have been modest. This remains an area for further improvement.

6.3 Dynamic Measurements

We ran each of the benchmarks under our co-simulation infrastructure with 1, 2, and 4 heaps. At each size we used an automated binary search to find the smallest heap size in which the application could run with 0 stall cycles (100% minimum mutator utilization or "MMU" [6]), measured as a multiple of the maximum live memory of the application (within a factor of 0.025). We then report statistics for each benchmark at that heap size in Table 1.

We see that the minimum heap sizes are in general quite reasonable – from just under 1.1 to 1.7 times the maximum live data set. This is considerably less than is typically required by software real-time collectors, or even non-real-time collectors when tuned for throughput.

Maximum collection times ("Max GC" – in cycles) generally go down considerably as the number of heaps increases. This indicates that the multiple heaps are achieving significant useful parallelism in their mark engines (the exception is SortedList, which is designed to be a pathological case of a single linked list with many cross-heap pointers).

The effects of parallelism are even more surprising given that the percentage of non-null pointers that are foreign ("Foreign Ptrs") varies from roughly 25 to 75%. Apparently each foreign pointer generates sufficient local work that there is some benefit.

On the other hand, the marking engines are stalled (have no pointers in their mark queues to process) a considerable fraction of the time ("Mark Stalled"). This is due to two factors: cross-heap pointers and the multi-stage pipeline of our design. However, this does not seem to harm the overall performance.

When we are unable to send foreign pointers to the remote heap, the object containing them must be re-enqueued in the local mark queue (as described in Section 4.2.1), leading to additional work.

We expected this extra work to occur primarily when the foreign barrier queue was pre-empting the marking engine's access to the *Foreign Out* port. While this does happen, the most significant effect is seen when the number of pointers per object increases, as with EM3D, which has 24 pointers per object. In this case, the foreign pointer sequencer becomes full and exerts back-pressure. In EM3D with $H = 4$, there are 155 re-queues with a maximum collection time of 706 cycles. Note however that since we have a seven stage pipeline, the work of the re-queues can be overlapped with other processing.

Another surprise is the occupancy of the foreign barrier queue ("Barrier Q Max"), which never exceeds one, even though we dedicated an entire BRAM capable of holding 1K pointers. This is true even in EM3D, which has a high mutation rate and a high percentage of cross-pointers, which would seem to imply that many write barriers would generate foreign pointers. It appears these are simply drained very quickly.

As a result, there is never any need for the application to perform dynamic scheduling of writes; for these benchmarks the system is well able to keep up with its mutation rate.

7. Related Work

The only prior work on garbage collection of on-chip FPGA data structures is our our own [2, 3]. Since we have already made extensive comparisons to these papers we do not discuss them further here.

Otherwise, there has been very little work on supporting high-level dynamic memory abstractions in reconfigurable hardware, and none on garbage collection. Simsa and Singh [15] and Cook et al.[9] have explored compilation of C subprograms that use malloc/free into VHDL or Bluespec for synthesis to FPGAs.

LegUp supports structs containing pointers, but does not support dynamic memory allocation or pointer return values [5].

Faes et al. [10] have built an "FPGA-aware" collector, with a completely different goal from ours: allowing the FPGA to maintain references into the CPU's main program heap. This facilitates co-processing by the FPGA.

There have been several systems which have micro-coded some or all of the collector in hardware [11, 13]. However, these collectors are designed for general-purpose DRAM heaps, and stall the application for times varying from 200 cycles up to 0.5 ms.

Most hardware support for garbage collection has been in the form of specialized memory barriers (particularly read barriers) because of their high throughput cost. The Symbolics Lisp Machine [12] introduced this kind of hardware barrier to implement Baker's algorithm [4]. Both the Lisp Machine and SOAR [17] also introduced hardware support for generational write barriers.

The Azul Vega processor and its associated collector [7] has hardware support for read barriers, fast user-mode trap handlers (4-10 cycles), cooperative pre-emption, and special TLB support – enabling a collector capable of handling very large heaps and large numbers of processors. However, it stalls the application for up to 79% of the cycles in a 50ms time window.

Schoeberl [14] extends the JOP Java processor with hardware support for non-blocking object copies in the memory controller. This allows compaction operations to be pre-empted at the granularity of a single write.

8. Conclusions

We have presented the first garbage collector for reconfigurable hardware that is capable of allocating objects in multiple heaps with inter-heap references. This makes hardware garbage collection feasible for the first time since we can now accommodate heterogeneous objects in a single system.

We have shown that the cost in terms of logic and memory resources is relatively modest. Clock frequency remains an area for further improvement.

Measurements showed that some aspects of the design which were of serious concern from a theoretical standpoint do not occur in practice. This may allow for further optimizations.

Now that we have a feasible collector, the next step is to integrate it with a high-level language compiler that is capable of synthesizing hardware. We hope this will allow a major step forward in the level of abstraction at which hardware can be programmed.

A. Exploring the Design Space

Due to the effort required to implement a hardware design in Verilog, it is much more difficult to experiment with design alternatives than in software. The collector design presented in this paper involved a number of implementation choices – sometimes based on experience, sometimes on intuition.

In this section, we describe some of those design choices which might either provide a path to superior implementation in the future, or help avoid blind alleys that we pursued.

A.1 Dynamic vs. Static Pointer Typing

In our design pointers are dynamically typed, in the sense that they have "heap identifier" bits and are steered to foreign heaps dynamically based on those values.

Pointers could also be statically typed, in which case each pointer field contains pointers to exactly one heap, either local or foreign. But this would actually complicate some aspects of the design, and also reduce the flexibility to map multiple types into a single heap.

An intermediate solution would be to tag objects rather than individual pointers. This would provide a smoother path to incorporating true object-orientation in hardware (the tag would effectively become the class identifier). On the other hand, it would require some sort of "decode" phase to interpret the object tag, which would almost certainly slow down the collector.

Until we have more experience with compiler integration of the collector, using dynamically typed pointers provides the maximum flexibility, good performance, and (as long as the number of heaps is modest) minimal storage overhead.

A.2 Connected vs. Isolated Heaps

A program could have multiple heaps, some of which might contain cross-pointers and others of which are completely isolated. In other cases pointers might exist from heap A to heap B but not vice-versa.

Our design is parameterizable to allow it to operate in the isolated case. More complex combinations of connectivities are possible, but would require additional macro processing or machine-generation of HDL in order to perform the wiring of the modules.

A.3 Unsynchronized Partial Mark Maps

We can absorb a higher mutation rate by having multiple "mark maps" whose function is to ensure that the same pointer is not placed in their associated queue more than once.

However, with k such maps there would need to be k times as much queue space. We would also need a centralized "complete" mark map, presumably at the head of queues just before the point where a new object pointer is looked up in the heap.

Since we saw that in practice the foreign barrier queue never had more than one entry (but could hold 1000), and in general that mutation rates were well below 1 per cycle, it does not seem worth incurring so much additional complexity and overhead until we have compelling use cases which require support of very high mutation rates.

A.4 Parallel Field Access

The design as presented only allows read or write to one pointer field per cycle. In fact, we could allow a read to each pointer field of an object in every cycle (on port **A** of the pointer BRAM).

However, allowing parallel field writes could cause as many as P write barrier pointers to be generated in every cycle. A local queue could be used to absorb short-term bursts in the allocation rate, or we could use the technique of Section A.3 to support a higher sustained write rate.

A.5 Parallel Object Writes

Since the BRAM is dual-ported, the objects at two different addresses can be read or written in a single cycle. The design as presented reserves port **B** for the collector. However, this port could also be exposed to the mutator (in read-only or read-write mode) if it were allowed to pre-empt the collector.

Of course, this means that mutator operations on port **B** would slow down marking – which increases collection time and therefore the required heap size. The trade-off is thus between more parallelism in the memory system versus more determinism in the garbage collector.

A.6 Steele Barrier

The Yuasa barrier we use traces the over-written pointer, which might be to a foreign heap. If we used a Dijsktra barrier, we would have to record the new (over-writing) pointer, which could also be to the foreign heap. But if we used a Steele barrier (which records the object into which the pointer is written), it would be guaranteed to be a heap-local object. Thus we could eliminate the foreign barrier queue and associated complexity, both in implementation and in analysis of real-time behavior.

However, we would sacrifice the snapshot property, since with incremental-update collectors reprocessing work is unbounded and termination is difficult. Real-time (stall-free) behavior might no longer be possible.

A.7 Per-Heap Clock Domains

In our design all heaps (and the application) run at the same clock frequency. However, we could place each heap into its own clock domain, and introduce FIFOs for clock-domain crossing where they are inter-connected. This would potentially allow some of the heaps to run at higher frequencies.

Decoupling the heaps from the mutator could also significantly improve the clock speed of the mutator. However, this could also increase the effective mutation and allocation rates, which would increase the load on the collector.

A.8 Multi-Pumping

Multi-pumping is a method for running a portion of a design at a multiple of the base clock frequency to increase its performance. We could apply this technique specifically to the pointer BRAMs by doubling their clock frequency (they are rated up to 500 MHz), which would give the appearance of doubling the number of reads and writes per cycle.

This would allow us to dedicate one "half cycle" entirely to the mutator (which could use ports A and B at the same time) and the other half-cycle entirely to the collector. However, this would raise the same issues around maximum mutation rate as other options outlined above.

References

[1] S. E. Abdullahi and G. A. Ringwood. Garbage collecting the internet: A survey of distributed garbage collection. *ACM Comput. Surv.*, 30(3):330–373, Sept. 1998.

[2] D. F. Bacon, P. Cheng, and S. Shukla. And then there were none: A stall-free real-time garbage collector for reconfigurable hardware. In *Proceedings of the 33rd ACM SIGPLAN Conference on Programming Language Design and Implementation*, pp. 23–34, 2012.

[3] D. F. Bacon, P. Cheng, and S. Shukla. A generalized high-performance garbage collector for FPGA data structures. Technical report, IBM Research, Jan. 2014.

[4] H. G. Baker. List processing in real-time on a serial computer. *Commun. ACM*, 21(4):280–294, Apr. 1978.

[5] A. Canis et al. LegUp: An open-source high-level synthesis tool for FPGA-based processor/accelerator systems. *TECS*, 13(2):1:1–1:25, Sept. 2013.

[6] P. Cheng and G. Blelloch. A parallel, real-time garbage collector. In *Proc. SIGPLAN Conference on Programming Language Design and Implementation*, pp. 125–136, Snowbird, Utah, June 2001.

[7] C. Click, G. Tene, and M. Wolf. The pauseless GC algorithm. In *Proceedings of the First ACM/USENIX International Conference on Virtual Execution Environments*, pp. 46–56, 2005.

[8] R. P. Colwell, R. P. Nix, J. J. O'Donnell, D. B. Papworth, and P. K. Rodman. A VLIW architecture for a trace scheduling compiler. *IEEE Trans. Computers*, 37(8):967–979, 1988.

[9] B. Cook et al. Finding heap-bounds for hardware synthesis. In *Formal Methods in Computer-Aided Design*, pp. 205–212, Nov. 2009.

[10] P. Faes, M. Christiaens, D. Buytaert, and D. Stroobandt. FPGA-aware garbage collection in Java. In T. Rissa, S. J. E. Wilton, and P. H. W. Leong, editors, *FPL*, pp. 675–680, 2005.

[11] M. Meyer. An on-chip garbage collection coprocessor for embedded real-time systems. In *Proceedings of the 11th IEEE International Conference on Embedded and Real-Time Computing Systems and Applications*, pp. 517–524, 2005.

[12] D. A. Moon. Garbage collection in a large LISP system. In *Conference Record of the 1984 ACM Symposium on LISP and Functional Programming*, Austin, Texas, Aug. 1984.

[13] W. J. Schmidt and K. D. Nilsen. Performance of a hardware-assisted real-time garbage collector. In *Proceedings of the Sixth International Conference on Architectural Support for Programming Languages and Operating Systems*, pp. 76–85, 1994.

[14] M. Schoeberl and W. Puffitsch. Nonblocking real-time garbage collection. *ACM Trans. Embedded Comput. Sys.*, 10:1–28, 2010.

[15] J. Simsa and S. Singh. Designing hardware with dynamic memory abstraction. In *Proceedings of the 18th Annual International Symposium on Field Programmable Gate Arrays*, pp. 69–72, 2010.

[16] G. L. Steele, Jr. Data representation in PDP-10 MACLISP. Technical report, MIT, 1977. AI Memo 420.

[17] D. Ungar et al. Architecture of SOAR: Smalltalk on a RISC. In *Proceedings of the 11th Annual International Symposium on Computer Architecture*, pp. 188–197, 1984.

[18] Xilinx. Virtex-5 family overview. Technical Report DS100, Feb. 2009.

[19] T. Yuasa. Real-time garbage collection on general-purpose machines. *J. Systems and Software*, 11(3):181–198, Mar. 1990.

[20] J. Zhou and B. Demsky. Locality-aware many-core garbage collection. Technical Report CECS 10-08, Center for Embedded Computer Systems University of California, Irvine, Aug. 2010.

Author Index

www.ingramcontent.com/pod-product-compliance
Lightning Source LLC
Chambersburg PA
CBHW081544220326
41598CB00036B/6558